D0400341

library wars

13

Love & War

STORY & ART BY *Kiiro Yumi*   ORIGINAL CONCEPT BY *Hiro Arikawa*

Library Wars

Love & War

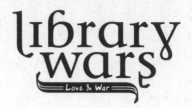

Contents

The Library Freedom Act

Libraries have the freedom to acquire their collections.

Libraries have the freedom to circulate
materials in their collections.

Libraries guarantee the privacy of their patrons.

Libraries oppose any type of censorship.

When libraries are imperiled,
librarians will join together
to secure their freedom.

library wars

Love & War

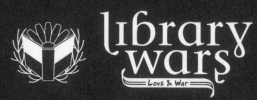

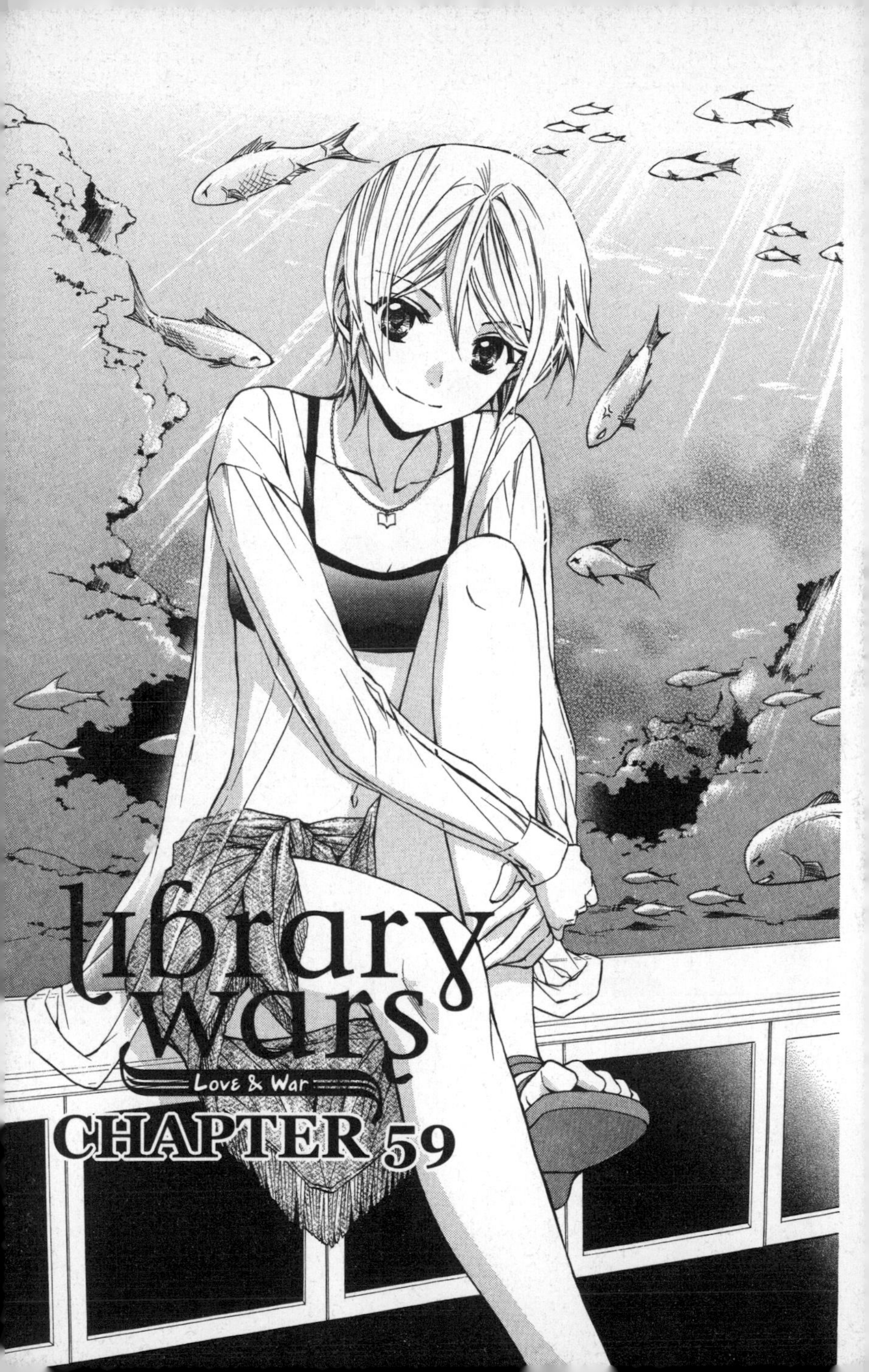
library wars
Love & War
CHAPTER 59

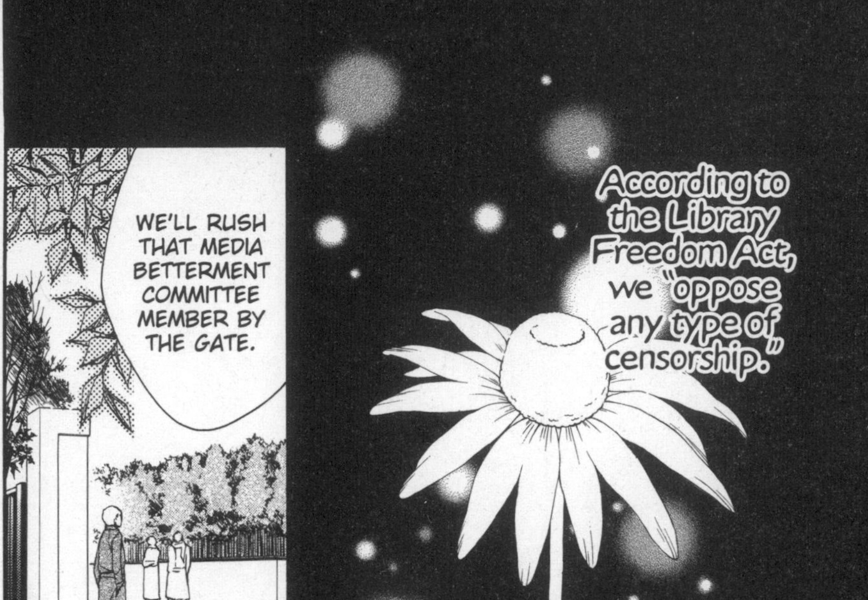
According to the Library Freedom Act, we "oppose any type of censorship."
I'm proud to be a member of the Library Forces.
WE'LL RUSH THAT MEDIA BETTERMENT COMMITTEE MEMBER BY THE GATE.
IT'LL BE A SHORT FIGHT, ORIKUCHI. DON'T MISS IT.

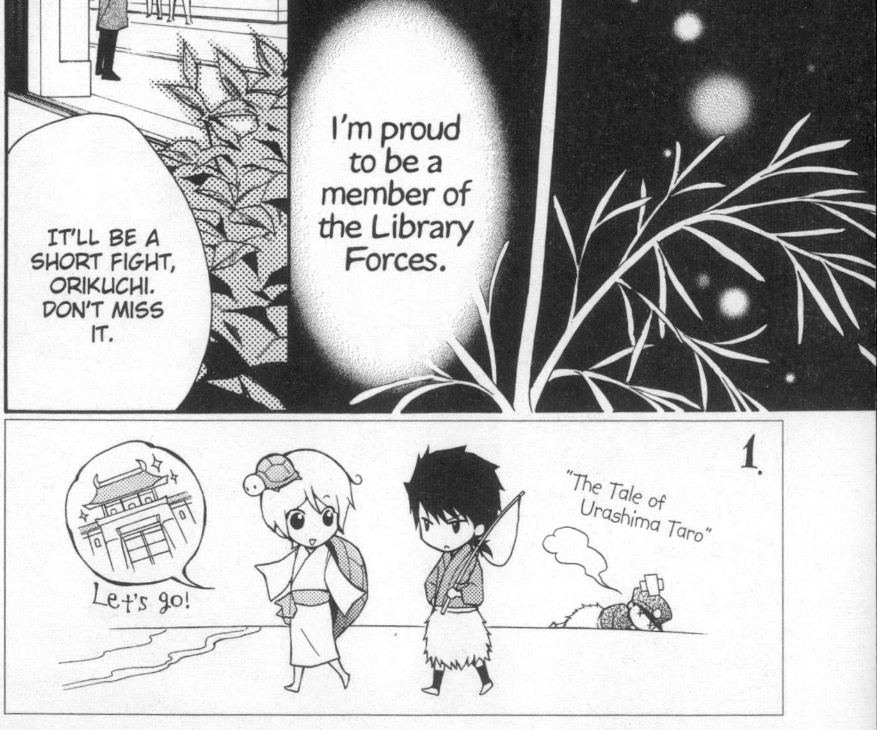
1.
"The Tale of Urashima Taro"
Let's go!

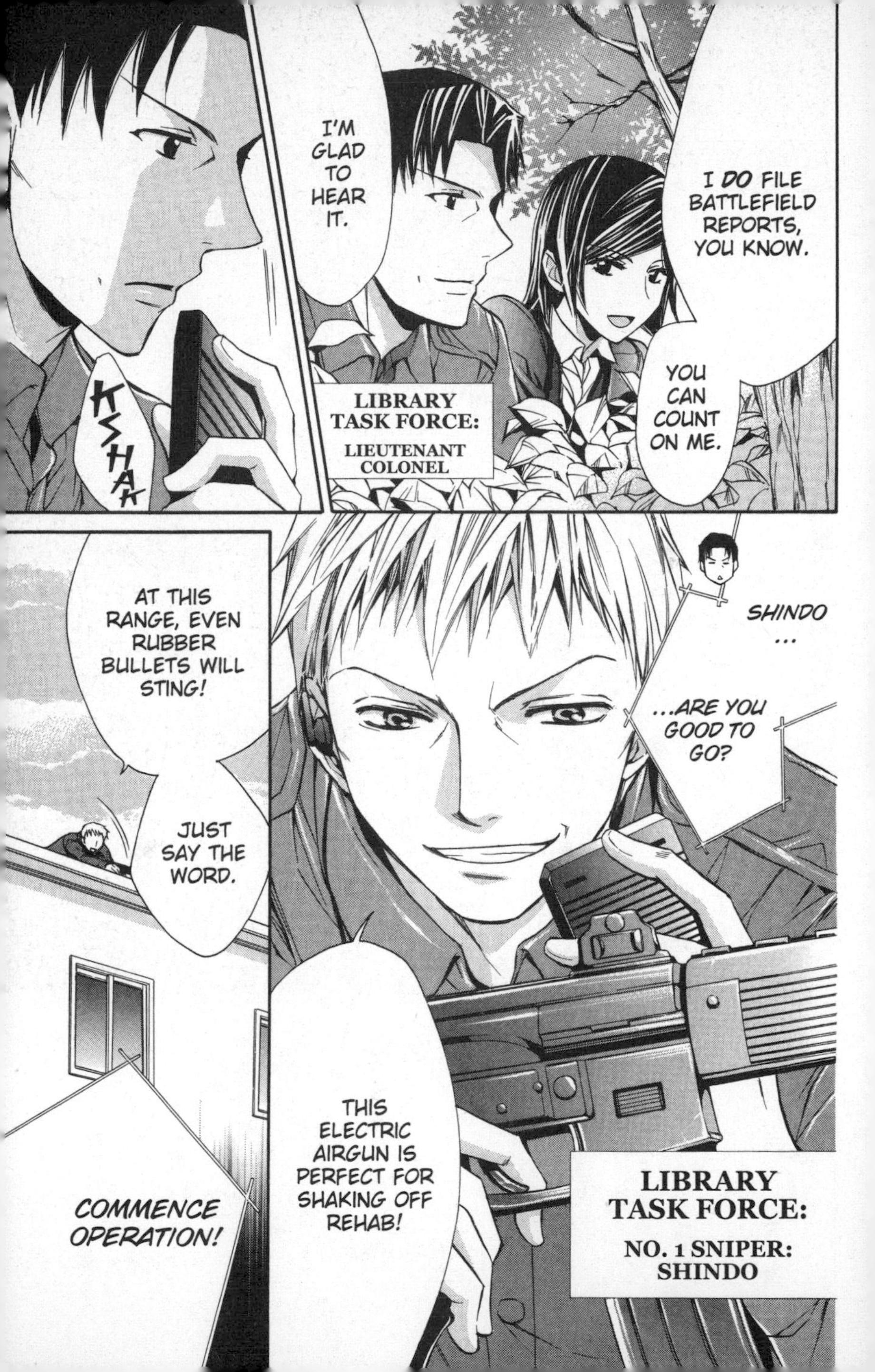
I DO FILE BATTLEFIELD REPORTS, YOU KNOW.
YOU CAN COUNT ON ME.
I'M GLAD TO HEAR IT.
LIBRARY TASK FORCE: LIEUTENANT COLONEL
KSHAK
SHINDO...
...ARE YOU GOOD TO GO?
THIS ELECTRIC AIRGUN IS PERFECT FOR SHAKING OFF REHAB!
LIBRARY TASK FORCE: NO. 1 SNIPER: SHINDO
AT THIS RANGE, EVEN RUBBER BULLETS WILL STING!
JUST SAY THE WORD.
COMMENCE OPERATION!

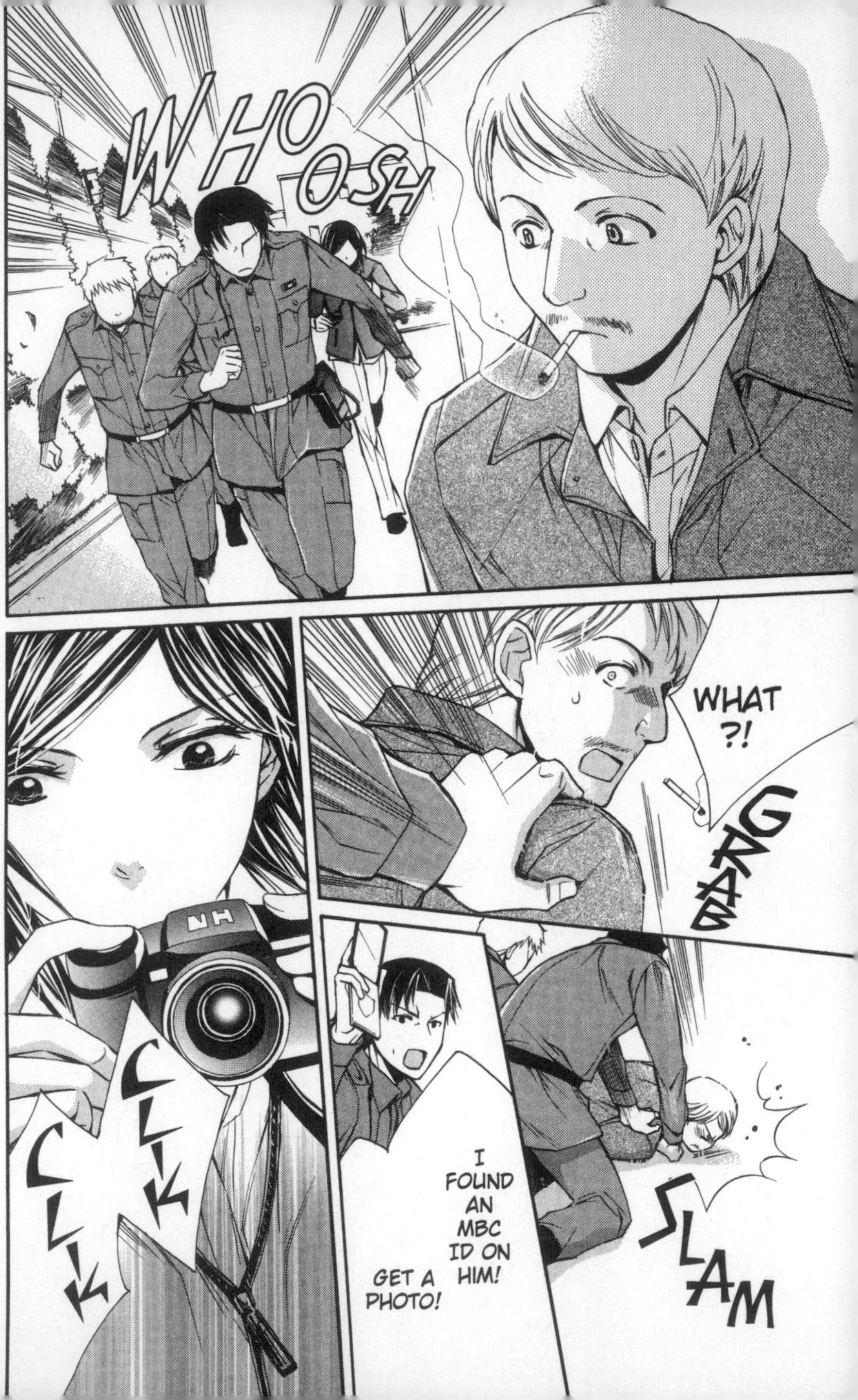
WHOOSH
WHAT?!
GRAB
SLAM
I FOUND AN MBC ID ON HIM!
GET A PHOTO!
CLIK
CLIK

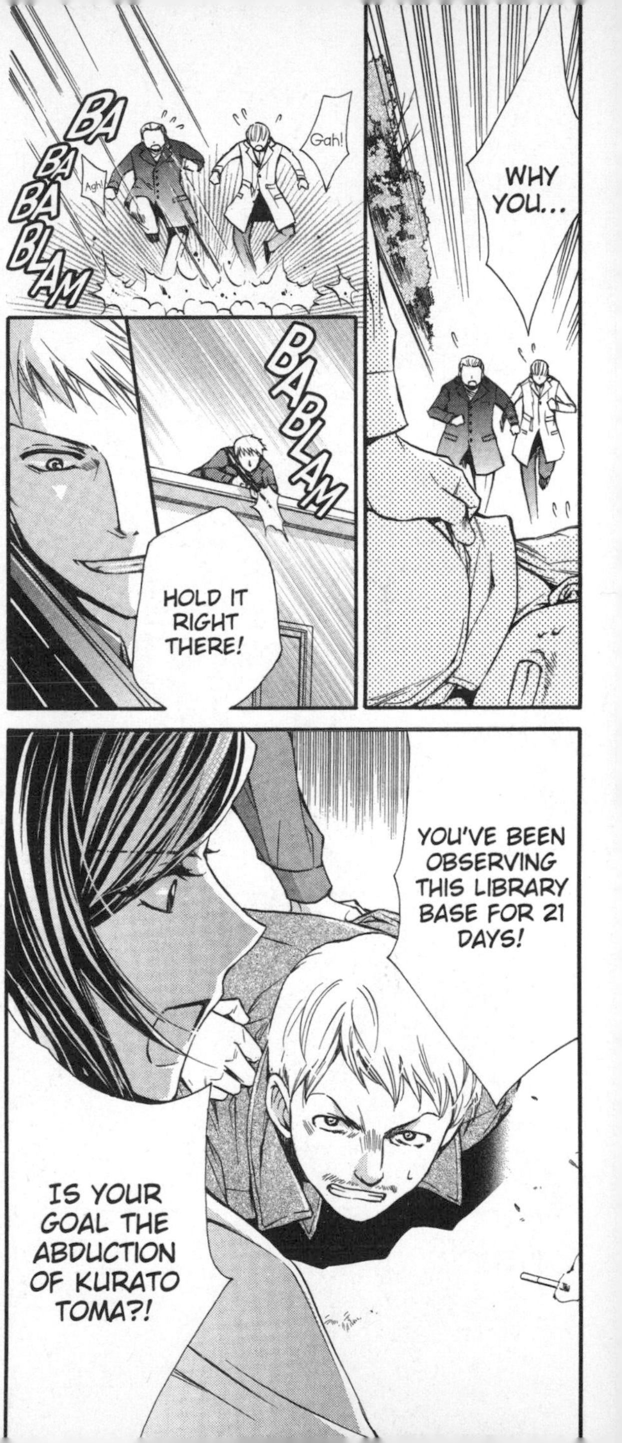
WHY YOU...
BA BA BA BLAM
Gah!
Agh!
BABLAM
HOLD IT RIGHT THERE!
YOU'VE BEEN OBSERVING THIS LIBRARY BASE FOR 21 DAYS!
IS YOUR GOAL THE ABDUCTION OF KURATO TOMA?!

1

*

Hello, I'm Yumi Kiiro and this is *Library Wars: Love & War*, Volume 13!

Every time a new volume comes out and I see the manga I authored all lined up on the bookstore shelves, I'm overjoyed! I'm so grateful to everyone involved with this manga and to all the readers. Thank you!

It's a clumsy manga, but please stick with it to the end!

*

*

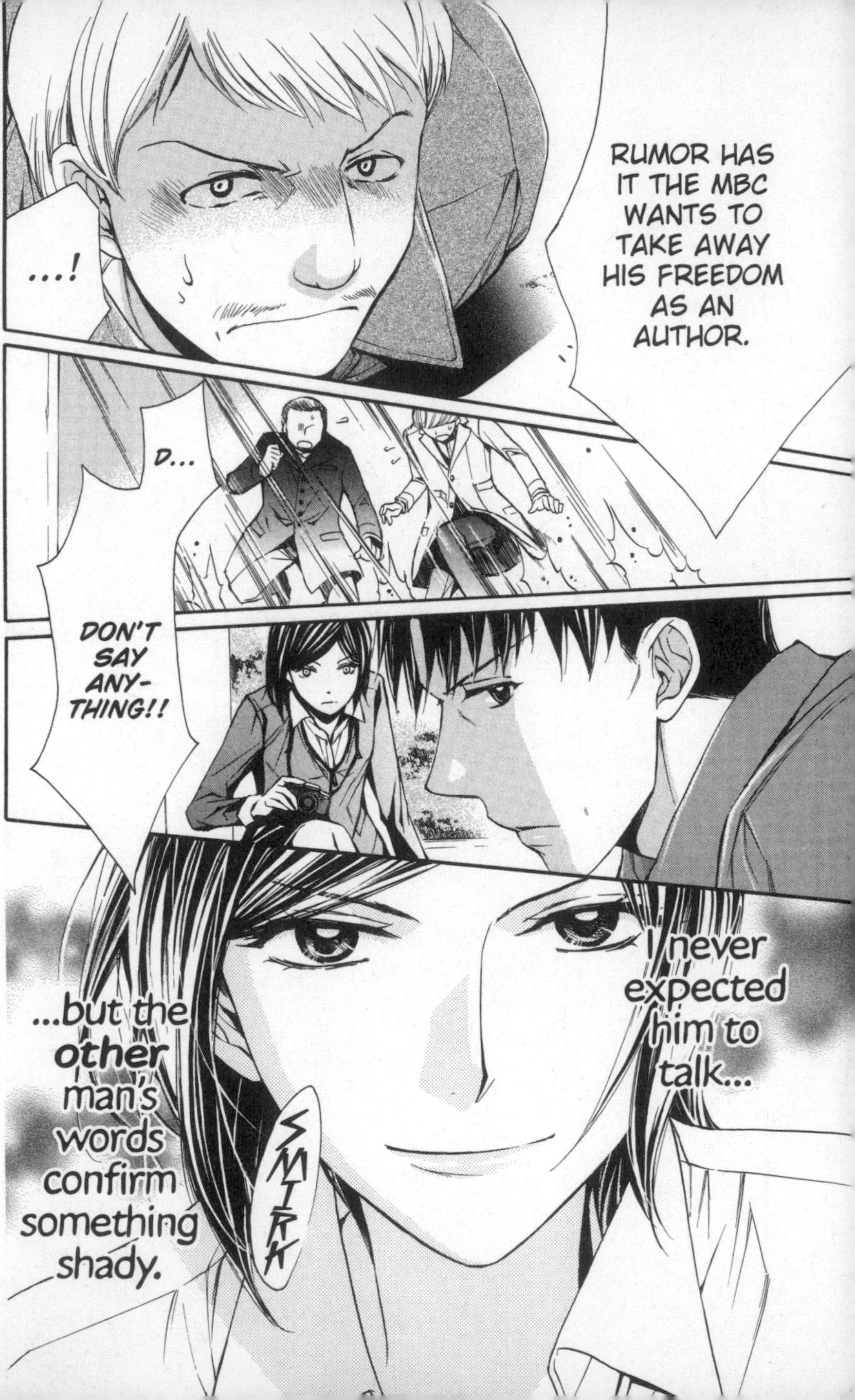
RUMOR HAS IT THE MBC WANTS TO TAKE AWAY HIS FREEDOM AS AN AUTHOR.
...!
D...
DON'T SAY ANY-THING!!
I never expected him to talk...
SMIRK
...but the **other** man's words confirm something shady.

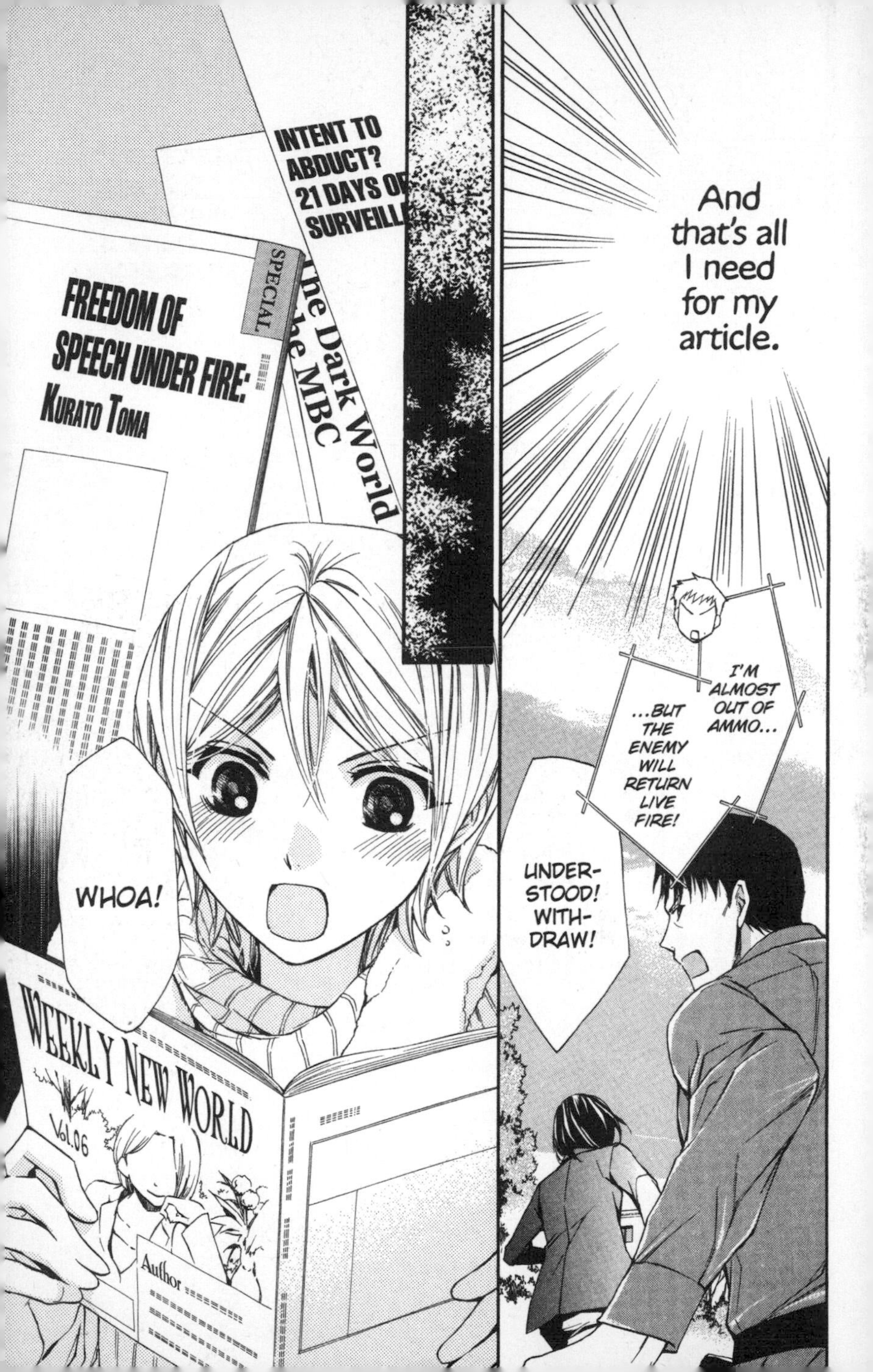
And that's all I need for my article.
I'M ALMOST OUT OF AMMO...
...BUT THE ENEMY WILL RETURN LIVE FIRE!
UNDER-STOOD! WITH-DRAW!
INTENT TO ABDUCT?
SPECIAL
FREEDOM OF SPEECH UNDER FIRE: KURATO TOMA
The Dark World
WHOA!
WEEKLY NEW WORLD
Vol.06
Author

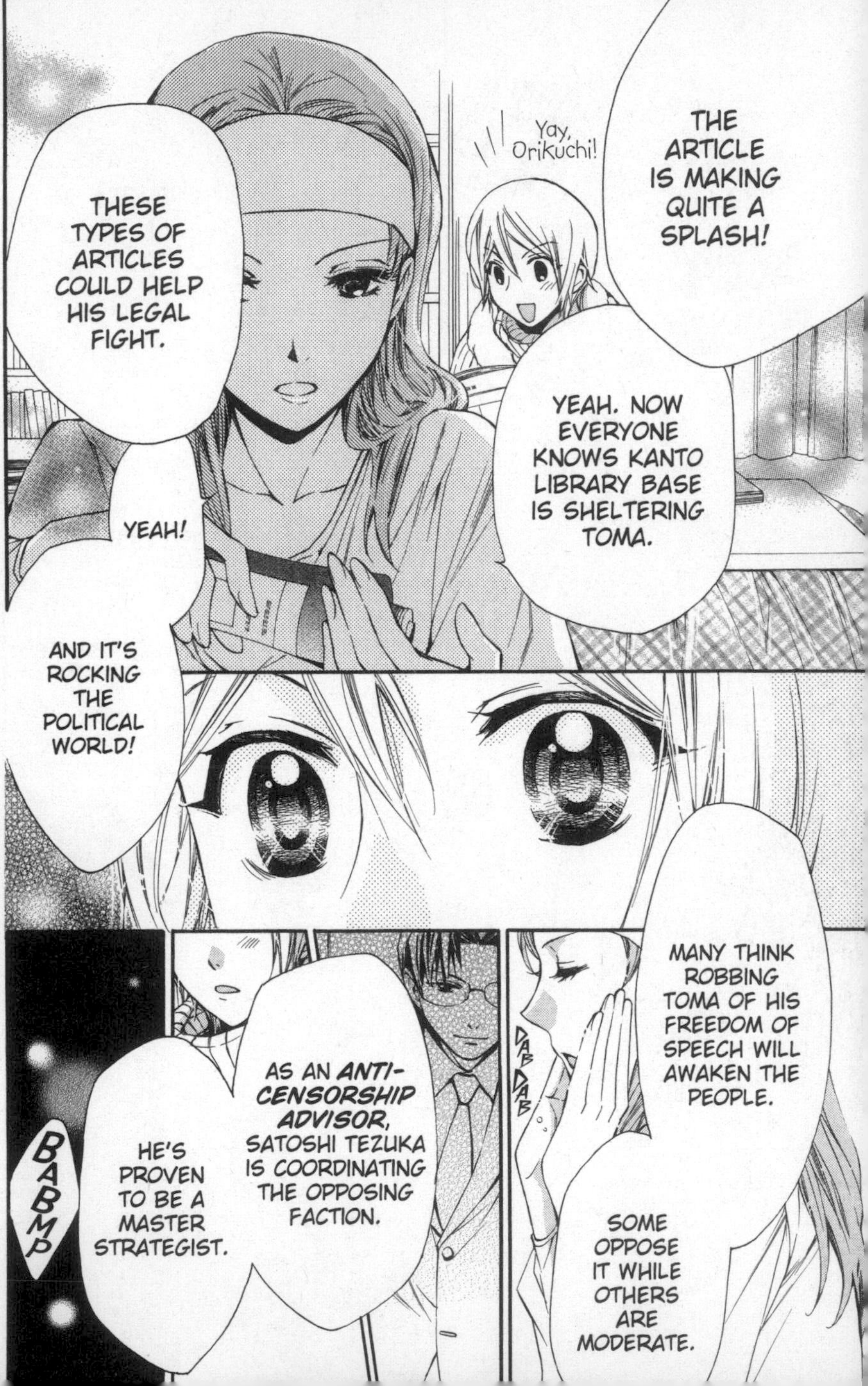
THE ARTICLE IS MAKING QUITE A SPLASH!
Yay, Orikuchi!
YEAH. NOW EVERYONE KNOWS KANTO LIBRARY BASE IS SHELTERING TOMA.
THESE TYPES OF ARTICLES COULD HELP HIS LEGAL FIGHT.
YEAH!
AND IT'S ROCKING THE POLITICAL WORLD!
MANY THINK ROBBING TOMA OF HIS FREEDOM OF SPEECH WILL AWAKEN THE PEOPLE.
DAB DAB
SOME OPPOSE IT WHILE OTHERS ARE MODERATE.
AS AN *ANTI-CENSORSHIP ADVISOR,* SATOSHI TEZUKA IS COORDINATING THE OPPOSING FACTION.
HE'S PROVEN TO BE A MASTER STRATEGIST.
BABMP

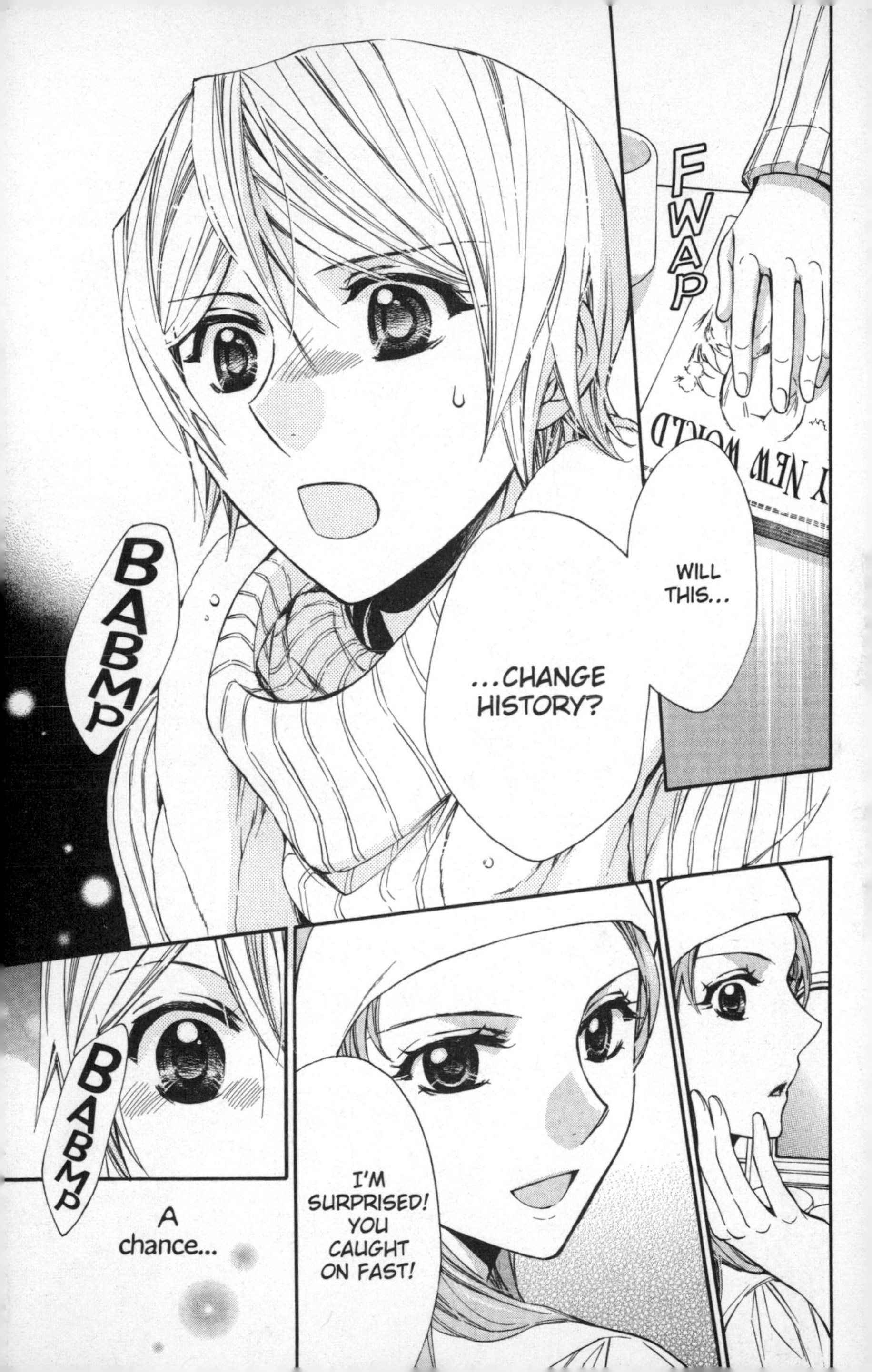
FWAP
WILL THIS...
...CHANGE HISTORY?
BABMP
I'M SURPRISED! YOU CAUGHT ON FAST!
BABMP
A chance...

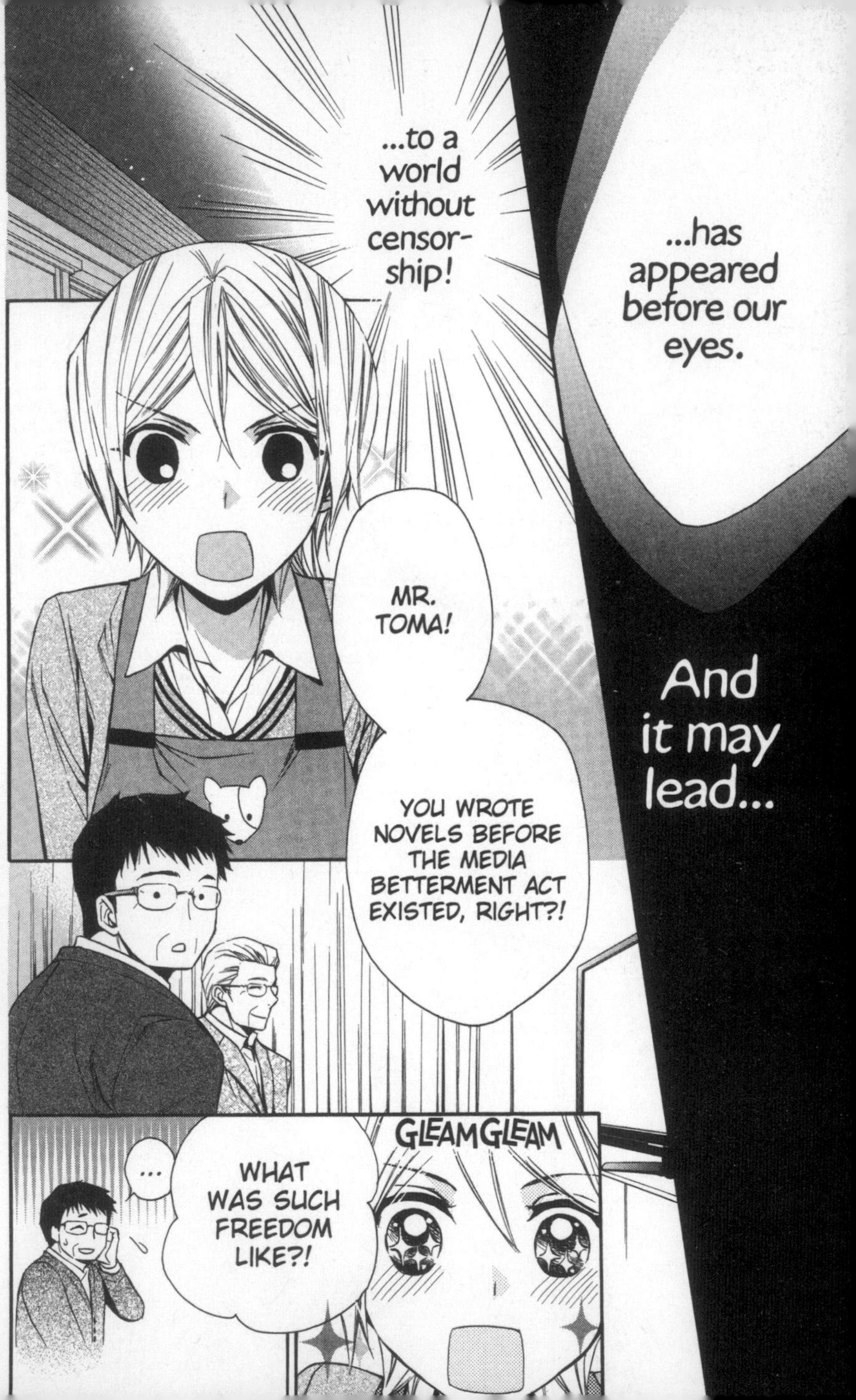
...has appeared before our eyes.
And it may lead...
...to a world without censor-ship!
MR. TOMA!
YOU WROTE NOVELS BEFORE THE MEDIA BETTERMENT ACT EXISTED, RIGHT?!
GLEAMGLEAM
WHAT WAS SUCH FREEDOM LIKE?!
...

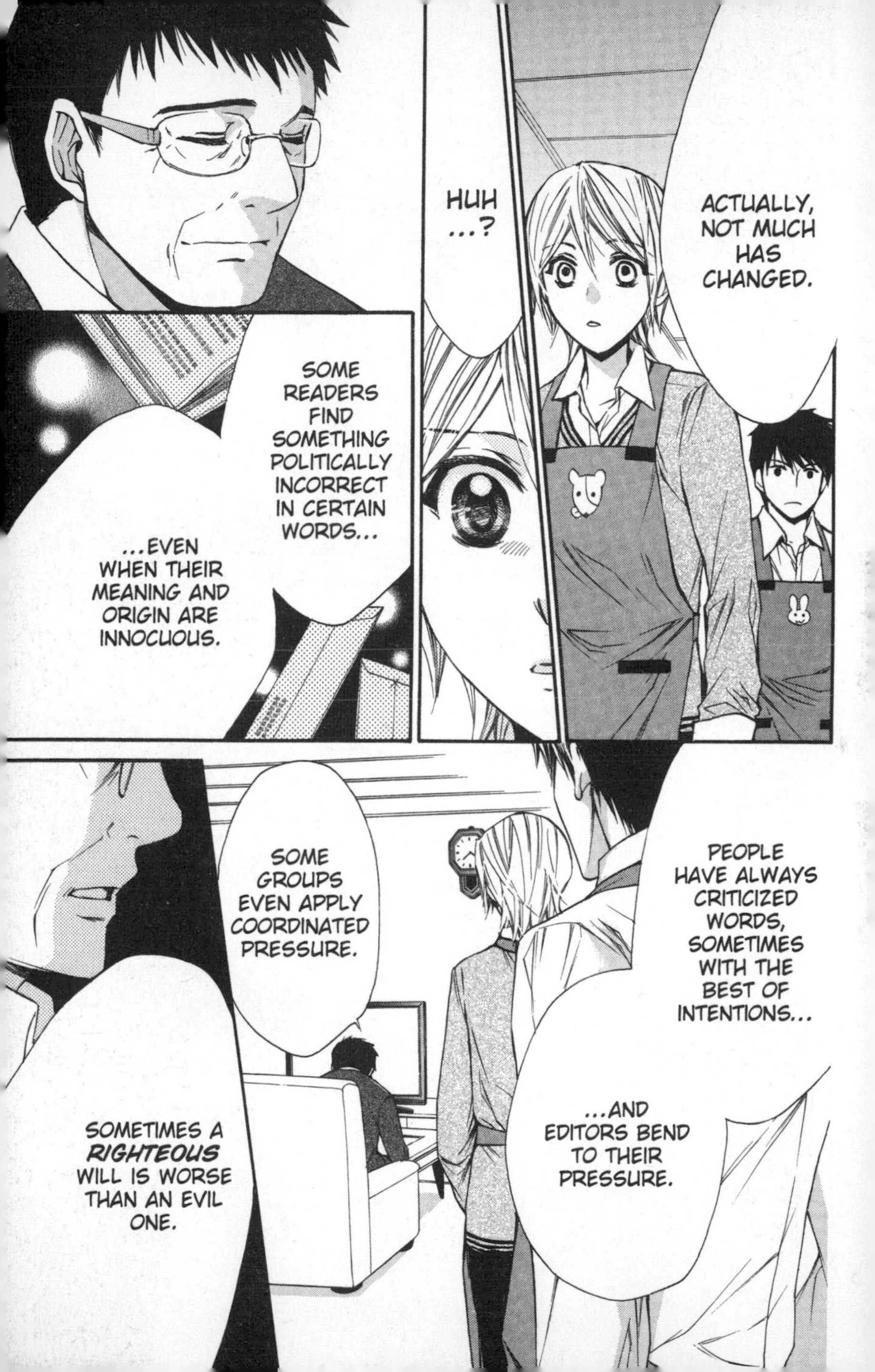
ACTUALLY, NOT MUCH HAS CHANGED.
HUH ...?
SOME READERS FIND SOMETHING POLITICALLY INCORRECT IN CERTAIN WORDS...
...EVEN WHEN THEIR MEANING AND ORIGIN ARE INNOCUOUS.
PEOPLE HAVE ALWAYS CRITICIZED WORDS, SOMETIMES WITH THE BEST OF INTENTIONS...
...AND EDITORS BEND TO THEIR PRESSURE.
SOME GROUPS EVEN APPLY COORDINATED PRESSURE.
SOMETIMES A *RIGHTEOUS* WILL IS WORSE THAN AN EVIL ONE.

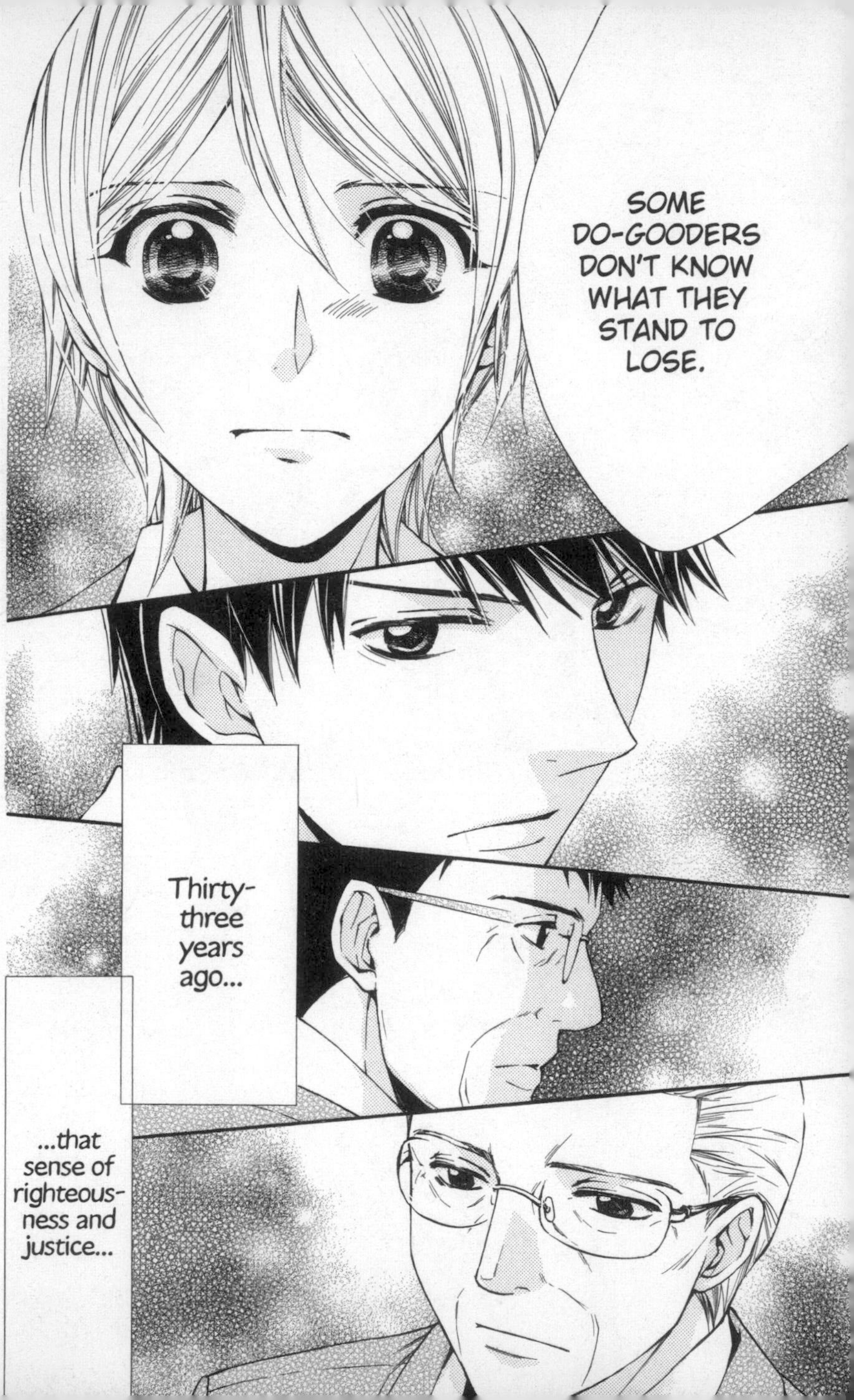
SOME DO-GOODERS DON'T KNOW WHAT THEY STAND TO LOSE.
Thirty-three years ago...
...that sense of righteousness and justice...

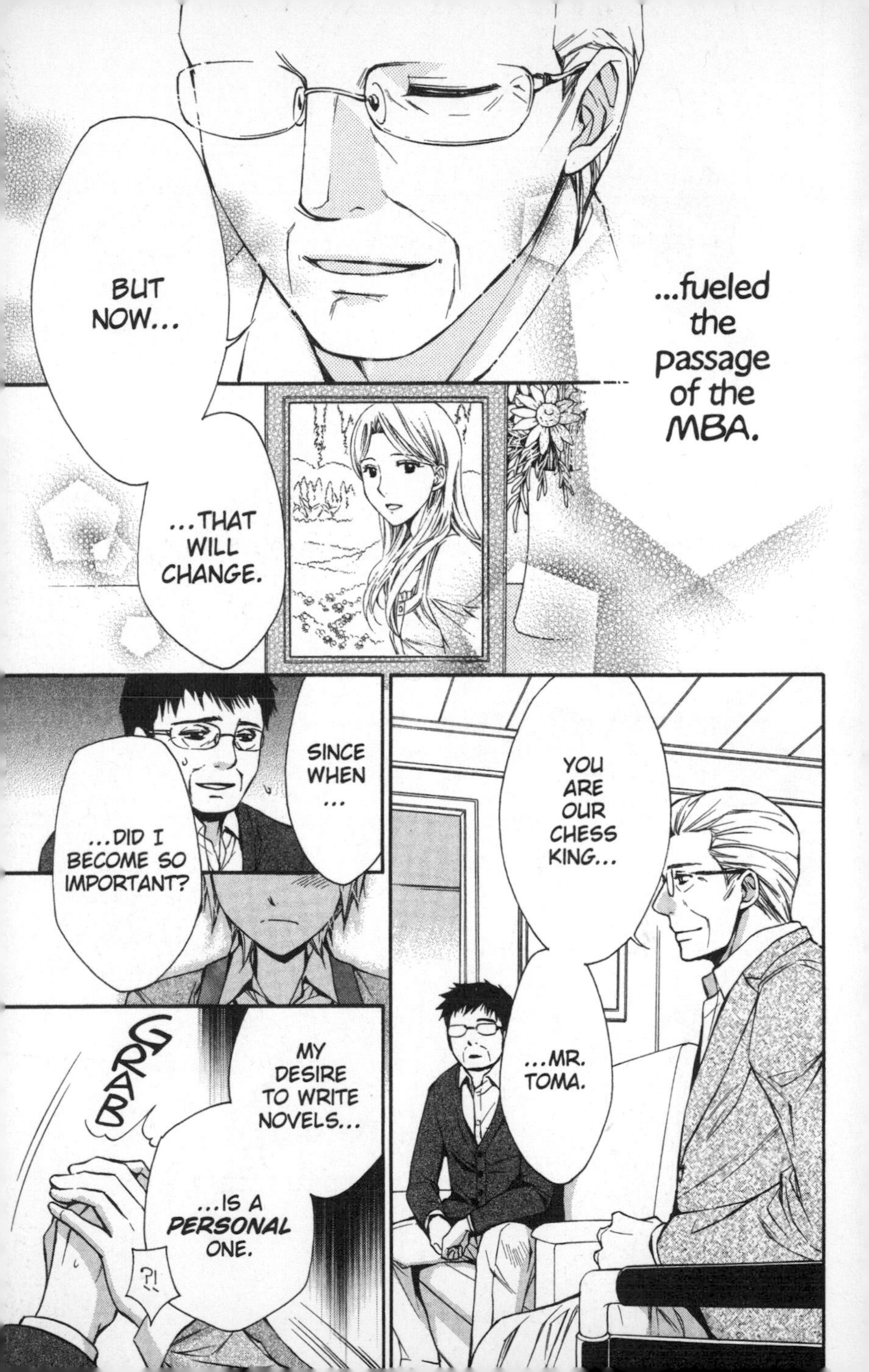
...fueled the passage of the MBA.
BUT NOW...
...THAT WILL CHANGE.
YOU ARE OUR CHESS KING...
...MR. TOMA.
SINCE WHEN...
...DID I BECOME SO IMPORTANT?
MY DESIRE TO WRITE NOVELS...
...IS A *PERSONAL* ONE.
GRAB
?!

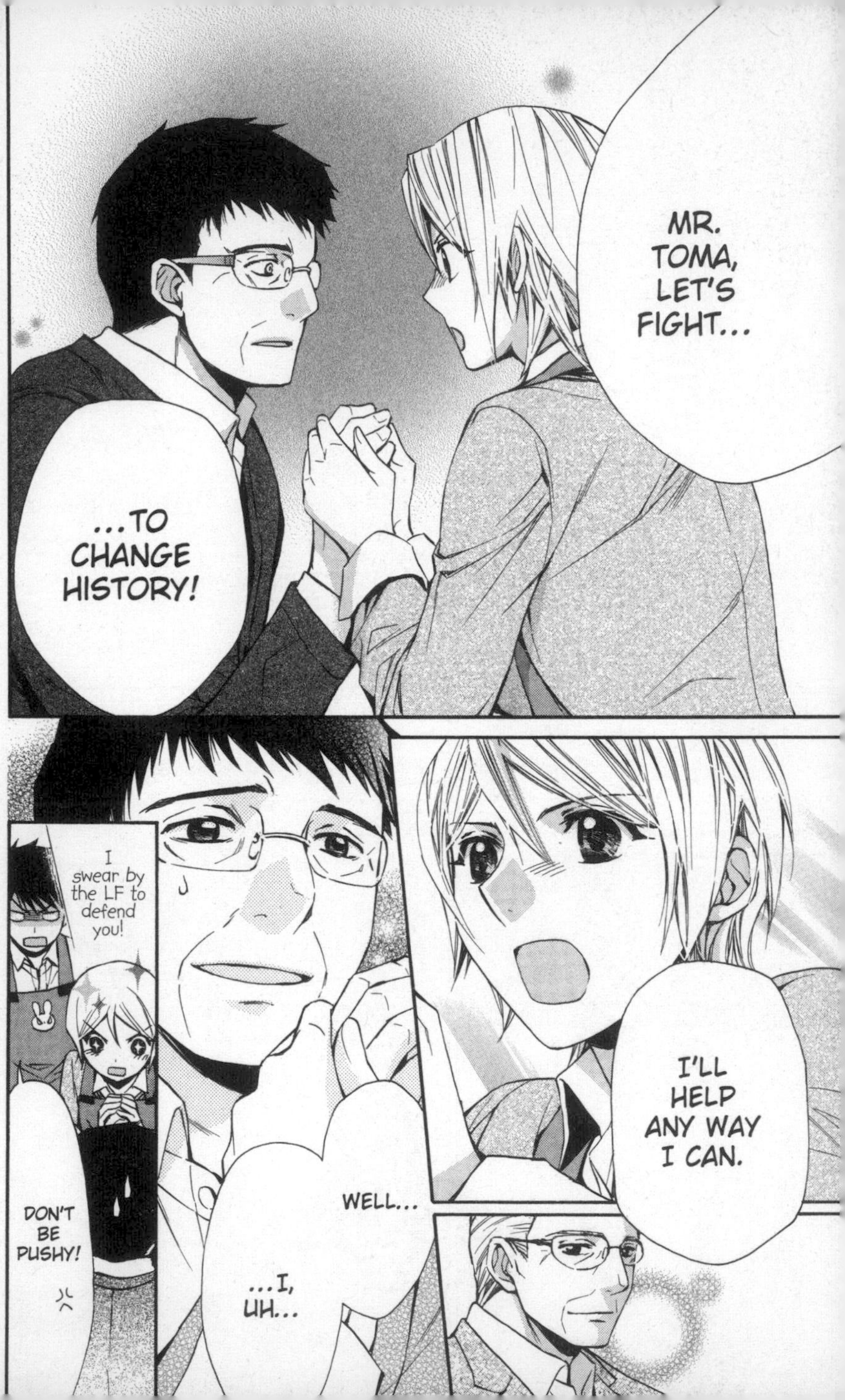
MR. TOMA, LET'S FIGHT...
...TO CHANGE HISTORY!
I'LL HELP ANY WAY I CAN.
WELL...
...I, UH...
I swear by the LF to defend you!
DON'T BE PUSHY!

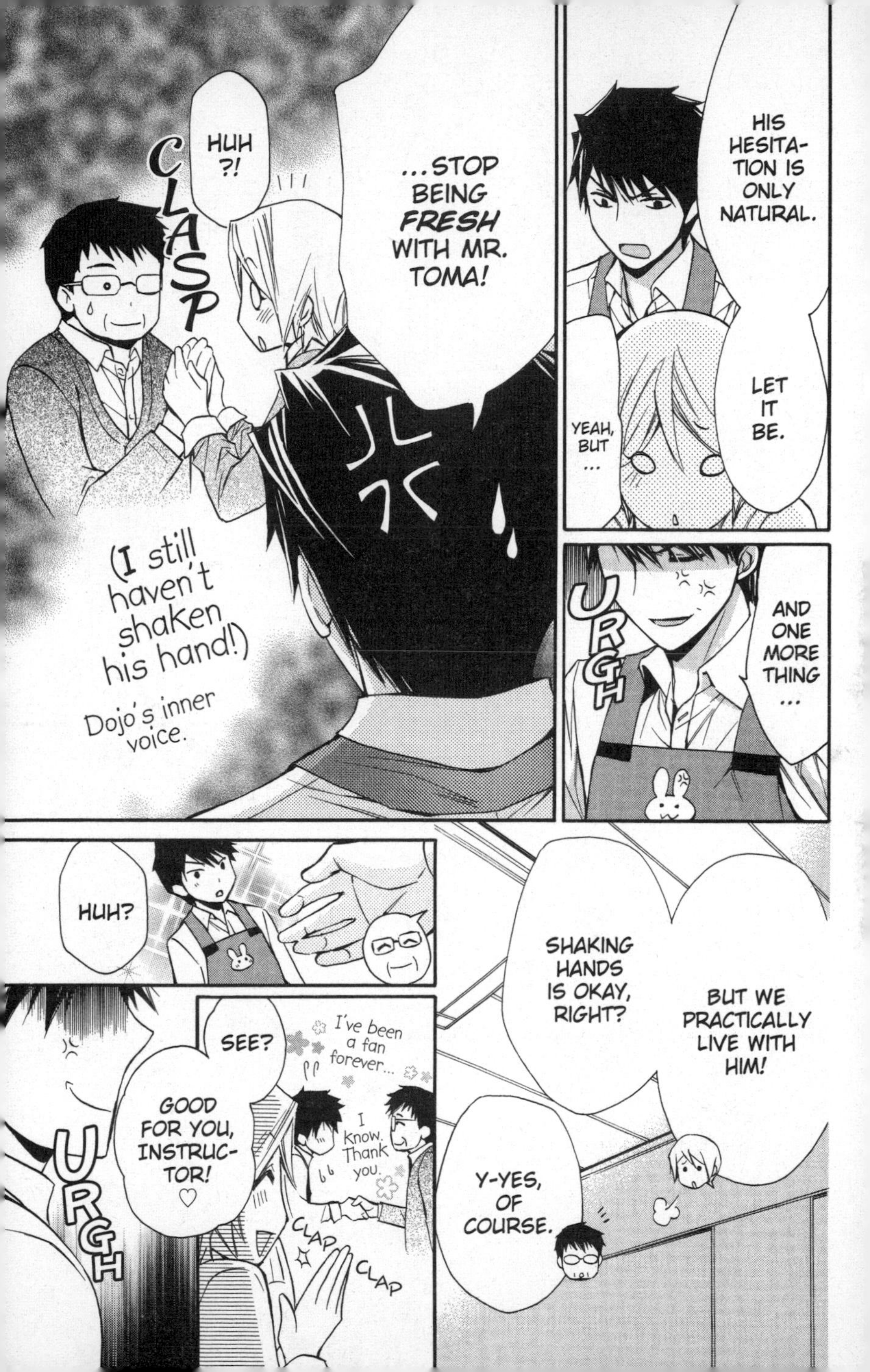
HIS HESITATION IS ONLY NATURAL.
LET IT BE.
YEAH, BUT ...
AND ONE MORE THING ...
URGH
...STOP BEING *FRESH* WITH MR. TOMA!
HUH ?!
CLASP
(I still haven't shaken his hand!)
Dojo's inner voice.
SHAKING HANDS IS OKAY, RIGHT?
BUT WE PRACTICALLY LIVE WITH HIM!
Y-YES, OF COURSE.
HUH?
SEE?
GOOD FOR YOU, INSTRUCTOR! ♡
I've been a fan forever...
I know. Thank you.
URGH
CLAP
CLAP

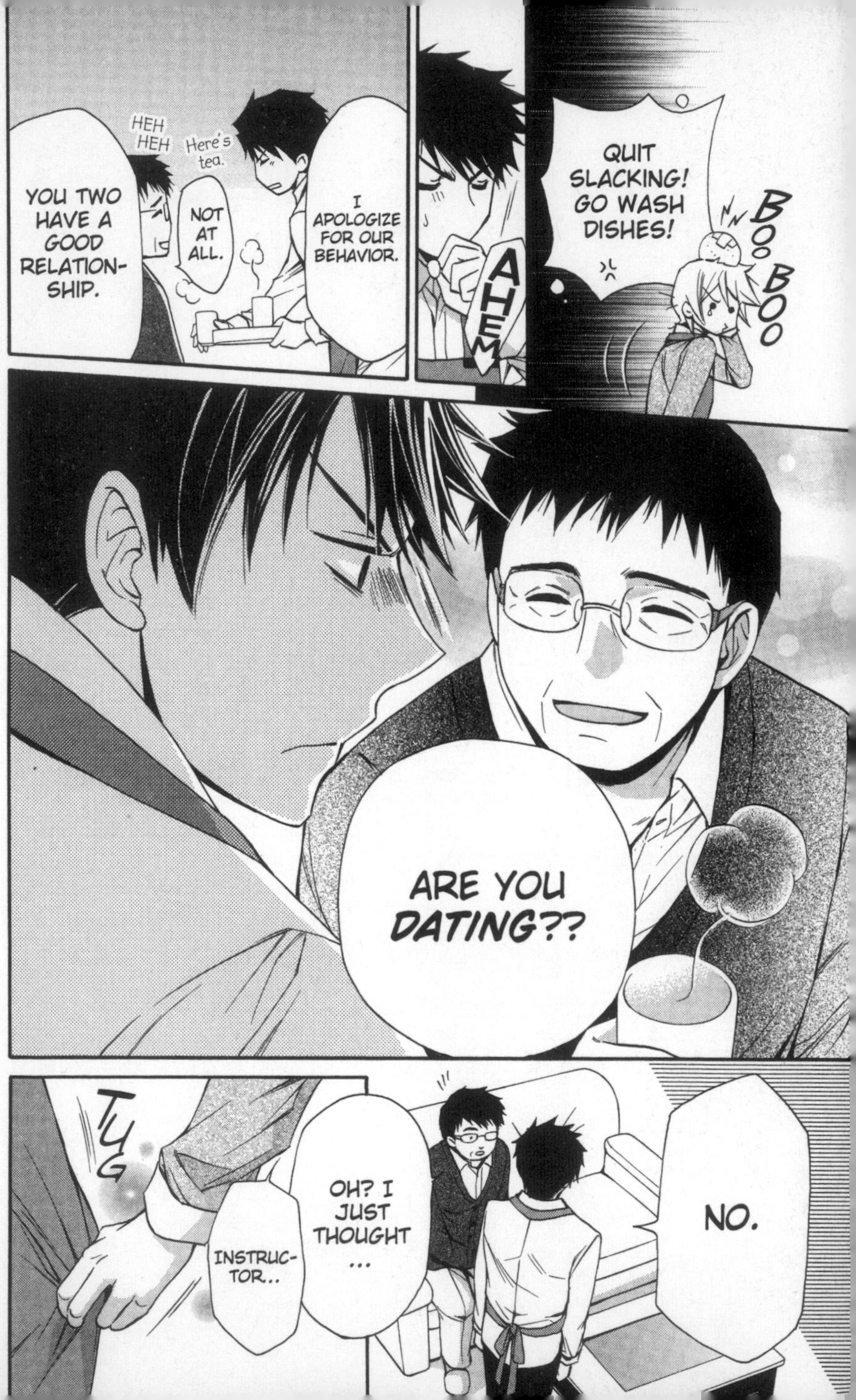
QUIT SLACKING! GO WASH DISHES!
BOO BOO
AHEM
I APOLOGIZE FOR OUR BEHAVIOR.
Here's tea.
NOT AT ALL.
HEH HEH
YOU TWO HAVE A GOOD RELATION-SHIP.
ARE YOU DATING??
NO.
OH? I JUST THOUGHT...
TUG
INSTRUC-TOR...

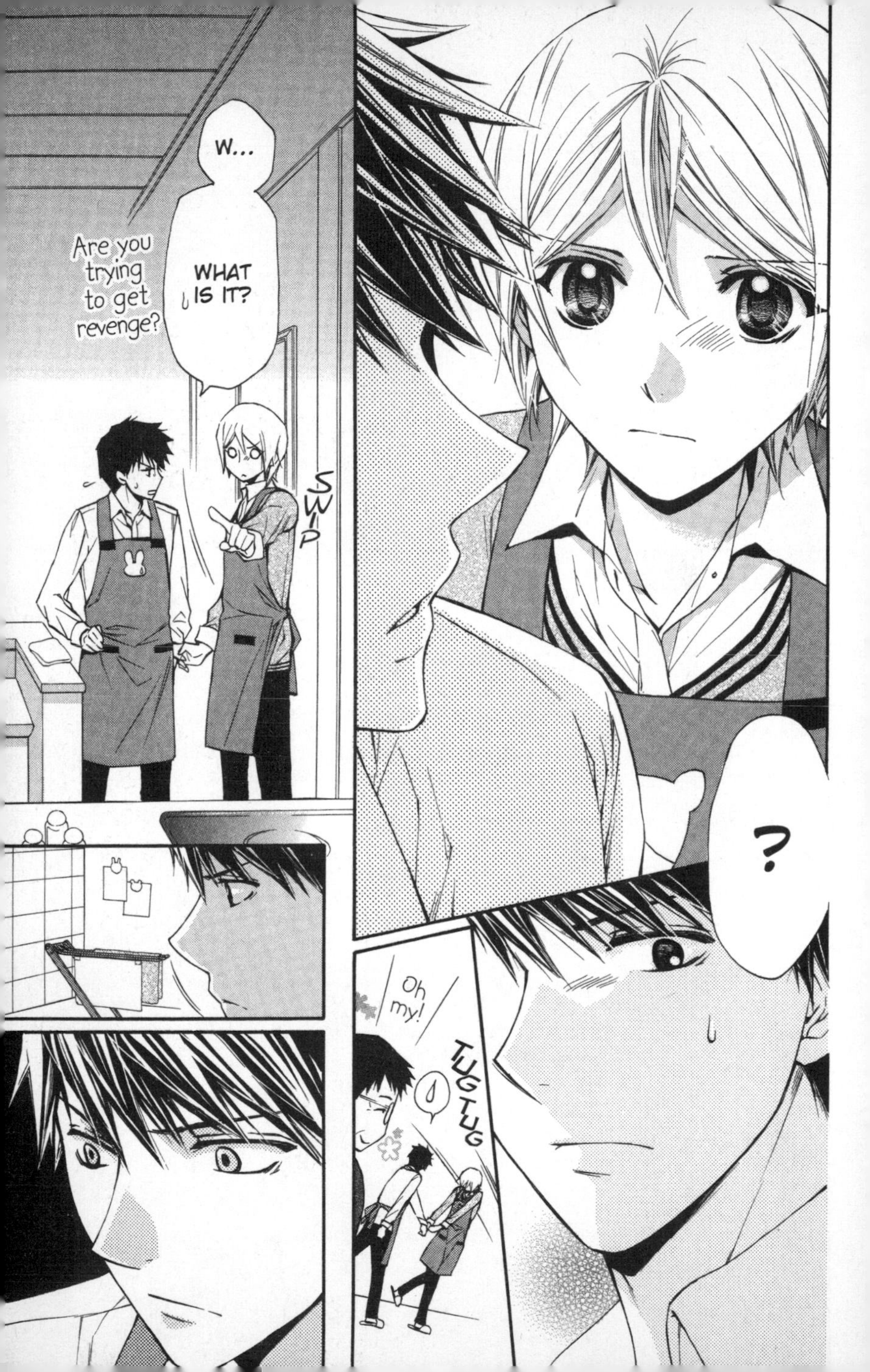
?
W...
WHAT IS IT?
Are you trying to get revenge?
SWIP
Oh my!
TUG TUG

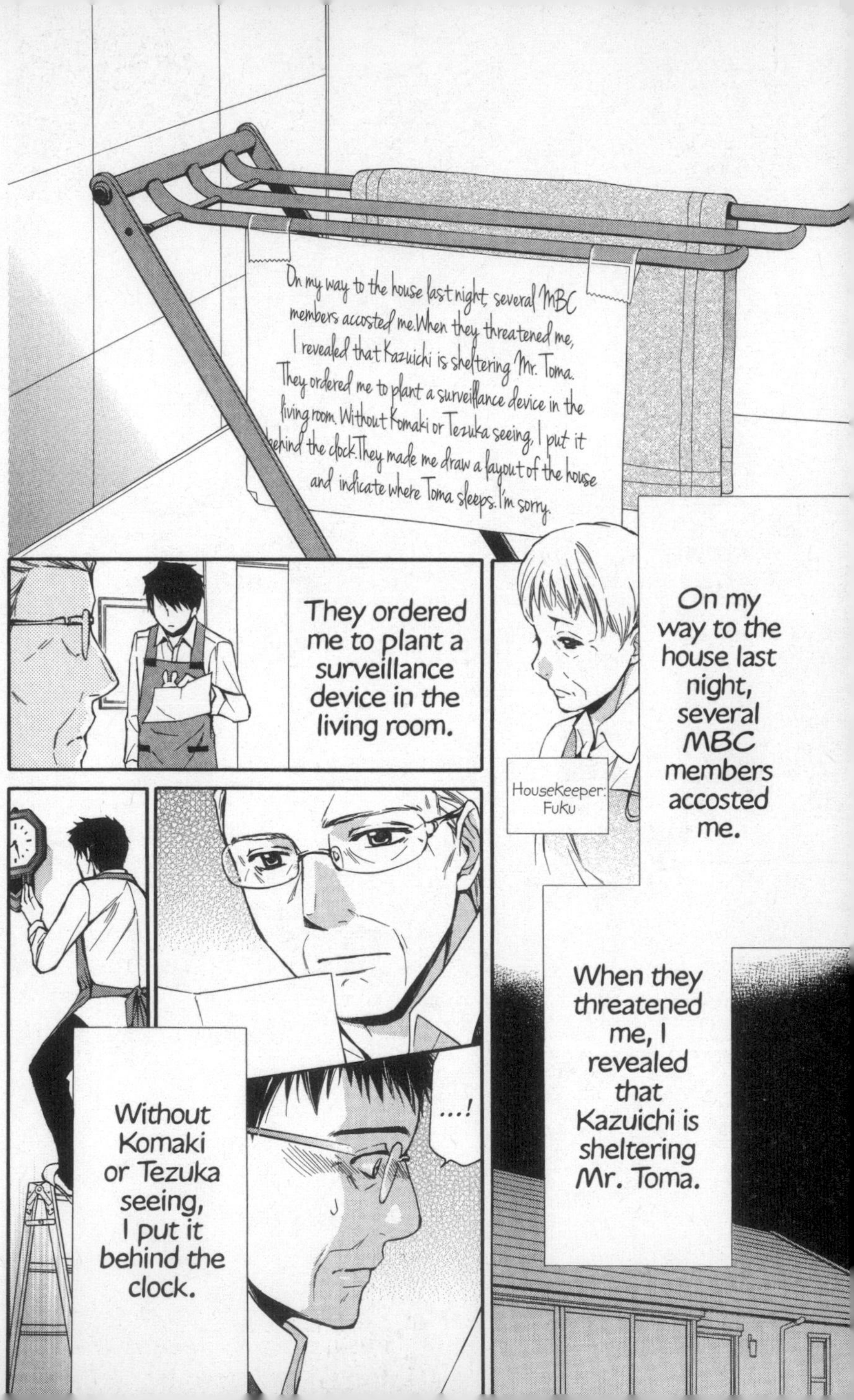
On my way to the house last night, several MBC members accosted me. When they threatened me, I revealed that Kazuichi is sheltering Mr. Toma. They ordered me to plant a surveillance device in the living room. Without Komaki or Tezuka seeing, I put it behind the clock. They made me draw a layout of the house and indicate where Toma sleeps. I'm sorry.
On my way to the house last night, several MBC members accosted me.
HouseKeeper: Fuku
When they threatened me, I revealed that Kazuichi is sheltering Mr. Toma.
They ordered me to plant a surveillance device in the living room.
Without Komaki or Tezuka seeing, I put it behind the clock.
...!

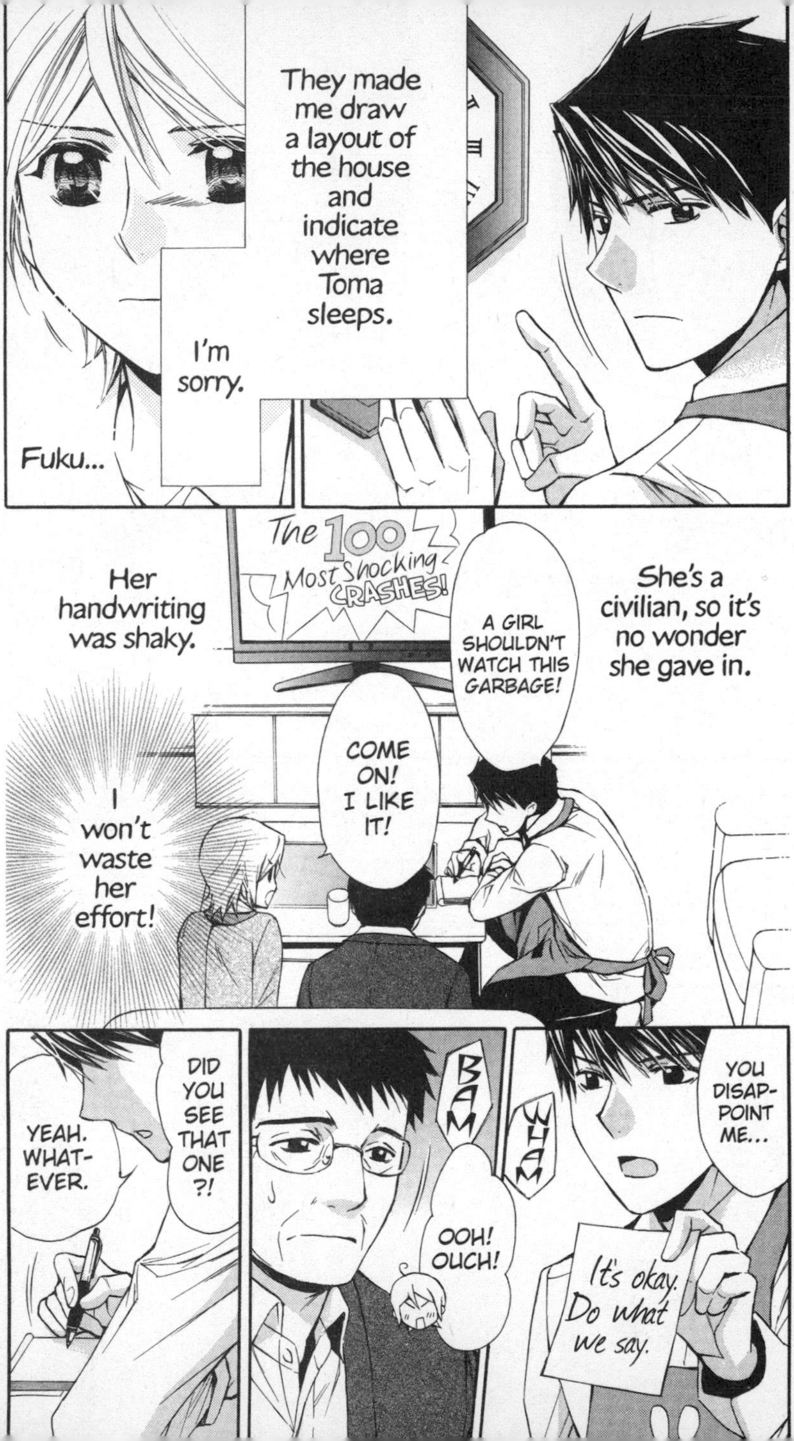
They made me draw a layout of the house and indicate where Toma sleeps.
I'm sorry.
Fuku...
She's a civilian, so it's no wonder she gave in.
A GIRL SHOULDN'T WATCH THIS GARBAGE!
The 100 Most Shocking CRASHES!
Her handwriting was shaky.
COME ON! I LIKE IT!
I won't waste her effort!
YOU DISAP-POINT ME...
It's okay. Do what we say.
WHAM
BAM
OOH! OUCH!
DID YOU SEE THAT ONE?!
YEAH. WHAT-EVER.

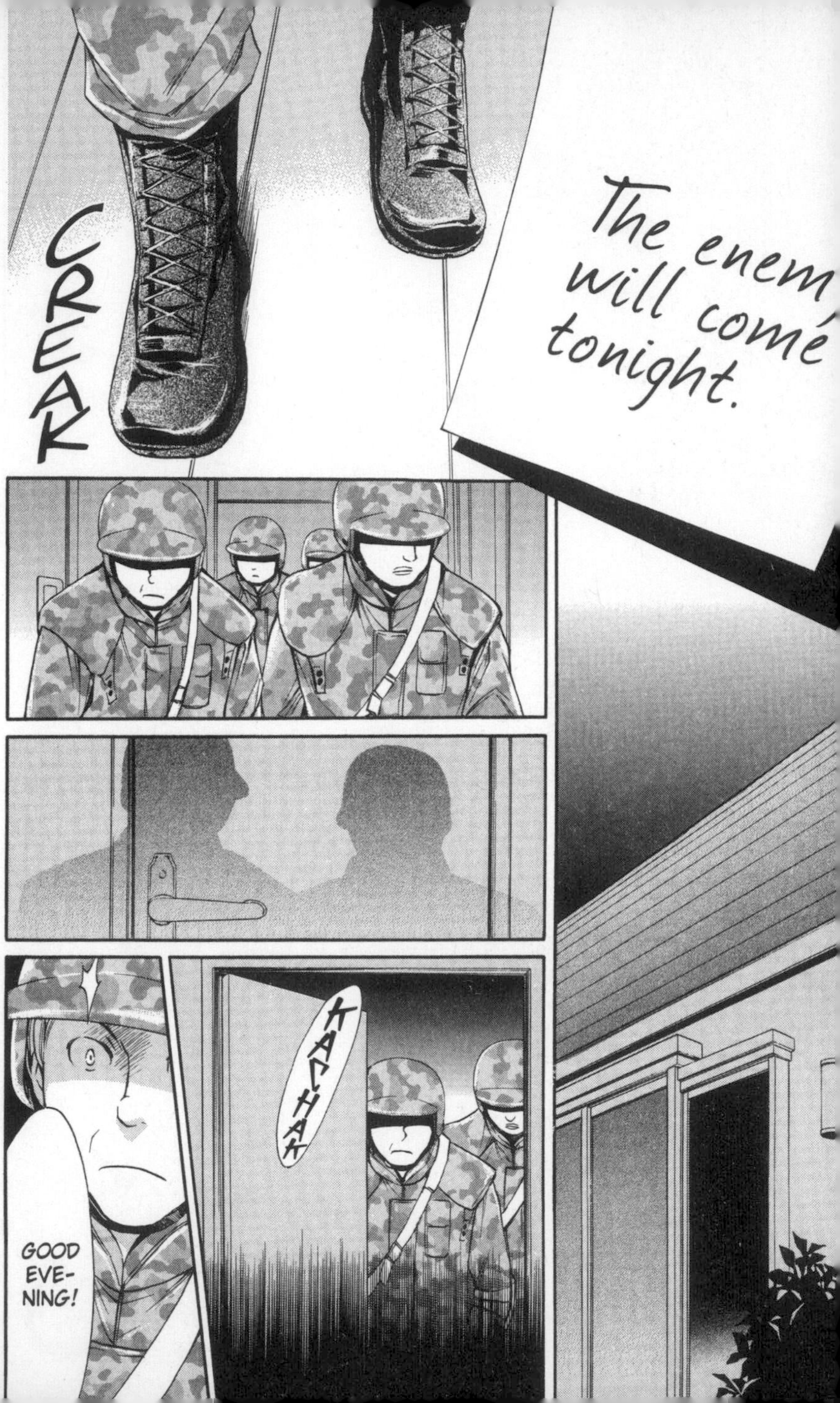
The enem
will comé
tonight.
CREAK
KACHAK
GOOD EVE-NING!

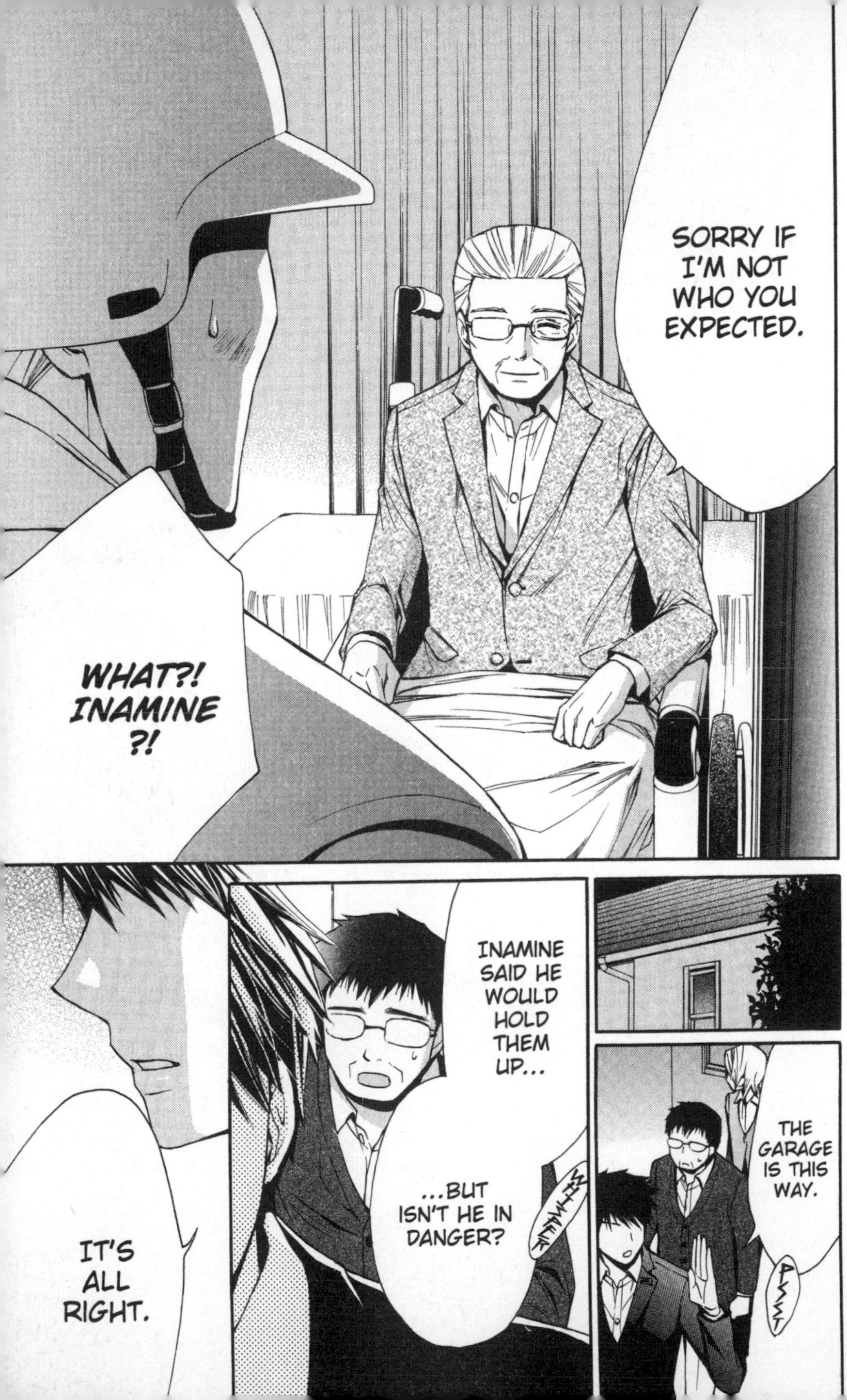
SORRY IF I'M NOT WHO YOU EXPECTED.
WHAT?! INAMINE ?!
THE GARAGE IS THIS WAY.
PSST
INAMINE SAID HE WOULD HOLD THEM UP...
...BUT ISN'T HE IN DANGER?
WHISPER
IT'S ALL RIGHT.

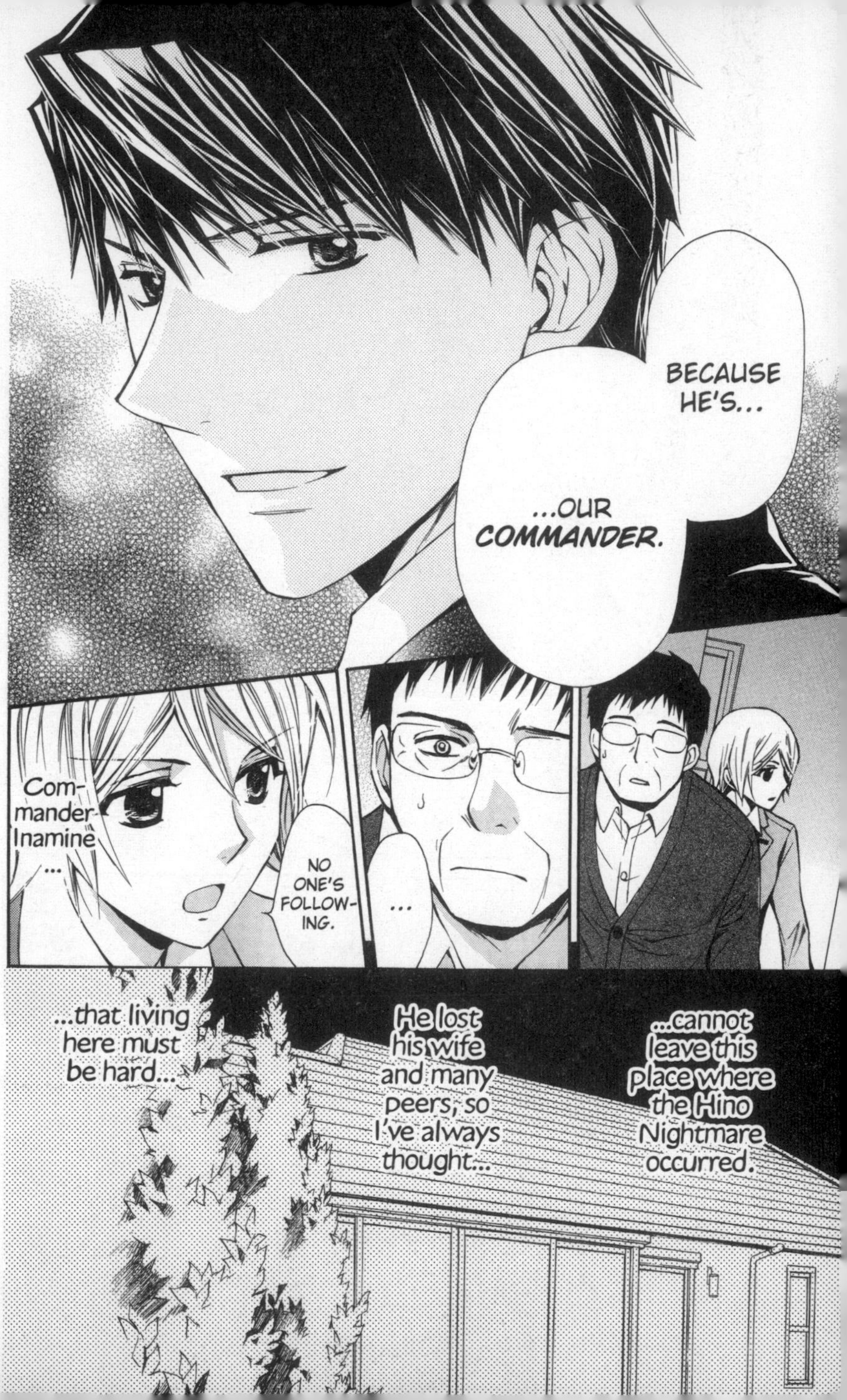
BECAUSE HE'S...
...OUR COMMANDER.
...
NO ONE'S FOLLOWING.
Commander Inamine...
...cannot leave this place where the Hino Nightmare occurred.
He lost his wife and many peers, so I've always thought...
...that living here must be hard...

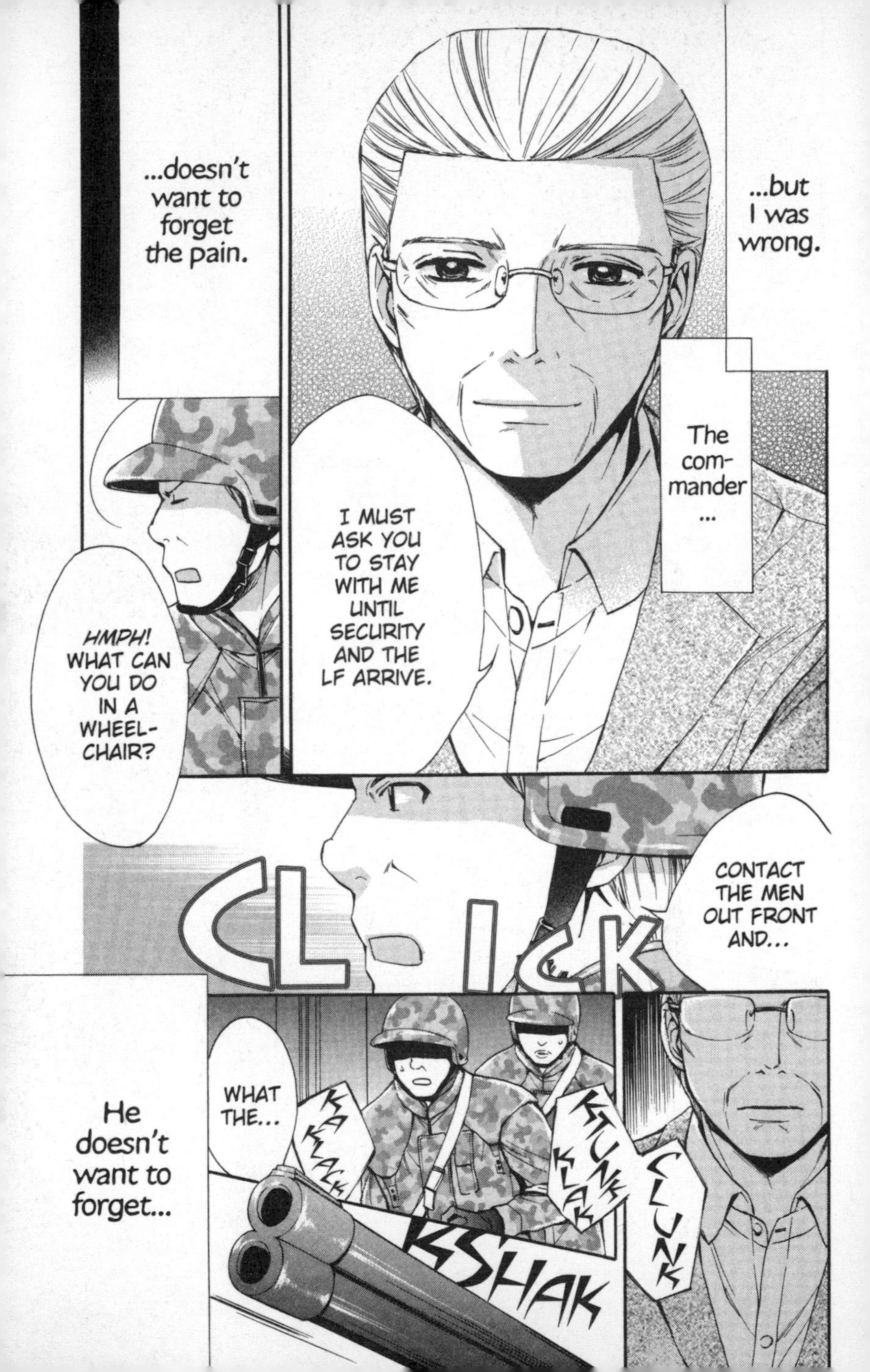
...but I was wrong.
The commander...
I MUST ASK YOU TO STAY WITH ME UNTIL SECURITY AND THE LF ARRIVE.
...doesn't want to forget the pain.
HMPH! WHAT CAN YOU DO IN A WHEELCHAIR?
CONTACT THE MEN OUT FRONT AND...
CLICK
CLUNK
KTUNK
KLAK
KSHAK
WHAT THE...
KA KLACK
He doesn't want to forget...

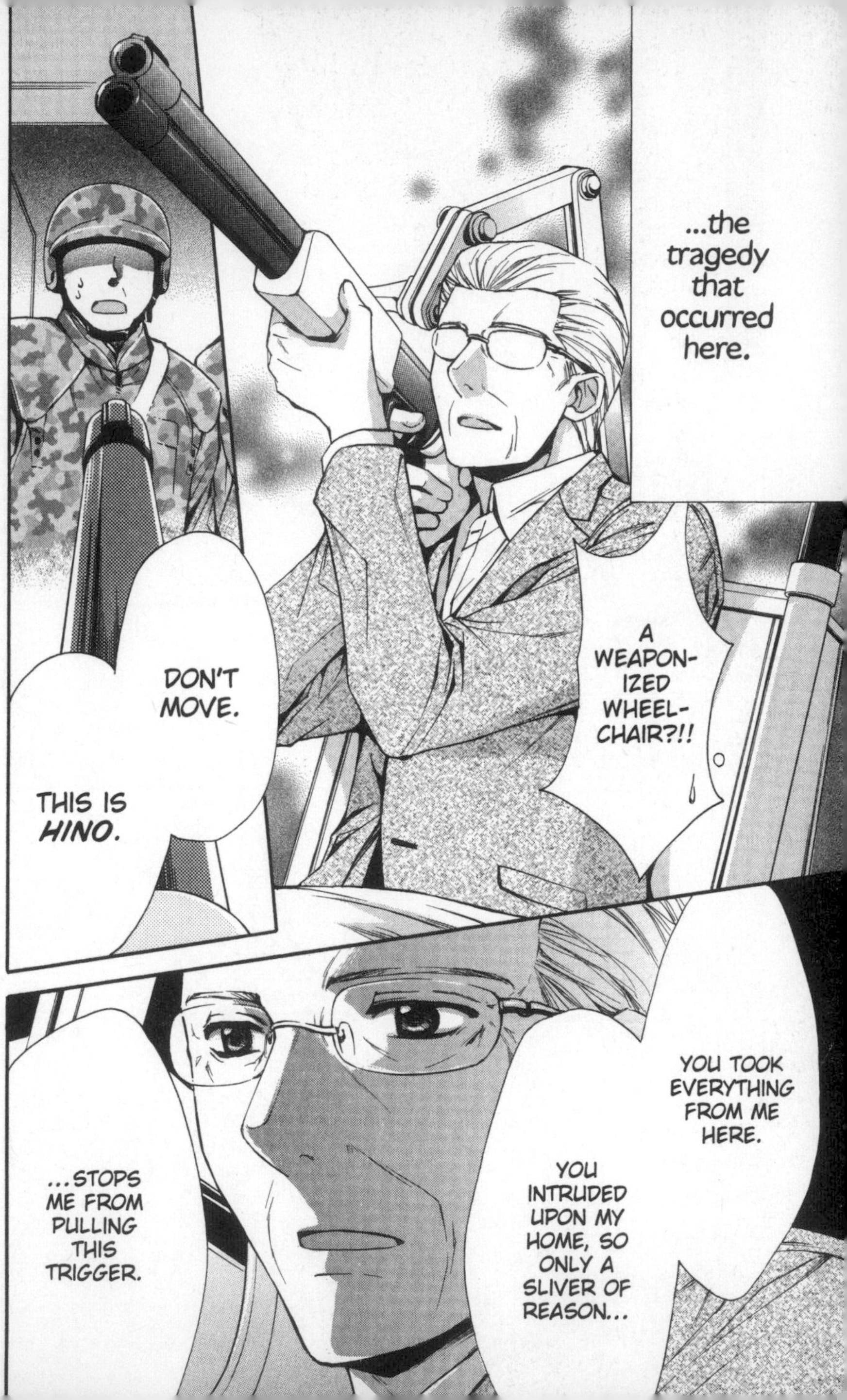
...the tragedy that occurred here.
A WEAPON-IZED WHEEL-CHAIR?!!
DON'T MOVE.
THIS IS *HINO*.
YOU TOOK EVERYTHING FROM ME HERE.
YOU INTRUDED UPON MY HOME, SO ONLY A SLIVER OF REASON...
...STOPS ME FROM PULLING THIS TRIGGER.

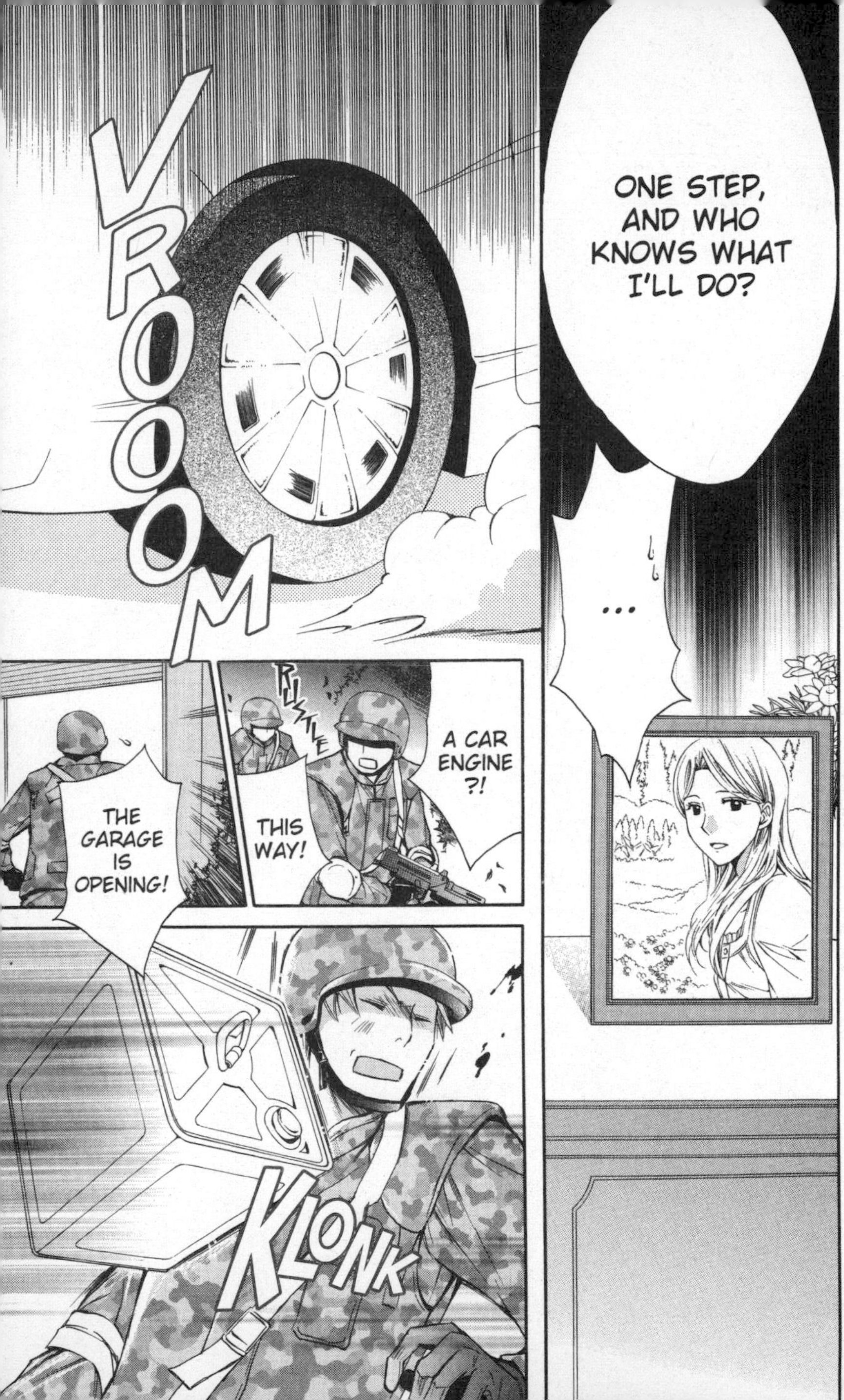
ONE STEP, AND WHO KNOWS WHAT I'LL DO?
...
VROOOOM
RUSTLE
A CAR ENGINE ?!
THIS WAY!
THE GARAGE IS OPENING!
KLONK

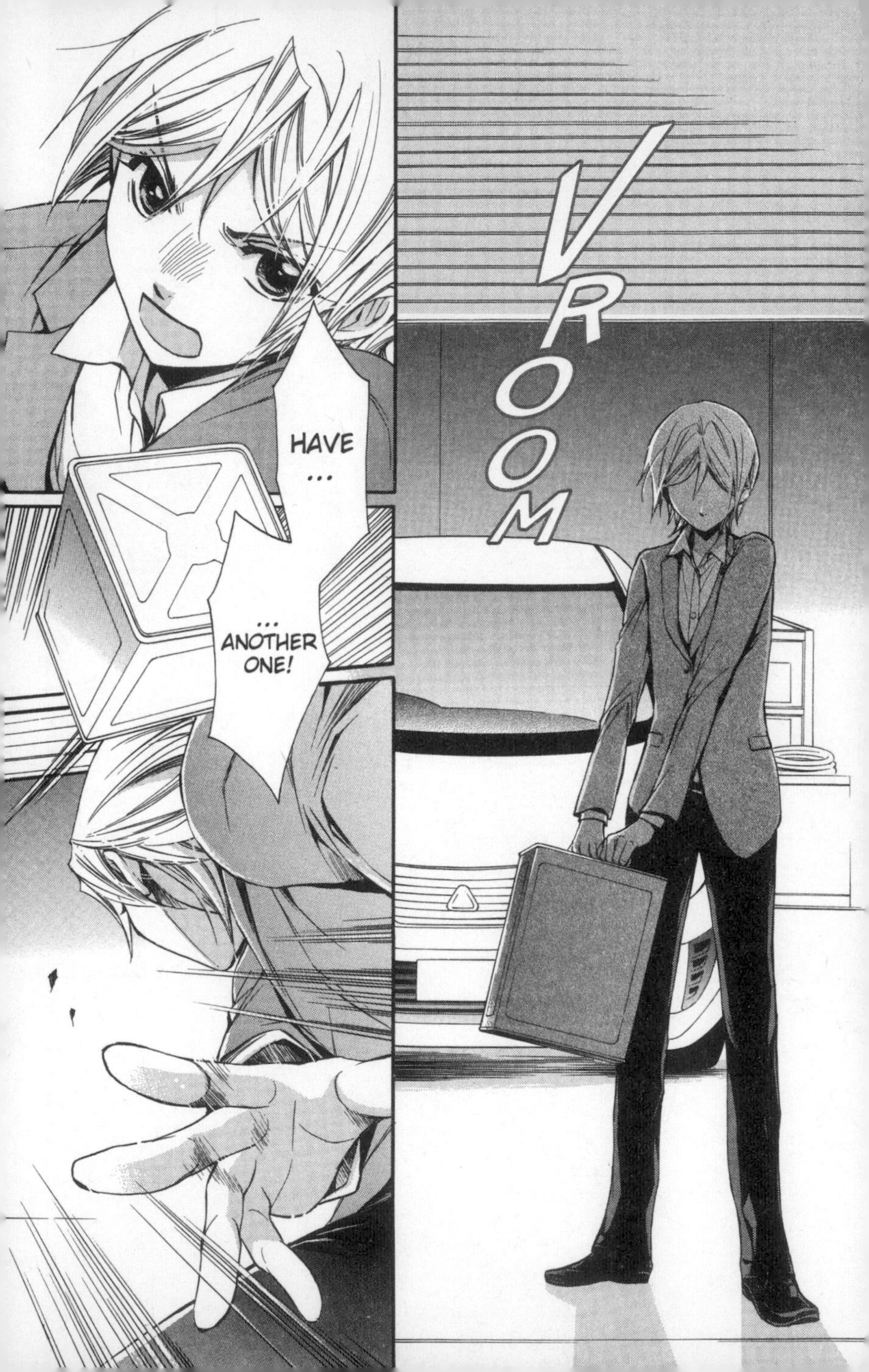
VROOM
HAVE ...
... ANOTHER ONE!

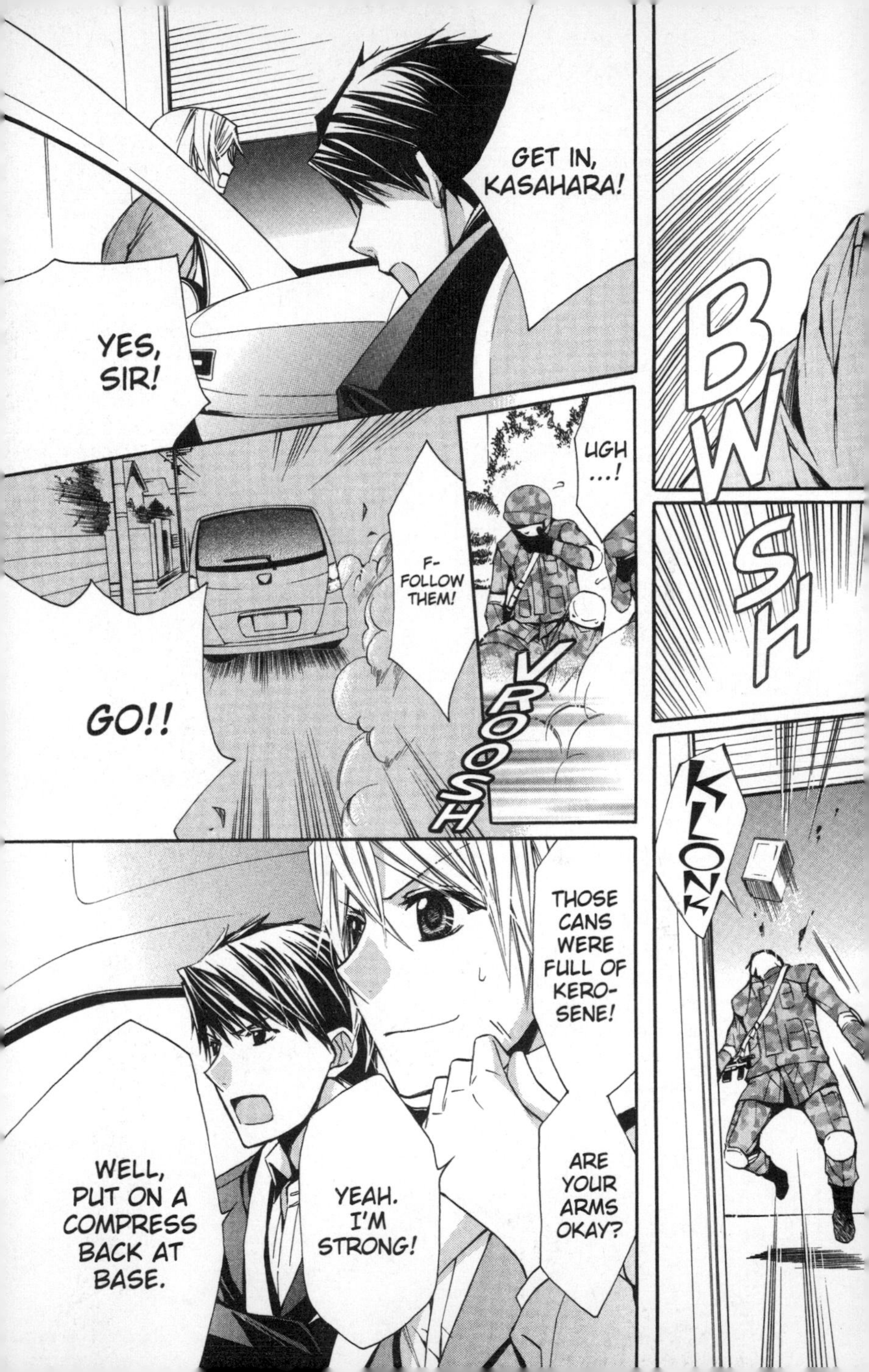
BWSH
KLONK
GET IN, KASAHARA!
YES, SIR!
UGH...!
F-FOLLOW THEM!
VROOSH
GO!!
THOSE CANS WERE FULL OF KERO-SENE!
ARE YOUR ARMS OKAY?
YEAH. I'M STRONG!
WELL, PUT ON A COMPRESS BACK AT BASE.

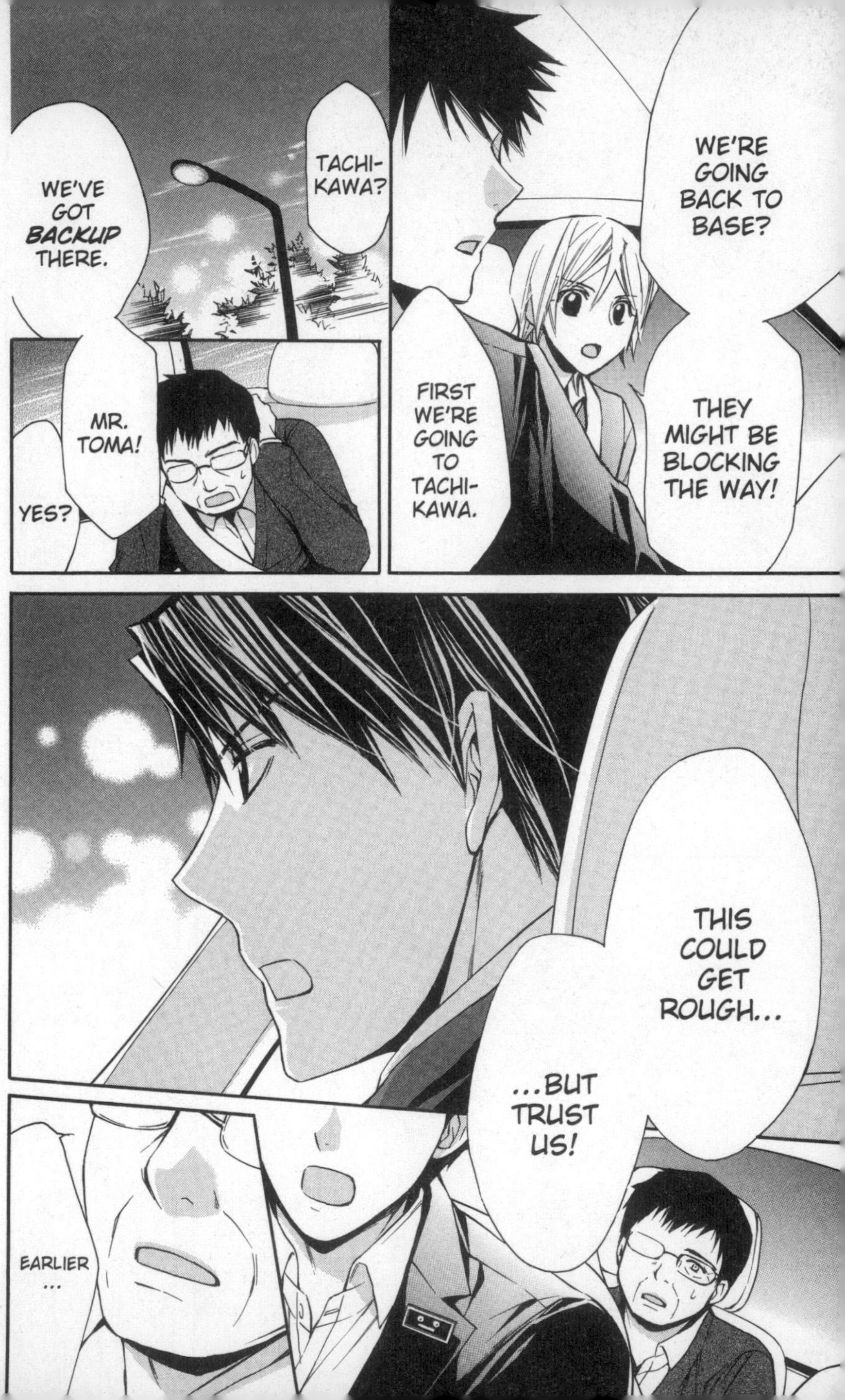
WE'RE GOING BACK TO BASE?
THEY MIGHT BE BLOCKING THE WAY!
FIRST WE'RE GOING TO TACHI-KAWA.
TACHI-KAWA?
WE'VE GOT *BACKUP* THERE.
MR. TOMA!
YES?
THIS COULD GET ROUGH...
...BUT TRUST US!
EARLIER ...

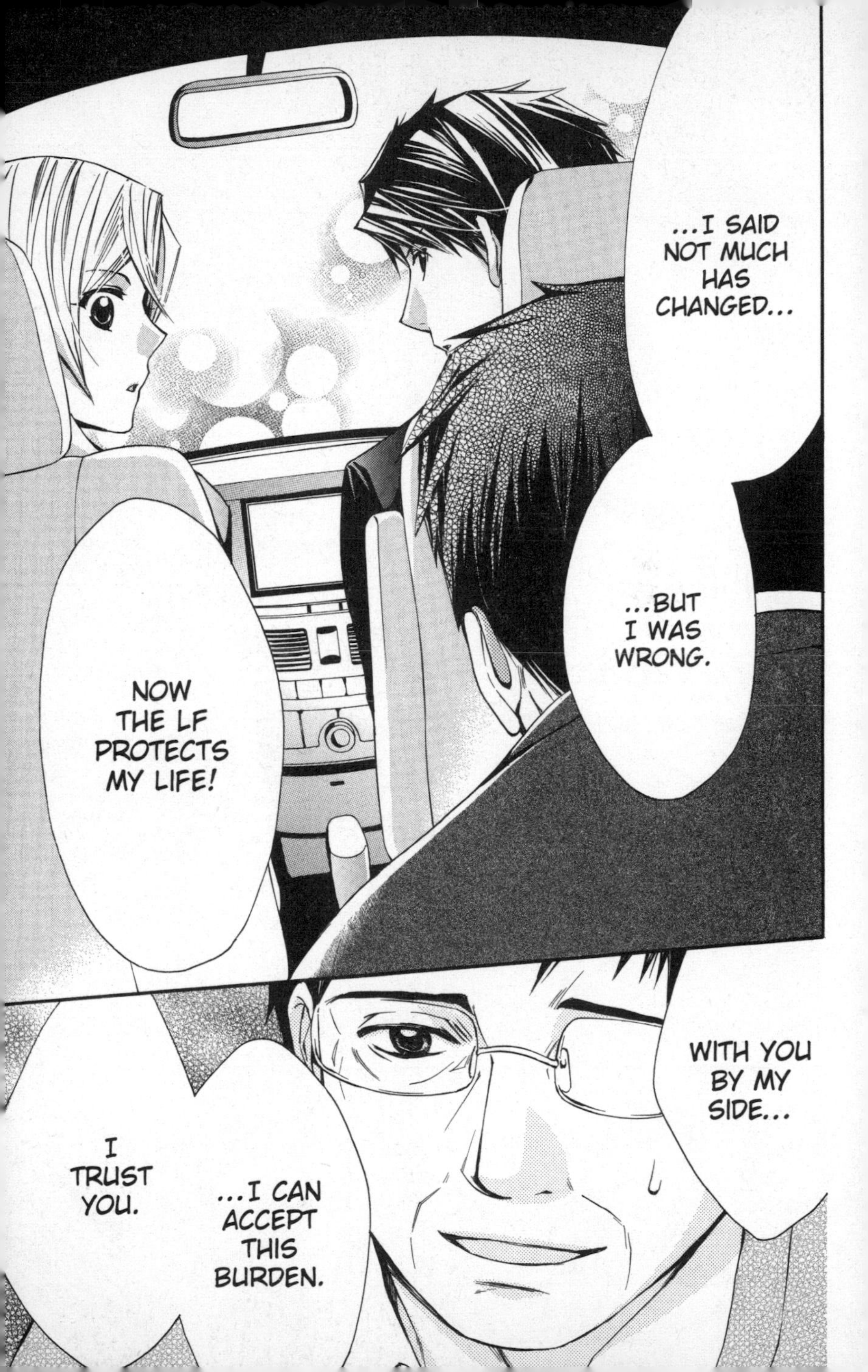
...I SAID NOT MUCH HAS CHANGED...
...BUT I WAS WRONG.
NOW THE LF PROTECTS MY LIFE!
WITH YOU BY MY SIDE...
...I CAN ACCEPT THIS BURDEN.
I TRUST YOU.

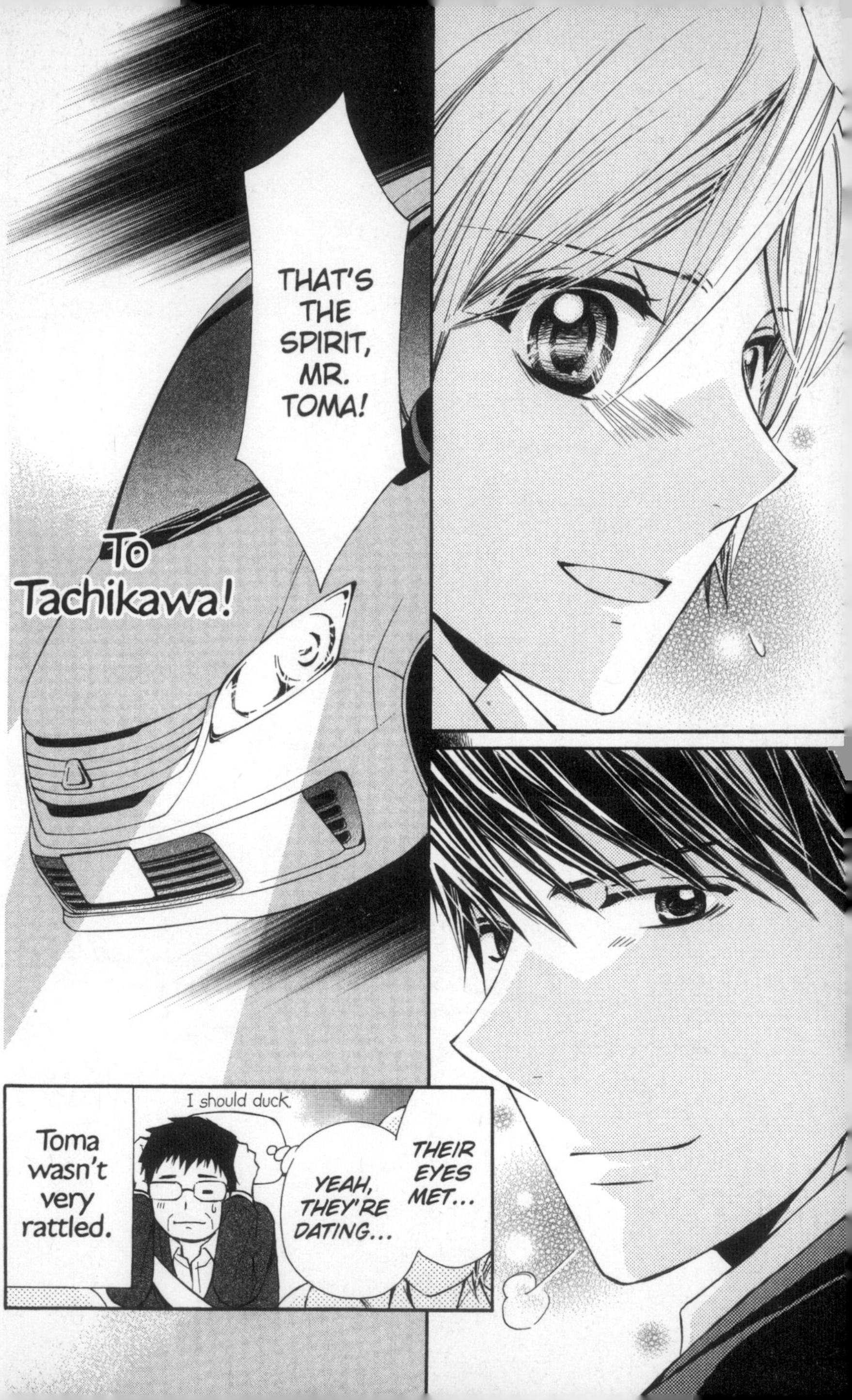
THAT'S THE SPIRIT, MR. TOMA!
To Tachikawa!
THEIR EYES MET...
YEAH, THEY'RE DATING...
I should duck.
Toma wasn't very rattled.

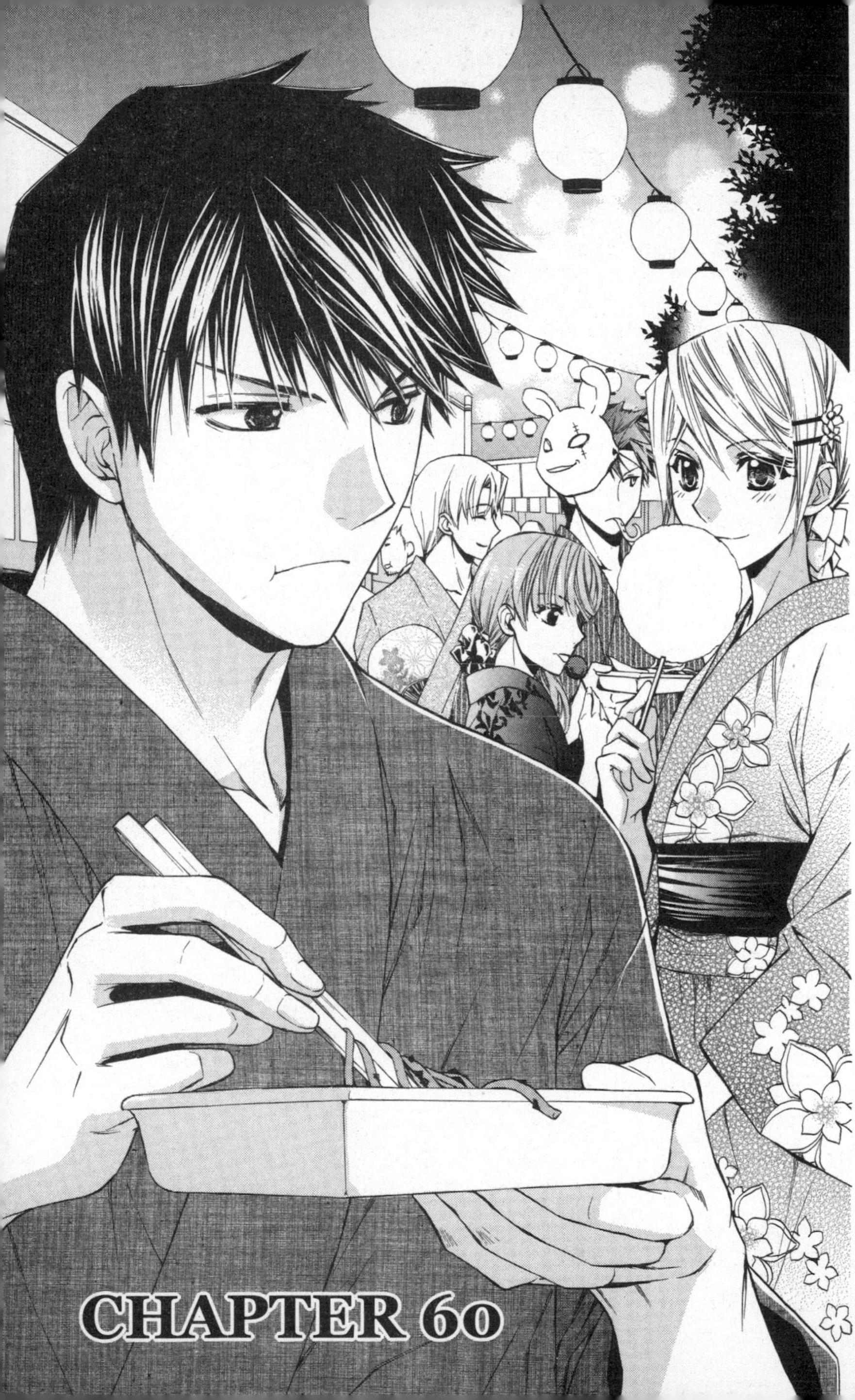
CHAPTER 60

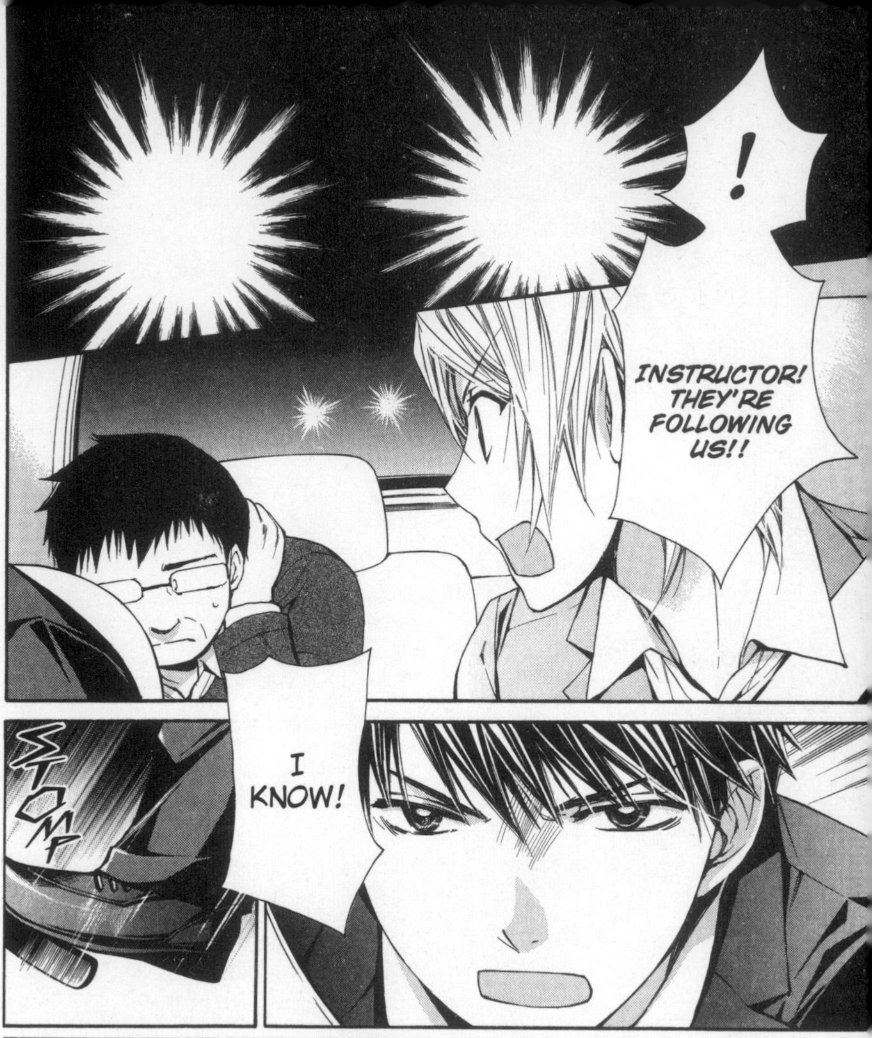
!
INSTRUCTOR! THEY'RE FOLLOWING US!!
I KNOW!
STOMP

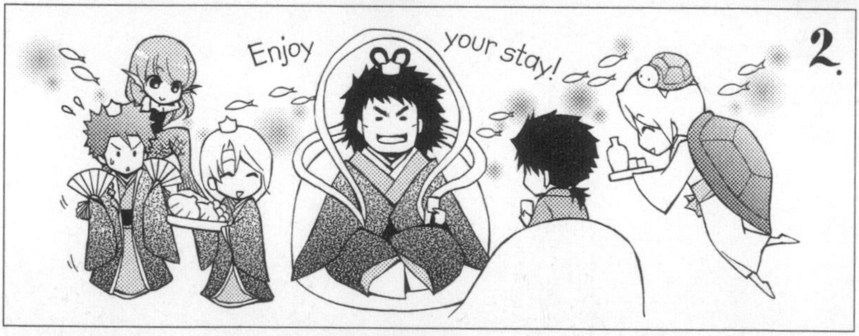
2.
Enjoy your stay!

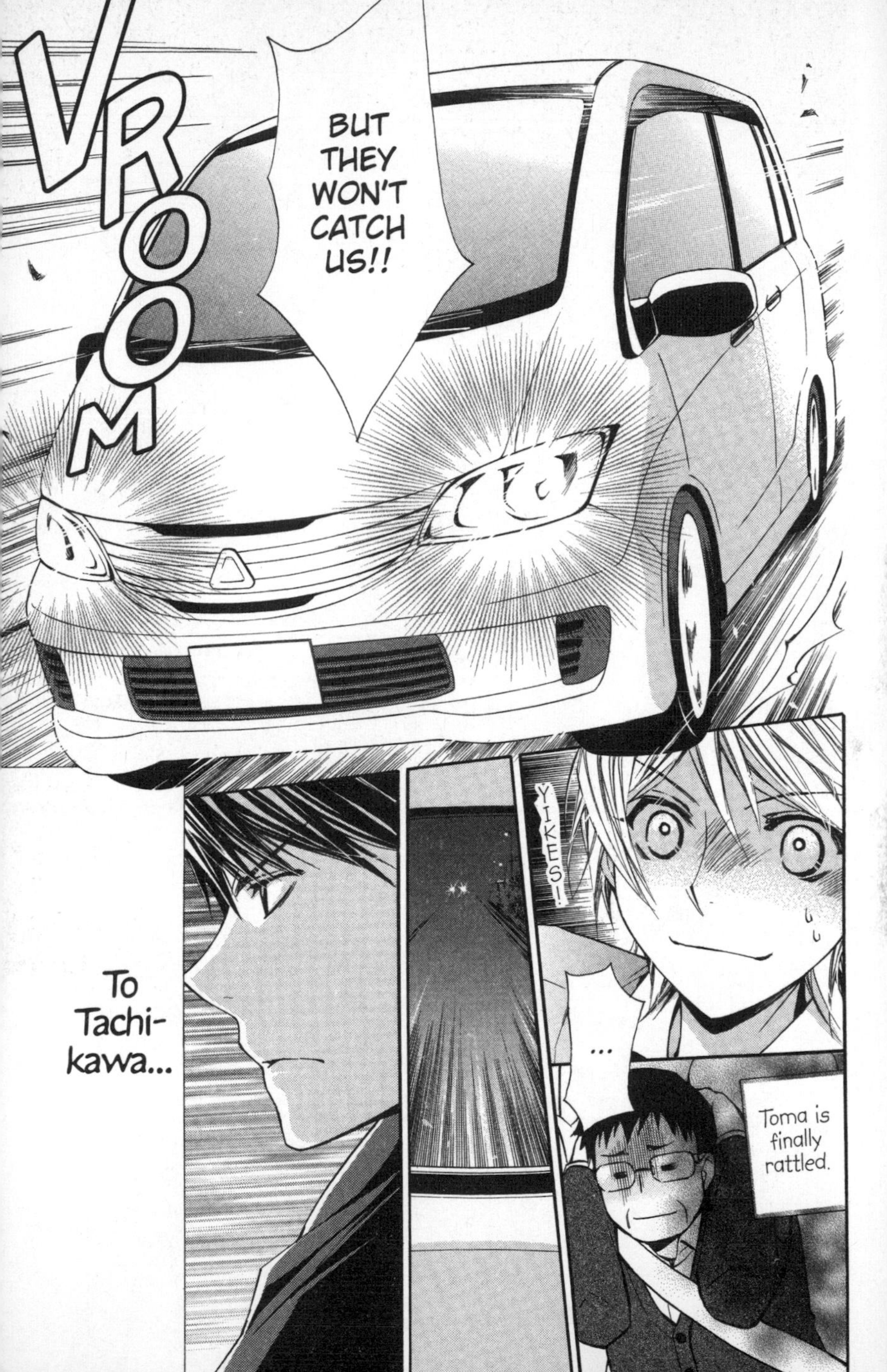
VROOM
BUT THEY WON'T CATCH US!!
YIKES!
...
Toma is finally rattled.
To Tachikawa...

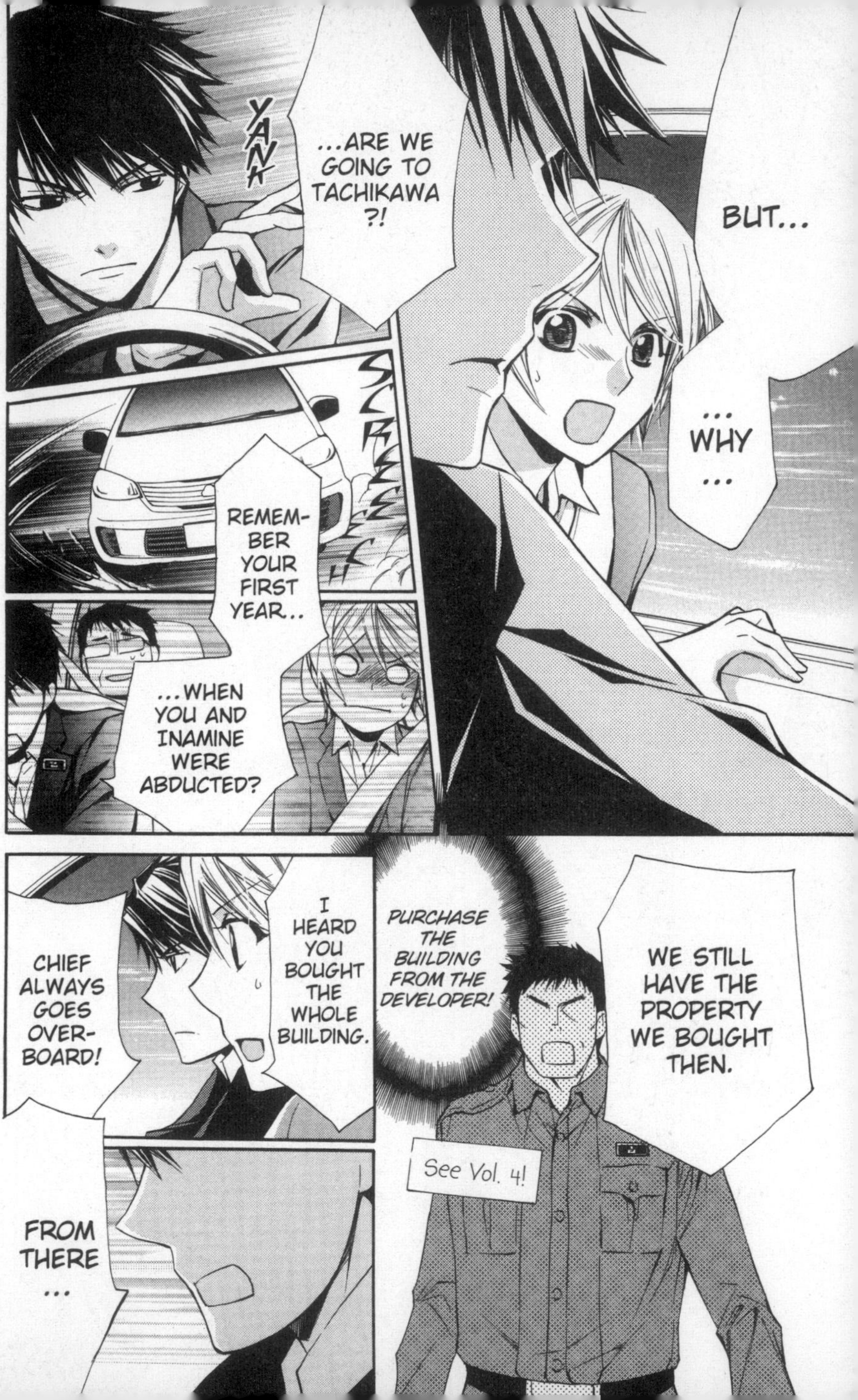
BUT...
...WHY...
YANK
...ARE WE GOING TO TACHIKAWA?!
SCREEECH
REMEMBER YOUR FIRST YEAR...
...WHEN YOU AND INAMINE WERE ABDUCTED?
WE STILL HAVE THE PROPERTY WE BOUGHT THEN.
PURCHASE THE BUILDING FROM THE DEVELOPER!
See Vol. 4!
I HEARD YOU BOUGHT THE WHOLE BUILDING.
CHIEF ALWAYS GOES OVERBOARD!
FROM THERE...

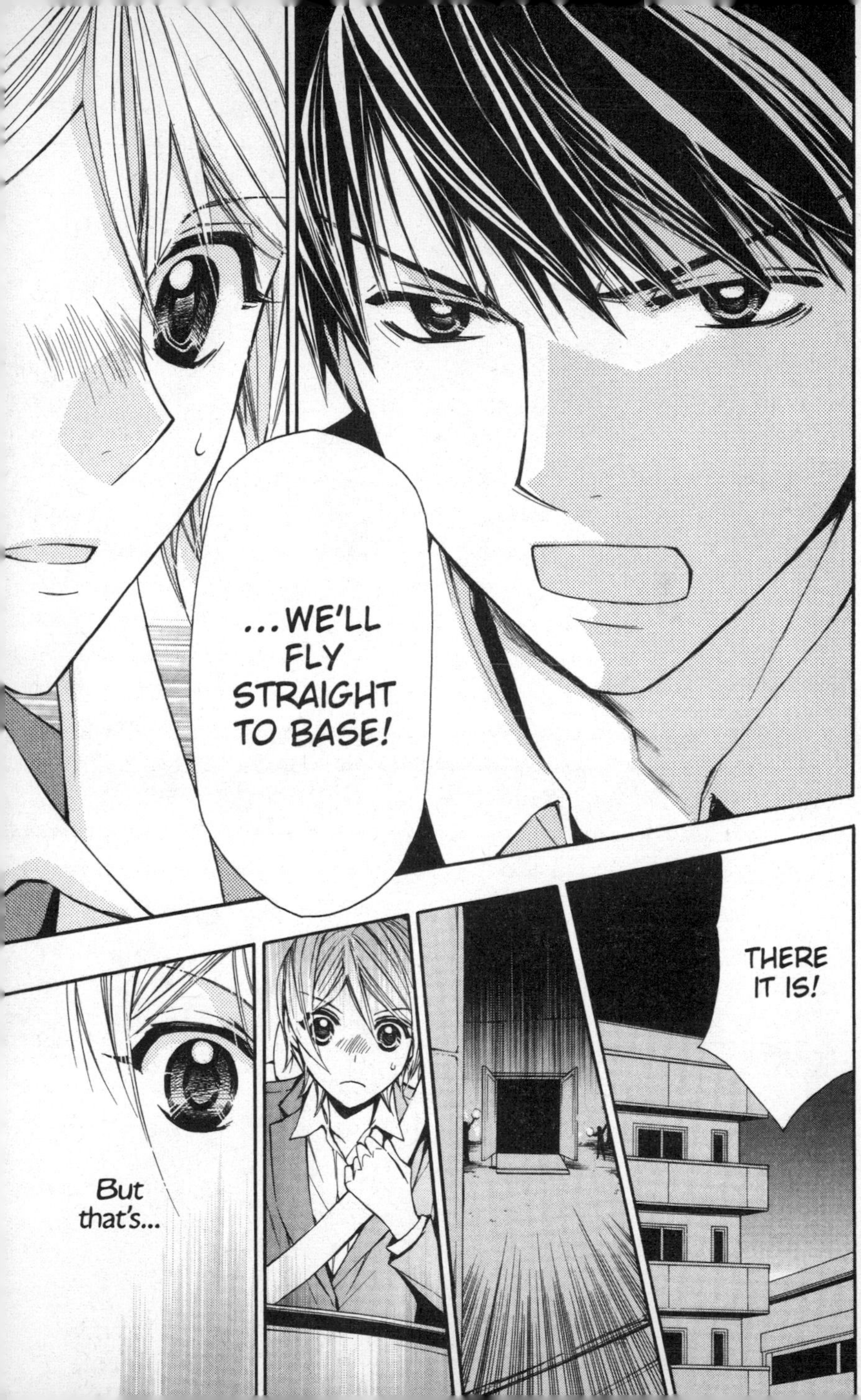
...WE'LL FLY STRAIGHT TO BASE!
THERE IT IS!
But that's...

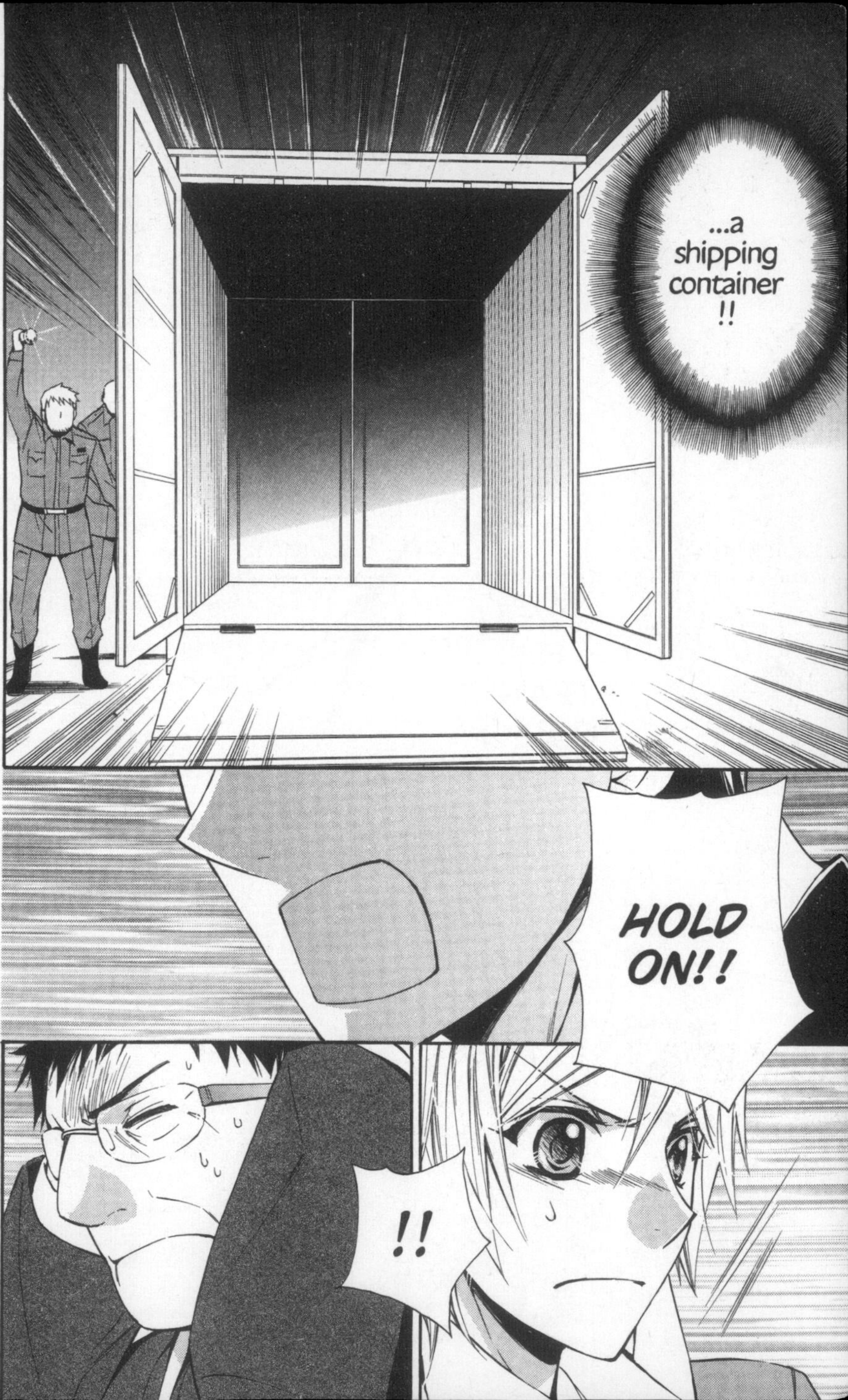
...a shipping container !!
HOLD ON!!
!!

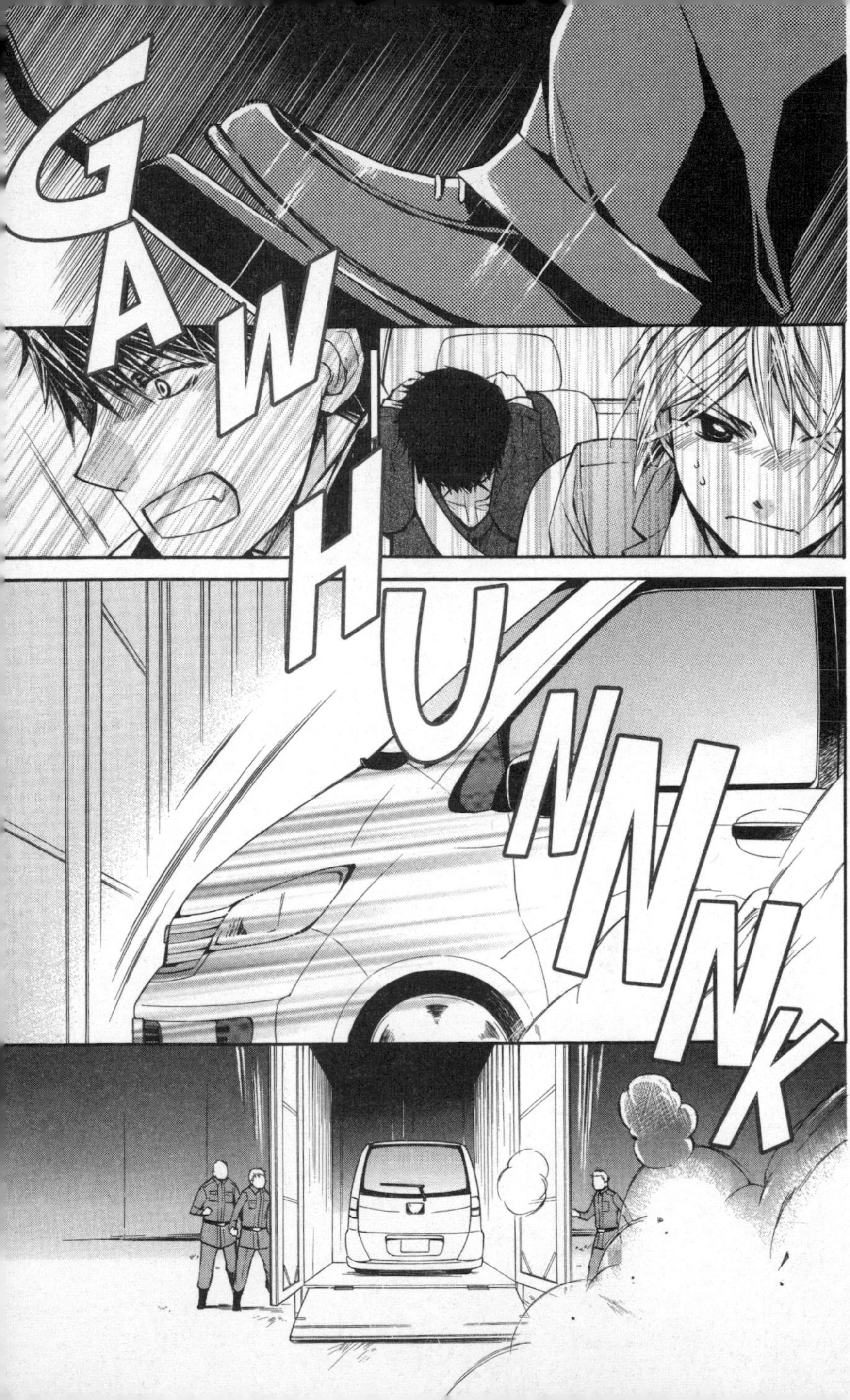
GAWHUNNNK

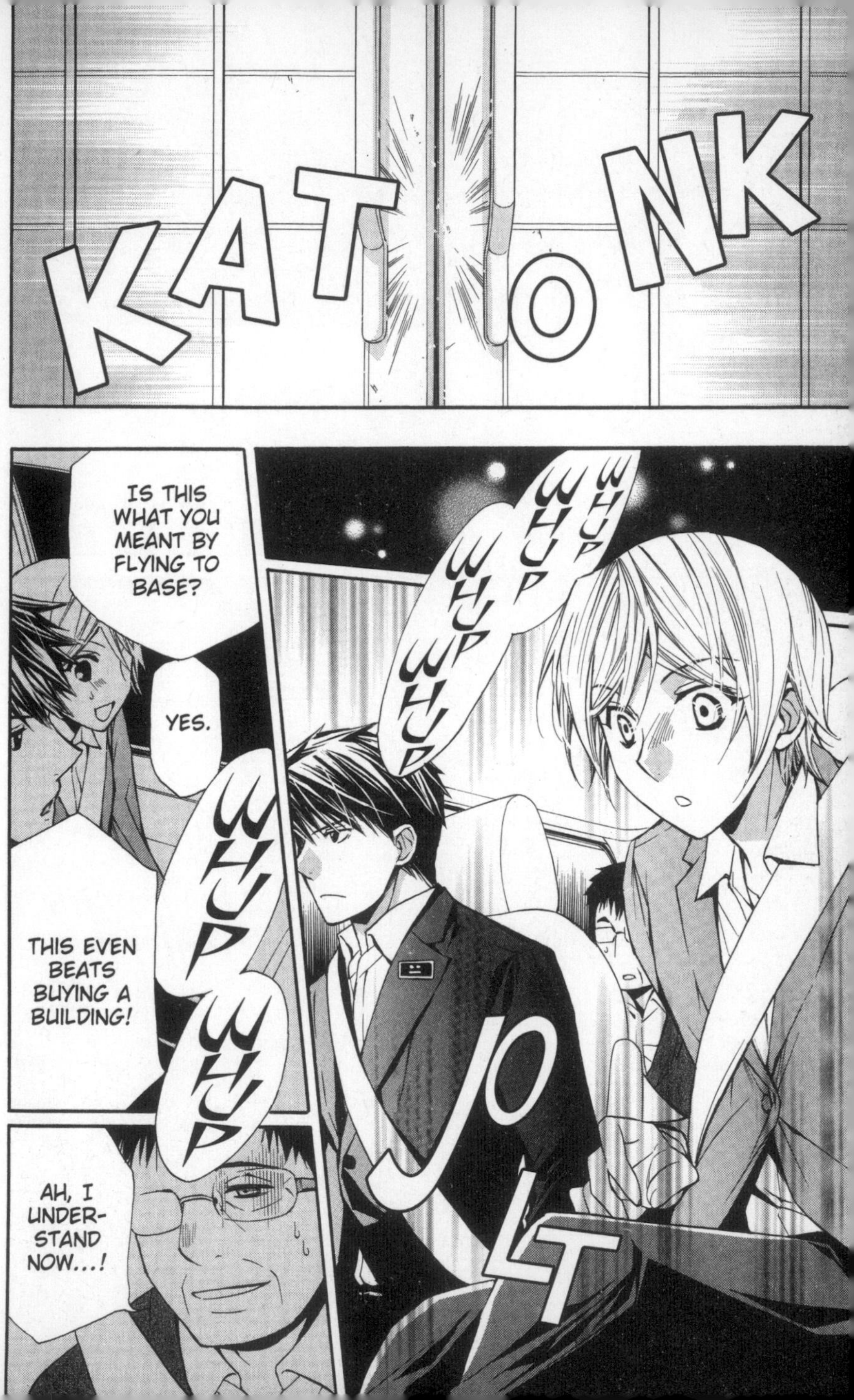
KATONK
WHUP WHUP WHUP
WHUP WHUP WHUP
WHUP WHUP
JOLT
IS THIS WHAT YOU MEANT BY FLYING TO BASE?
YES.
THIS EVEN BEATS BUYING A BUILDING!
AH, I UNDER-STAND NOW...!

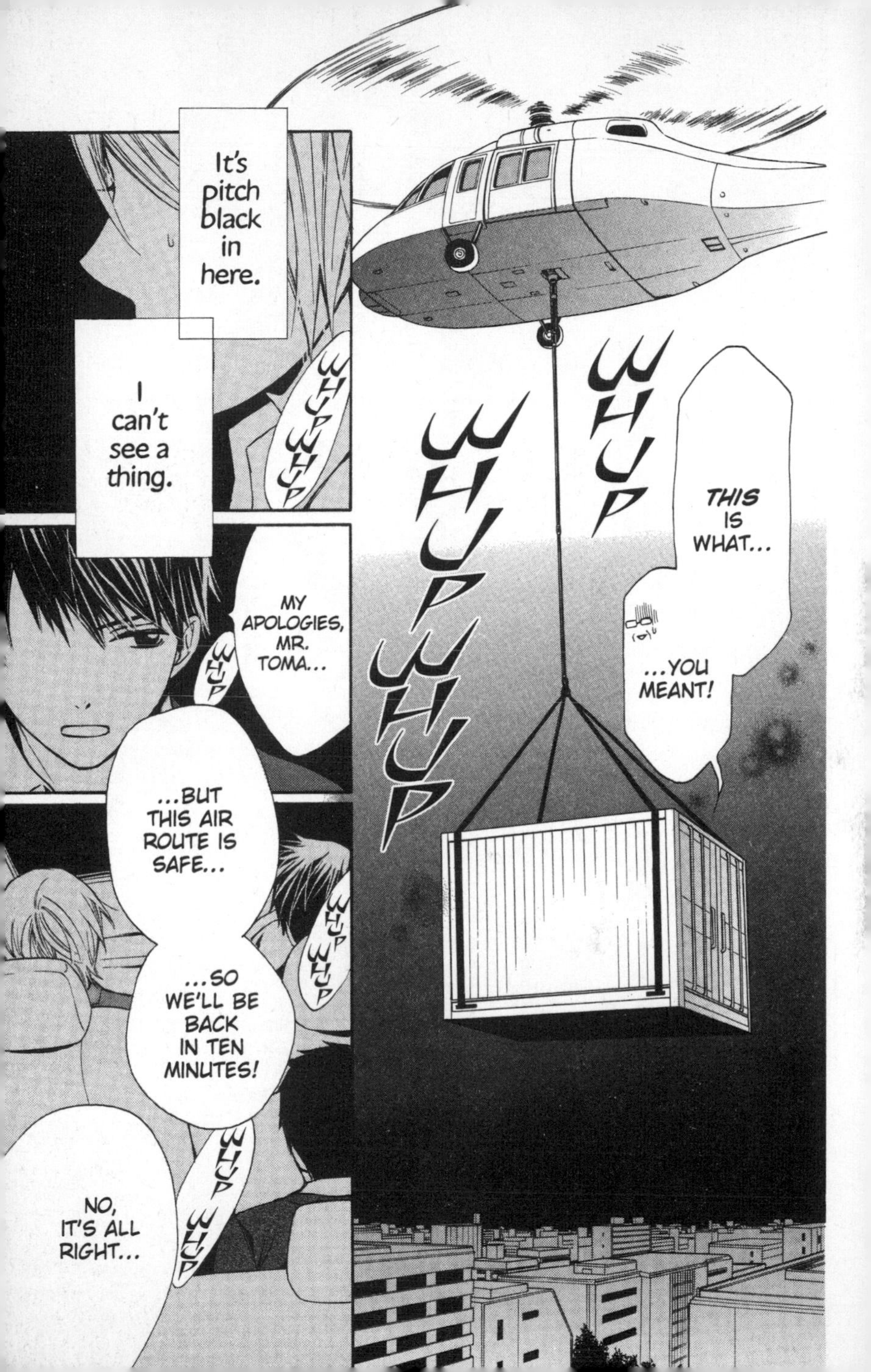
WHUP
THIS IS WHAT...
...YOU MEANT!
WHUP WHUP WHUP
It's pitch black in here.
I can't see a thing.
WHUP WHUP WHUP
MY APOLOGIES, MR. TOMA...
WHUP
...BUT THIS AIR ROUTE IS SAFE...
WHUP WHUP
...SO WE'LL BE BACK IN TEN MINUTES!
WHUP WHUP
NO, IT'S ALL RIGHT...

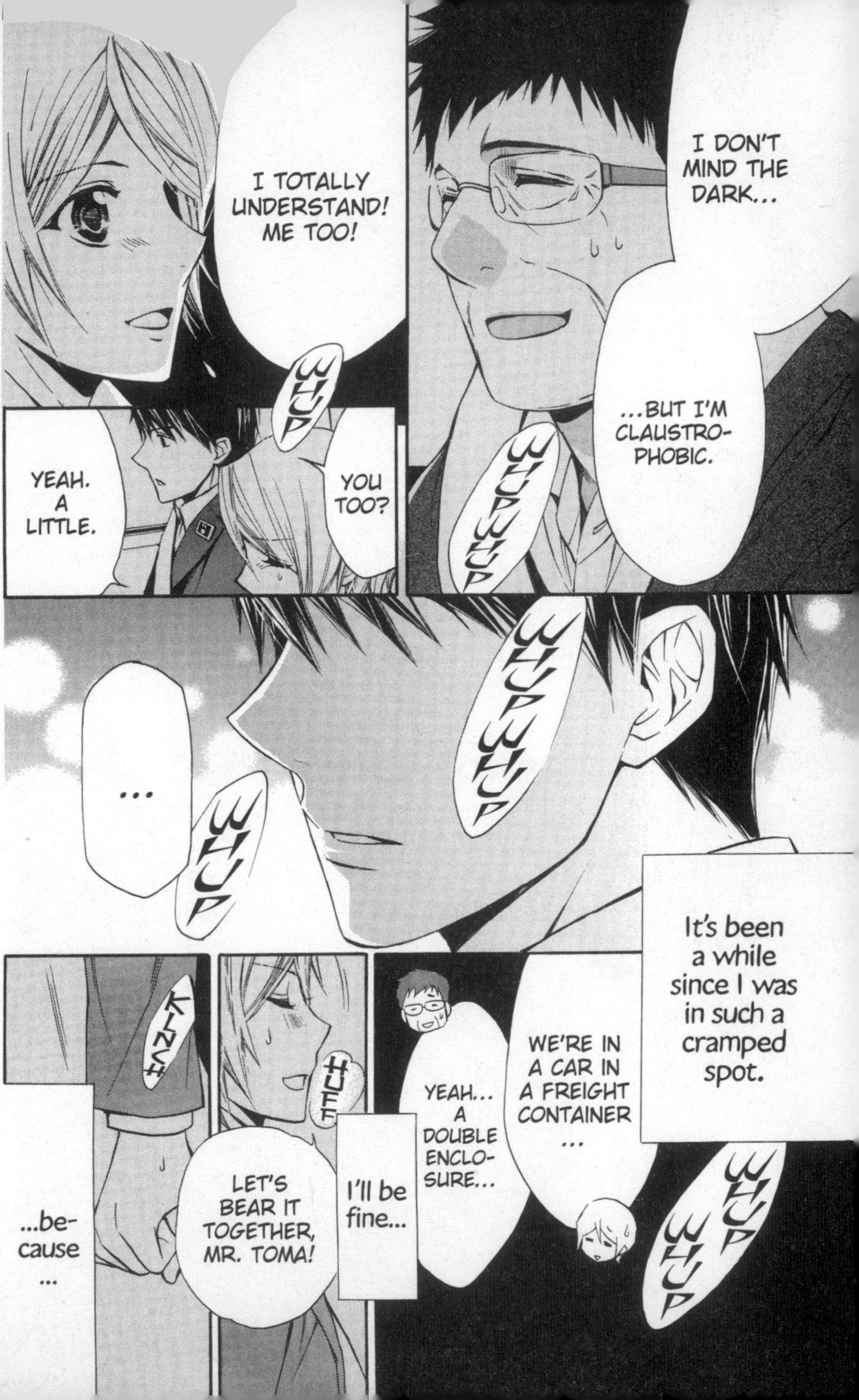
I DON'T MIND THE DARK...
...BUT I'M CLAUSTRO-PHOBIC.
WHUPWHUP
I TOTALLY UNDERSTAND! ME TOO!
WHUP
YOU TOO?
YEAH. A LITTLE.
WHUPWHUP
...
WHUP
It's been a while since I was in such a cramped spot.
WE'RE IN A CAR IN A FREIGHT CONTAINER...
YEAH... A DOUBLE ENCLO-SURE...
WHUP WHUP WHUP
HUFF
I'll be fine...
LET'S BEAR IT TOGETHER, MR. TOMA!
KLINCH
...be-cause...

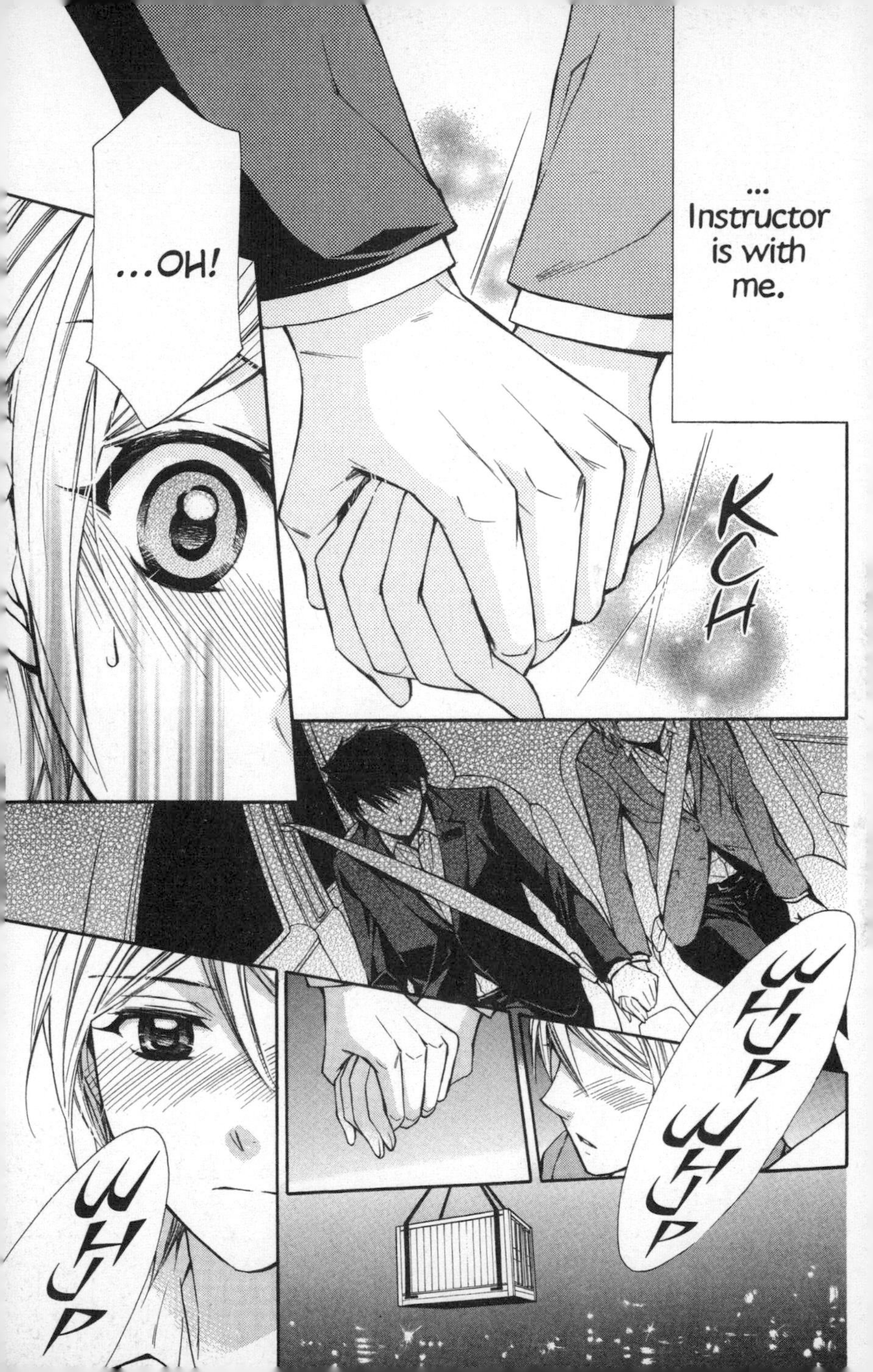
... Instructor is with me.
KCH
...OH!
WHUP WHUP
WHUP

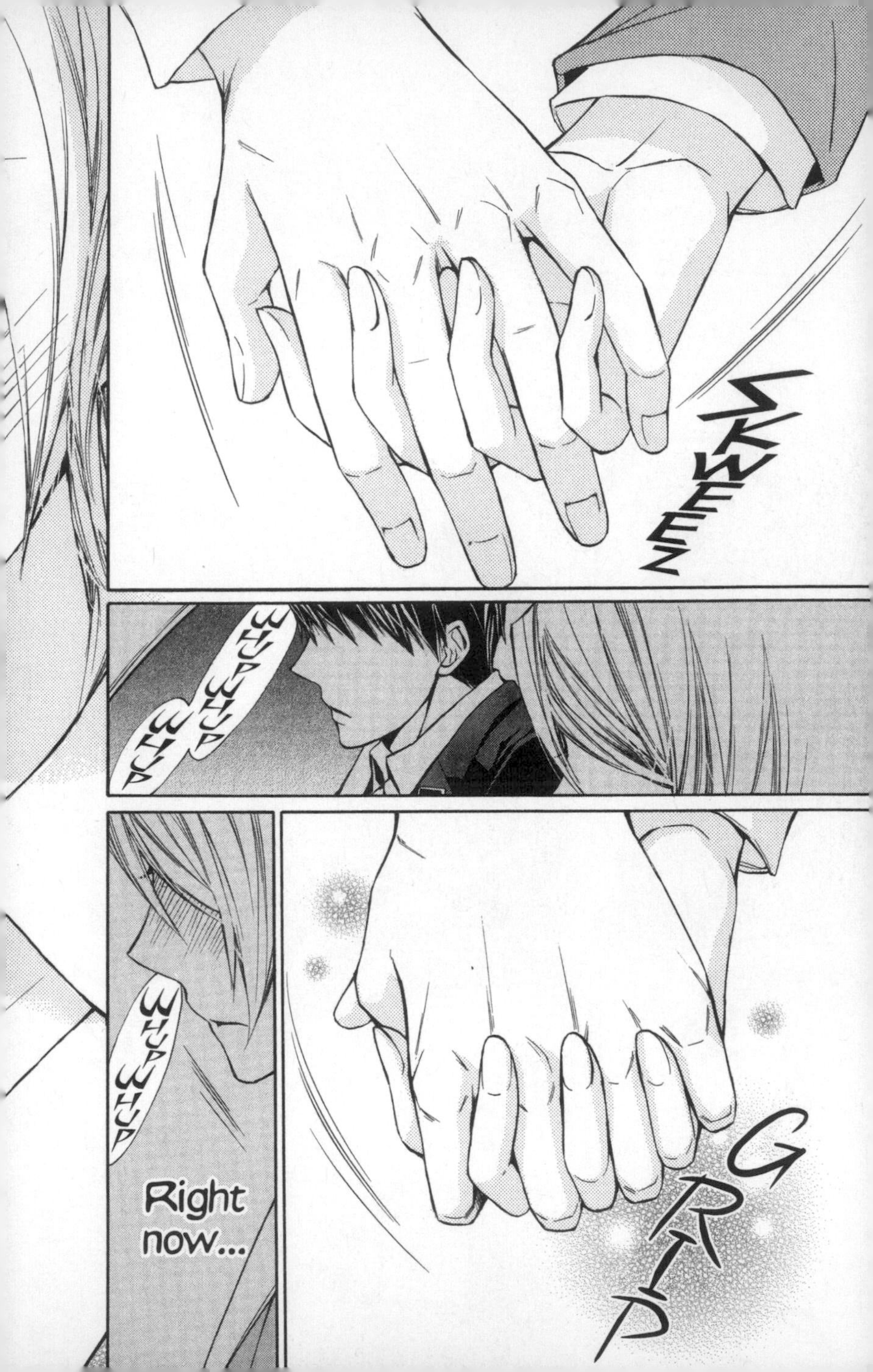
SKWEEZ
WHUP WHUP WHUP
GRIP
WHUP WHUP
Right now...

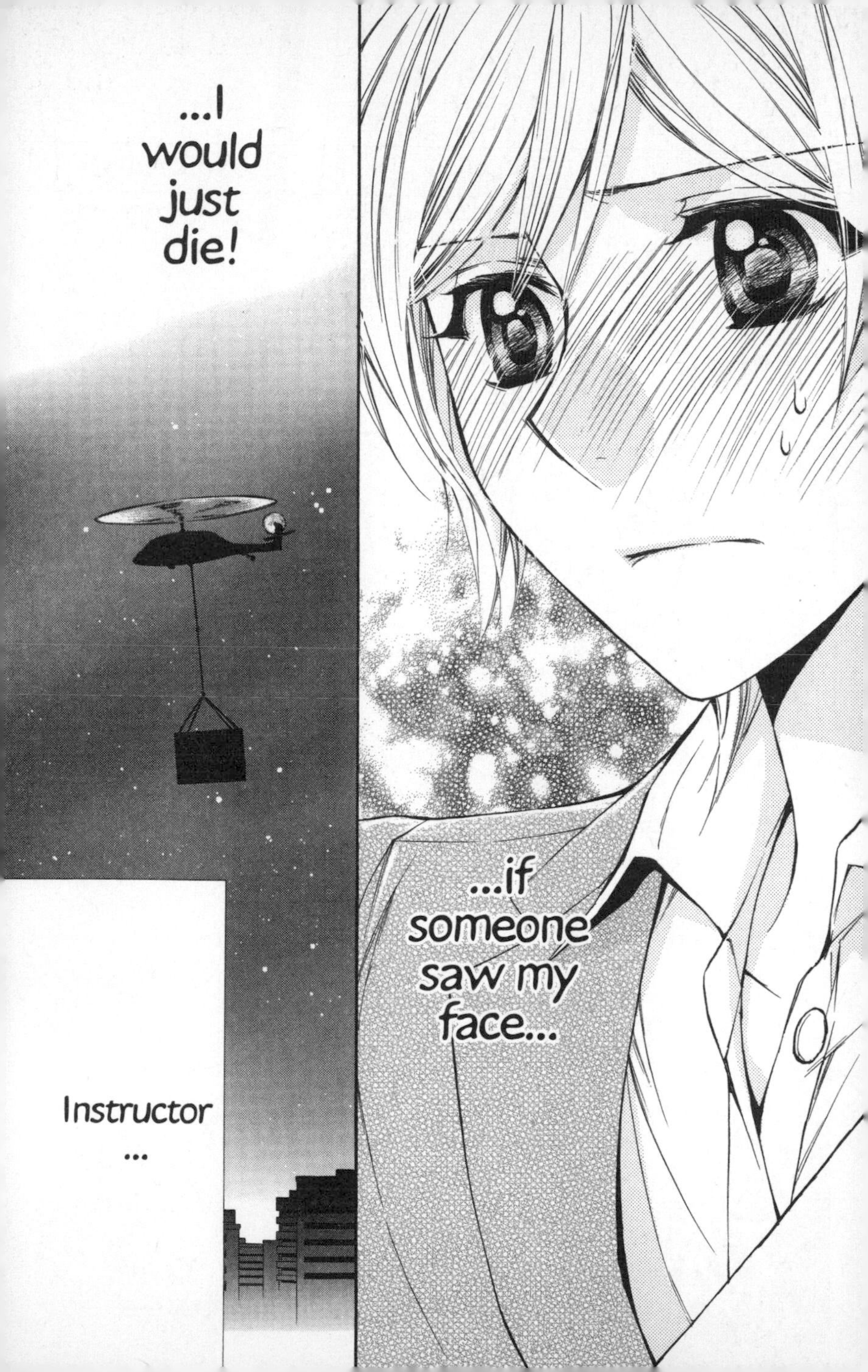
...if someone saw my face...
...I would just die!
Instructor ...

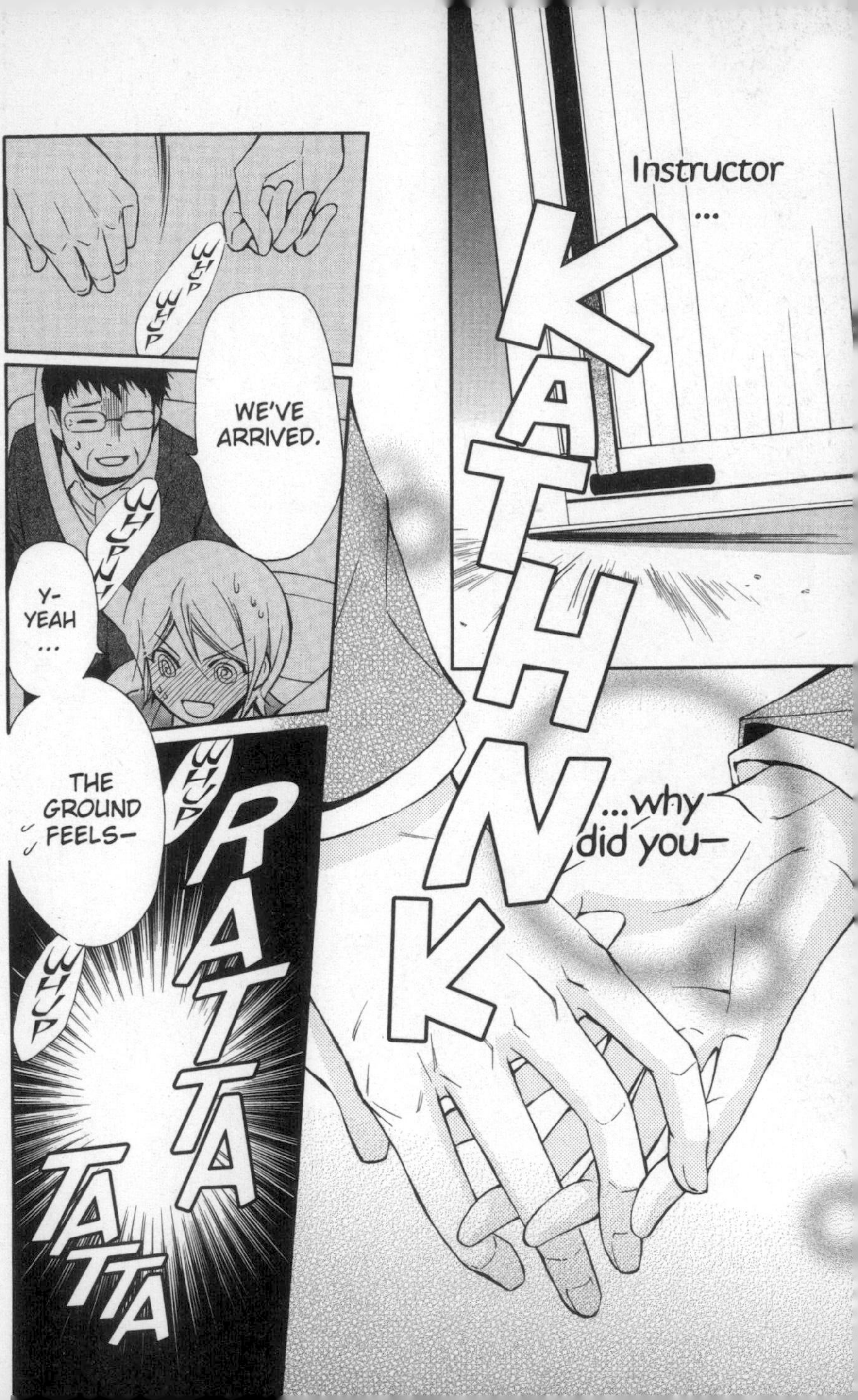
Instructor ...
KATHUNK
...why did you—
WHUP WHUP WHUP
WE'VE ARRIVED.
WHUP WHUP
Y-YEAH ...
THE GROUND FEELS—
WHUP
RATTA TATTA
WHUP

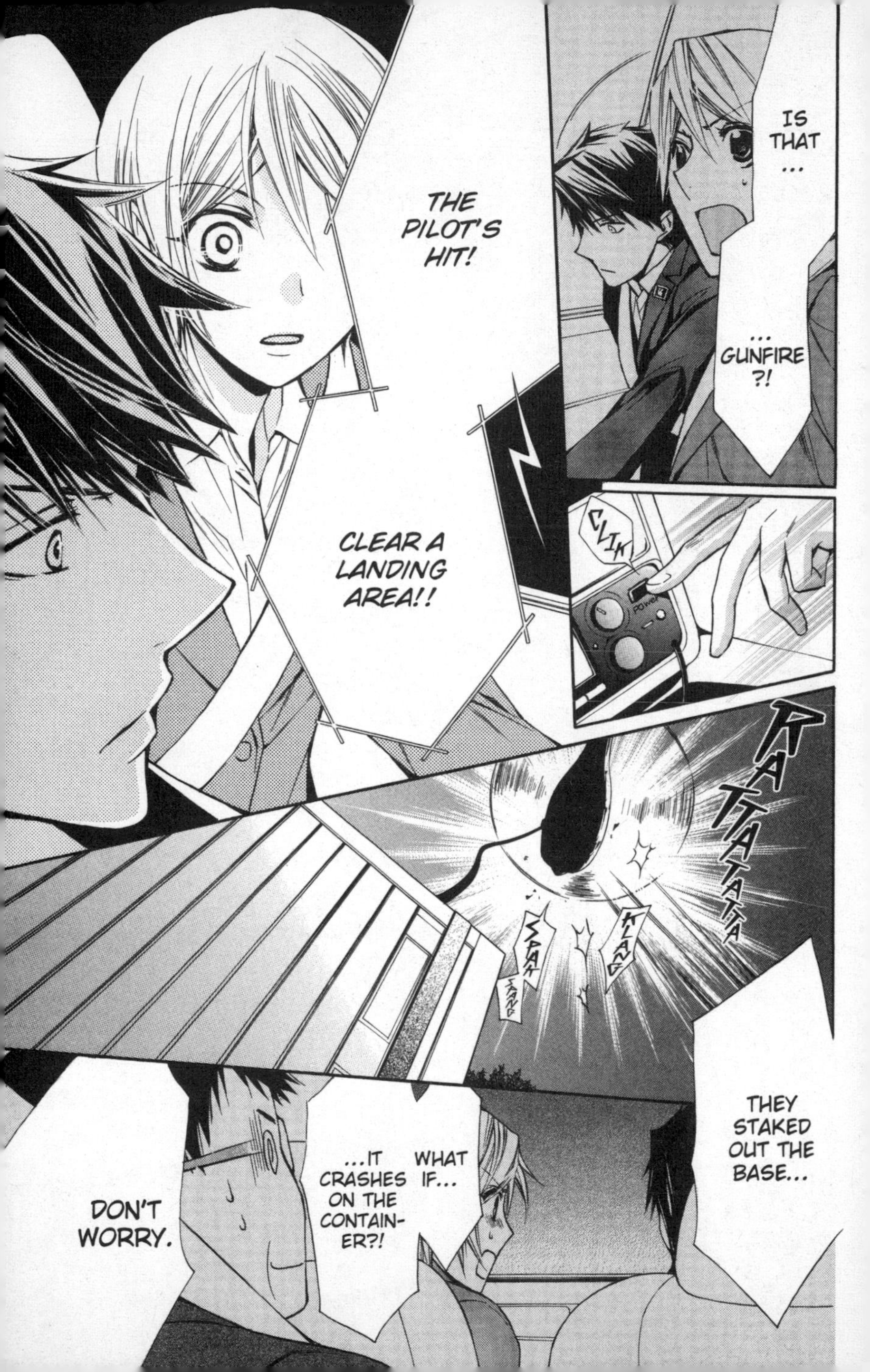
IS THAT ...
... GUNFIRE ?!
THE PILOT'S HIT!
CLEAR A LANDING AREA!!
CLIK
POWER
RATATATATA
KLANG
SPAK
TANG
THEY STAKED OUT THE BASE...
WHAT IF...
...IT CRASHES ON THE CONTAINER?!
DON'T WORRY.

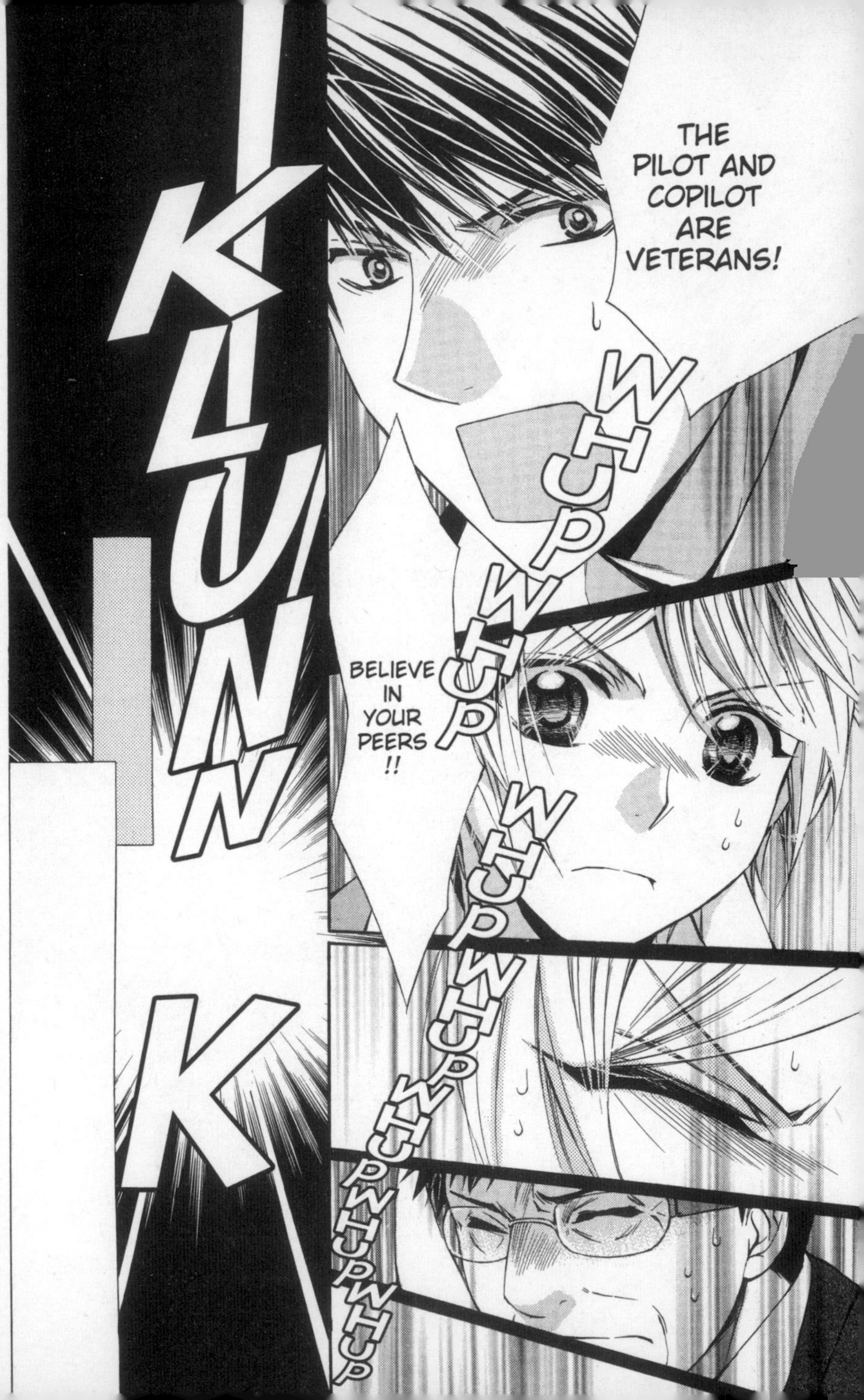
THE PILOT AND COPILOT ARE VETERANS!
WHUPWHUPWHUPWHUPWHUPWHUPWHUP
BELIEVE IN YOUR PEERS!!
KLUNNK

OFFICE
YOU'RE BACK!
EVERY-ONE IN ONE PIECE?
YES, SIR!
THE HELICOPTER MISSED THE CONTAINER.
THE PILOTS ARE ALIVE BUT INJURED.
MR. TOMA IS IN THE NAP ROOM.
GOOD WORK.
ADVISOR INAMINE IS SAFE AS WELL.
This civilian is tired...
THEY DID WELL. PRAISES ARE DUE.
TUMP TUMP TUMP TUMP
OH ...
... HERE THEY ARE!

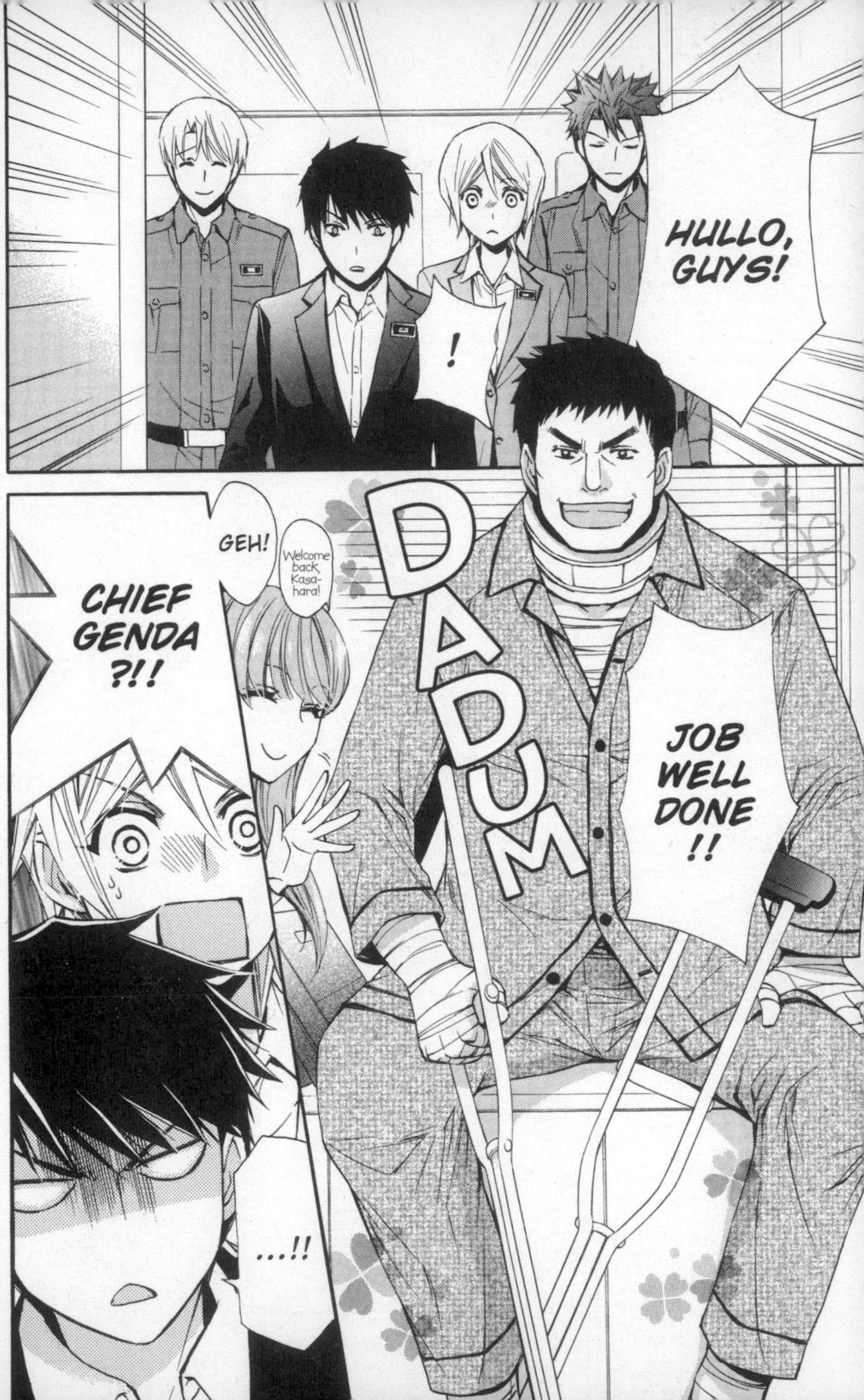
HULLO, GUYS!
!
JOB WELL DONE !!
DADUM
Welcome back, Kasa-hara!
GEH!
CHIEF GENDA ?!!
...!!

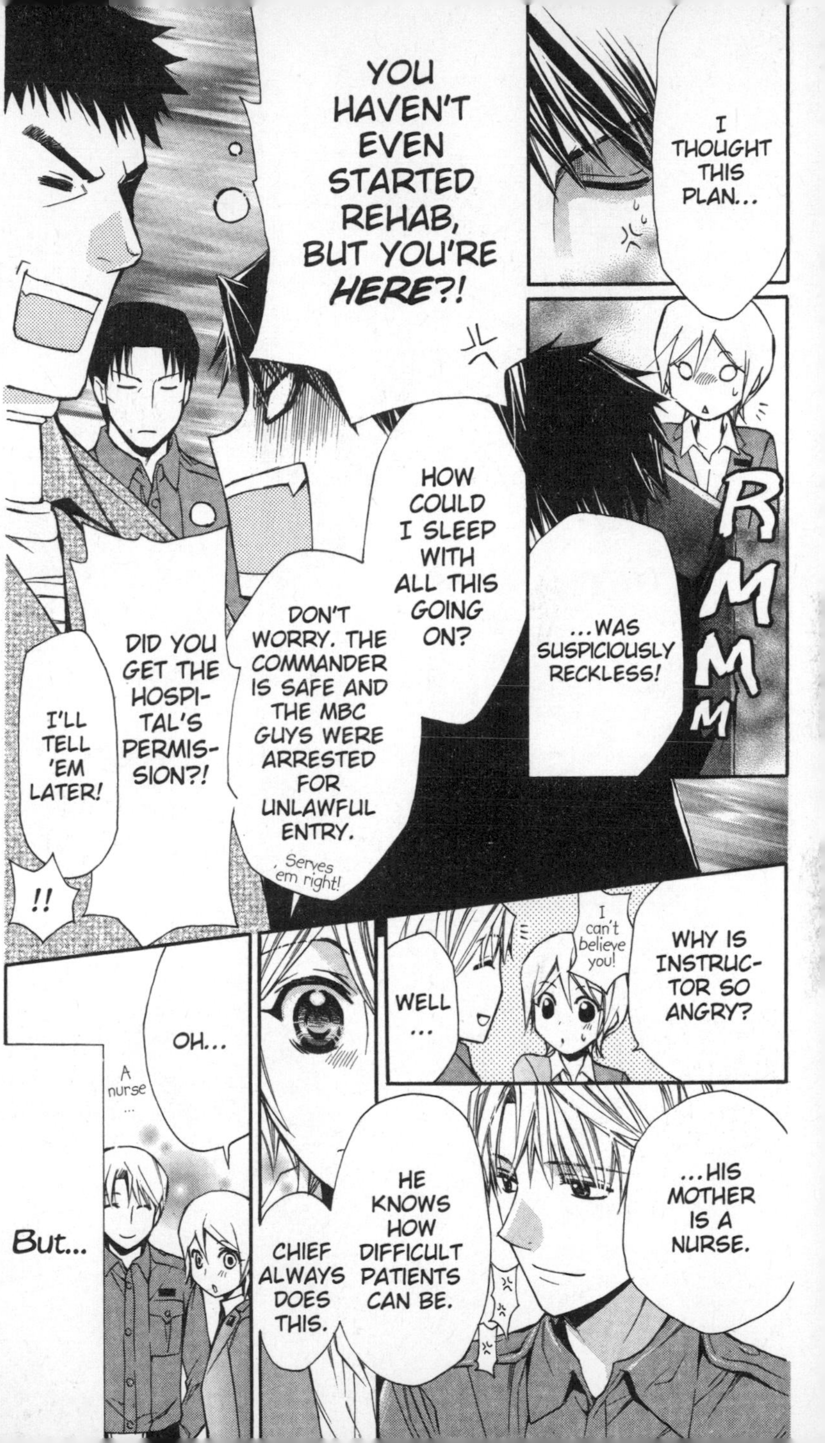
I THOUGHT THIS PLAN...
...WAS SUSPICIOUSLY RECKLESS!
RMMM
YOU HAVEN'T EVEN STARTED REHAB, BUT YOU'RE *HERE*?!
HOW COULD I SLEEP WITH ALL THIS GOING ON?
DON'T WORRY. THE COMMANDER IS SAFE AND THE MBC GUYS WERE ARRESTED FOR UNLAWFUL ENTRY.
Serves 'em right!
DID YOU GET THE HOSPITAL'S PERMISSION?!
I'LL TELL 'EM LATER!
!!
WHY IS INSTRUCTOR SO ANGRY?
I can't believe you!
WELL...
...HIS MOTHER IS A NURSE.
HE KNOWS HOW DIFFICULT PATIENTS CAN BE.
CHIEF ALWAYS DOES THIS.
OH...
A nurse...
But...

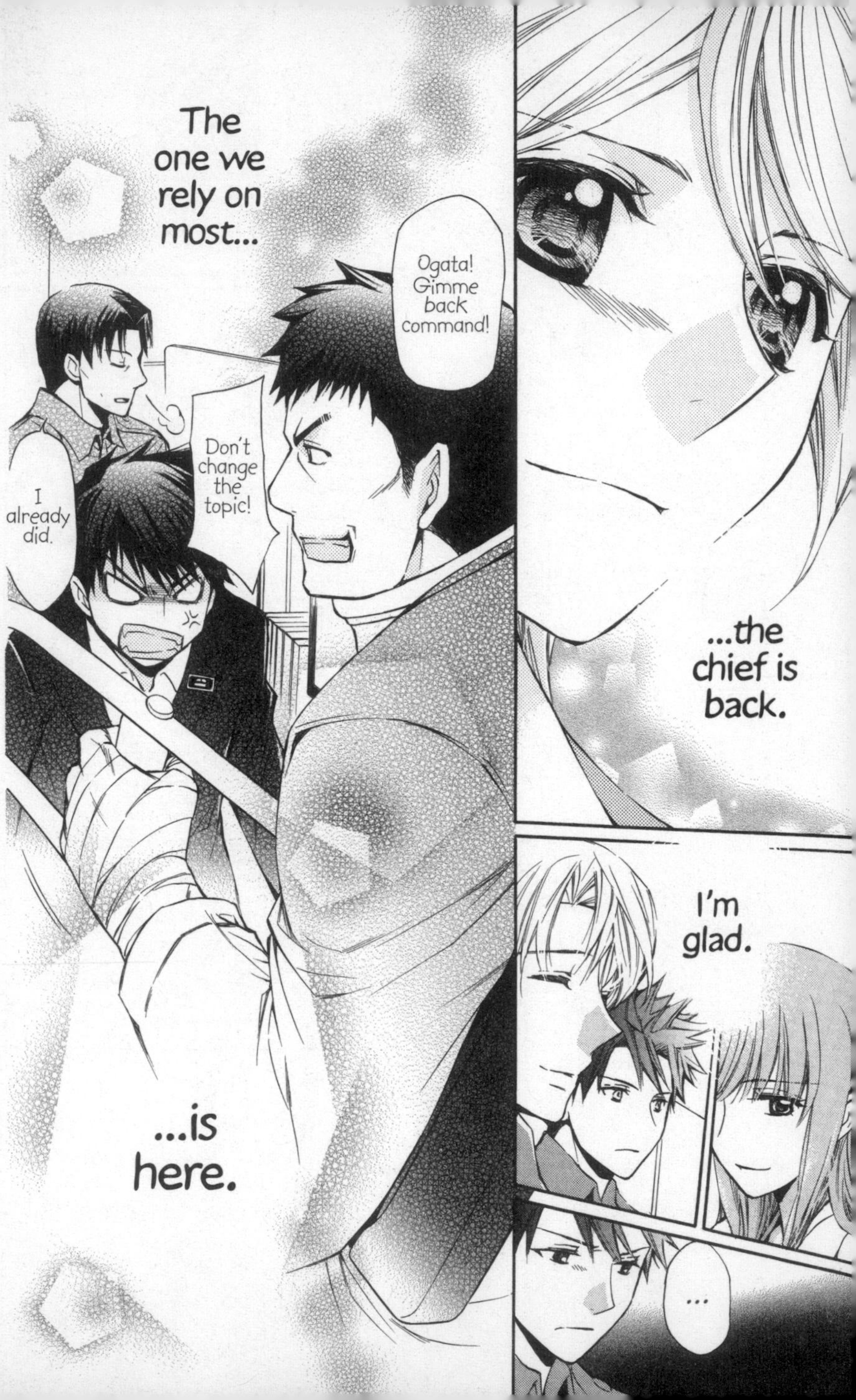
...the chief is back.
I'm glad.
...
The one we rely on most...
Ogata! Gimme back command!
Don't change the topic!
I already did.
...is here.

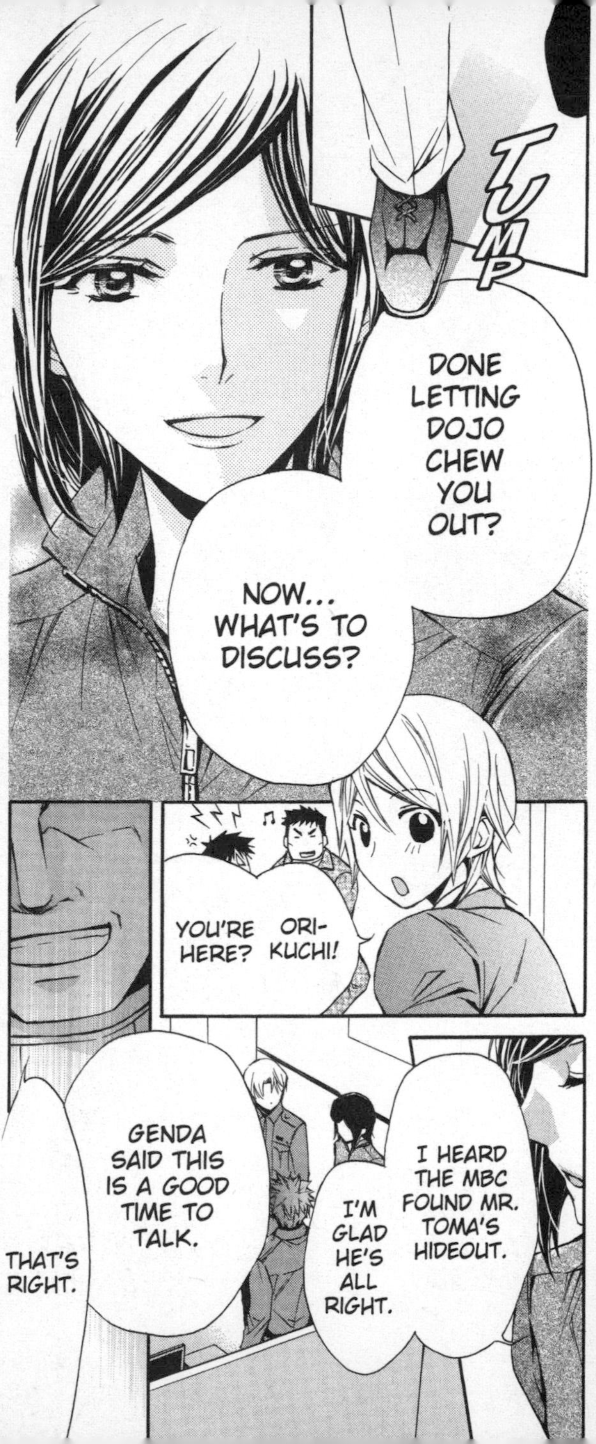
TUMP
DONE LETTING DOJO CHEW YOU OUT?
NOW... WHAT'S TO DISCUSS?
ORI-KUCHI!
YOU'RE HERE?
I HEARD THE MBC FOUND MR. TOMA'S HIDEOUT.
I'M GLAD HE'S ALL RIGHT.
GENDA SAID THIS IS A GOOD TIME TO TALK.
THAT'S RIGHT.

2

*

As usual, I've been using my time away from work to watch TV and play video games. Around New Year's there are so many special programs that I have a blast! I love comedians, so there's a ton I want to watch. I don't have any memory left to record them. I would like to see more programs with new gags, though!

About the time Volume 13 comes out, the *Thor* and *Hobbit* movies will be out, and I'm looking forward to the new *Aibo* movie a little later!!

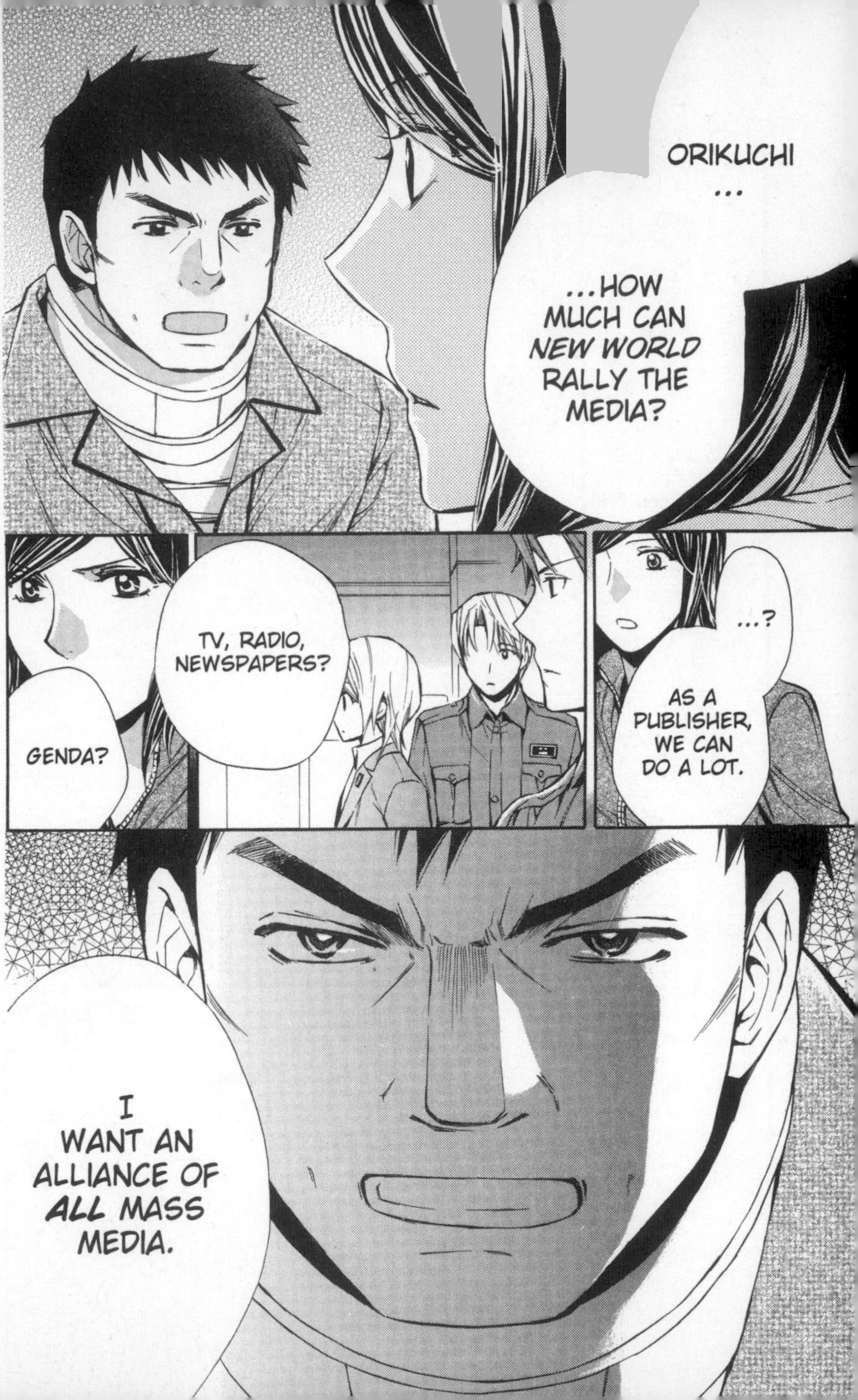
ORIKUCHI ...
...HOW MUCH CAN *NEW WORLD* RALLY THE MEDIA?
...?
AS A PUBLISHER, WE CAN DO A LOT.
TV, RADIO, NEWSPAPERS?
GENDA?
I WANT AN ALLIANCE OF *ALL* MASS MEDIA.

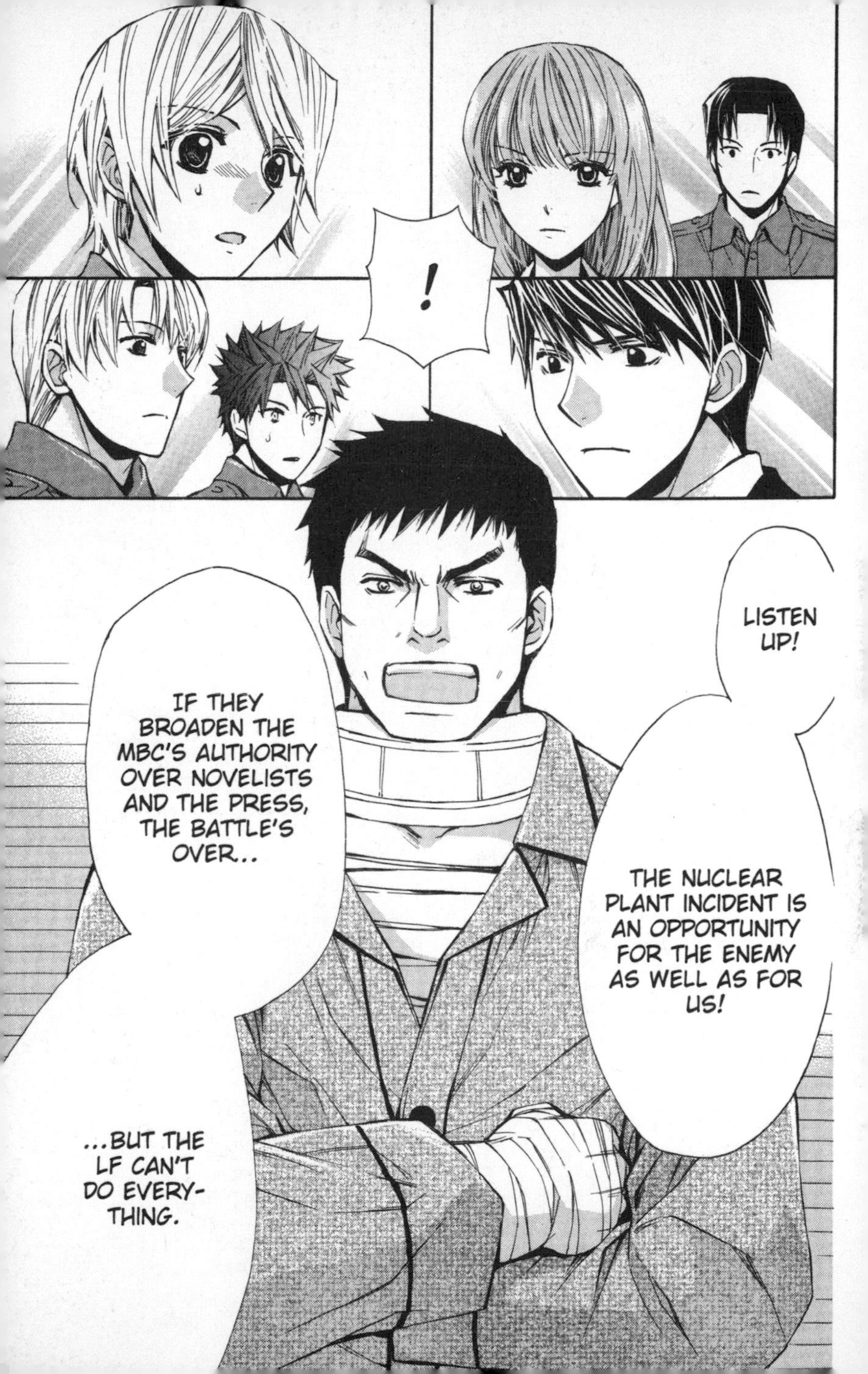
!
LISTEN UP!
THE NUCLEAR PLANT INCIDENT IS AN OPPORTUNITY FOR THE ENEMY AS WELL AS FOR US!
IF THEY BROADEN THE MBC'S AUTHORITY OVER NOVELISTS AND THE PRESS, THE BATTLE'S OVER...
...BUT THE LF CAN'T DO EVERY-THING.

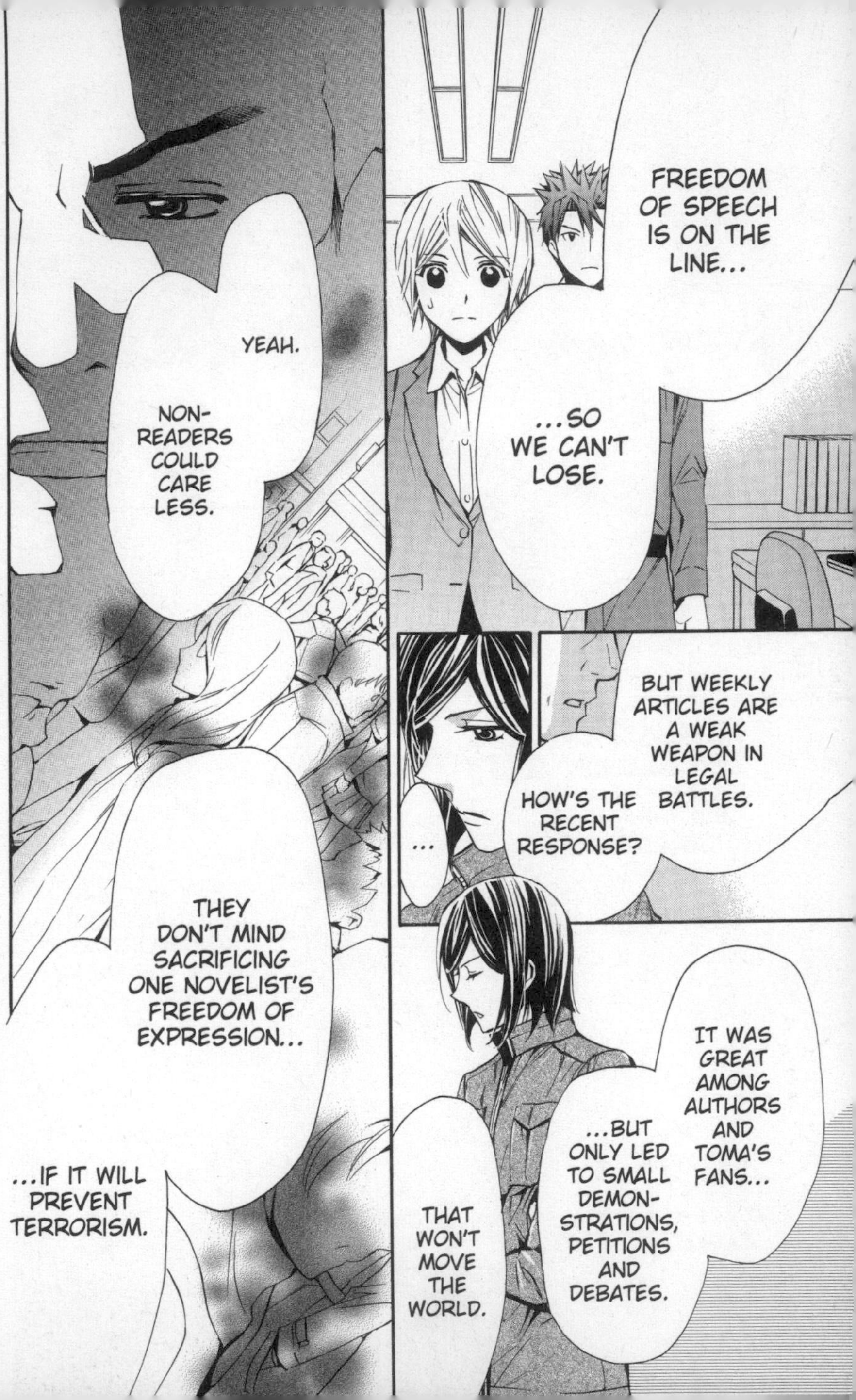
FREEDOM OF SPEECH IS ON THE LINE...
...SO WE CAN'T LOSE.
BUT WEEKLY ARTICLES ARE A WEAK WEAPON IN LEGAL BATTLES.
HOW'S THE RECENT RESPONSE?
...
IT WAS GREAT AMONG AUTHORS AND TOMA'S FANS...
...BUT ONLY LED TO SMALL DEMON-STRATIONS, PETITIONS AND DEBATES.
THAT WON'T MOVE THE WORLD.
YEAH.
NON-READERS COULD CARE LESS.
THEY DON'T MIND SACRIFICING ONE NOVELIST'S FREEDOM OF EXPRESSION...
...IF IT WILL PREVENT TERRORISM.

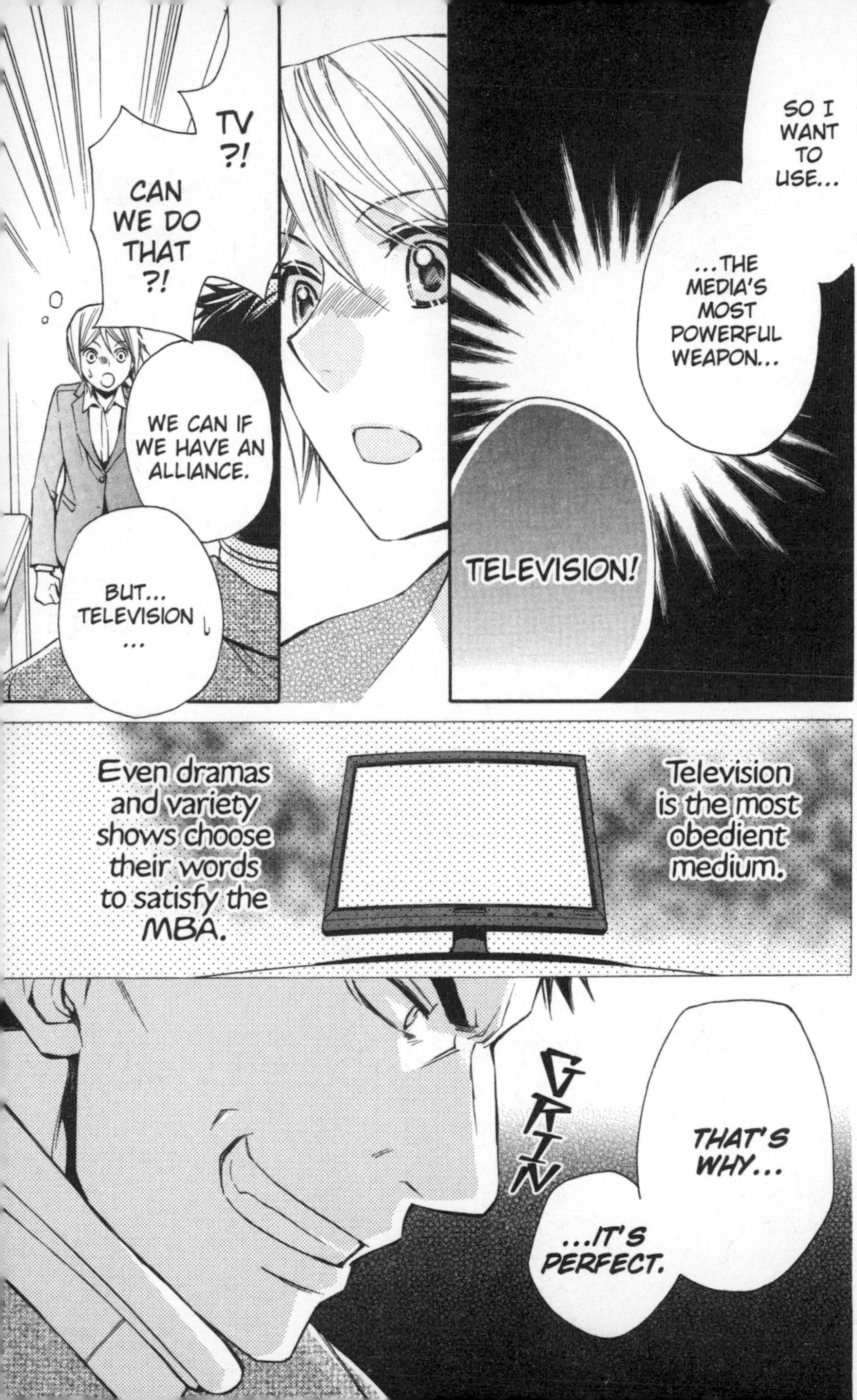
SO I WANT TO USE...
...THE MEDIA'S MOST POWERFUL WEAPON...
TELEVISION!
TV?!
CAN WE DO THAT?!
WE CAN IF WE HAVE AN ALLIANCE.
BUT... TELEVISION...
Television is the most obedient medium.
Even dramas and variety shows choose their words to satisfy the MBA.
GRIN
THAT'S WHY...
...IT'S PERFECT.

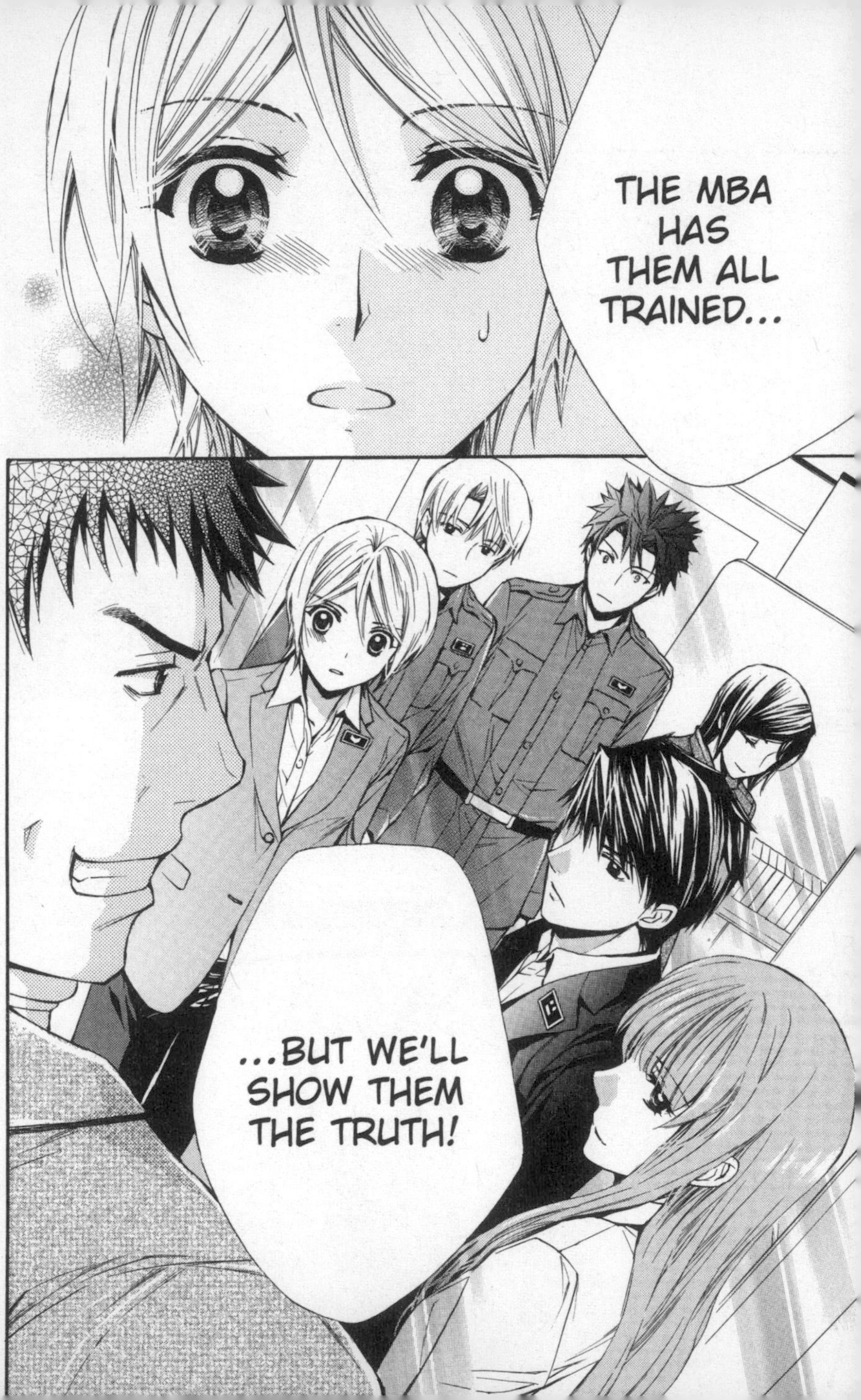
THE MBA HAS THEM ALL TRAINED...
...BUT WE'LL SHOW THEM THE TRUTH!

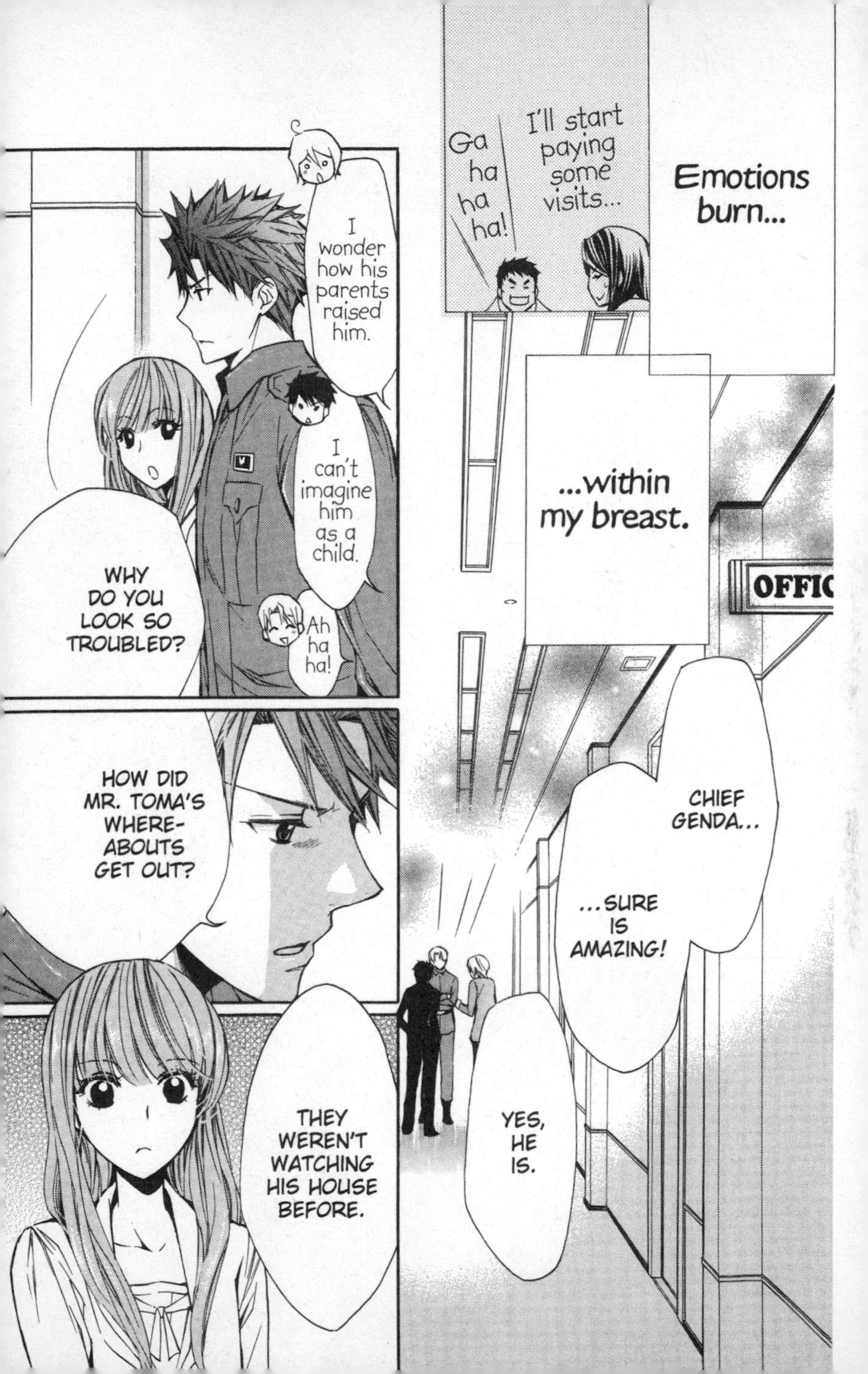
Emotions burn...
I'll start paying some visits...
Ga ha ha ha!
...within my breast.
OFFIC
CHIEF GENDA...
...SURE IS AMAZING!
YES, HE IS.
I wonder how his parents raised him.
I can't imagine him as a child.
Ah ha ha!
WHY DO YOU LOOK SO TROUBLED?
HOW DID MR. TOMA'S WHERE-ABOUTS GET OUT?
THEY WEREN'T WATCHING HIS HOUSE BEFORE.

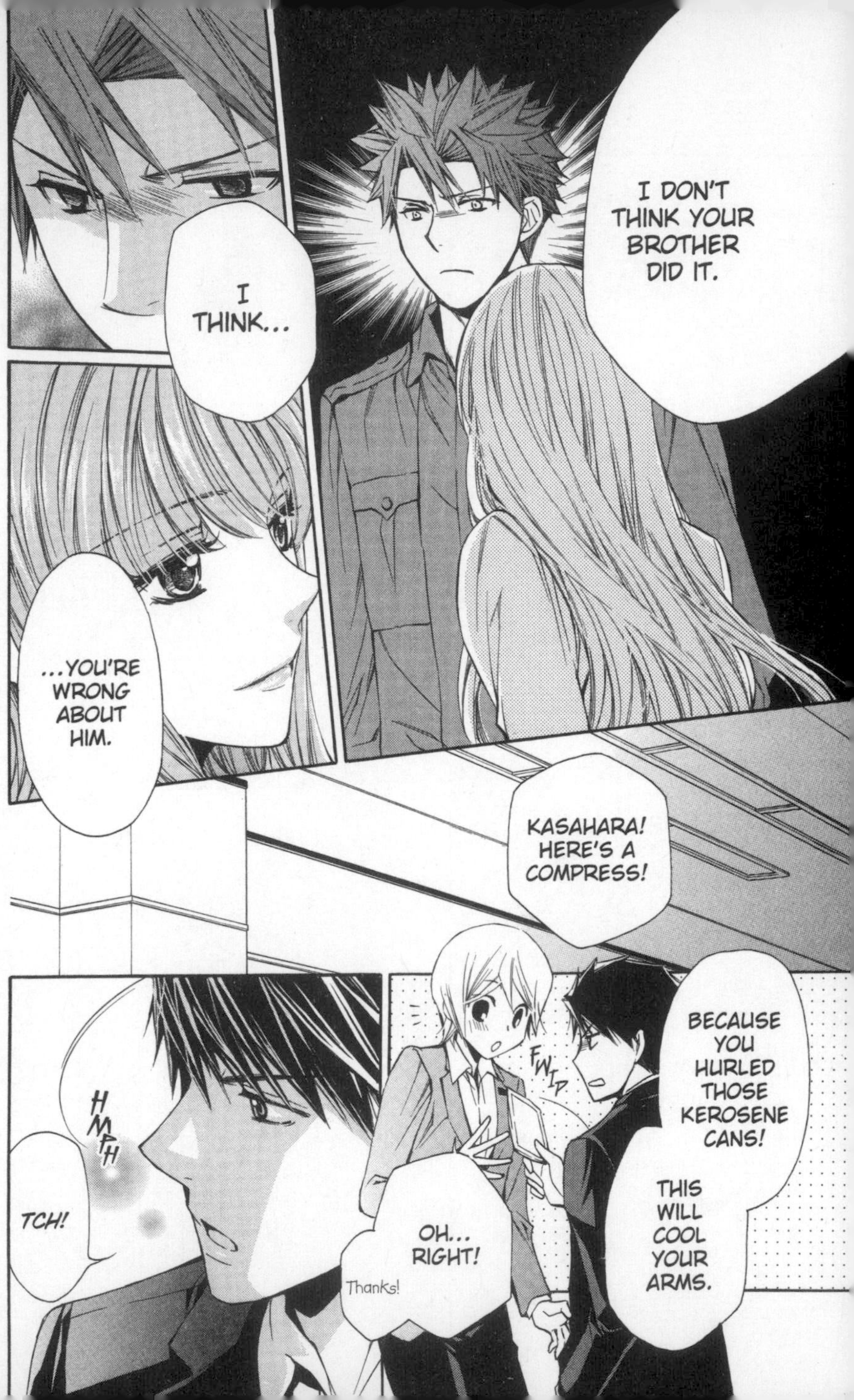
I DON'T THINK YOUR BROTHER DID IT.
I THINK...
...YOU'RE WRONG ABOUT HIM.
KASAHARA! HERE'S A COMPRESS!
BECAUSE YOU HURLED THOSE KEROSENE CANS!
FWIP
THIS WILL COOL YOUR ARMS.
OH... RIGHT!
Thanks!
HMPH
TCH!

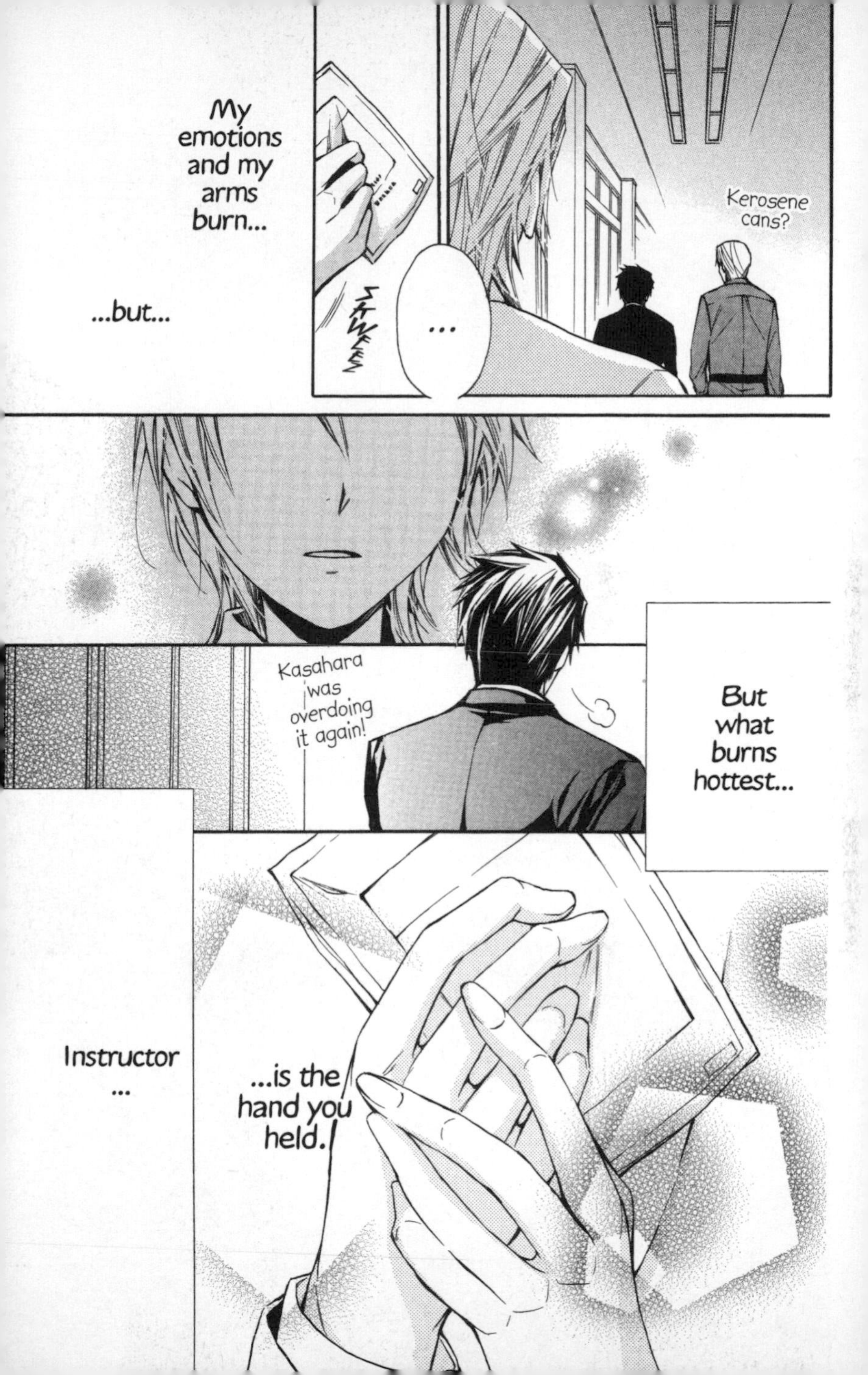
Kerosene cans?
SKWEEZ
...
My emotions and my arms burn...
...but...
But what burns hottest...
Kasahara was overdoing it again!
...is the hand you held.
Instructor ...

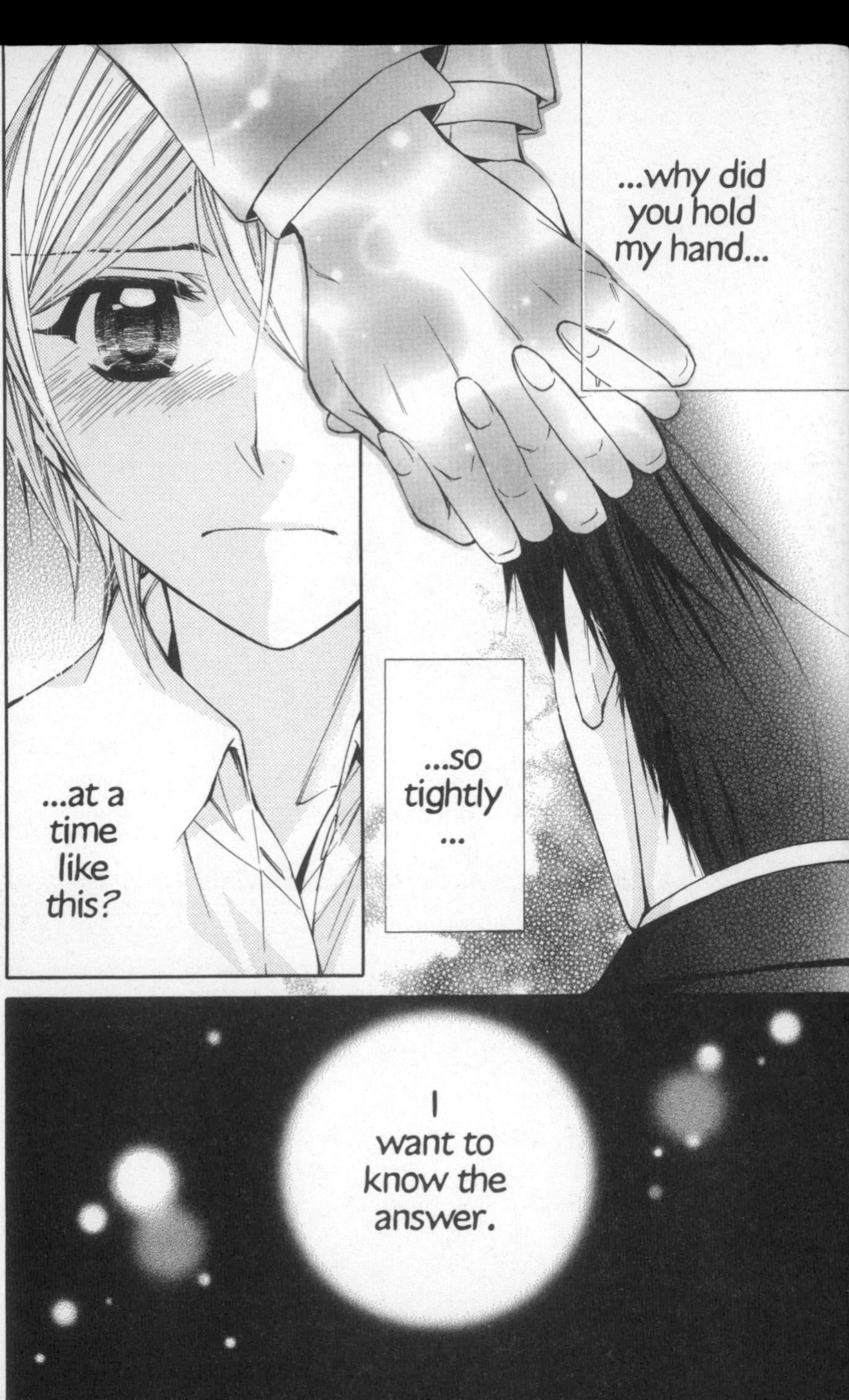
...why did you hold my hand...
...so tightly ...
...at a time like this?
I want to know the answer.

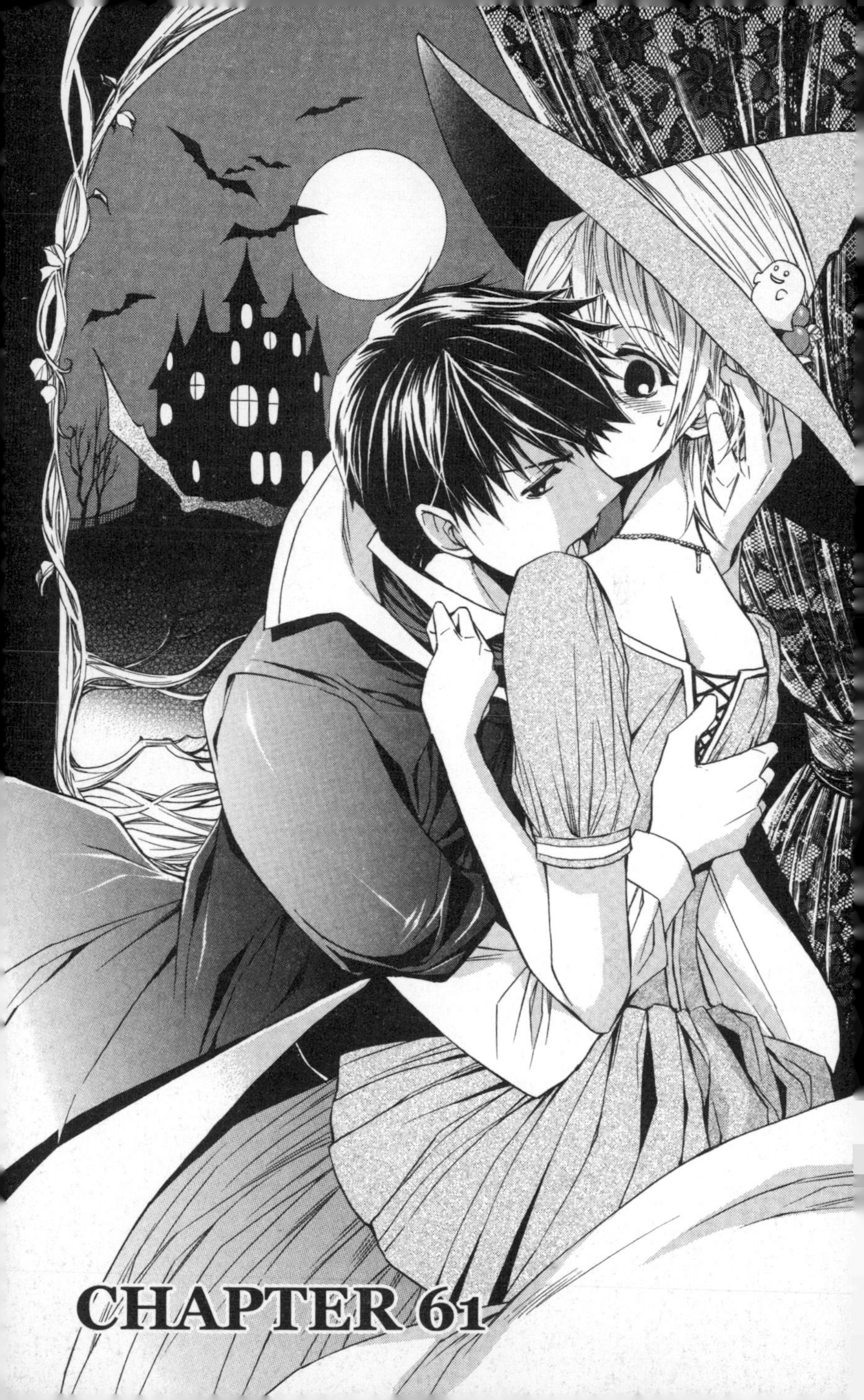
CHAPTER 61

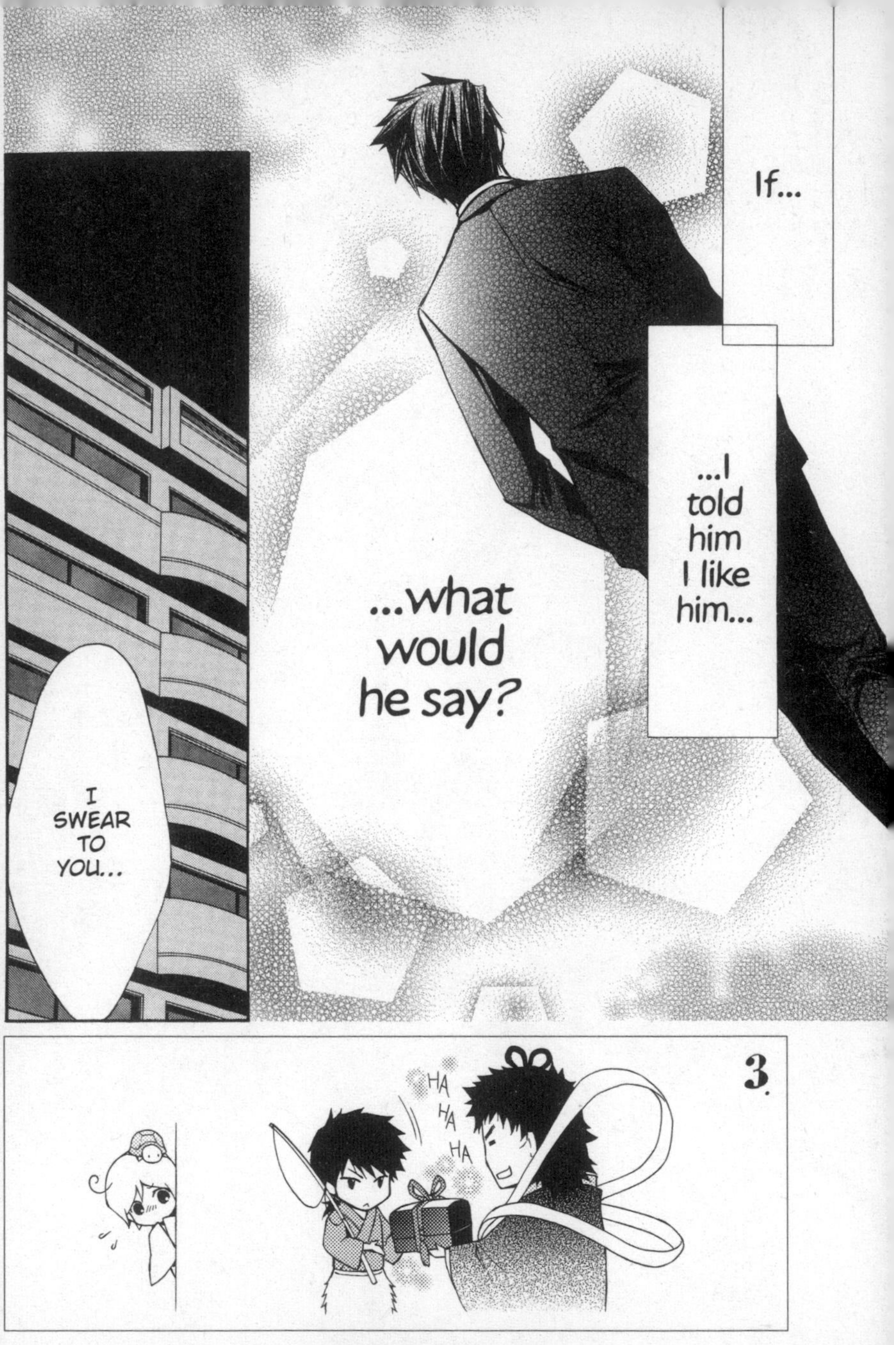
If...
...I told him I like him...
...what would he say?
I SWEAR TO YOU...
3.
HA HA HA

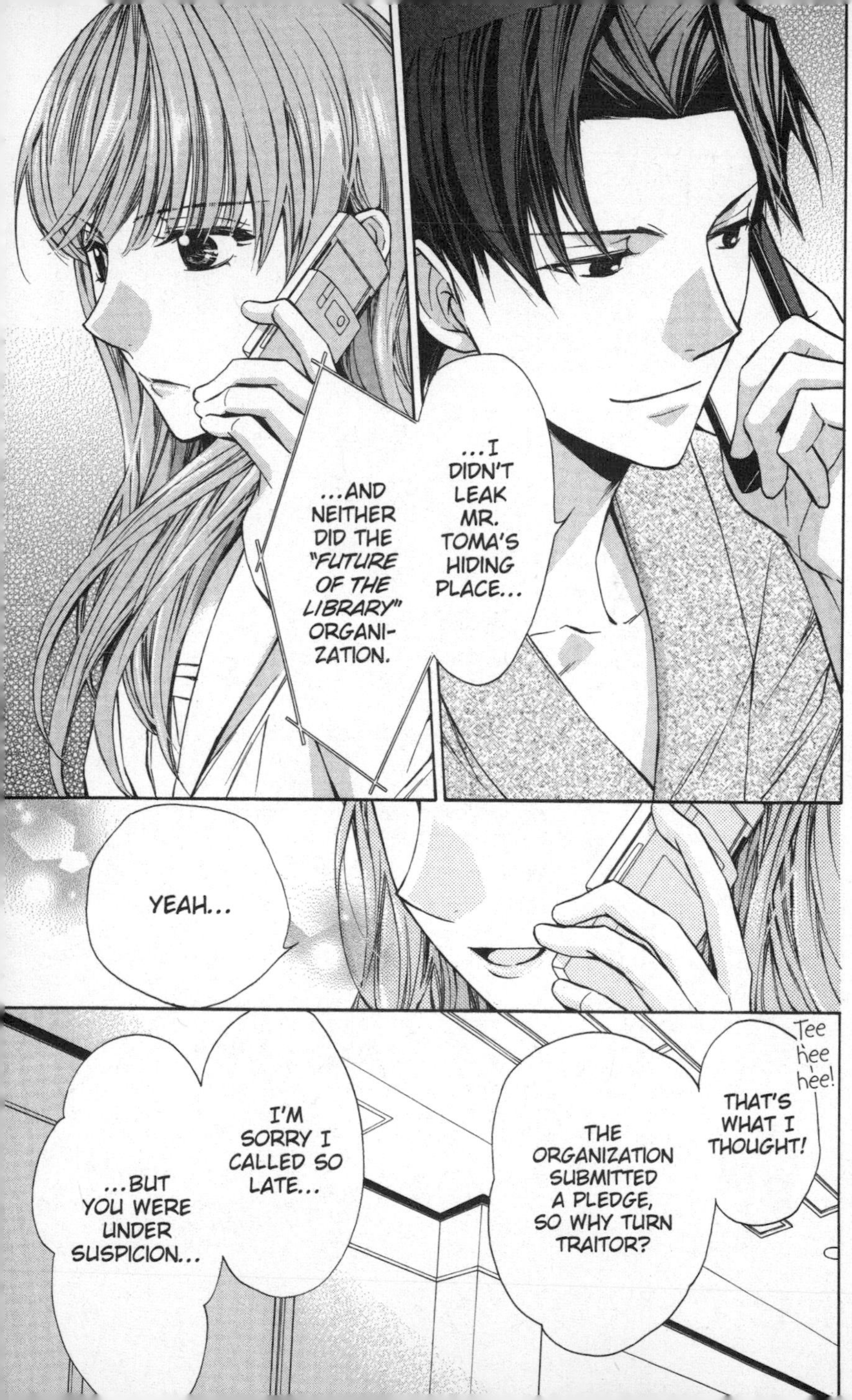
...I DIDN'T LEAK MR. TOMA'S HIDING PLACE...
...AND NEITHER DID THE "FUTURE OF THE LIBRARY" ORGANIZATION.
YEAH...
Tee hee hee!
THAT'S WHAT I THOUGHT!
THE ORGANIZATION SUBMITTED A PLEDGE, SO WHY TURN TRAITOR?
I'M SORRY I CALLED SO LATE...
...BUT YOU WERE UNDER SUSPICION...

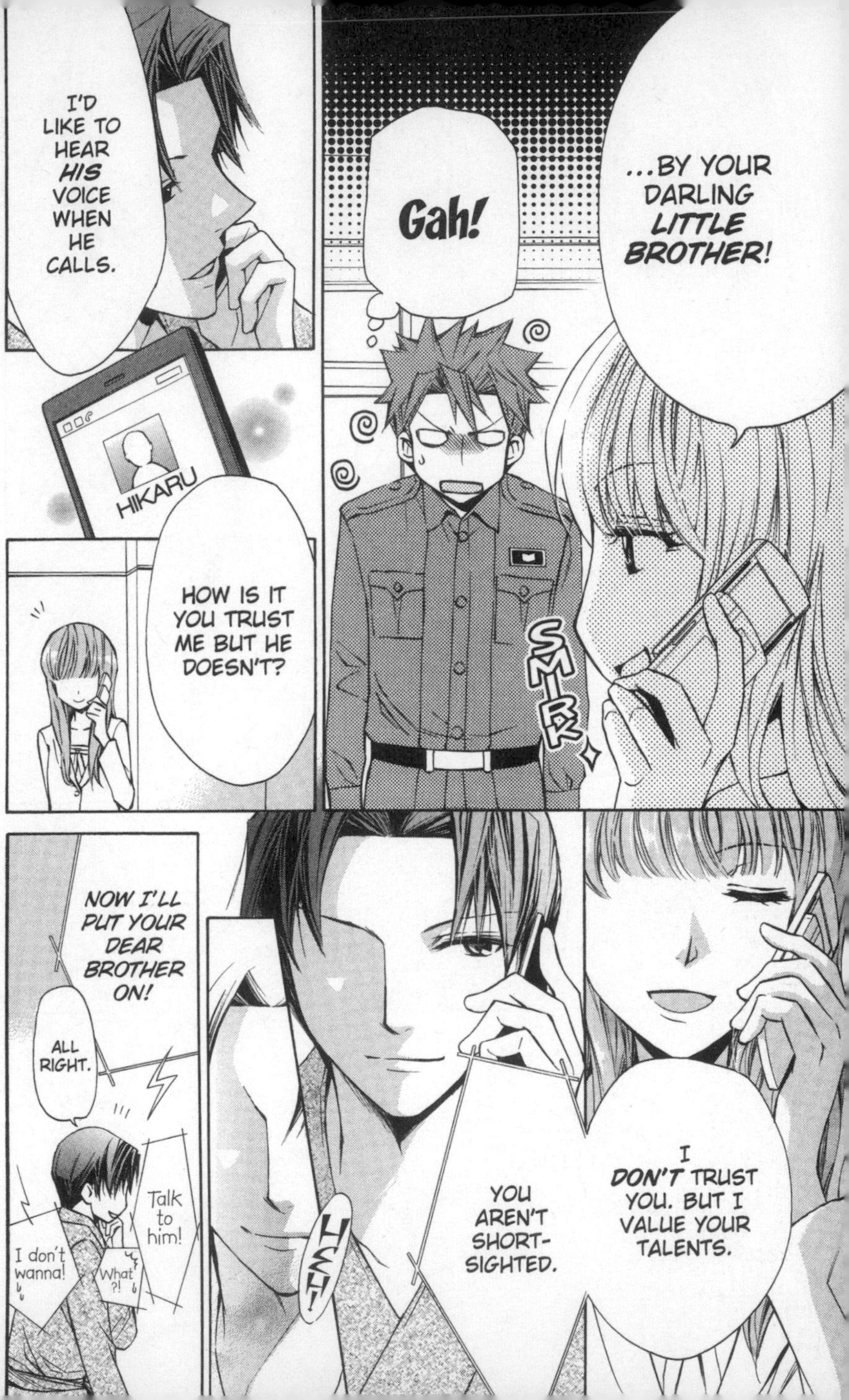

...BY YOUR DARLING LITTLE BROTHER!
Gah!
SMIRK
I'D LIKE TO HEAR HIS VOICE WHEN HE CALLS.
HIKARU
HOW IS IT YOU TRUST ME BUT HE DOESN'T?
I DON'T TRUST YOU. BUT I VALUE YOUR TALENTS.
YOU AREN'T SHORT-SIGHTED.
HEH!
NOW I'LL PUT YOUR DEAR BROTHER ON!
ALL RIGHT.
Talk to him!
What?!
I don't wanna!

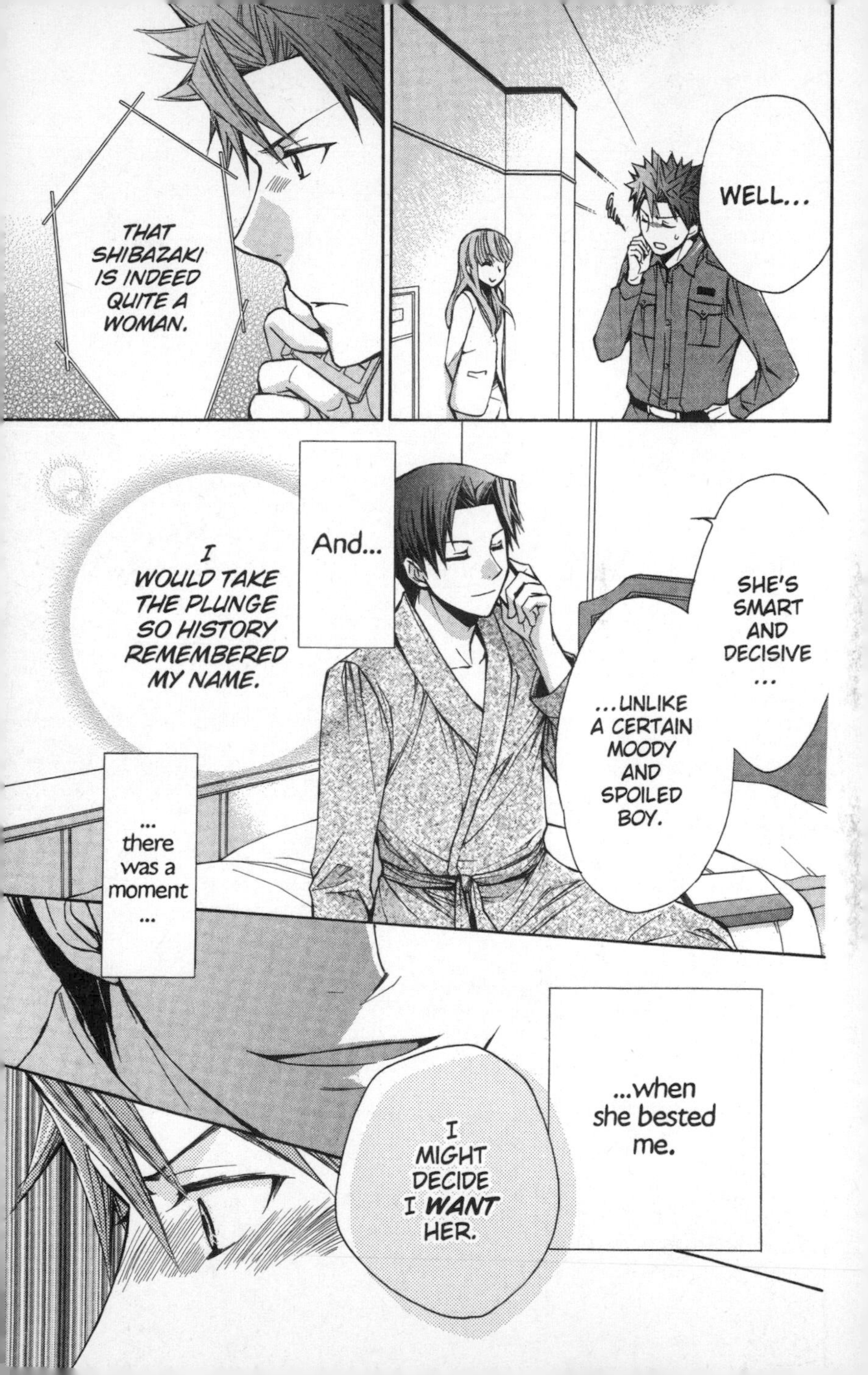
WELL...
THAT SHIBAZAKI IS INDEED QUITE A WOMAN.
SHE'S SMART AND DECISIVE ...
...UNLIKE A CERTAIN MOODY AND SPOILED BOY.
And...
I WOULD TAKE THE PLUNGE SO HISTORY REMEMBERED MY NAME.
... there was a moment ...
...when she bested me.
I MIGHT DECIDE I *WANT* HER.

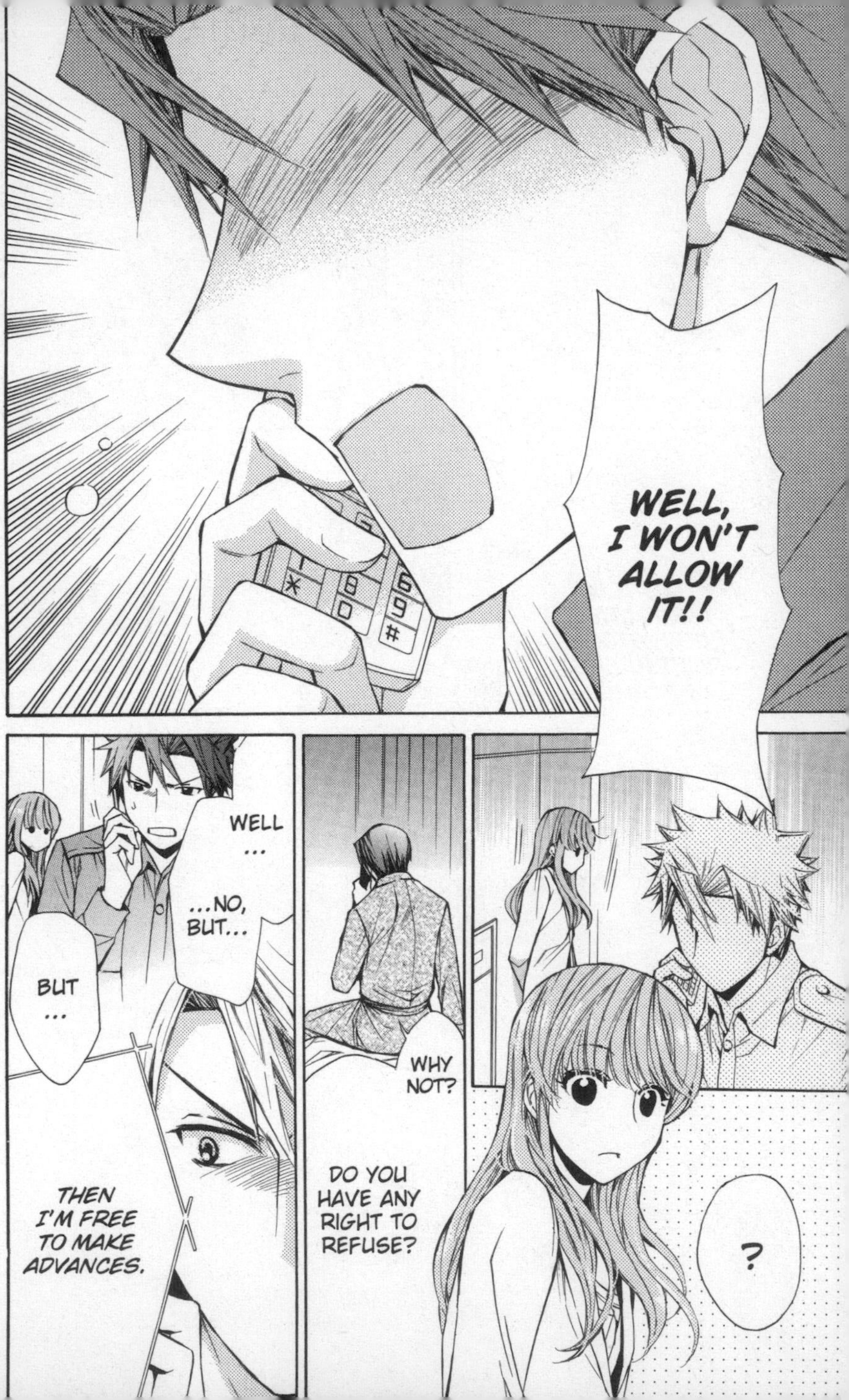
WELL, I WON'T ALLOW IT!!
?
WHY NOT?
DO YOU HAVE ANY RIGHT TO REFUSE?
WELL ...
...NO, BUT...
BUT ...
THEN I'M FREE TO MAKE ADVANCES.

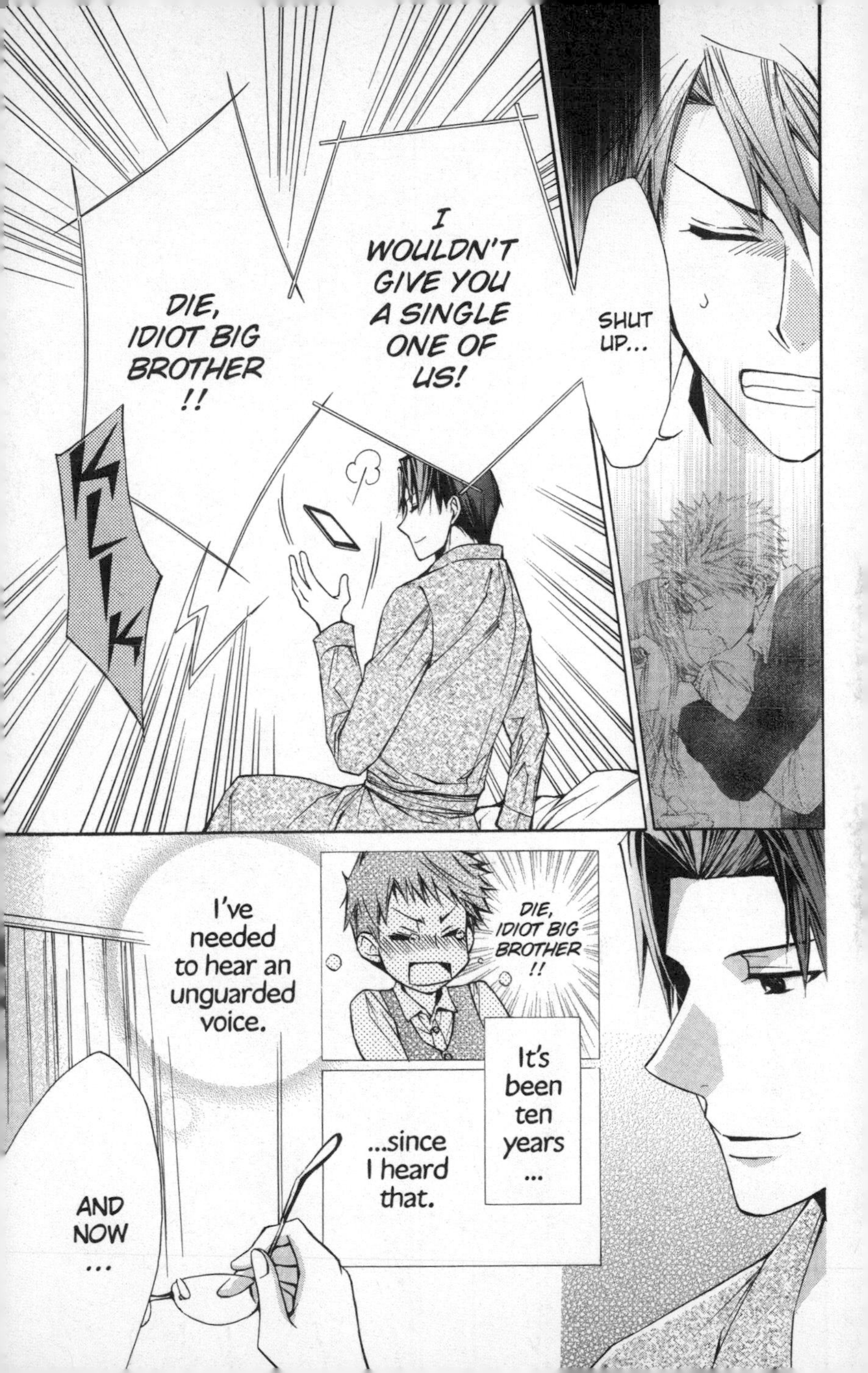
SHUT UP...
I WOULDN'T GIVE YOU A SINGLE ONE OF US!
DIE, IDIOT BIG BROTHER !!
DIE, IDIOT BIG BROTHER !!
It's been ten years ...
...since I heard that.
I've needed to hear an unguarded voice.
AND NOW ...

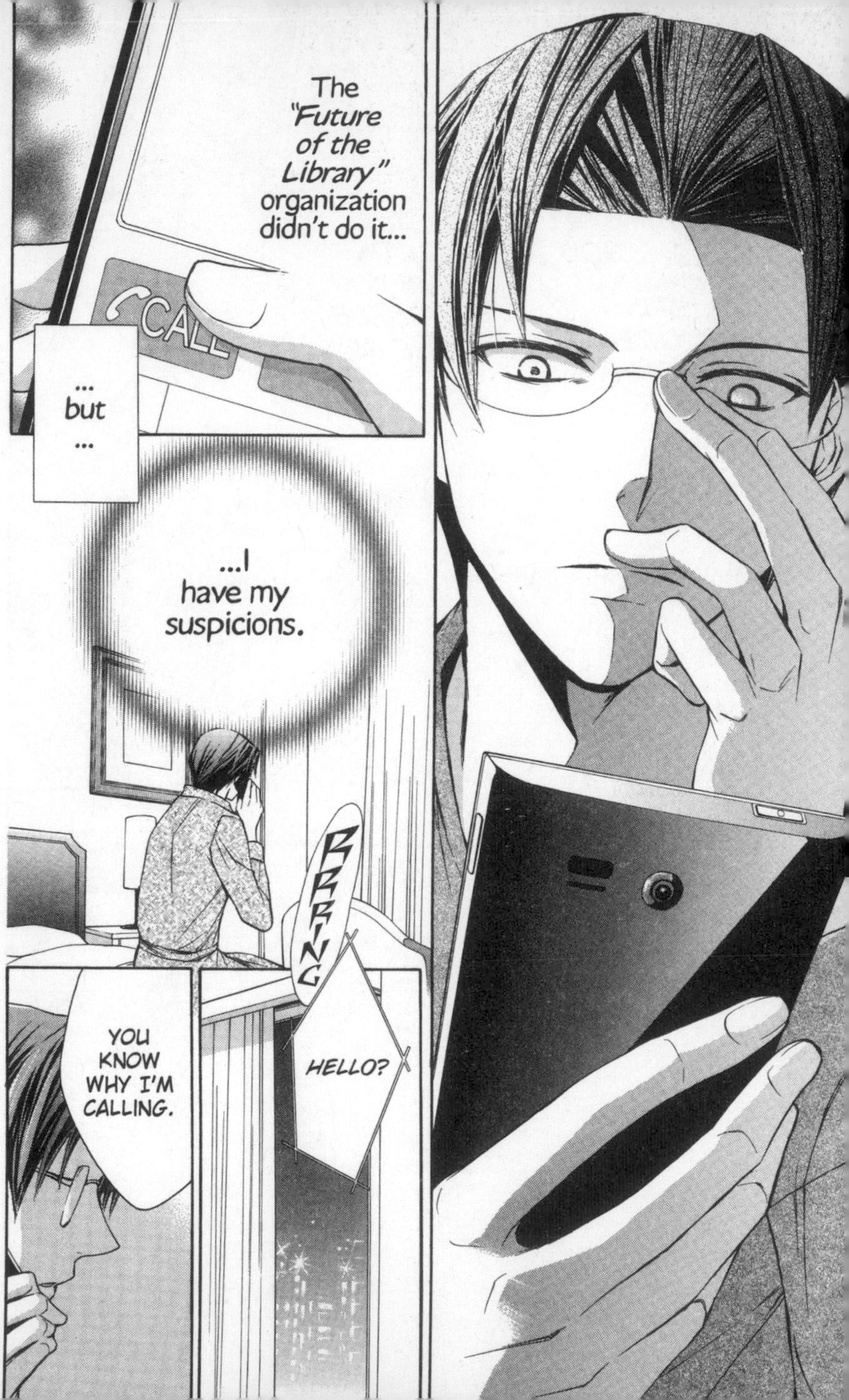
The "Future of the Library" organization didn't do it...
CALL
... but ...
...I have my suspicions.
RRRING
HELLO?
YOU KNOW WHY I'M CALLING.

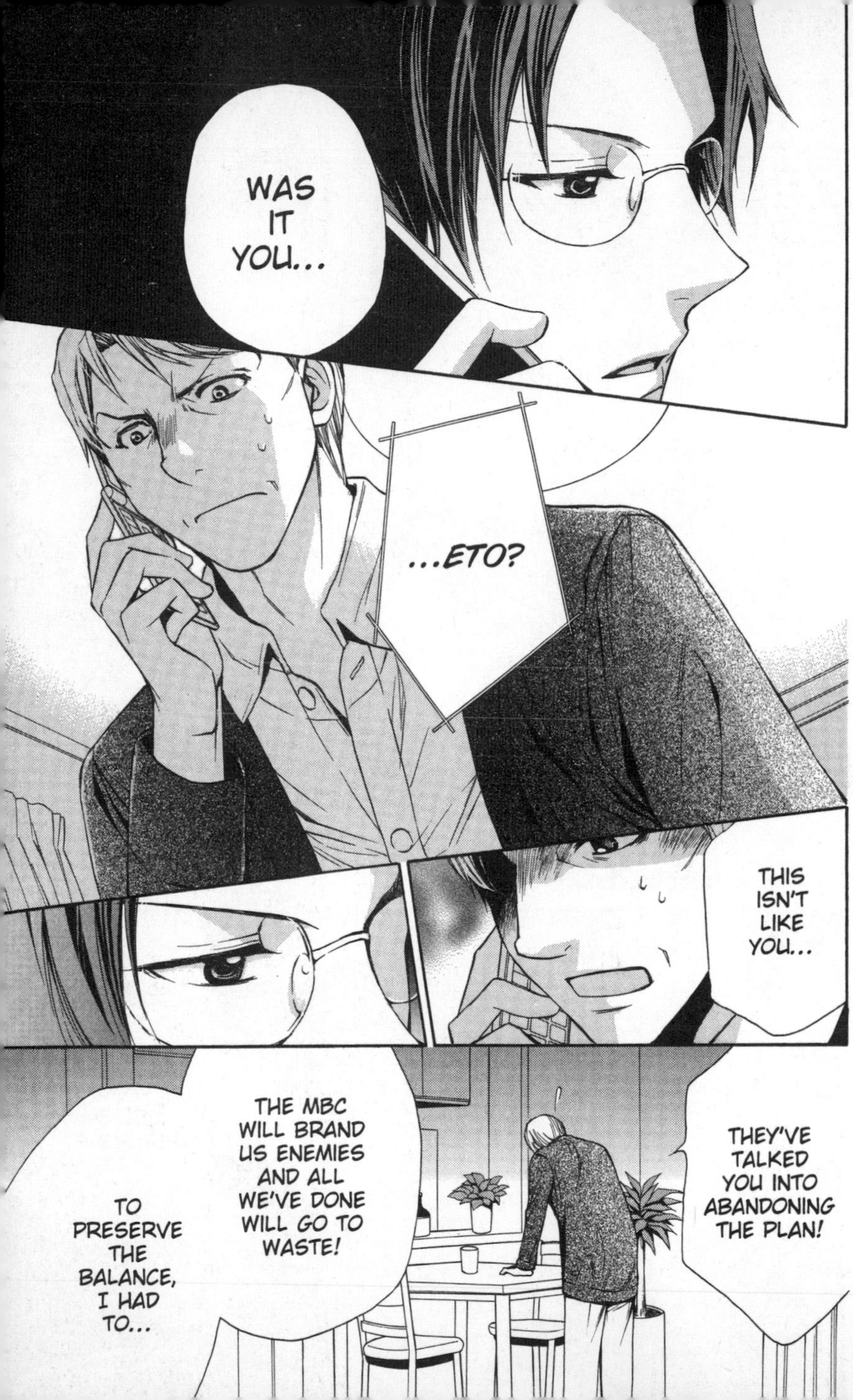
WAS IT YOU...
...ETO?
THIS ISN'T LIKE YOU...
THEY'VE TALKED YOU INTO ABANDONING THE PLAN!
THE MBC WILL BRAND US ENEMIES AND ALL WE'VE DONE WILL GO TO WASTE!
TO PRESERVE THE BALANCE, I HAD TO...

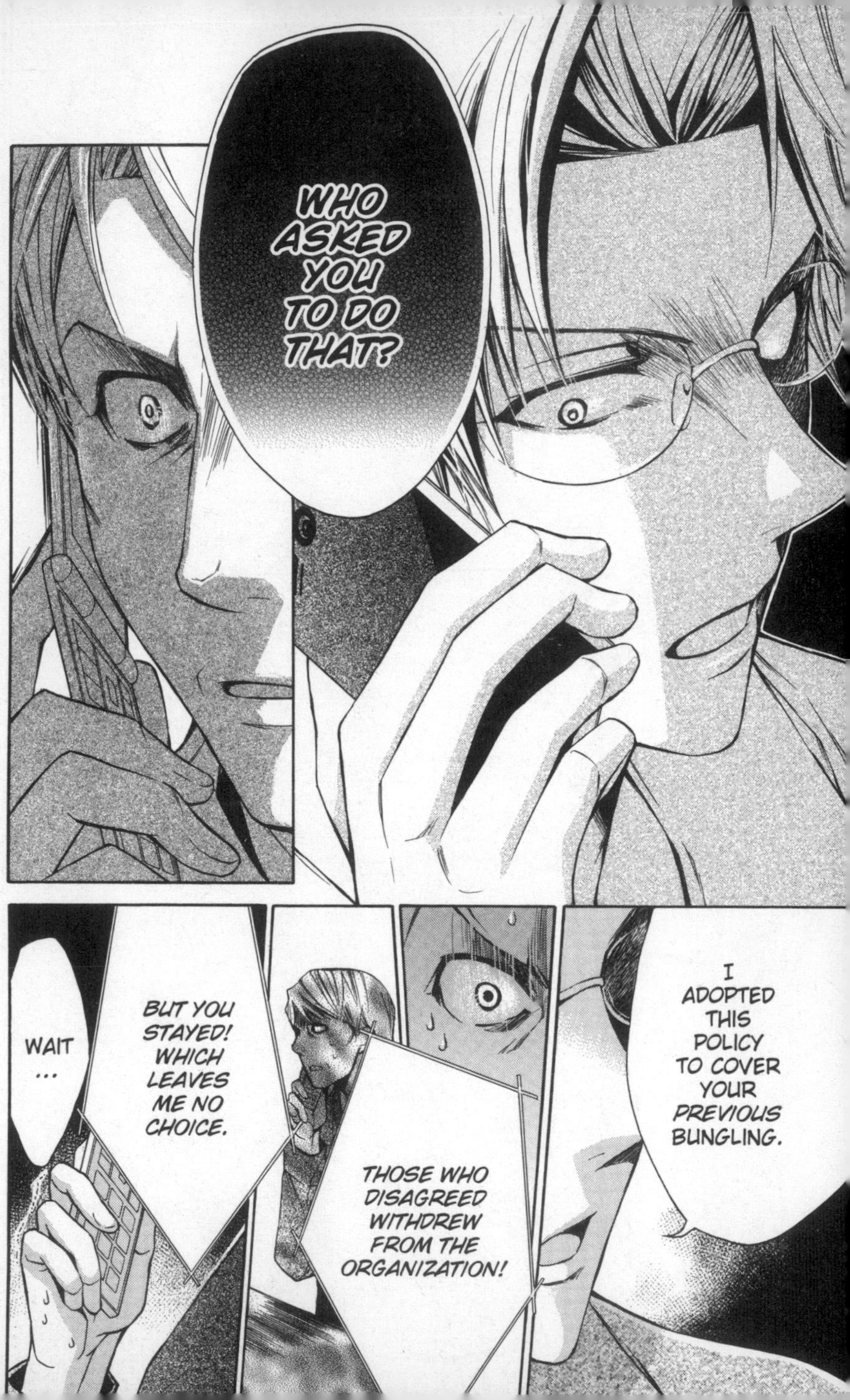
WHO ASKED YOU TO DO THAT?
I ADOPTED THIS POLICY TO COVER YOUR PREVIOUS BUNGLING.
THOSE WHO DISAGREED WITHDREW FROM THE ORGANIZATION!
BUT YOU STAYED! WHICH LEAVES ME NO CHOICE.
WAIT ...

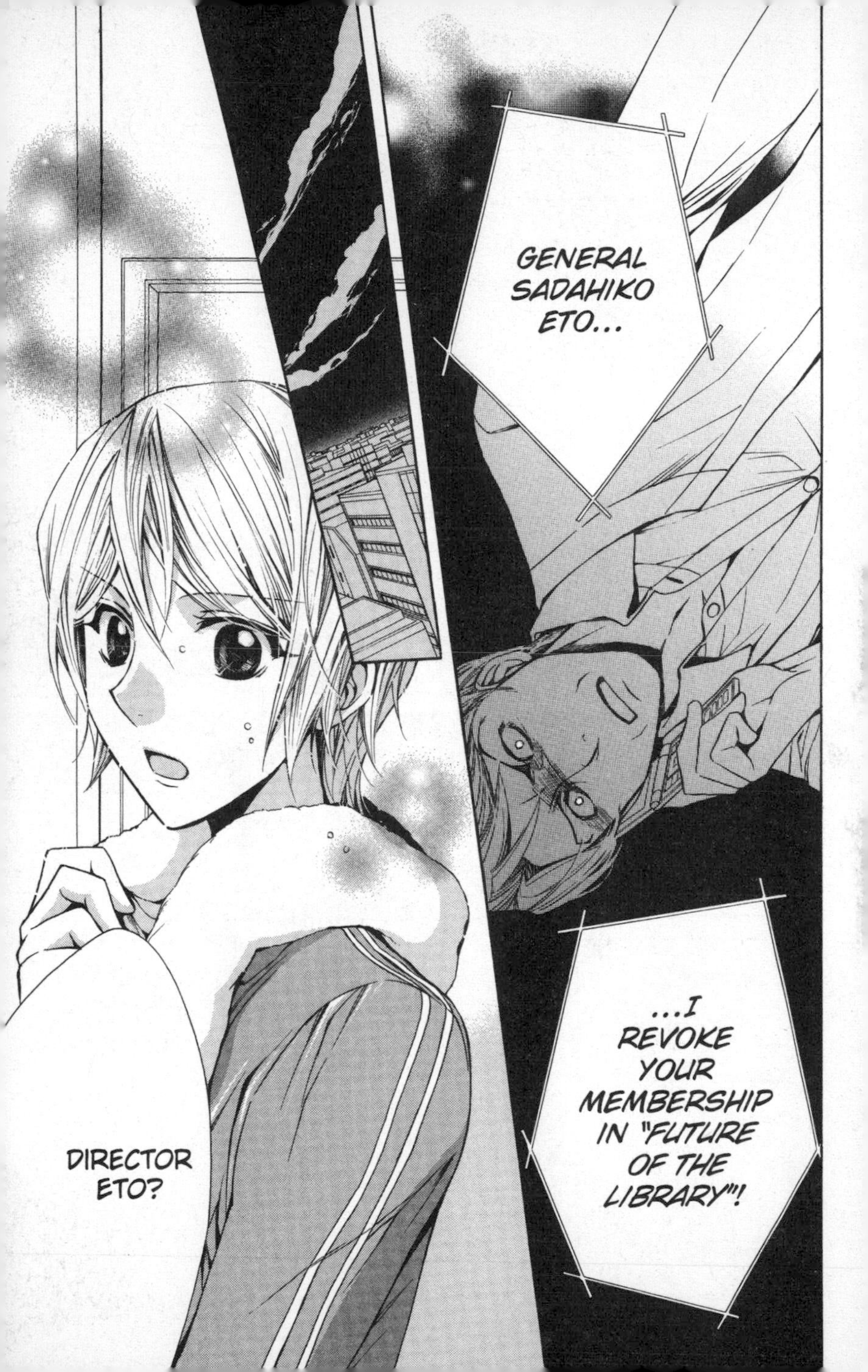
GENERAL SADAHIKO ETO...
...I REVOKE YOUR MEMBERSHIP IN "FUTURE OF THE LIBRARY"!
DIRECTOR ETO?

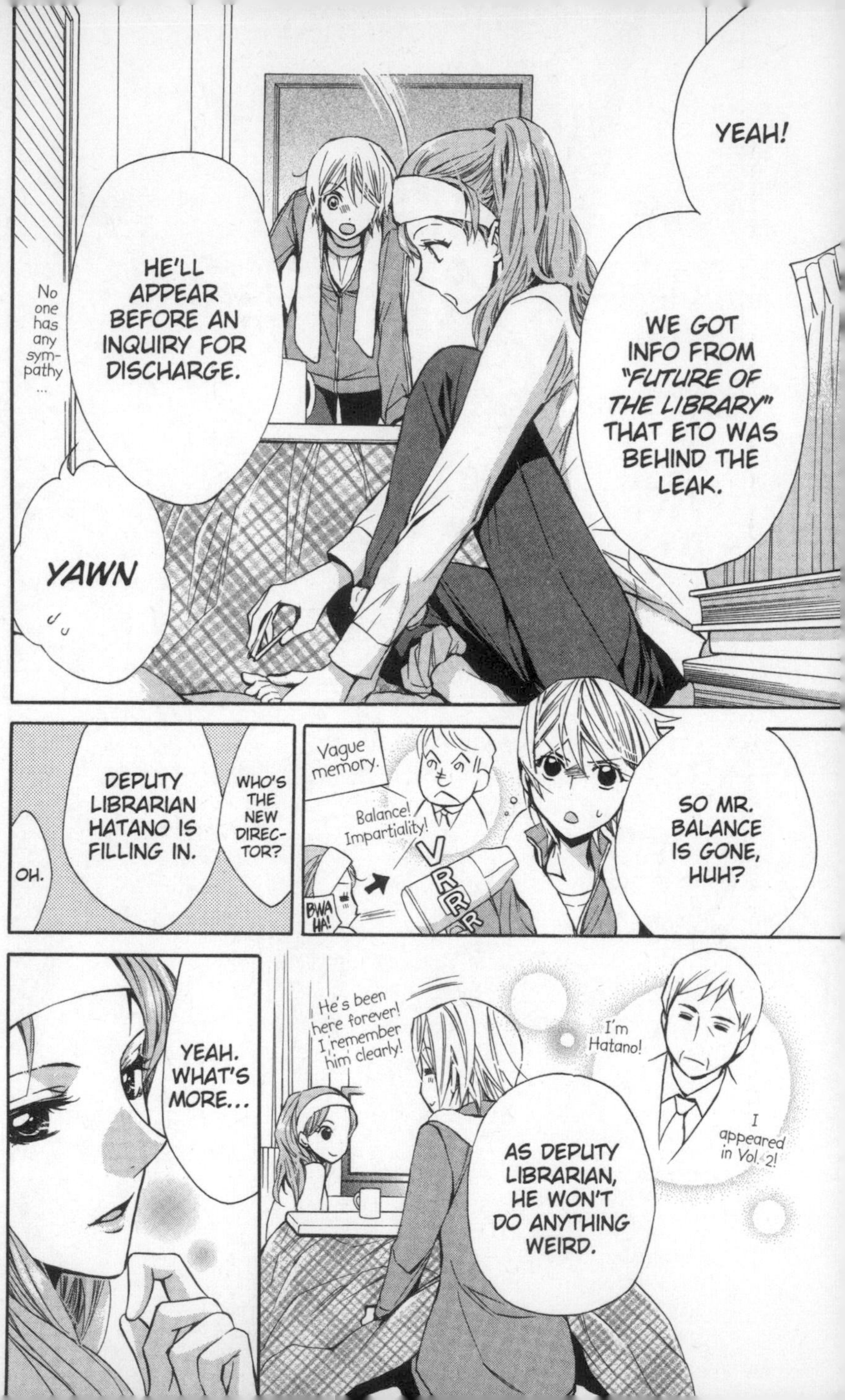
YEAH!
WE GOT INFO FROM "FUTURE OF THE LIBRARY" THAT ETO WAS BEHIND THE LEAK.
HE'LL APPEAR BEFORE AN INQUIRY FOR DISCHARGE.
No one has any sym-pathy...
YAWN
SO MR. BALANCE IS GONE, HUH?
Vague memory.
Balance! Impartiality!
VRRR
BWA HA!
WHO'S THE NEW DIREC-TOR?
DEPUTY LIBRARIAN HATANO IS FILLING IN.
OH.
I'm Hatano!
I appeared in Vol. 2!
AS DEPUTY LIBRARIAN, HE WON'T DO ANYTHING WEIRD.
He's been here forever! I remember him clearly!
YEAH. WHAT'S MORE...

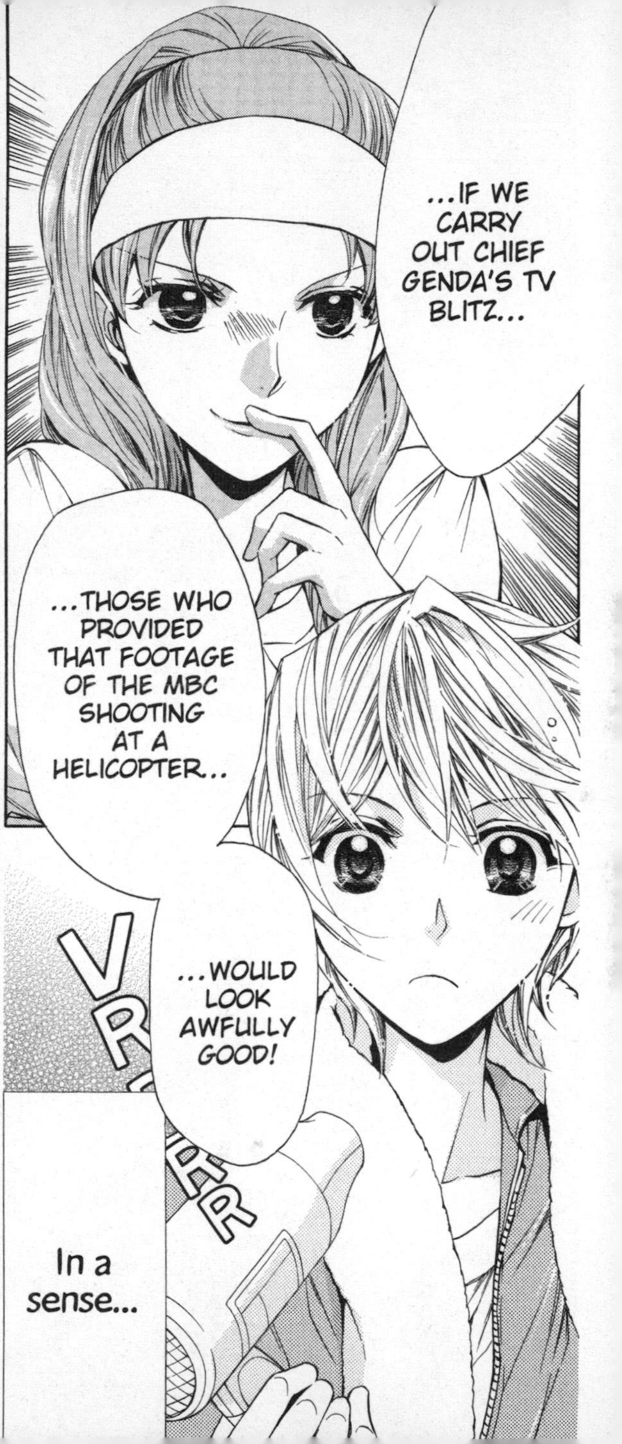
...IF WE CARRY OUT CHIEF GENDA'S TV BLITZ...
...THOSE WHO PROVIDED THAT FOOTAGE OF THE MBC SHOOTING AT A HELICOPTER...
...WOULD LOOK AWFULLY GOOD!
In a sense...

3

I don't have much to write about, so I might as well rattle on about *Monster Hunter*, the video game I've been devoting the most energy to. It won't make any sense if you don't play *MonHun*, so if you don't, just skip the sidebars!

I started playing *MonHun* with *Monster Hunter Freedom Unite*. I've always liked video games, but I'm not good at action games, so I rarely play them. But all my friends started playing *MonHun* and I wanted to join. At first, I really stunk at it... (to be continued)

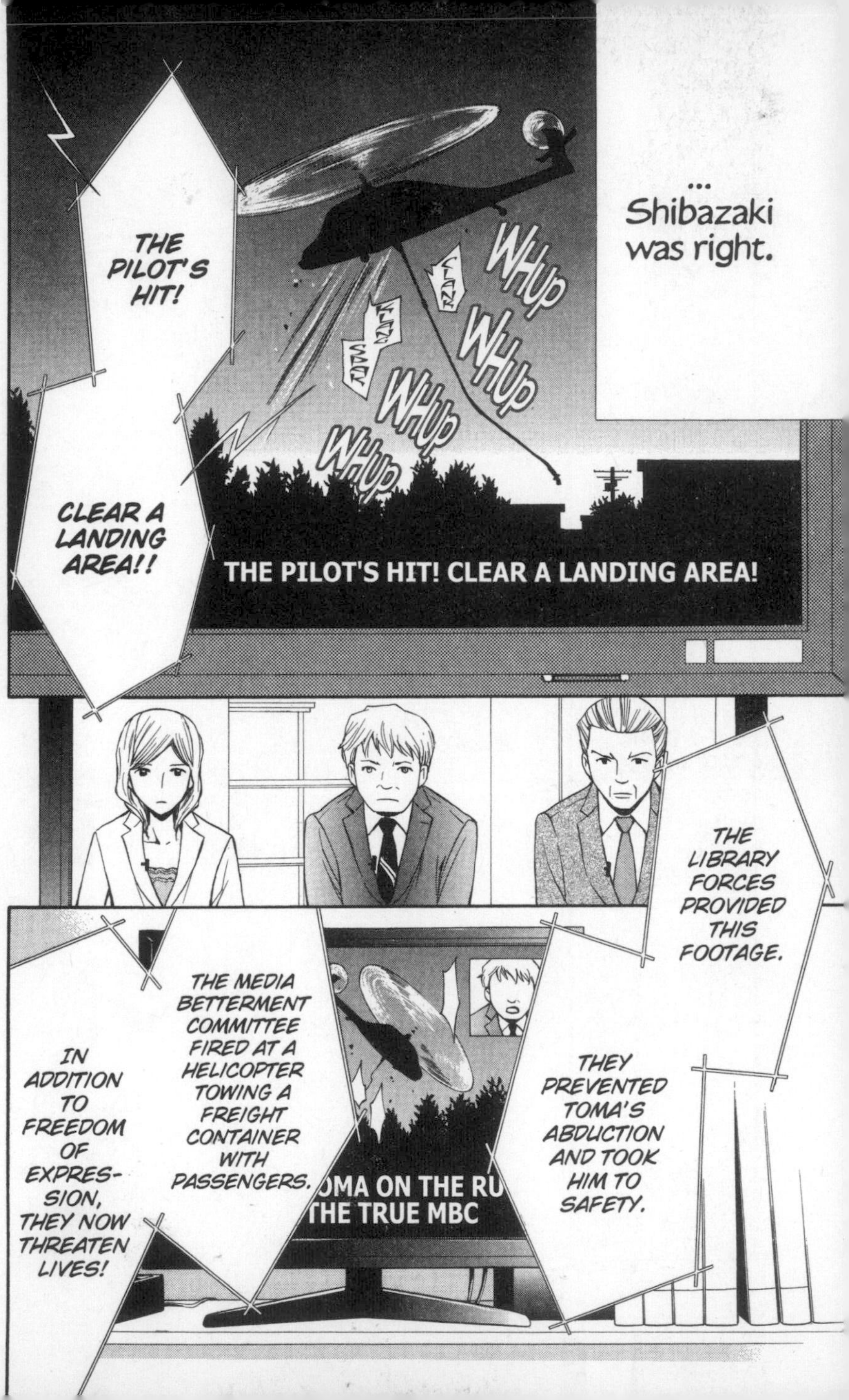
... Shibazaki was right.
WHUP WHUP WHUP WHUP
CLANK
THE PILOT'S HIT!
CLEAR A LANDING AREA!!
THE PILOT'S HIT! CLEAR A LANDING AREA!
THE LIBRARY FORCES PROVIDED THIS FOOTAGE.
THEY PREVENTED TOMA'S ABDUCTION AND TOOK HIM TO SAFETY.
THE MEDIA BETTERMENT COMMITTEE FIRED AT A HELICOPTER TOWING A FREIGHT CONTAINER WITH PASSENGERS.
OMA ON THE RU
THE TRUE MBC
IN ADDITION TO FREEDOM OF EXPRESSION, THEY NOW THREATEN LIVES!

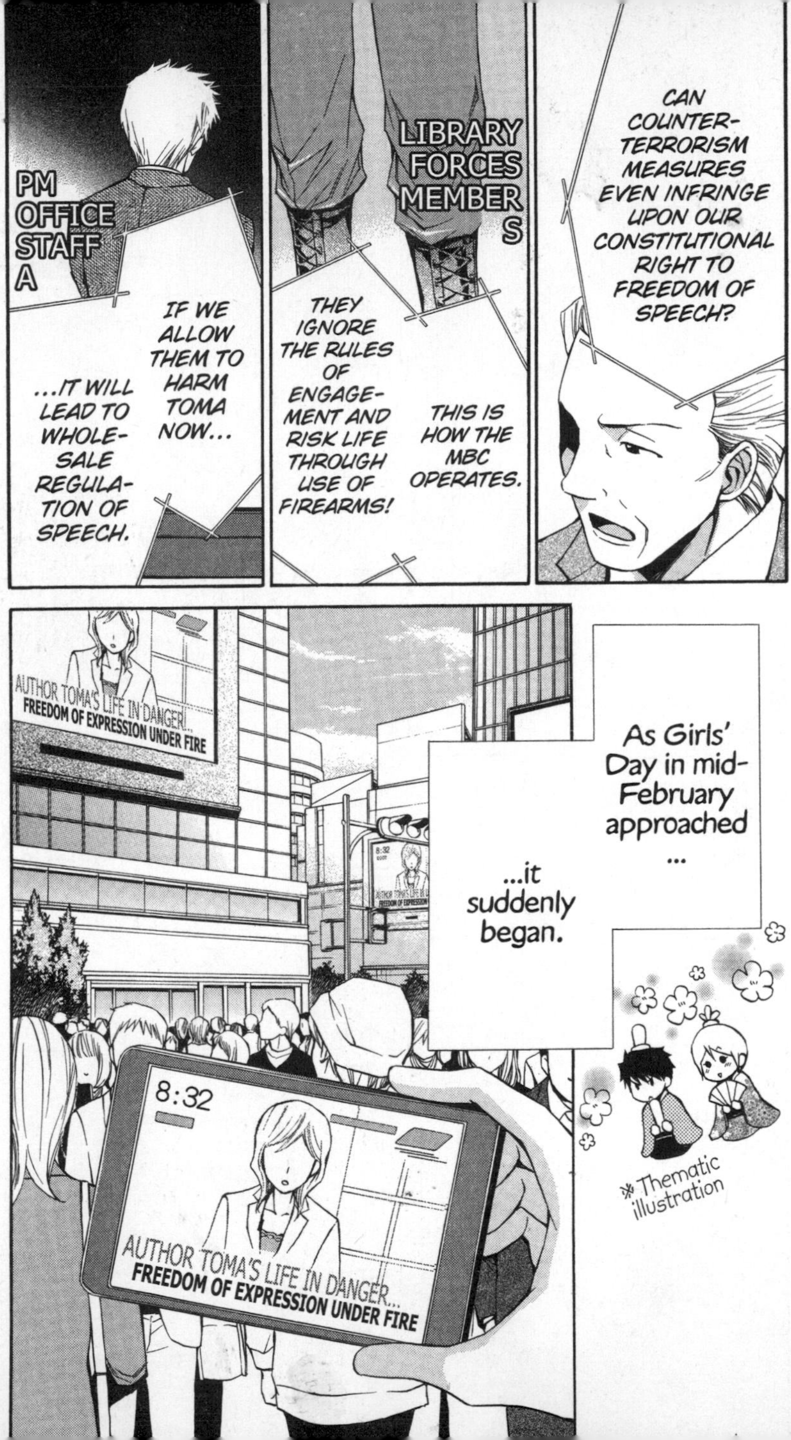
CAN COUNTER-TERRORISM MEASURES EVEN INFRINGE UPON OUR CONSTITUTIONAL RIGHT TO FREEDOM OF SPEECH?
LIBRARY FORCES MEMBER S
THIS IS HOW THE MBC OPERATES.
THEY IGNORE THE RULES OF ENGAGE-MENT AND RISK LIFE THROUGH USE OF FIREARMS!
PM OFFICE STAFF A
IF WE ALLOW THEM TO HARM TOMA NOW...
...IT WILL LEAD TO WHOLE-SALE REGULA-TION OF SPEECH.
As Girls' Day in mid-February approached...
...it suddenly began.
AUTHOR TOMA'S LIFE IN DANGER...
FREEDOM OF EXPRESSION UNDER FIRE
8:32
AUTHOR TOMA'S LIFE IN DANGER...
FREEDOM OF EXPRESSION UNDER FIRE
※ Thematic illustration

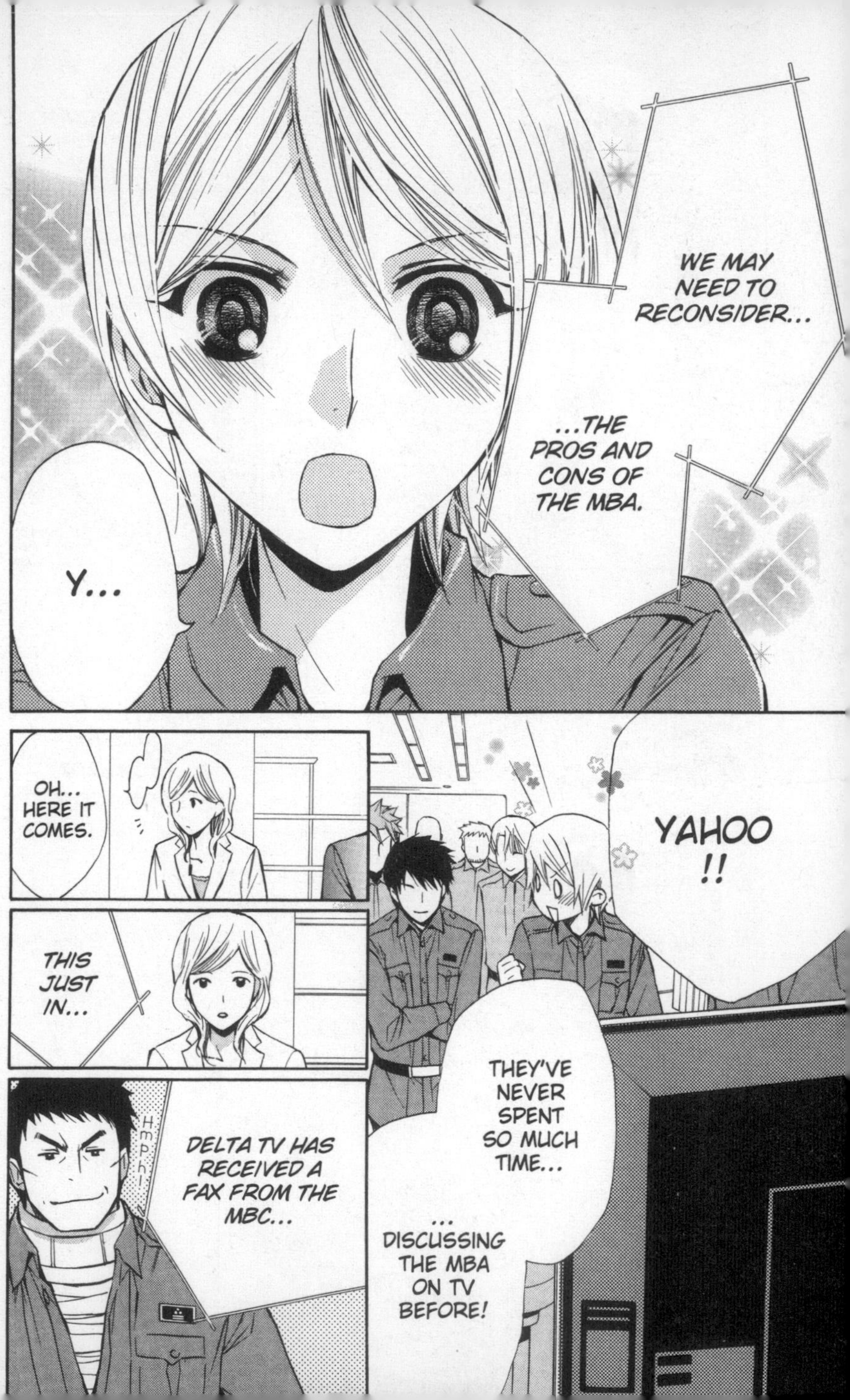
WE MAY NEED TO RECONSIDER...
...THE PROS AND CONS OF THE MBA.
Y...
YAHOO !!
THEY'VE NEVER SPENT SO MUCH TIME...
...DISCUSSING THE MBA ON TV BEFORE!
OH... HERE IT COMES.
THIS JUST IN...
Hmph!
DELTA TV HAS RECEIVED A FAX FROM THE MBC...

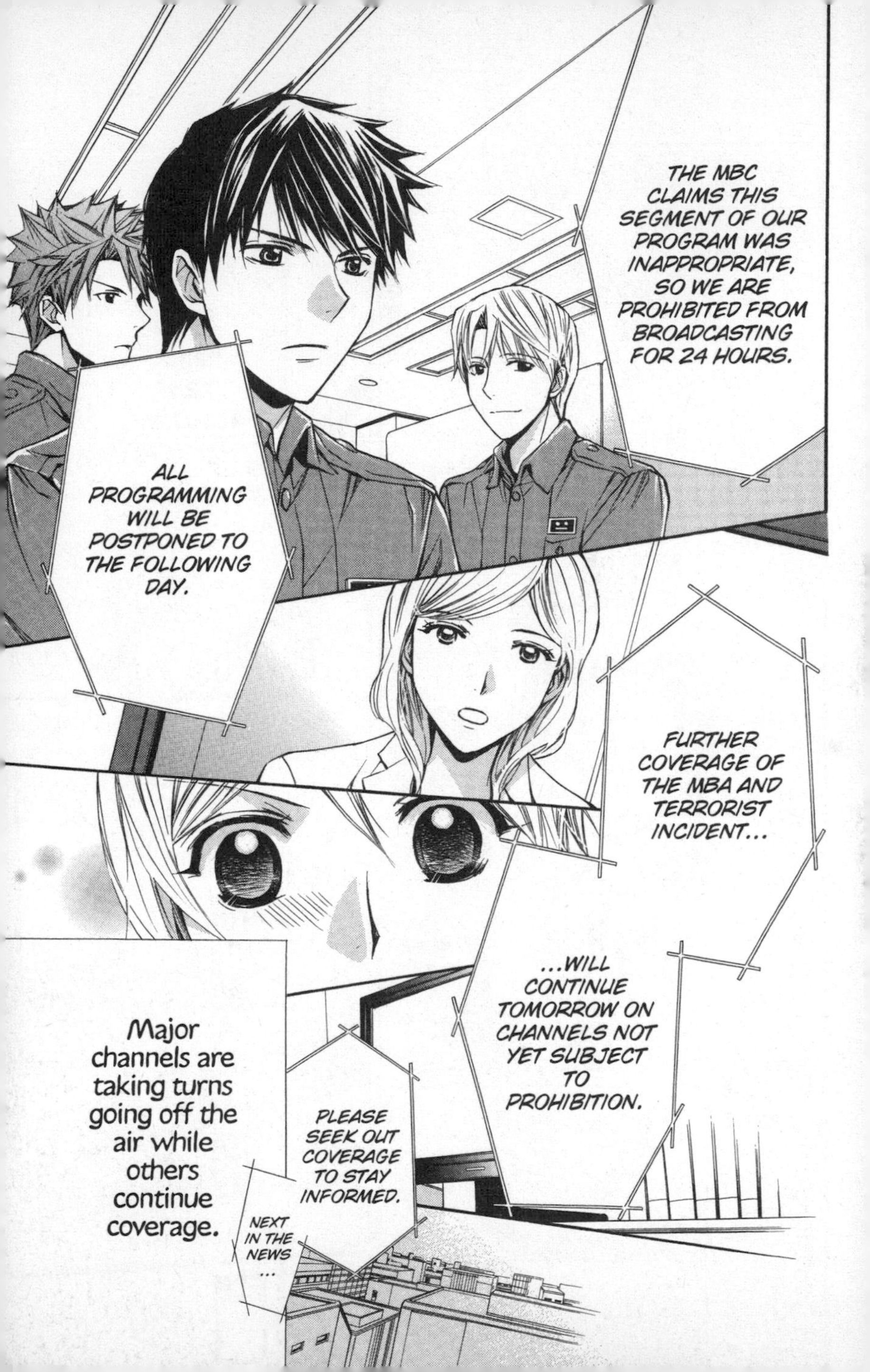
THE MBC CLAIMS THIS SEGMENT OF OUR PROGRAM WAS INAPPROPRIATE, SO WE ARE PROHIBITED FROM BROADCASTING FOR 24 HOURS.
ALL PROGRAMMING WILL BE POSTPONED TO THE FOLLOWING DAY.
FURTHER COVERAGE OF THE MBA AND TERRORIST INCIDENT...
...WILL CONTINUE TOMORROW ON CHANNELS NOT YET SUBJECT TO PROHIBITION.
PLEASE SEEK OUT COVERAGE TO STAY INFORMED.
Major channels are taking turns going off the air while others continue coverage.
NEXT IN THE NEWS ...

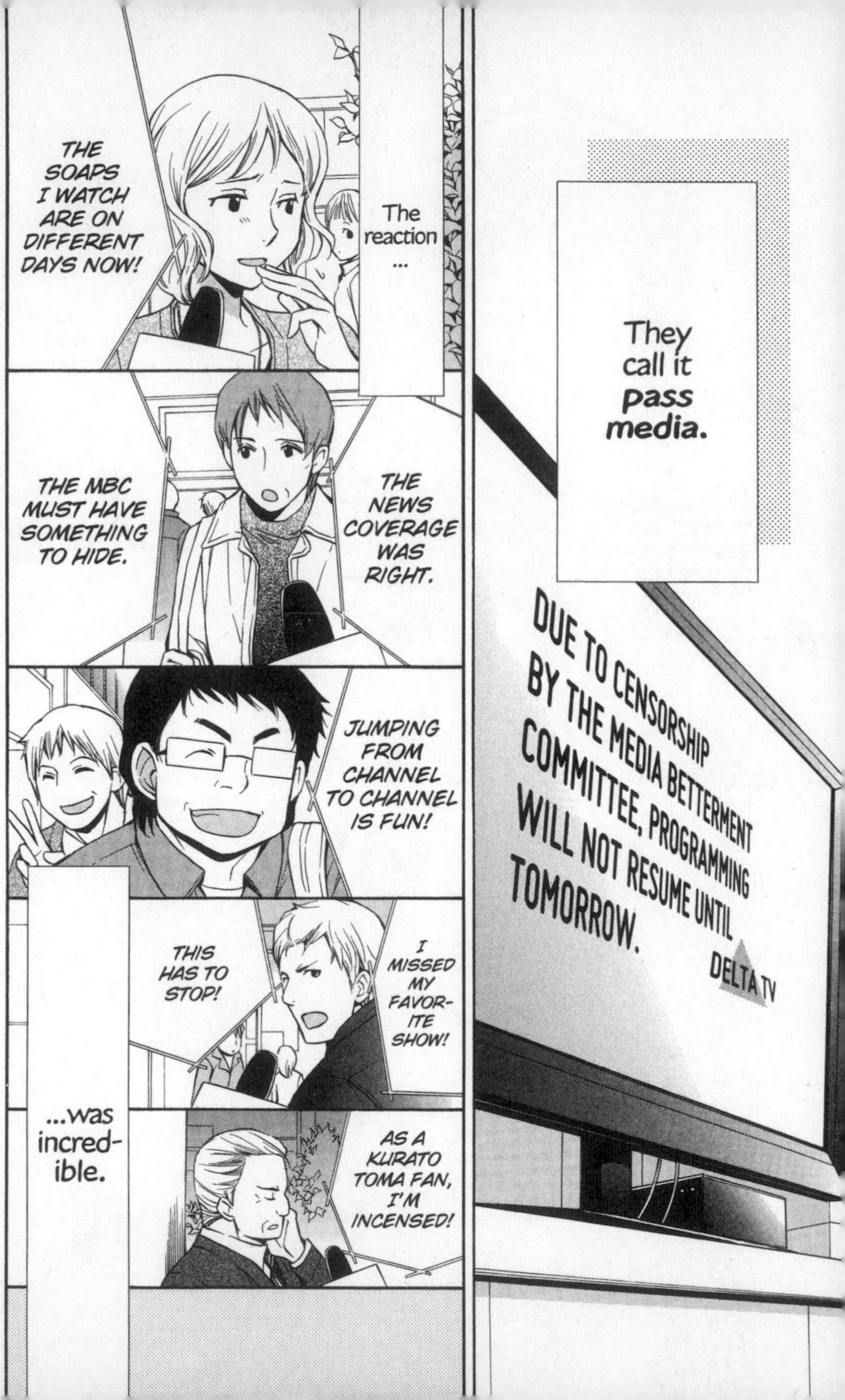
They call it **pass media.**
DUE TO CENSORSHIP BY THE MEDIA BETTERMENT COMMITTEE, PROGRAMMING WILL NOT RESUME UNTIL TOMORROW.
DELTA TV
The reaction ...
THE SOAPS I WATCH ARE ON DIFFERENT DAYS NOW!
THE NEWS COVERAGE WAS RIGHT.
THE MBC MUST HAVE SOMETHING TO HIDE.
JUMPING FROM CHANNEL TO CHANNEL IS FUN!
I MISSED MY FAVOR-ITE SHOW!
THIS HAS TO STOP!
AS A KURATO TOMA FAN, I'M INCENSED!
...was incred-ible.

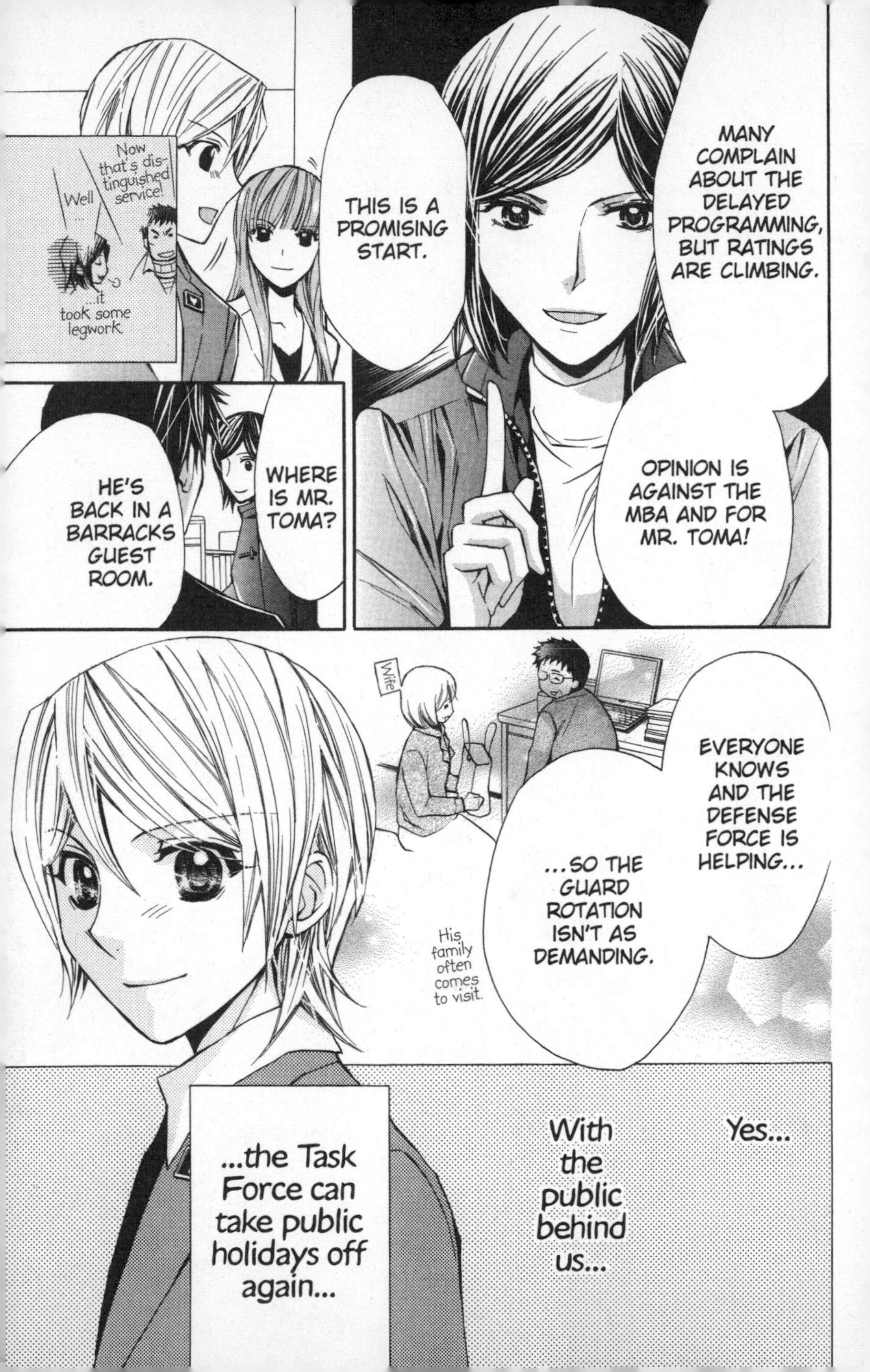
MANY COMPLAIN ABOUT THE DELAYED PROGRAMMING, BUT RATINGS ARE CLIMBING.
OPINION IS AGAINST THE MBA AND FOR MR. TOMA!
THIS IS A PROMISING START.
Now that's distinguished service!
Well...
...it took some legwork.
WHERE IS MR. TOMA?
HE'S BACK IN A BARRACKS GUEST ROOM.
EVERYONE KNOWS AND THE DEFENSE FORCE IS HELPING...
...SO THE GUARD ROTATION ISN'T AS DEMANDING.
Wife
His family often comes to visit.
Yes...
With the public behind us...
...the Task Force can take public holidays off again...

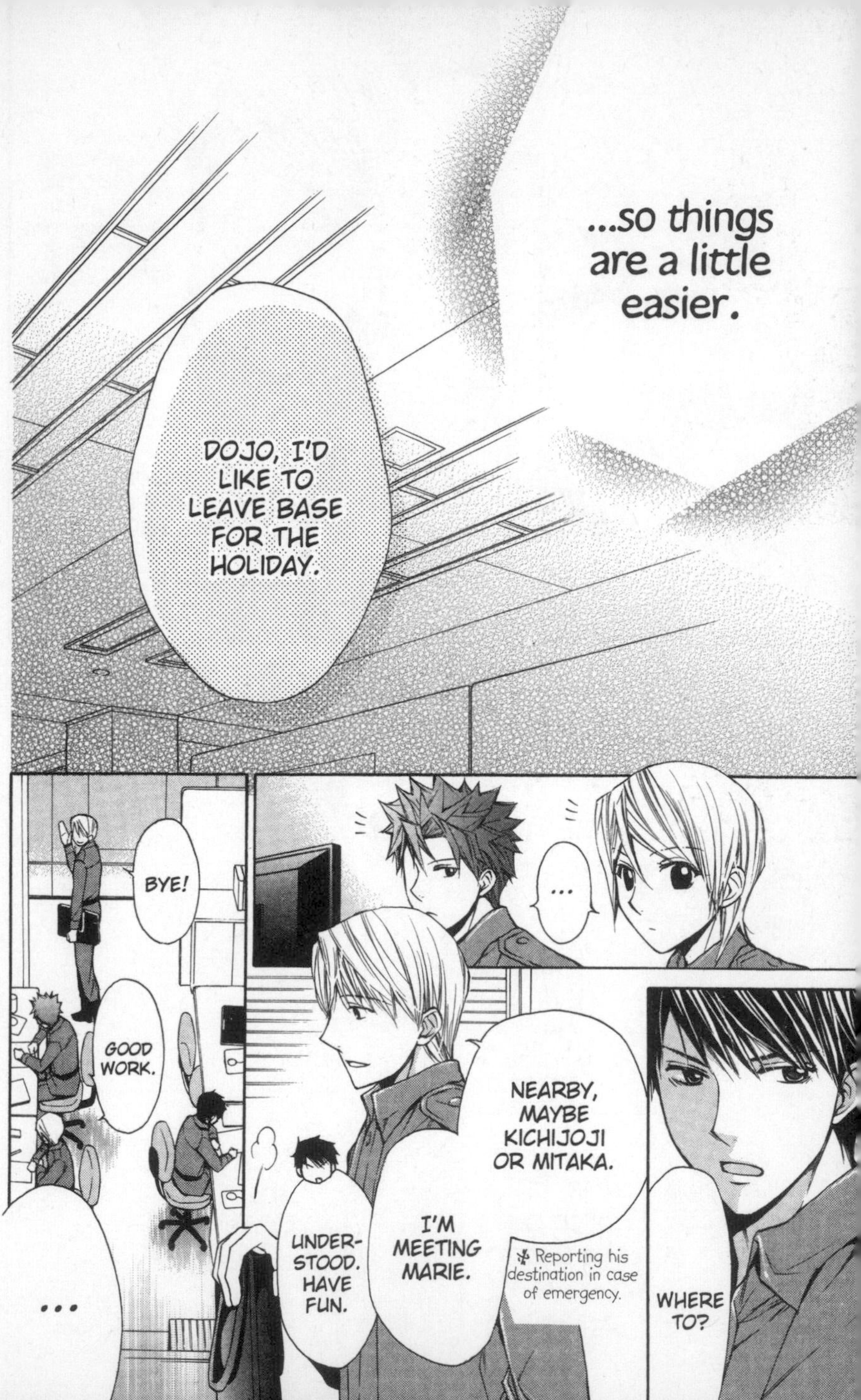
...so things are a little easier.
DOJO, I'D LIKE TO LEAVE BASE FOR THE HOLIDAY.
...
WHERE TO?
I'M MEETING MARIE.
NEARBY, MAYBE KICHIJOJI OR MITAKA.
* Reporting his destination in case of emergency.
UNDER-STOOD. HAVE FUN.
BYE!
GOOD WORK.
...

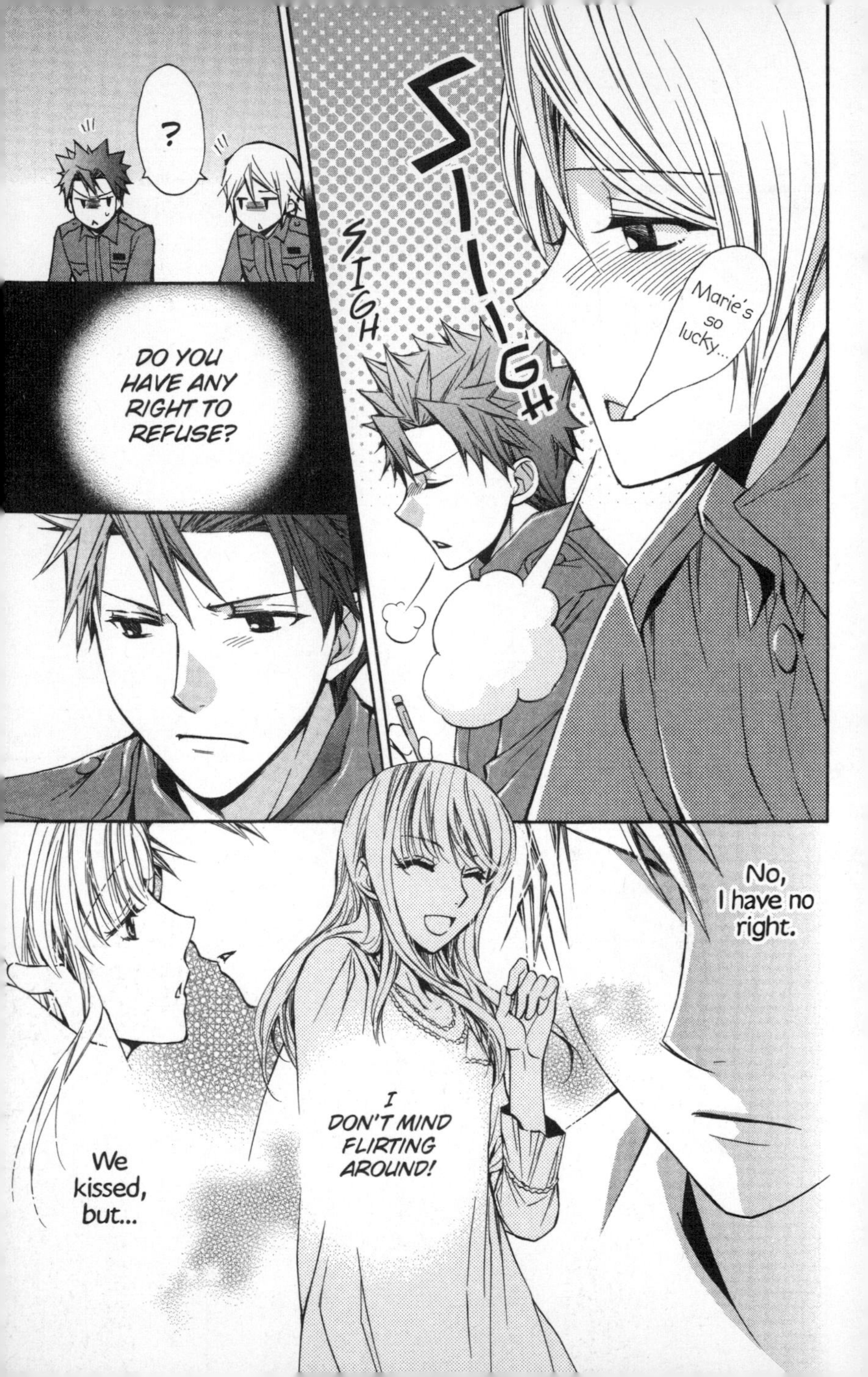
S—I—GH
SIGH
Marie's so lucky...
?
DO YOU HAVE ANY RIGHT TO REFUSE?
No, I have no right.
I DON'T MIND FLIRTING AROUND!
We kissed, but...

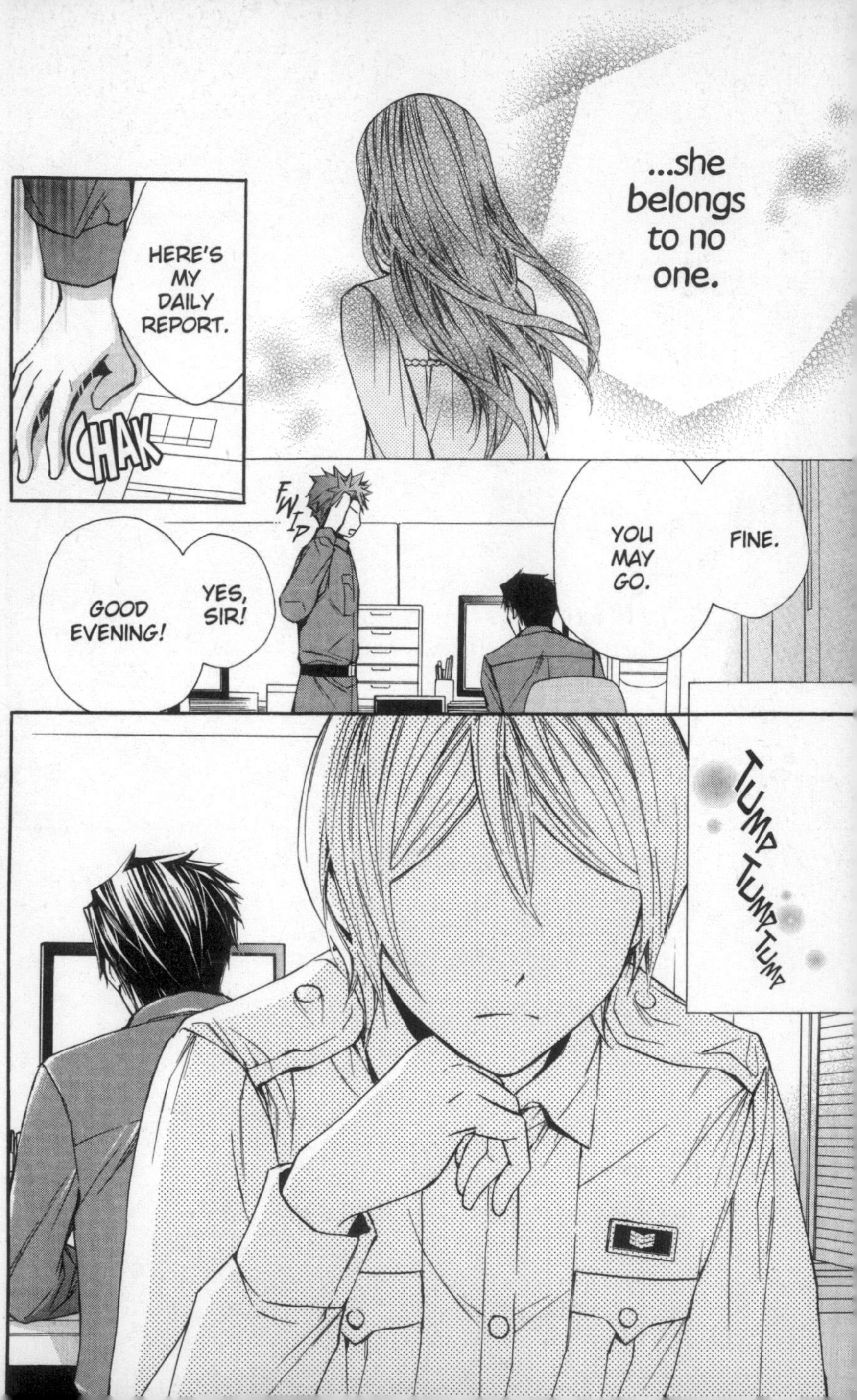
...she belongs to no one.
HERE'S MY DAILY REPORT.
CHAK
FINE. YOU MAY GO.
FWIP
YES, SIR! GOOD EVENING!
TUMP TUMP TUMP TUMP

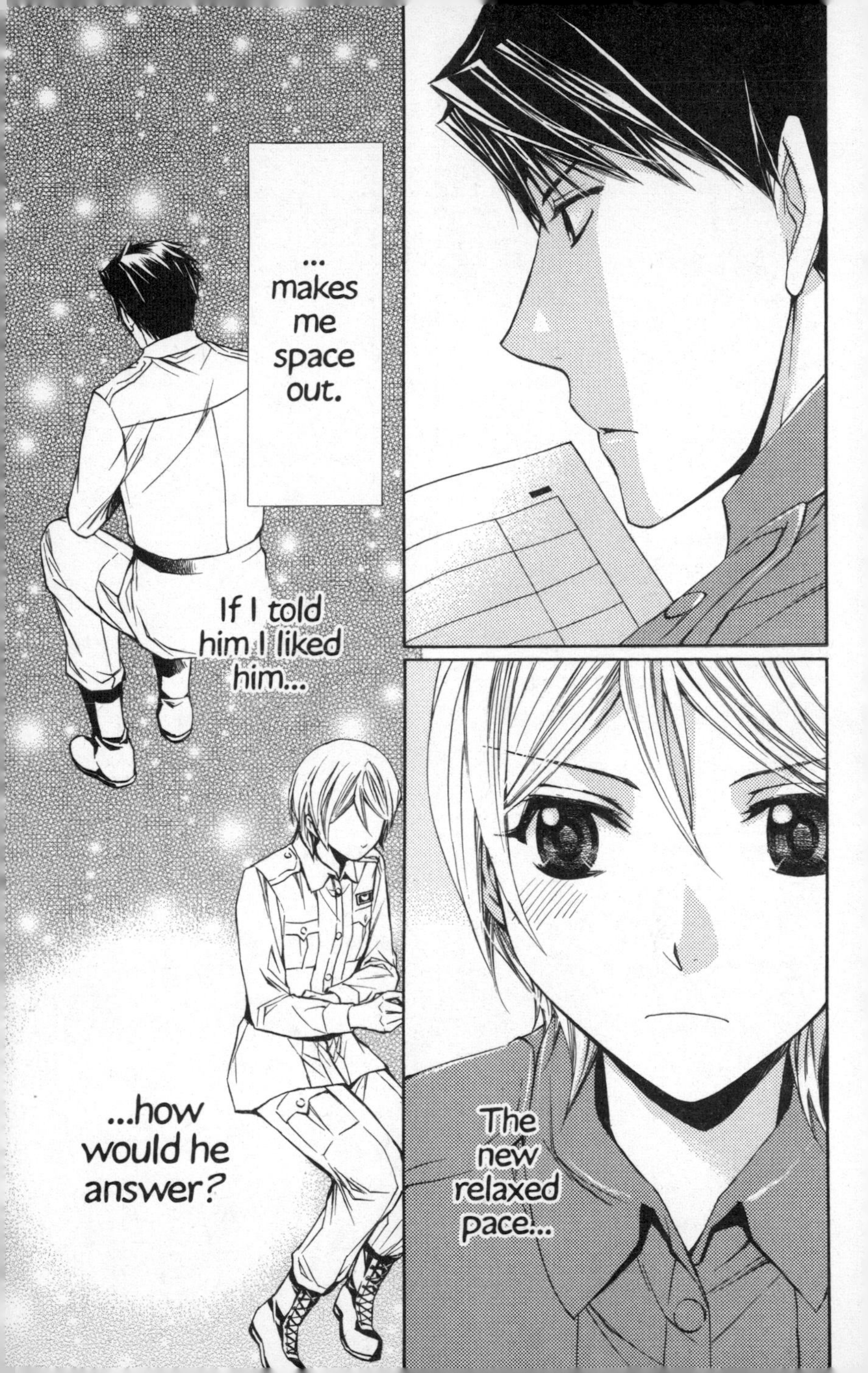
The new relaxed pace...
... makes me space out.
If I told him I liked him...
...how would he answer?

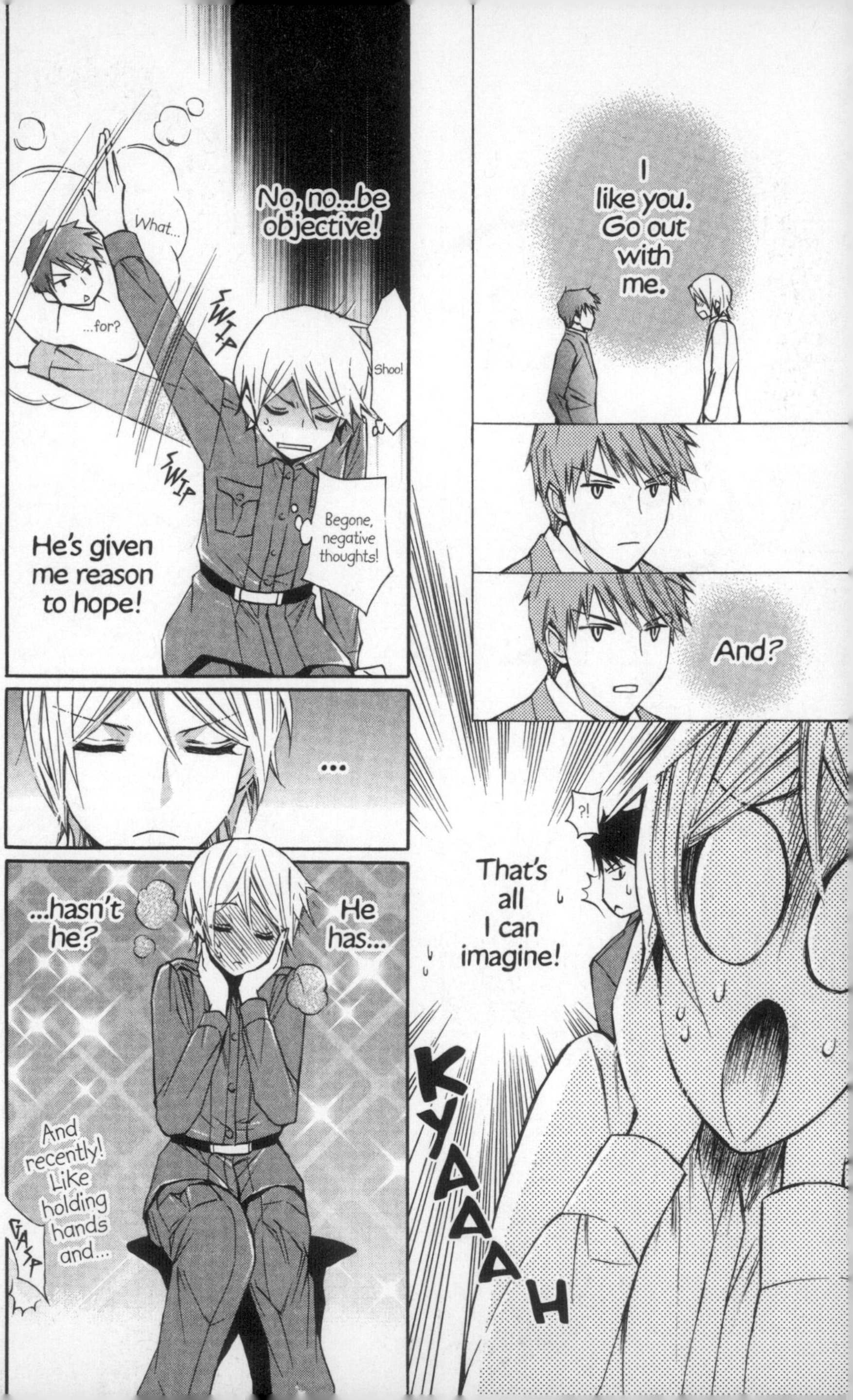
I like you. Go out with me.
And?
?!
That's all I can imagine!
KYAAAH
No, no...be objective!
What...
...for?
SWIP
Shoo!
SWIP
Begone, negative thoughts!
He's given me reason to hope!
...
He has...
...hasn't he?
And recently! Like holding hands and...
GASP

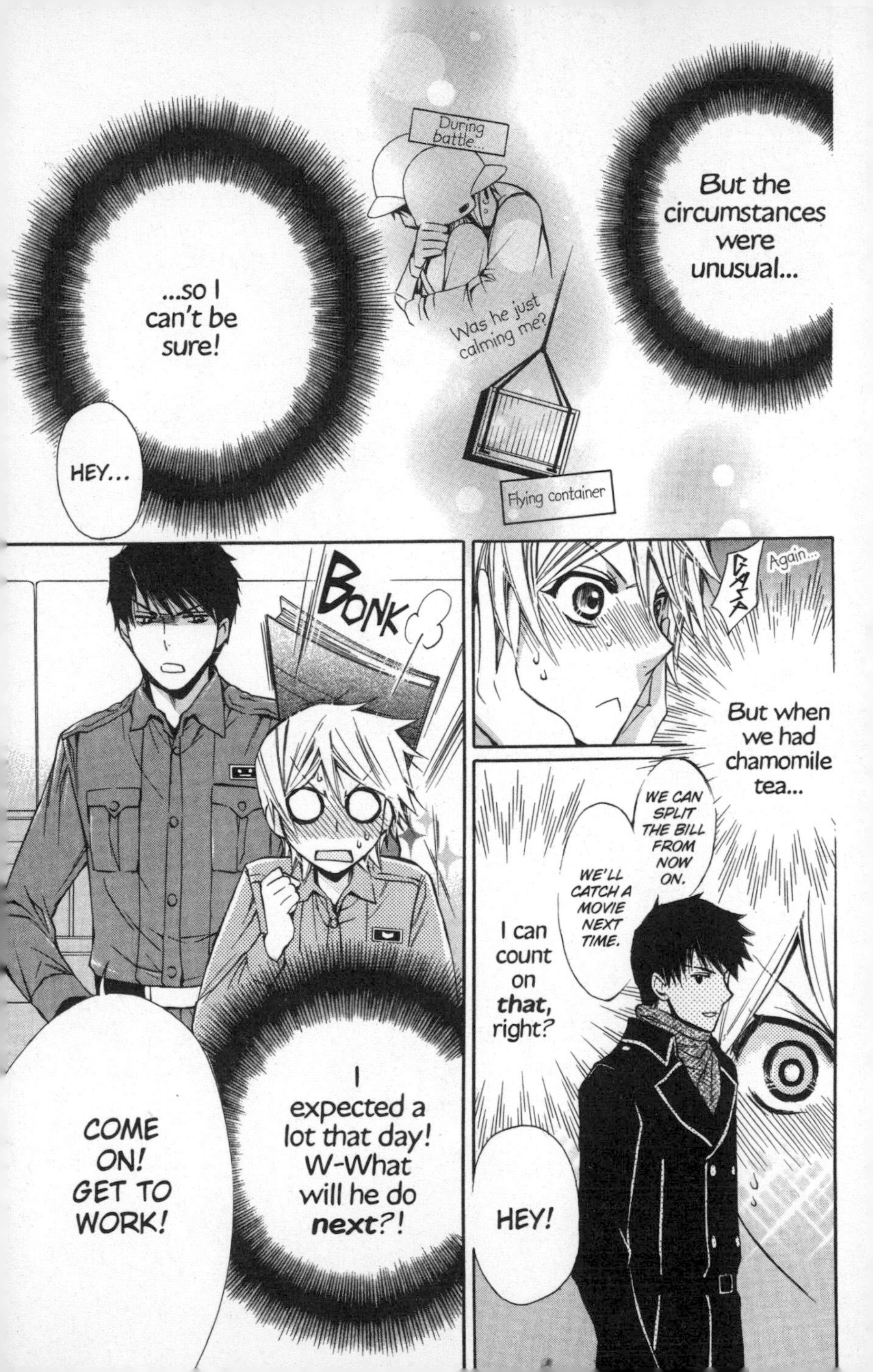
But the circumstances were unusual...
During battle...
Was he just calming me?
Flying container
...so I can't be sure!
HEY...
Again...
But when we had chamomile tea...
WE CAN SPLIT THE BILL FROM NOW ON.
WE'LL CATCH A MOVIE NEXT TIME.
I can count on **that**, right?
HEY!
BONK
I expected a lot that day! W-What will he do **next**?!
COME ON! GET TO WORK!

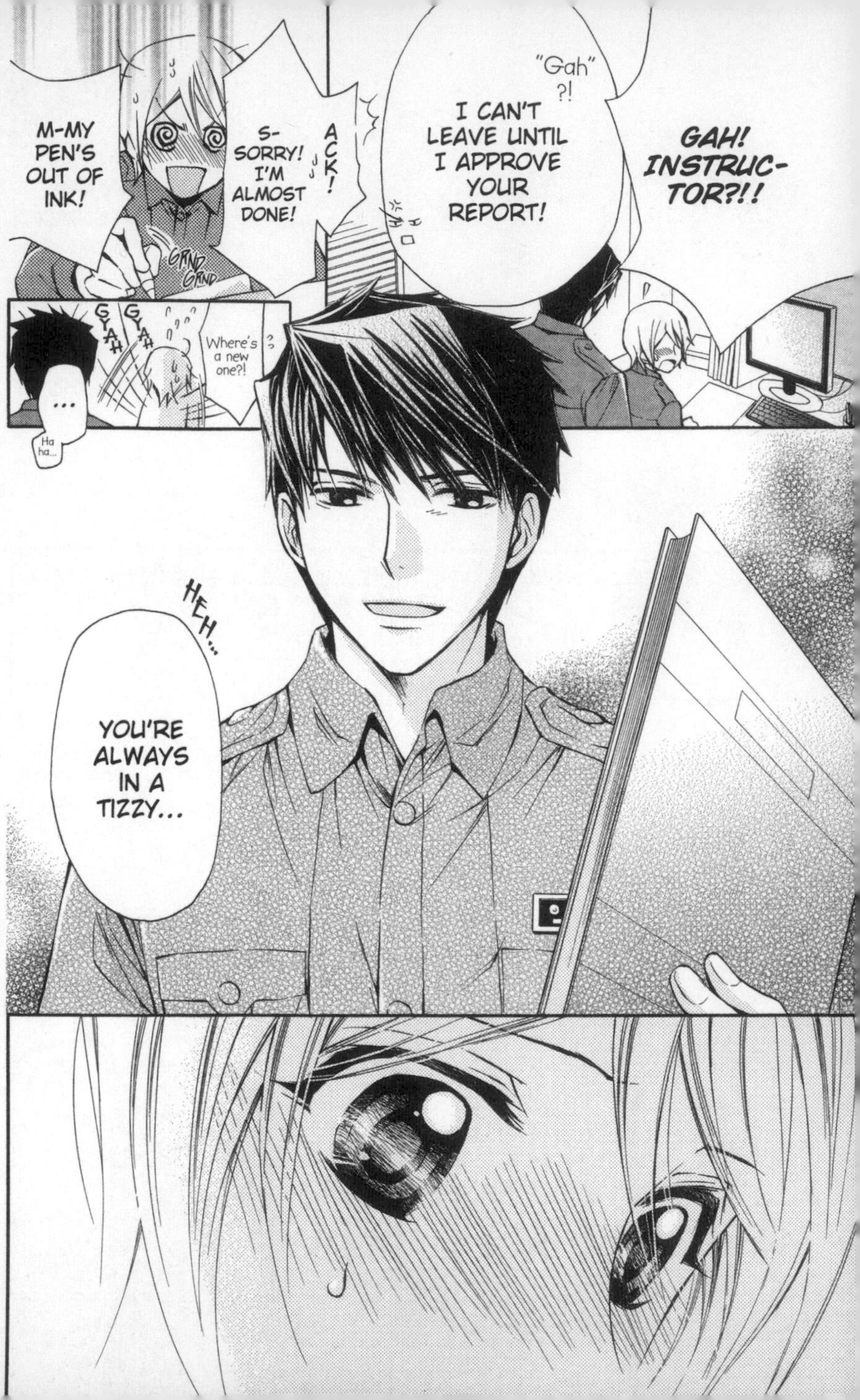
GAH! INSTRUCTOR?!!
"Gah" ?!
I CAN'T LEAVE UNTIL I APPROVE YOUR REPORT!
ACK!
S-SORRY! I'M ALMOST DONE!
M-MY PEN'S OUT OF INK!
GRND GRND
Where's a new one?!
GYAH GYAH
...
Ha ha...
HEH...
YOU'RE ALWAYS IN A TIZZY...

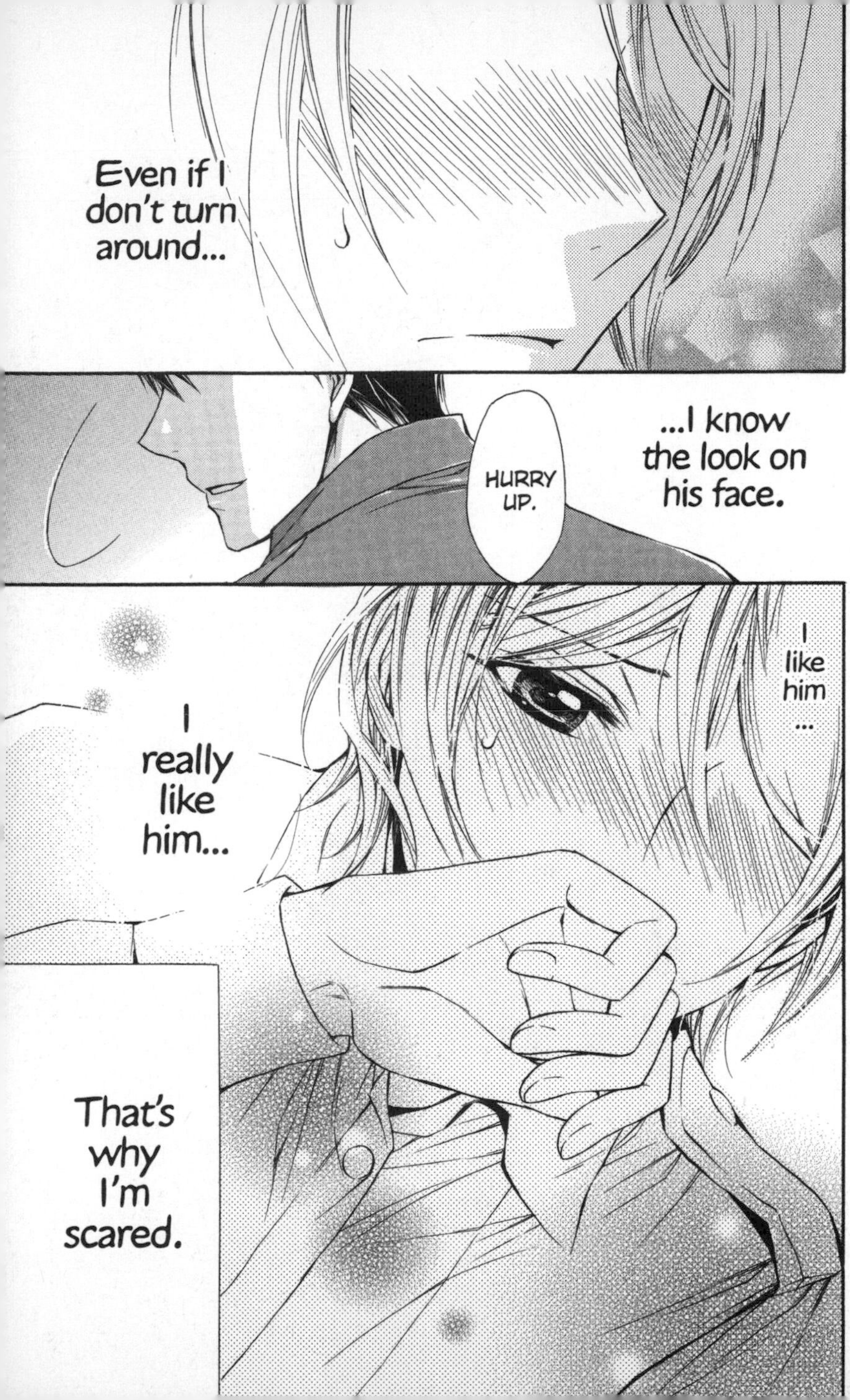
Even if I don't turn around...
...I know the look on his face.
HURRY UP.
I like him...
I really like him...
That's why I'm scared.

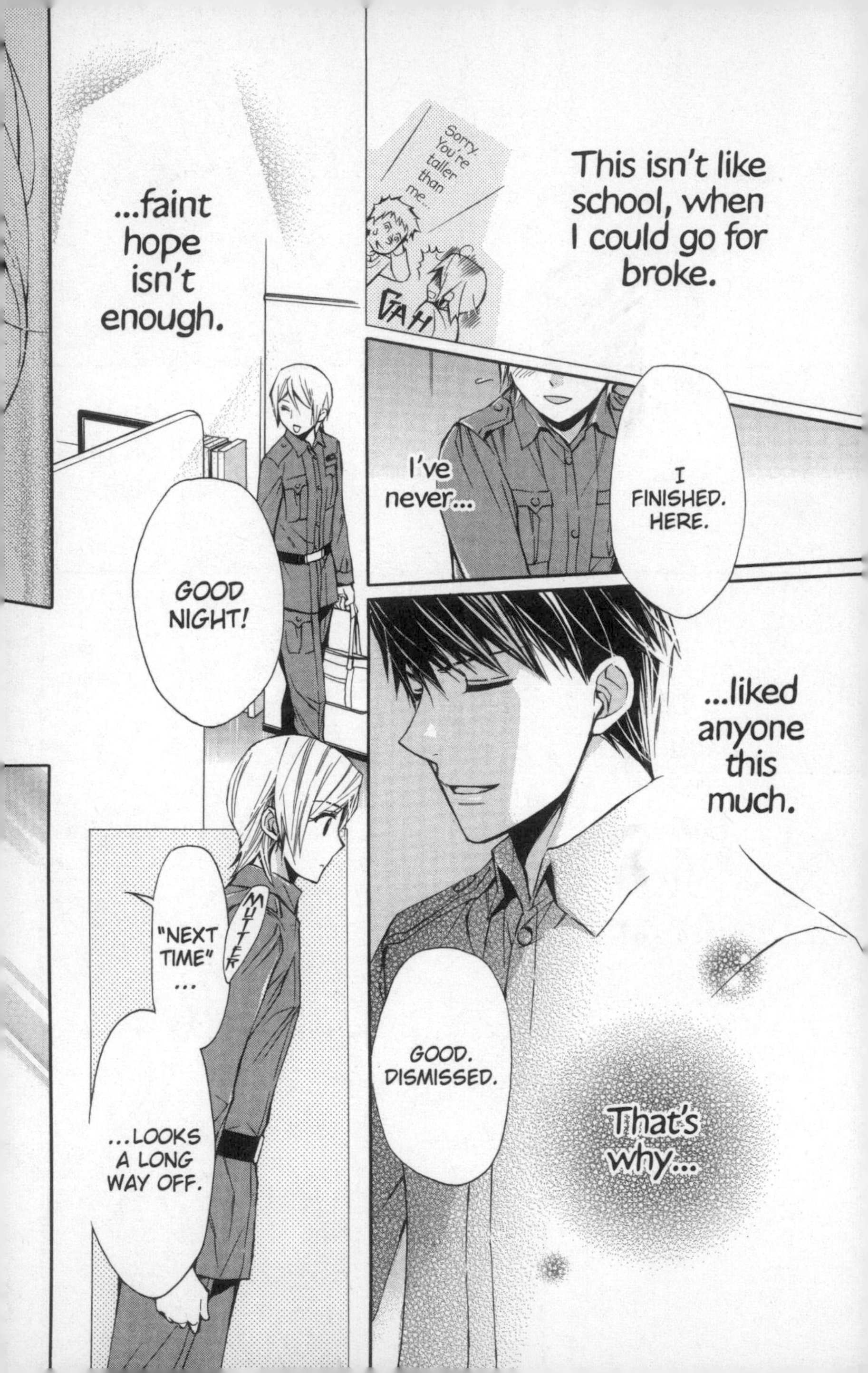
This isn't like school, when I could go for broke.
Sorry. You're taller than me..
GAH
I FINISHED. HERE.
I've never...
...liked anyone this much.
GOOD. DISMISSED.
That's why...
...faint hope isn't enough.
GOOD NIGHT!
MUTTER
"NEXT TIME"...
...LOOKS A LONG WAY OFF.

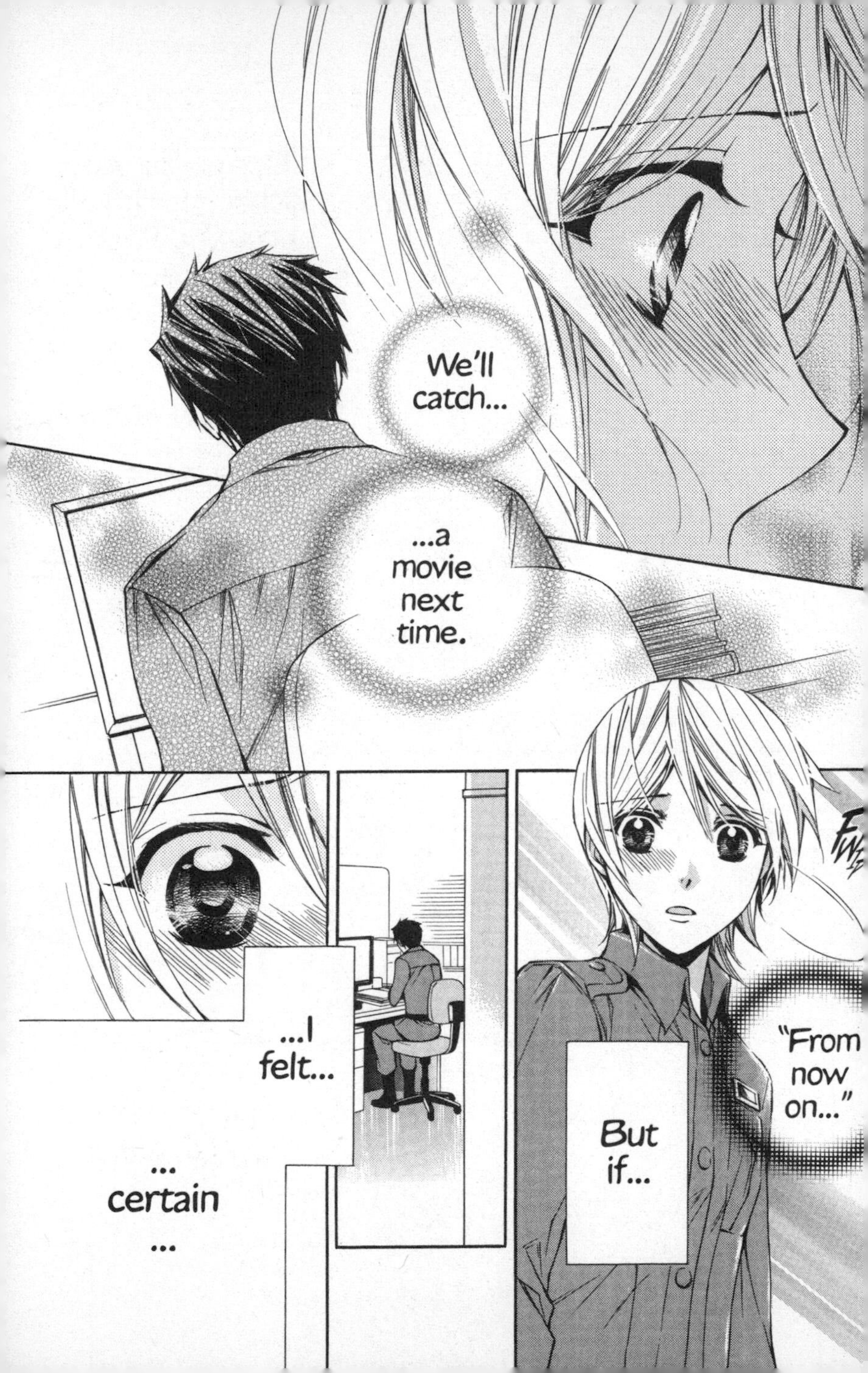
We'll catch...
...a movie next time.
"From now on..."
But if...
...I felt...
... certain ...

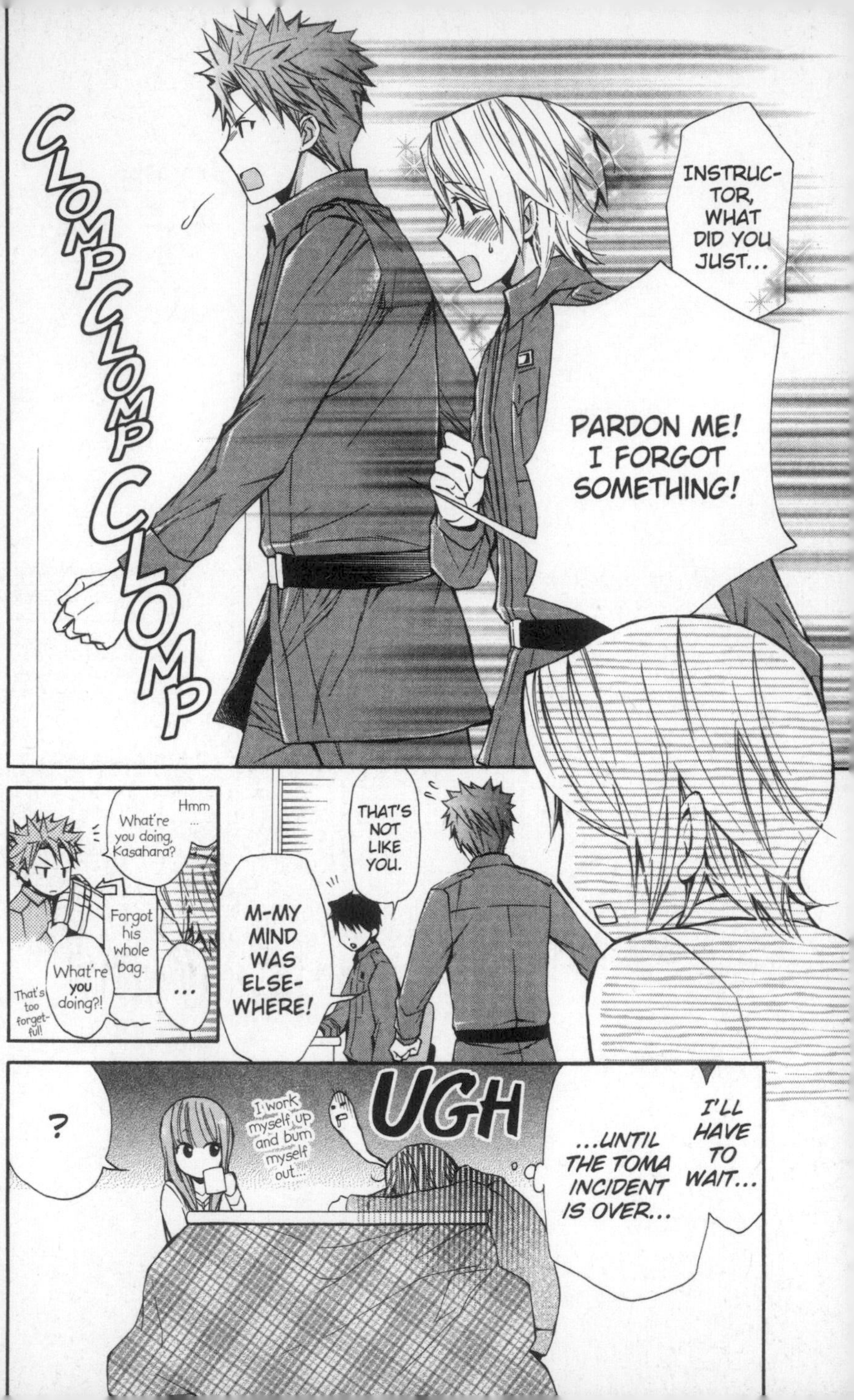
INSTRUCTOR, WHAT DID YOU JUST...
PARDON ME! I FORGOT SOMETHING!
CLOMP CLOMP CLOMP CLOMP
THAT'S NOT LIKE YOU.
M-MY MIND WAS ELSEWHERE!
Hmm ...
What're you doing, Kasahara?
Forgot his whole bag.
...
What're you doing?!
That's too forgetful!
I'LL HAVE TO WAIT...
...UNTIL THE TOMA INCIDENT IS OVER...
UGH
I work myself up and burn myself out...
?

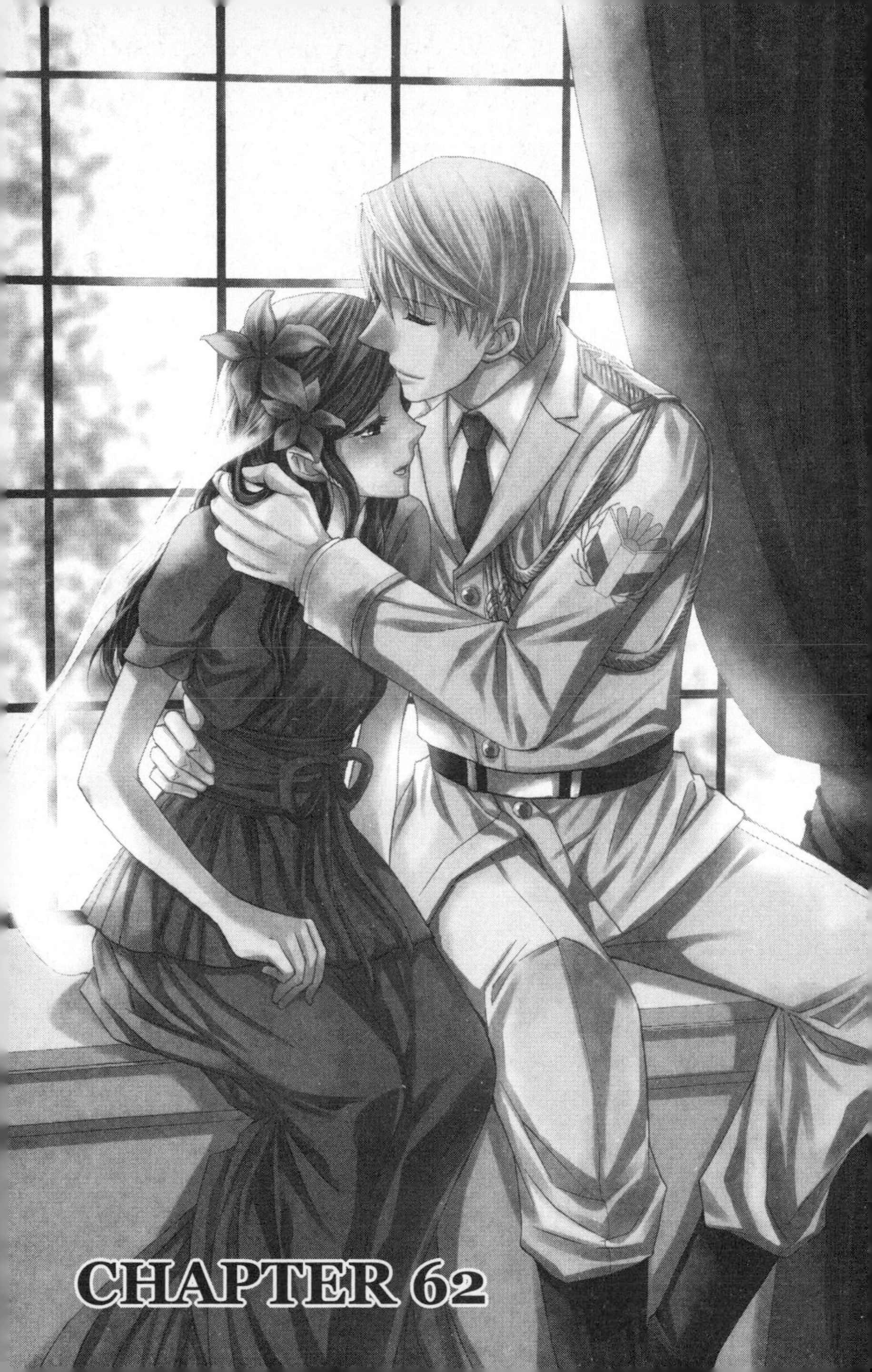
CHAPTER 62

KASAHARA THE PSYCHIC

Even if I don't turn around, I know the look on his face.

※ During break

Dojo now

?!!

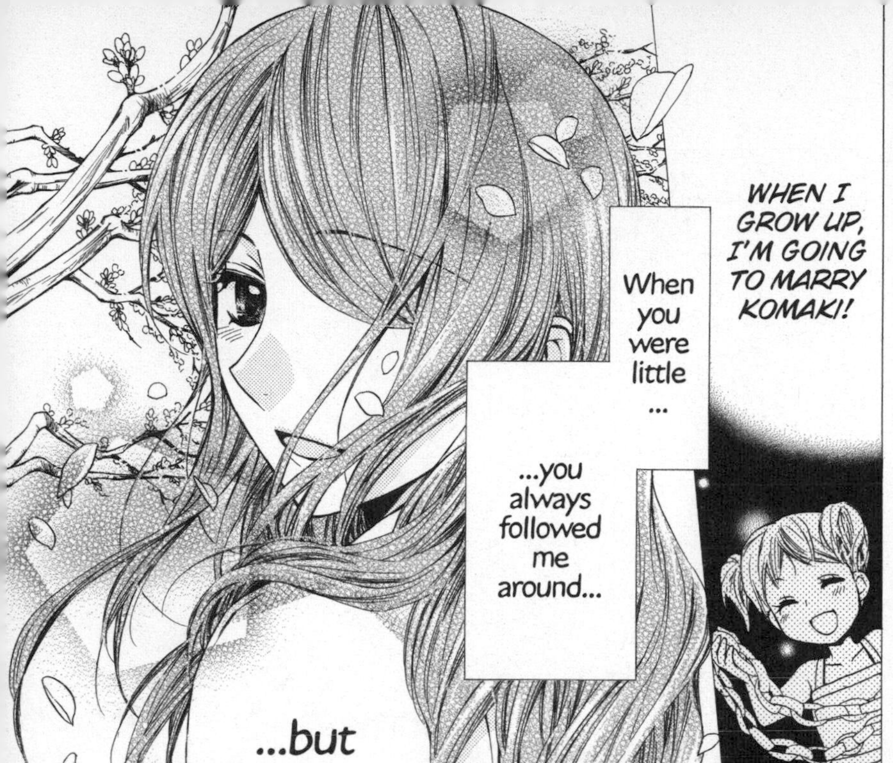
WHEN I GROW UP, I'M GOING TO MARRY KOMAKI!
When you were little ...
...you always followed me around...
...but now...

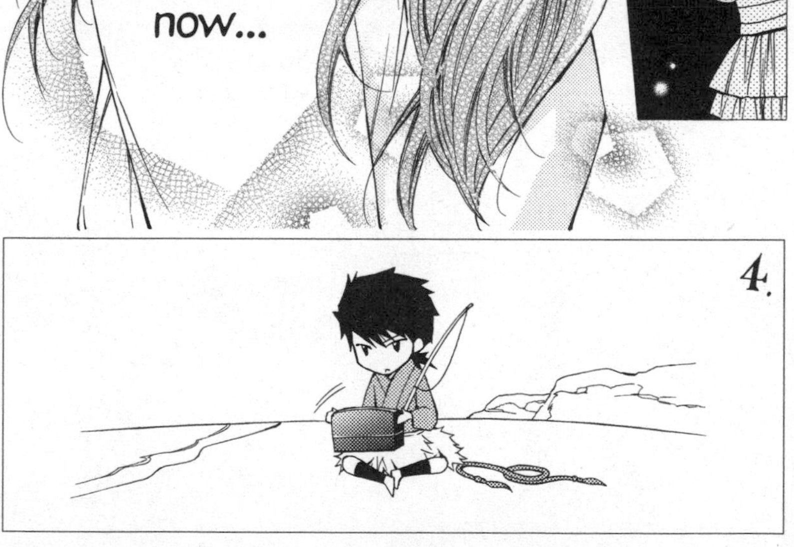
4.

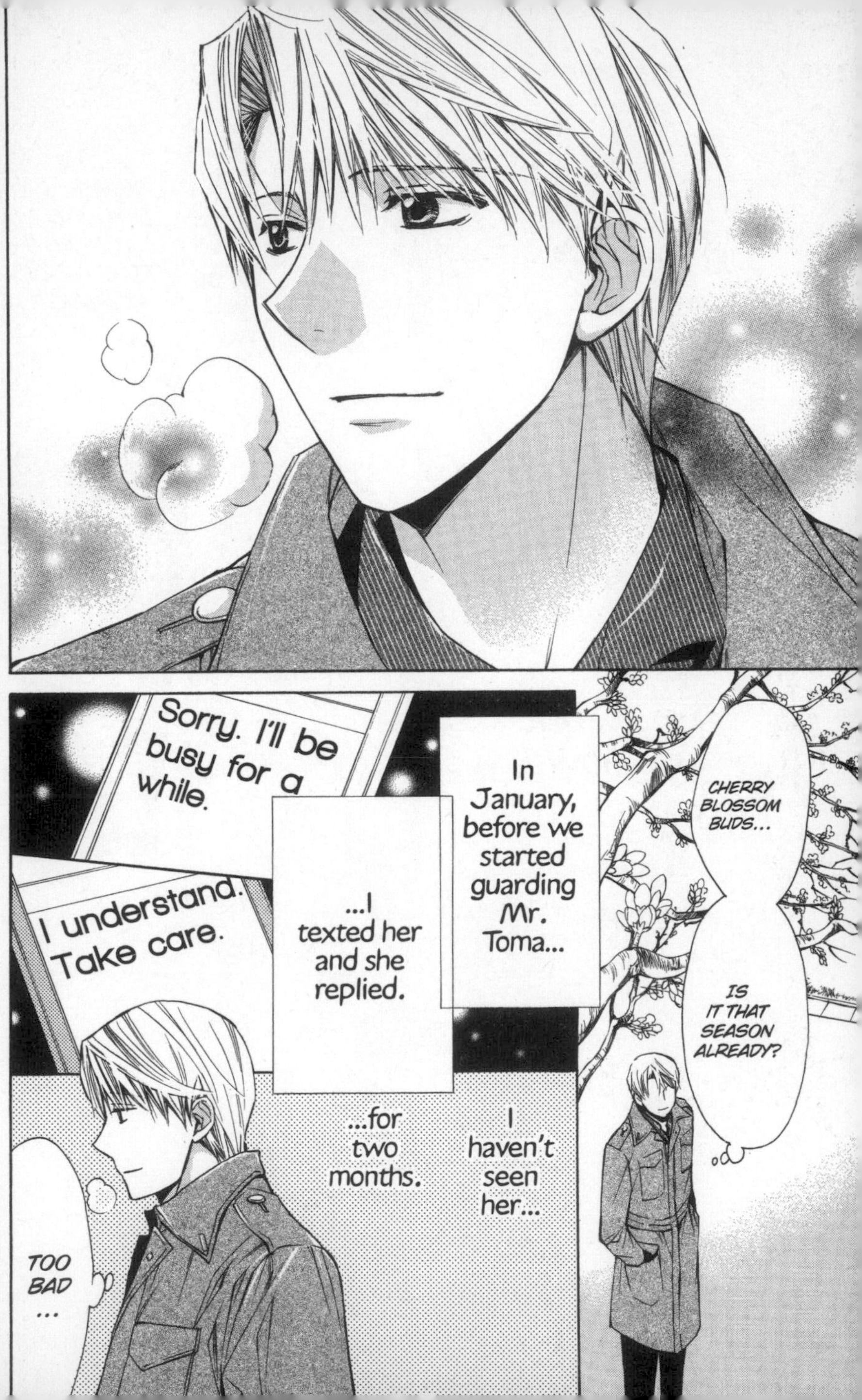
CHERRY BLOSSOM BUDS...
IS IT THAT SEASON ALREADY?
In January, before we started guarding Mr. Toma...
Sorry. I'll be busy for a while.
...I texted her and she replied.
I understand. Take care.
I haven't seen her...
...for two months.
TOO BAD...

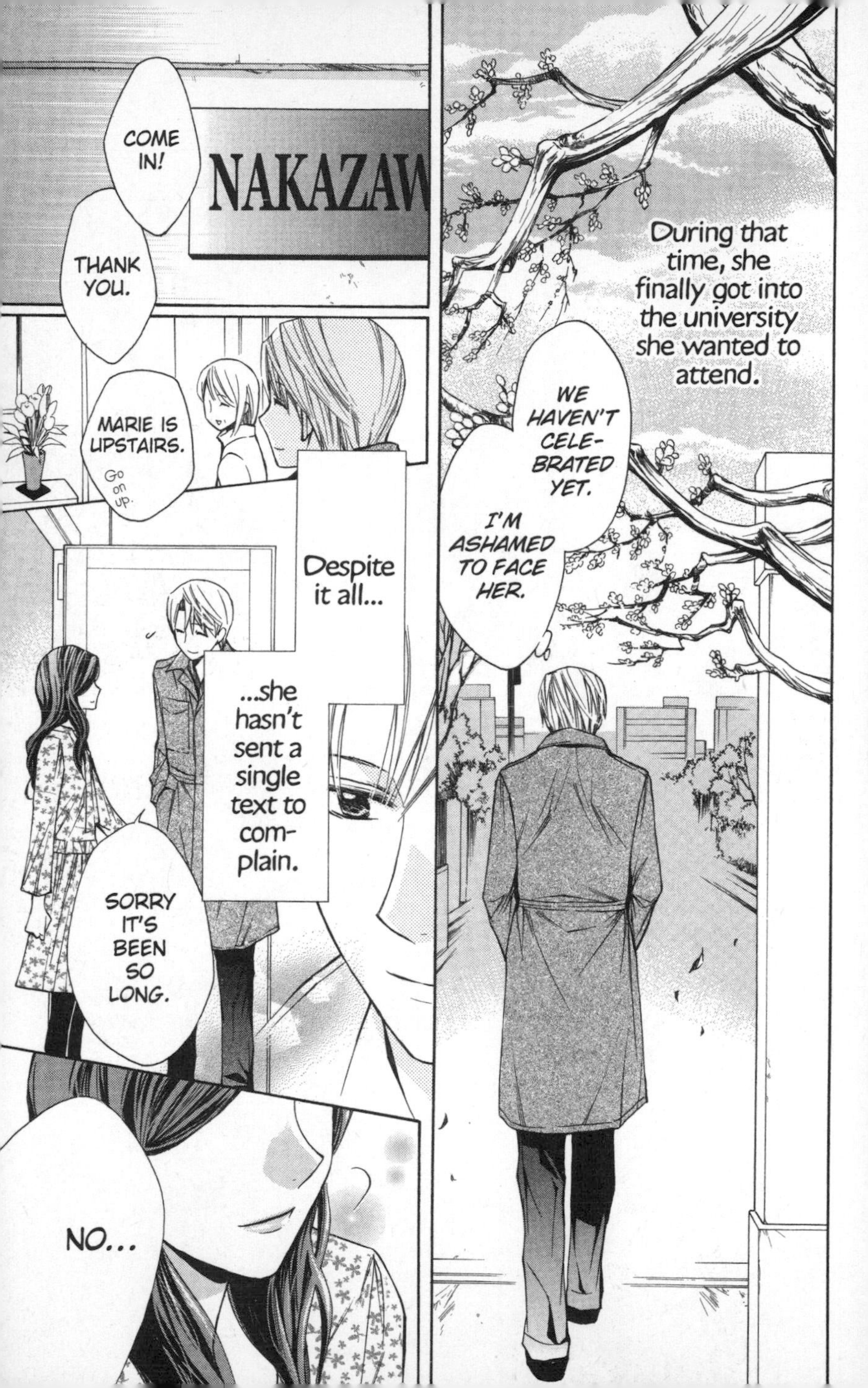
During that time, she finally got into the university she wanted to attend.
WE HAVEN'T CELE-BRATED YET.
I'M ASHAMED TO FACE HER.
NAKAZAW
COME IN!
THANK YOU.
MARIE IS UPSTAIRS.
Go on up.
Despite it all...
...she hasn't sent a single text to com-plain.
SORRY IT'S BEEN SO LONG.
NO...

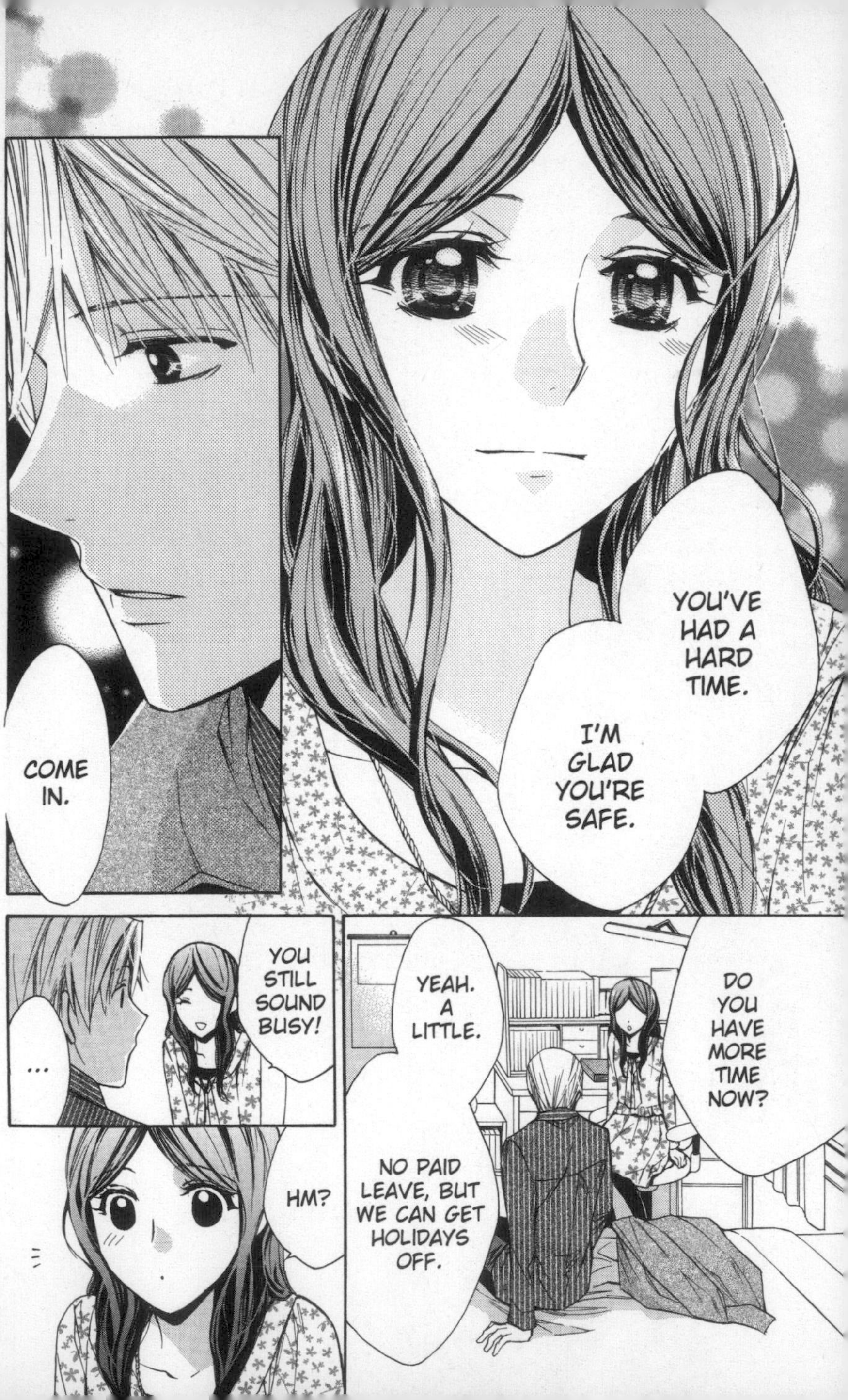
YOU'VE HAD A HARD TIME.
I'M GLAD YOU'RE SAFE.
COME IN.
DO YOU HAVE MORE TIME NOW?
YEAH. A LITTLE.
NO PAID LEAVE, BUT WE CAN GET HOLIDAYS OFF.
YOU STILL SOUND BUSY!
...
HM?

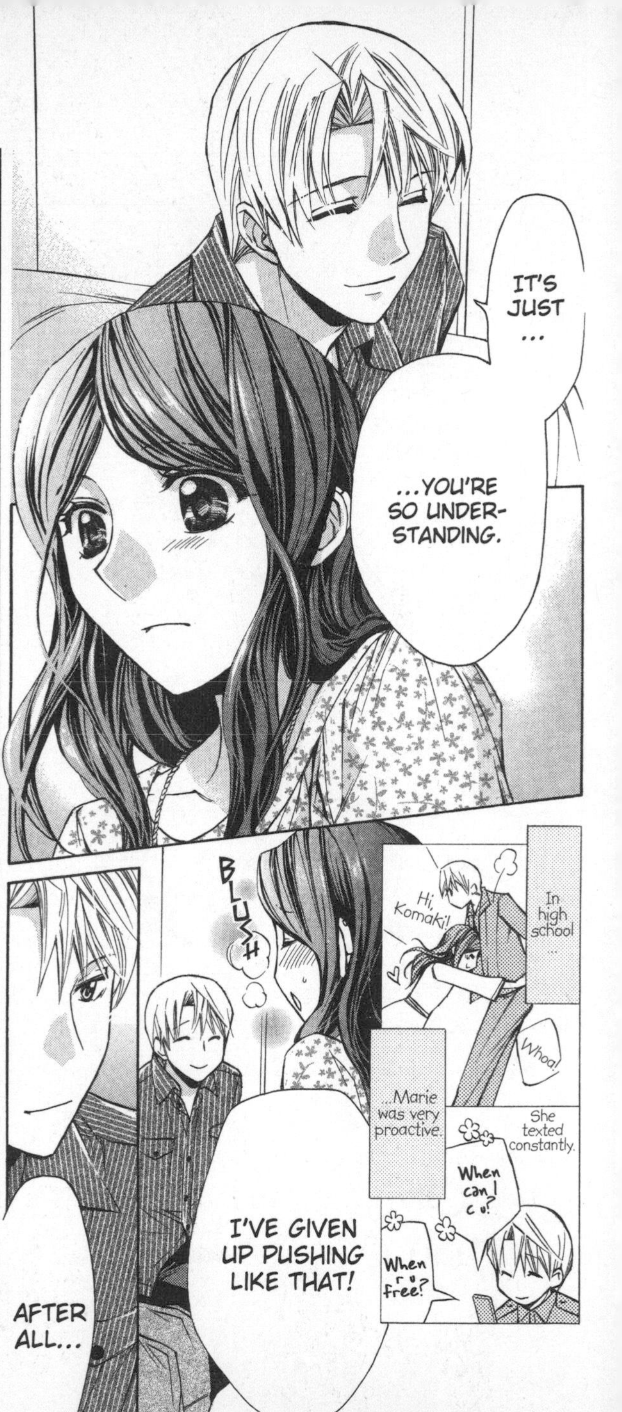
IT'S JUST ...
...YOU'RE SO UNDER-STANDING.
In high school ...
Hi, Komaki!
Whoa!
...Marie was very proactive.
She texted constantly.
When can I c u?
When r u free?
BLUSH
I'VE GIVEN UP PUSHING LIKE THAT!
AFTER ALL...

4

I was the kind of hunter to let my friends handle the key quest while I went someplace safe to gather mushrooms. But at some point... when was it? I built up experience and realized I could take down a G-rank Narga all by myself. I was totally into the *MonHun* world!

The years have flown by since then...

Soon after, I got into *Monster Hunter Frontier Online* and I've played all the games in the series since. My weapons are as follows:

Freedom Unite... Dual Blades

Tri...Hammer, Long Sword

3rd...Long Sword, Axe

3 Ultimate...Axe

MonHun 4 (now)... Axe and the new weapon Insect Glaive

(to be continued)

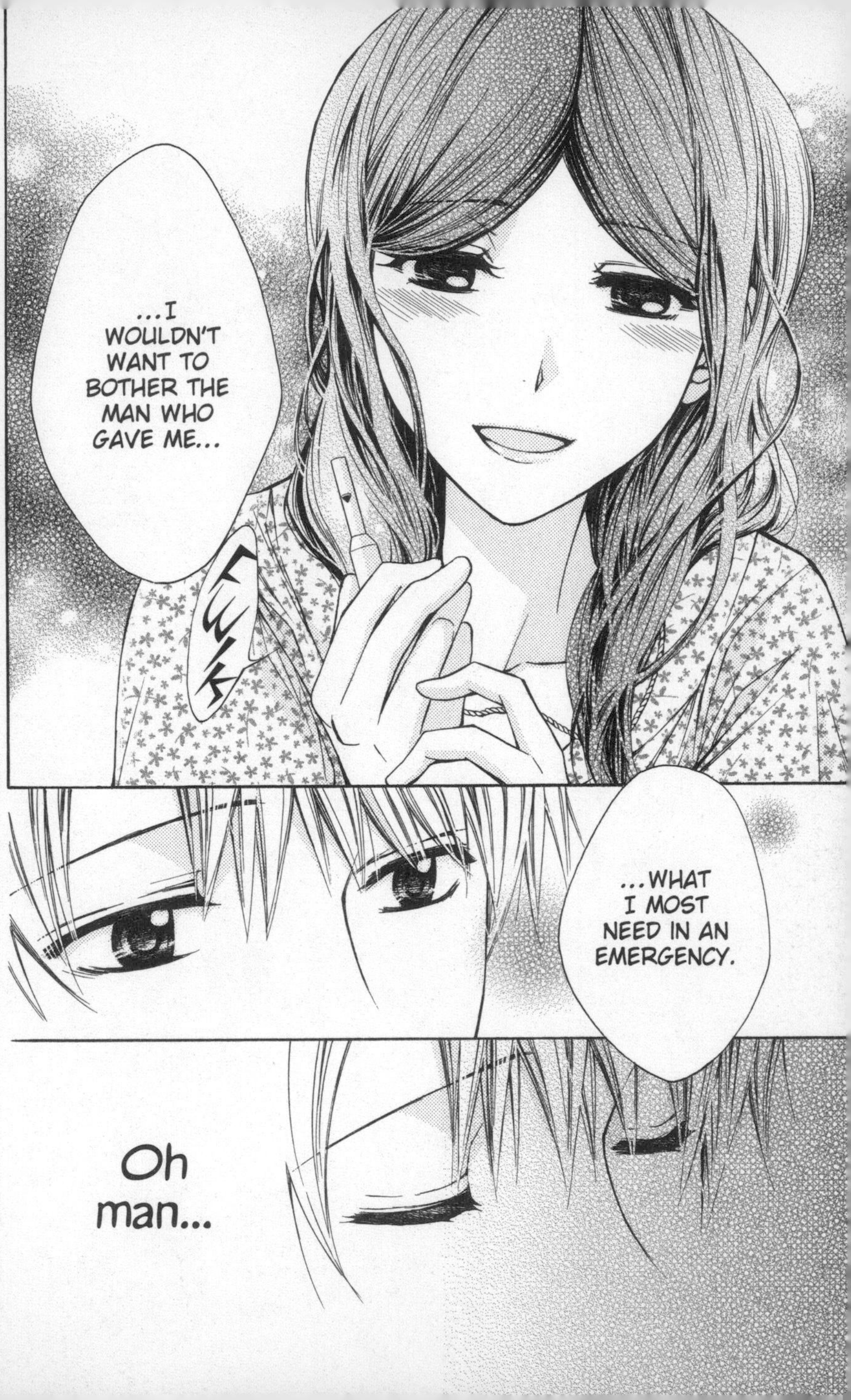
...I WOULDN'T WANT TO BOTHER THE MAN WHO GAVE ME...
FWIK
...WHAT I MOST NEED IN AN EMERGENCY.
Oh man...

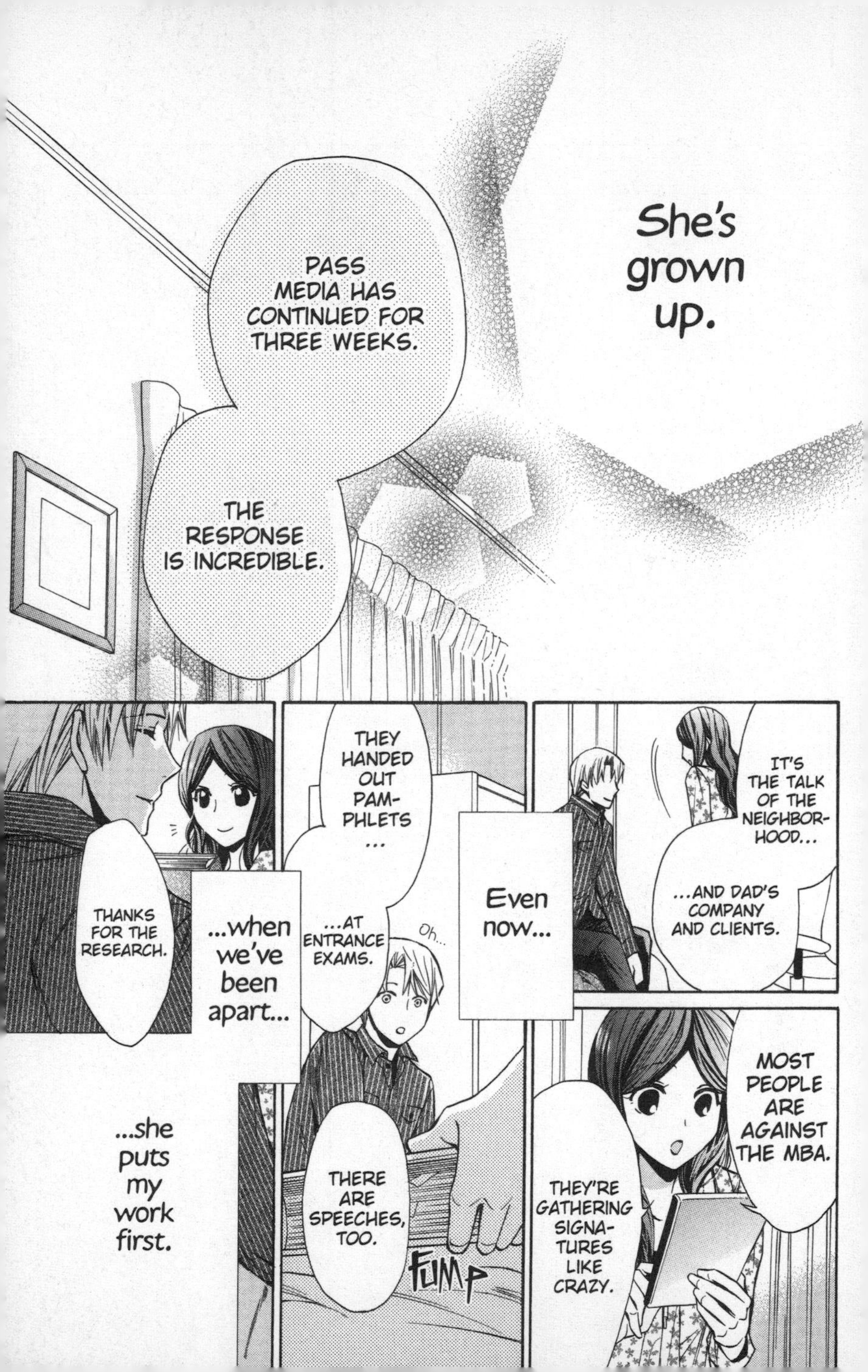
She's grown up.
PASS MEDIA HAS CONTINUED FOR THREE WEEKS.
THE RESPONSE IS INCREDIBLE.
IT'S THE TALK OF THE NEIGHBORHOOD...
...AND DAD'S COMPANY AND CLIENTS.
MOST PEOPLE ARE AGAINST THE MBA.
THEY'RE GATHERING SIGNATURES LIKE CRAZY.
Even now...
THEY HANDED OUT PAMPHLETS...
...AT ENTRANCE EXAMS.
THERE ARE SPEECHES, TOO.
FUMP
Oh...
...when we've been apart...
THANKS FOR THE RESEARCH.
...she puts my work first.

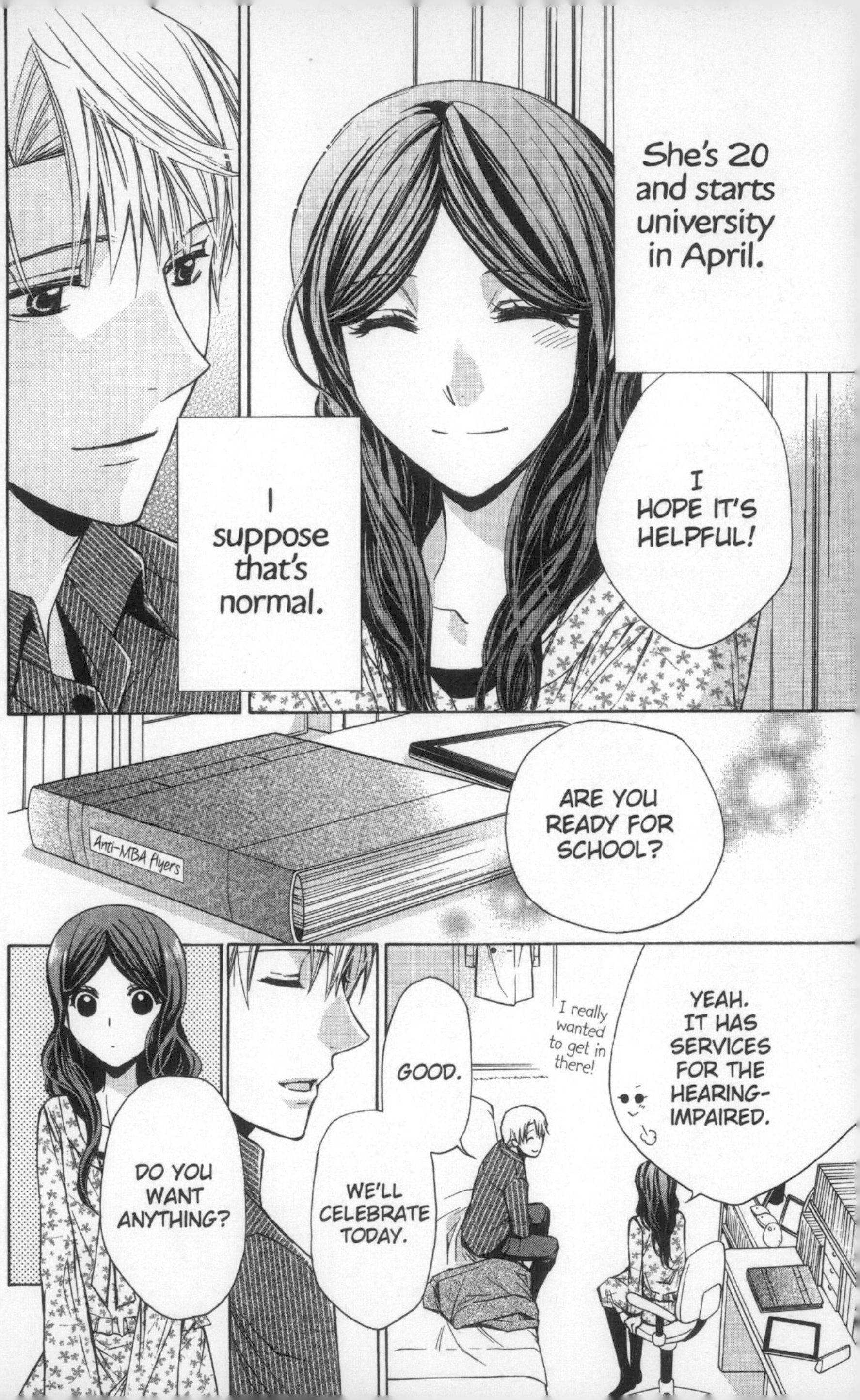
She's 20 and starts university in April.
I HOPE IT'S HELPFUL!
I suppose that's normal.
ARE YOU READY FOR SCHOOL?
Anti-MBA flyers
YEAH. IT HAS SERVICES FOR THE HEARING-IMPAIRED.
I really wanted to get in there!
GOOD.
WE'LL CELEBRATE TODAY.
DO YOU WANT ANYTHING?

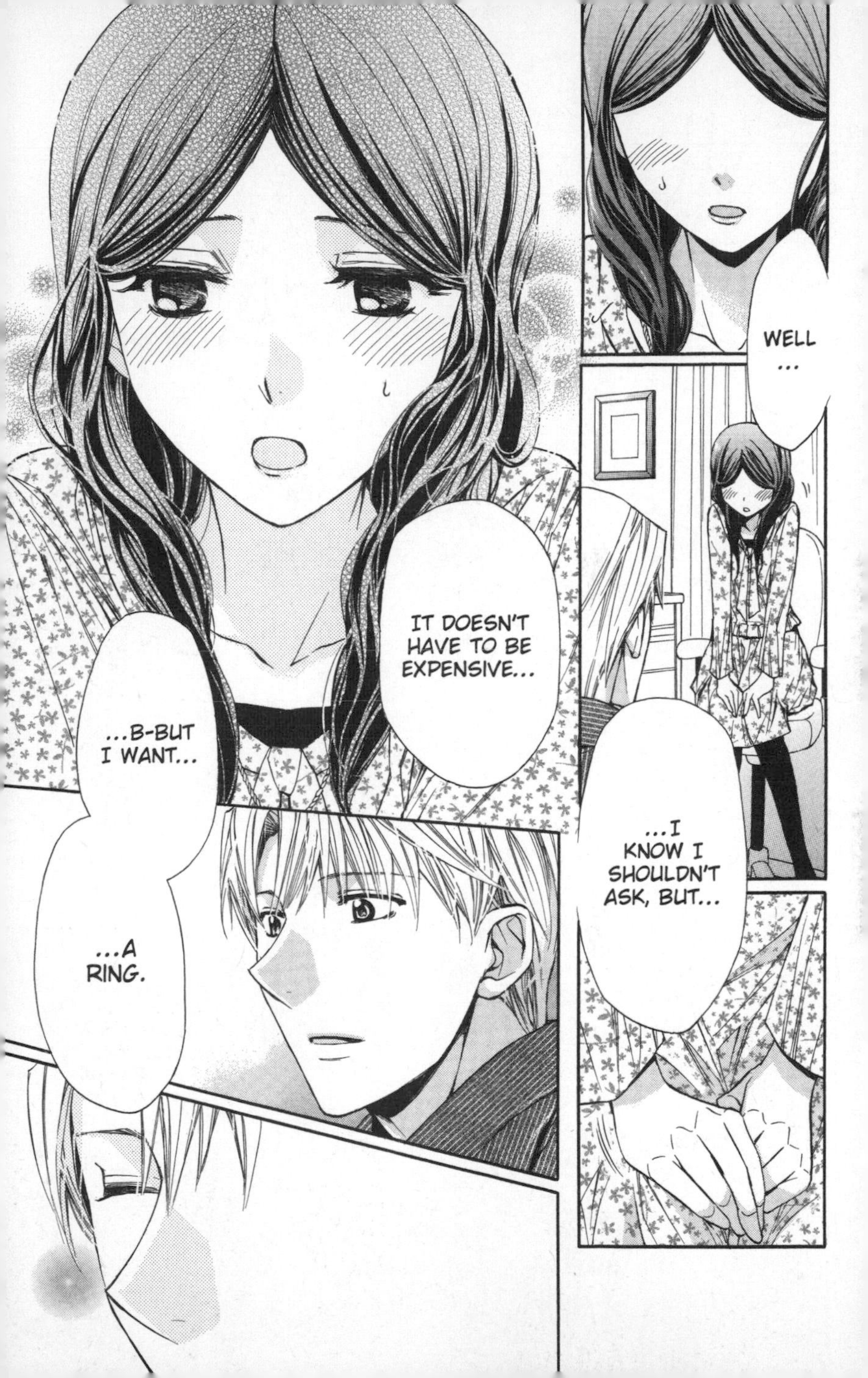
WELL ...
...I KNOW I SHOULDN'T ASK, BUT...
IT DOESN'T HAVE TO BE EXPENSIVE...
...B-BUT I WANT...
...A RING.

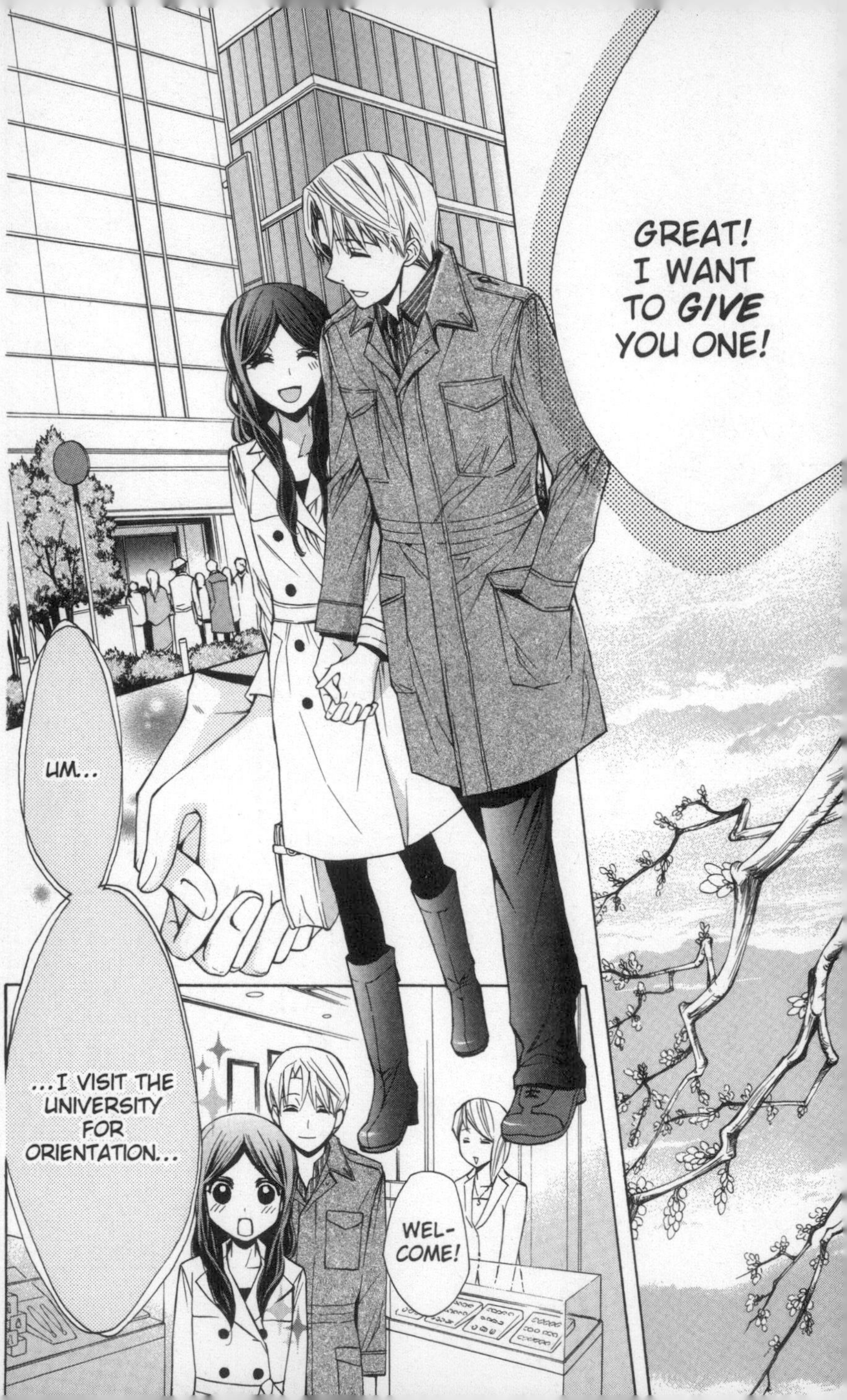
GREAT! I WANT TO GIVE YOU ONE!
UM...
...I VISIT THE UNIVERSITY FOR ORIENTATION...
WEL-COME!

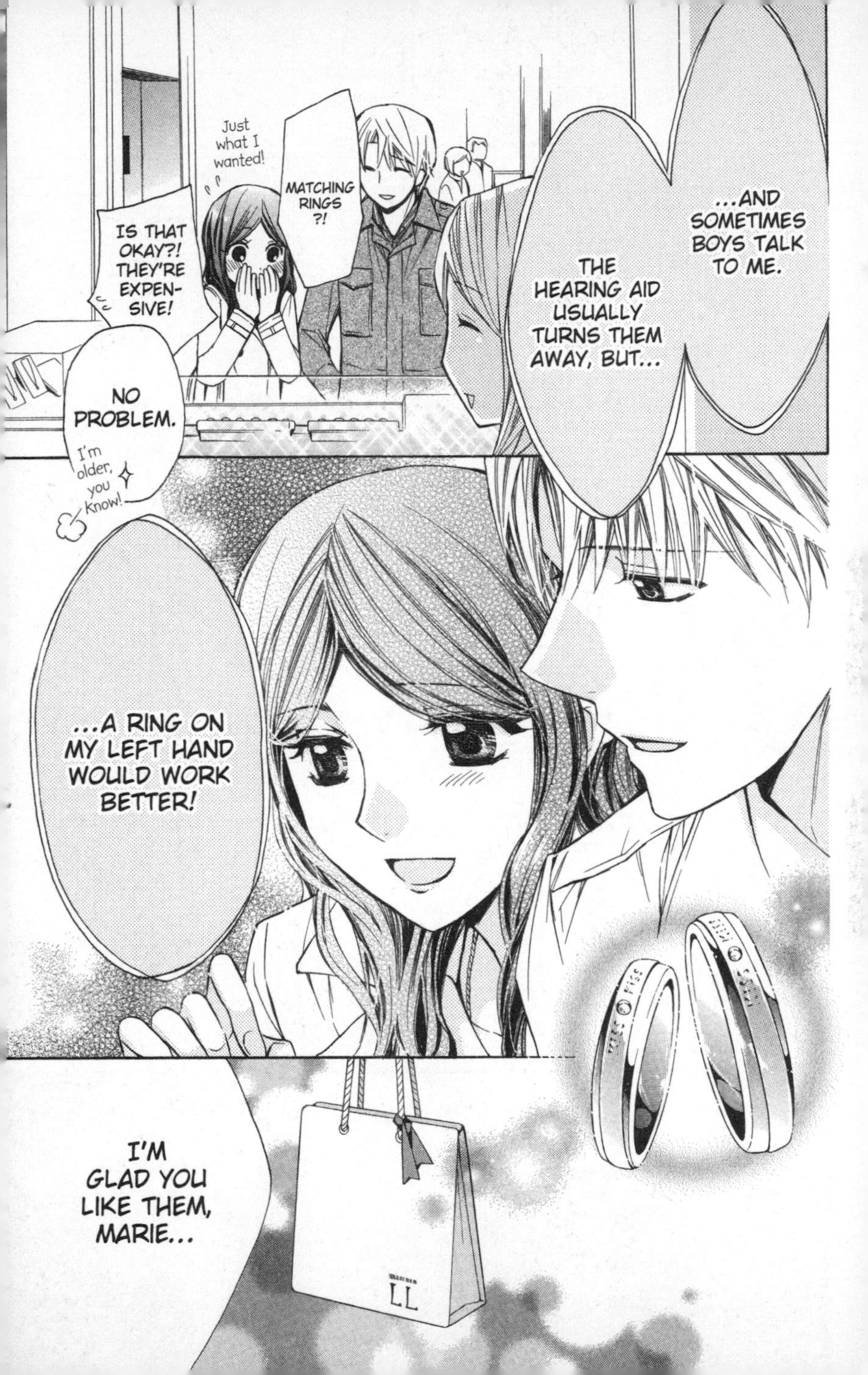
...AND SOMETIMES BOYS TALK TO ME.
THE HEARING AID USUALLY TURNS THEM AWAY, BUT...
MATCHING RINGS ?!
Just what I wanted!
IS THAT OKAY?! THEY'RE EXPEN-SIVE!
NO PROBLEM.
I'm older, you know!
...A RING ON MY LEFT HAND WOULD WORK BETTER!
I'M GLAD YOU LIKE THEM, MARIE...
LL

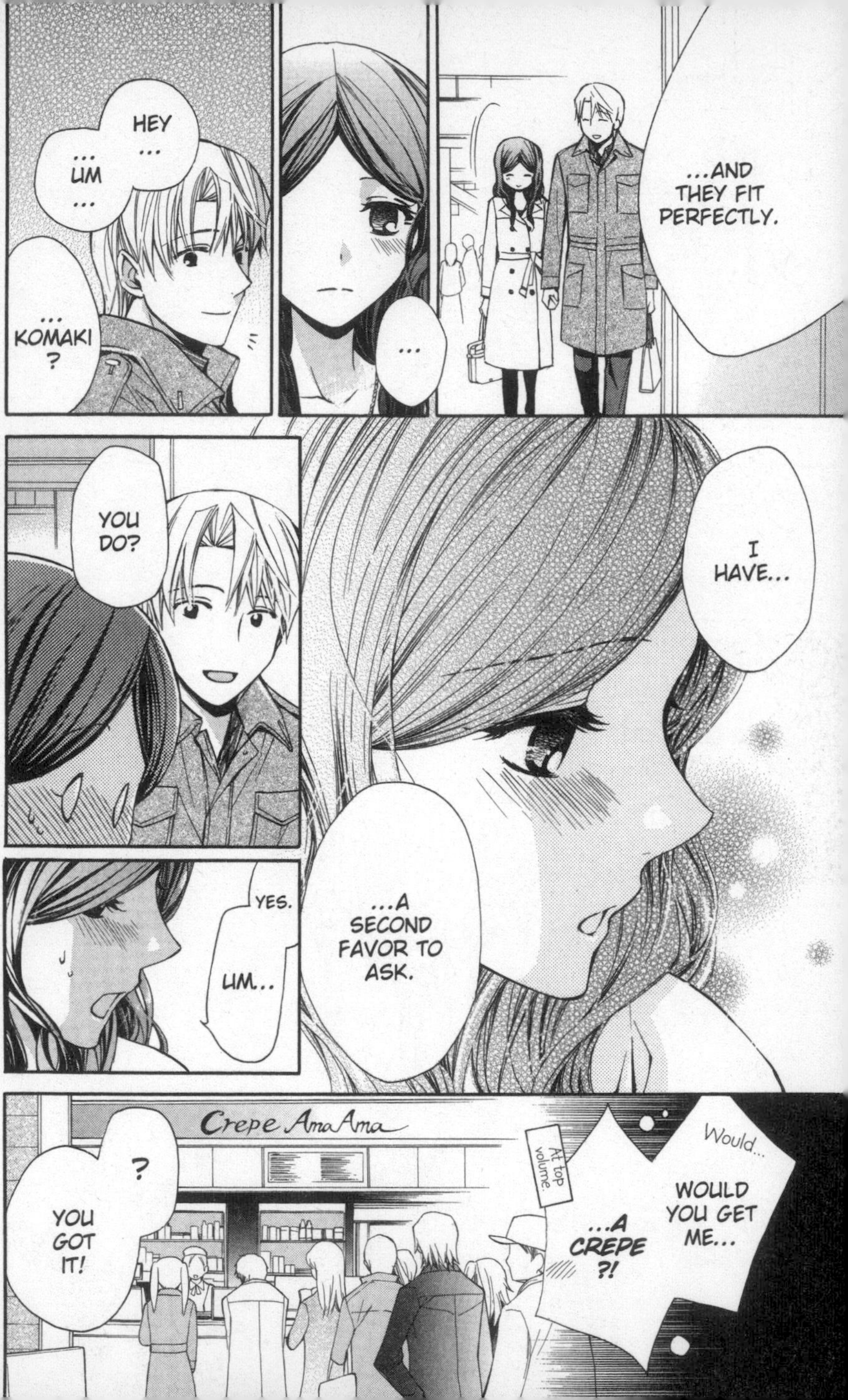
...AND THEY FIT PERFECTLY.
...
HEY ...
... UM ...
... KOMAKI ?
I HAVE...
...A SECOND FAVOR TO ASK.
YOU DO?
YES.
UM...
Would...
WOULD YOU GET ME...
...A CREPE ?!
At top volume.
Crepe AmaAma
?
YOU GOT IT!

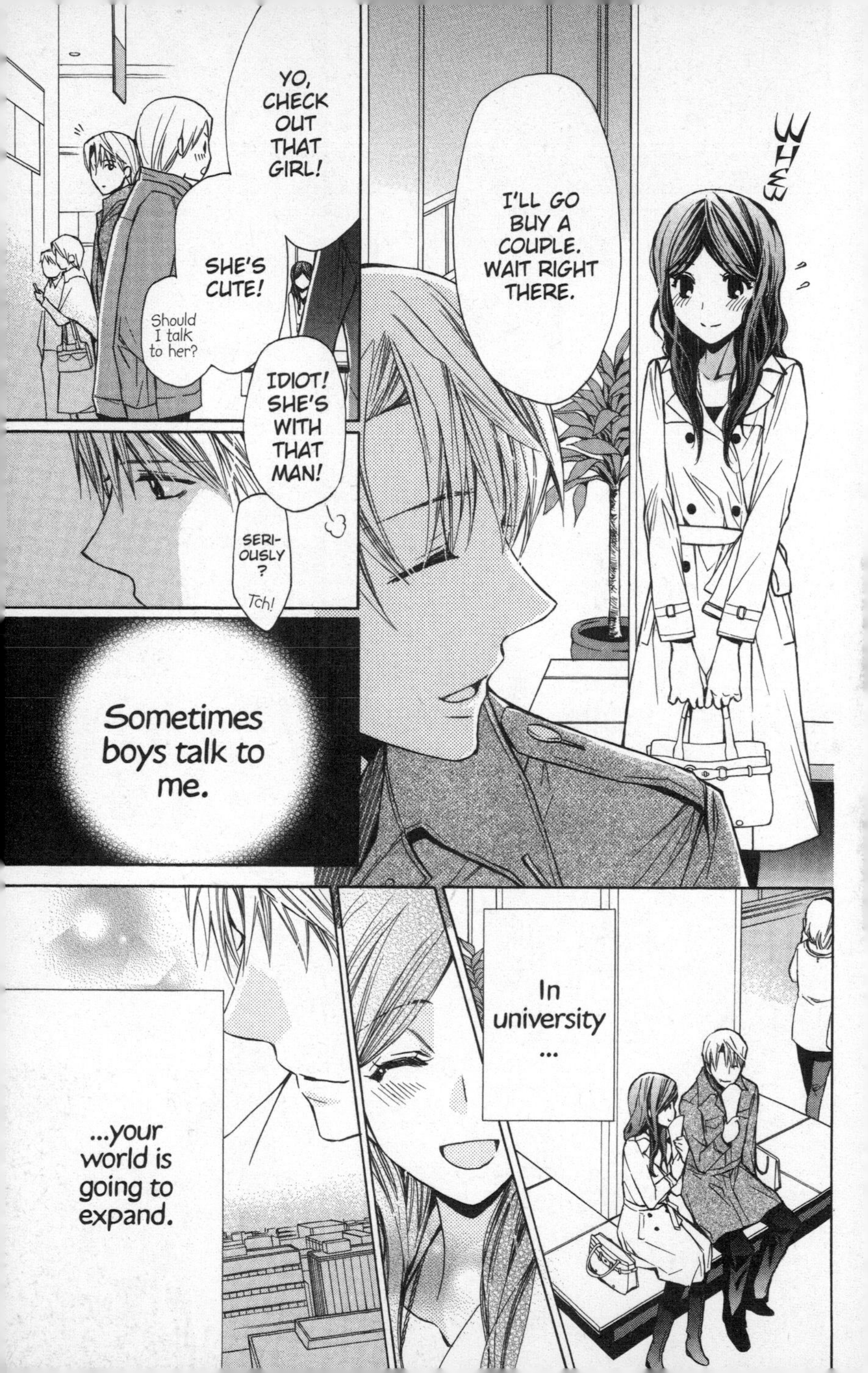
WHEW
I'LL GO BUY A COUPLE. WAIT RIGHT THERE.
YO, CHECK OUT THAT GIRL!
SHE'S CUTE!
Should I talk to her?
IDIOT! SHE'S WITH THAT MAN!
SERIOUSLY?
Tch!
Sometimes boys talk to me.
In university...
...your world is going to expand.

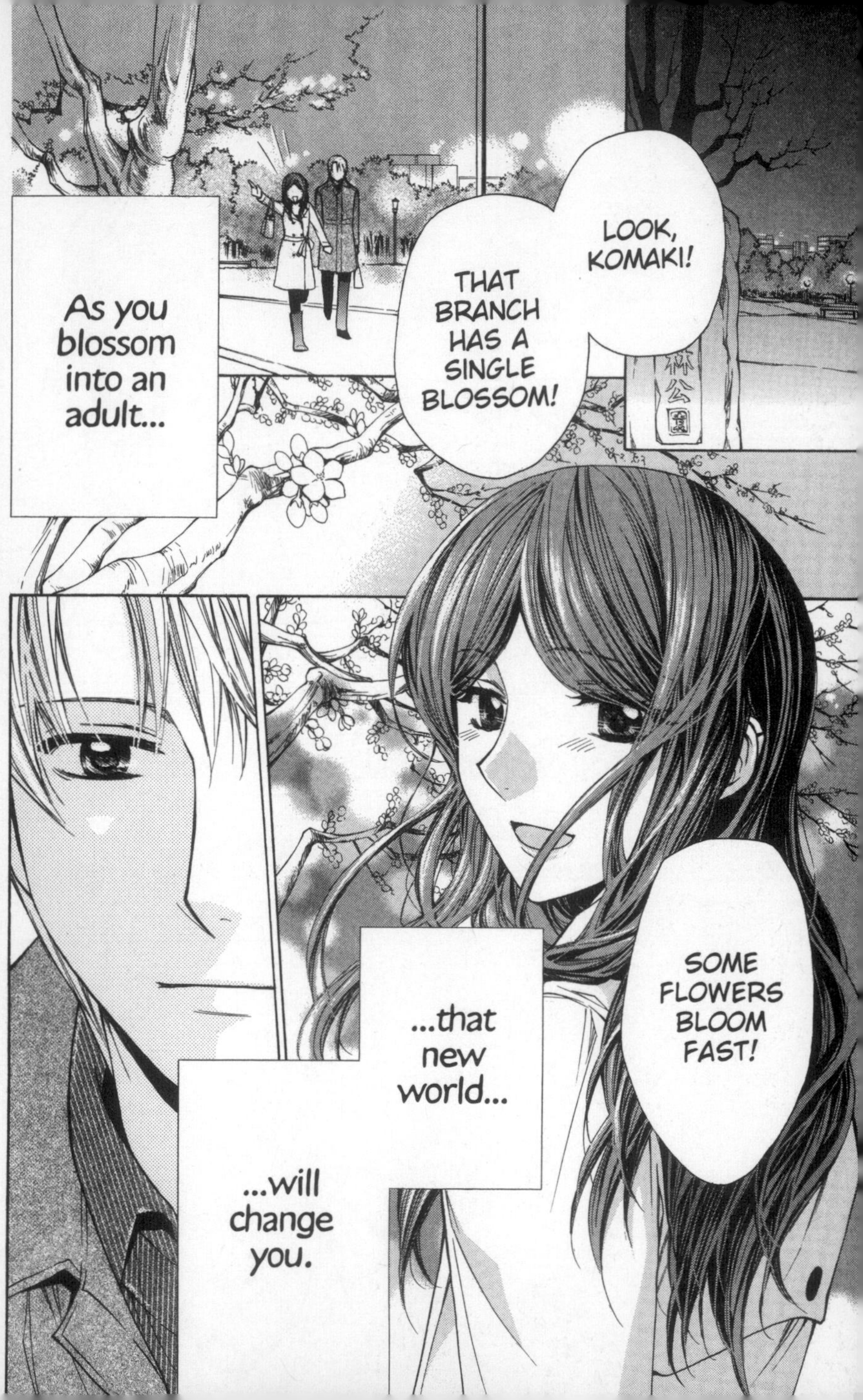
LOOK, KOMAKI!
THAT BRANCH HAS A SINGLE BLOSSOM!
As you blossom into an adult...
SOME FLOWERS BLOOM FAST!
...that new world...
...will change you.

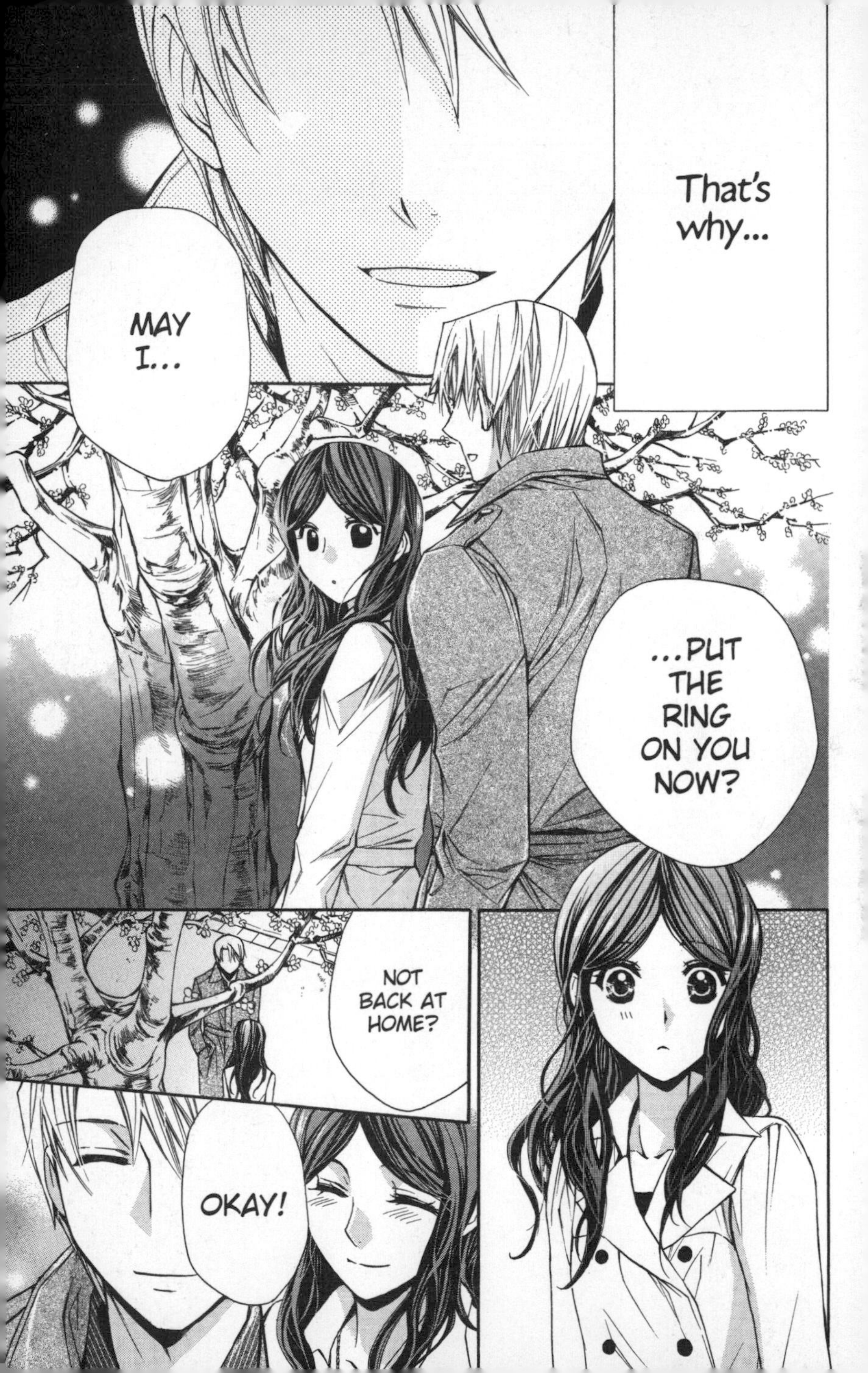
That's why...
MAY I...
...PUT THE RING ON YOU NOW?
NOT BACK AT HOME?
OKAY!

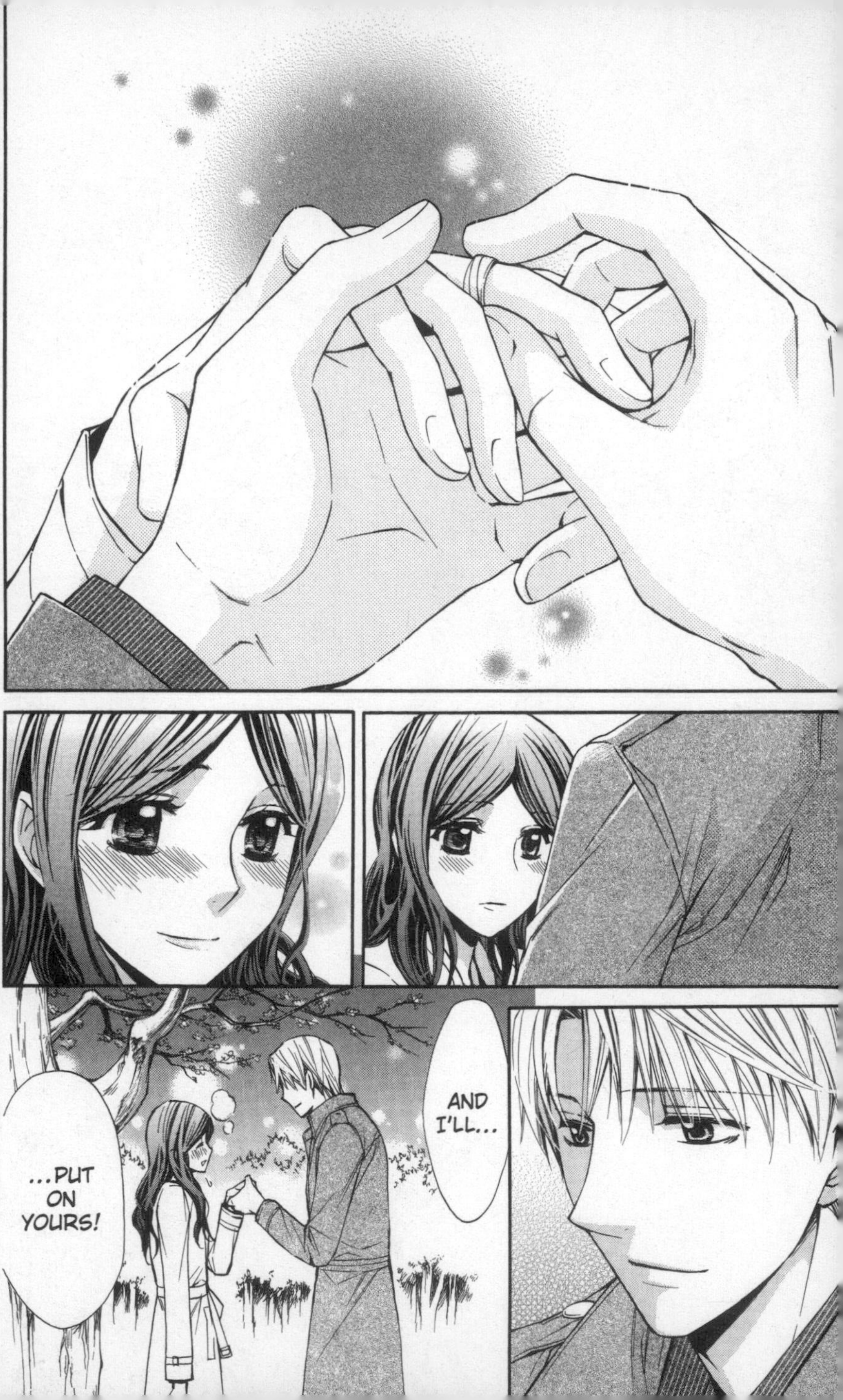
AND I'LL...
...PUT ON YOURS!

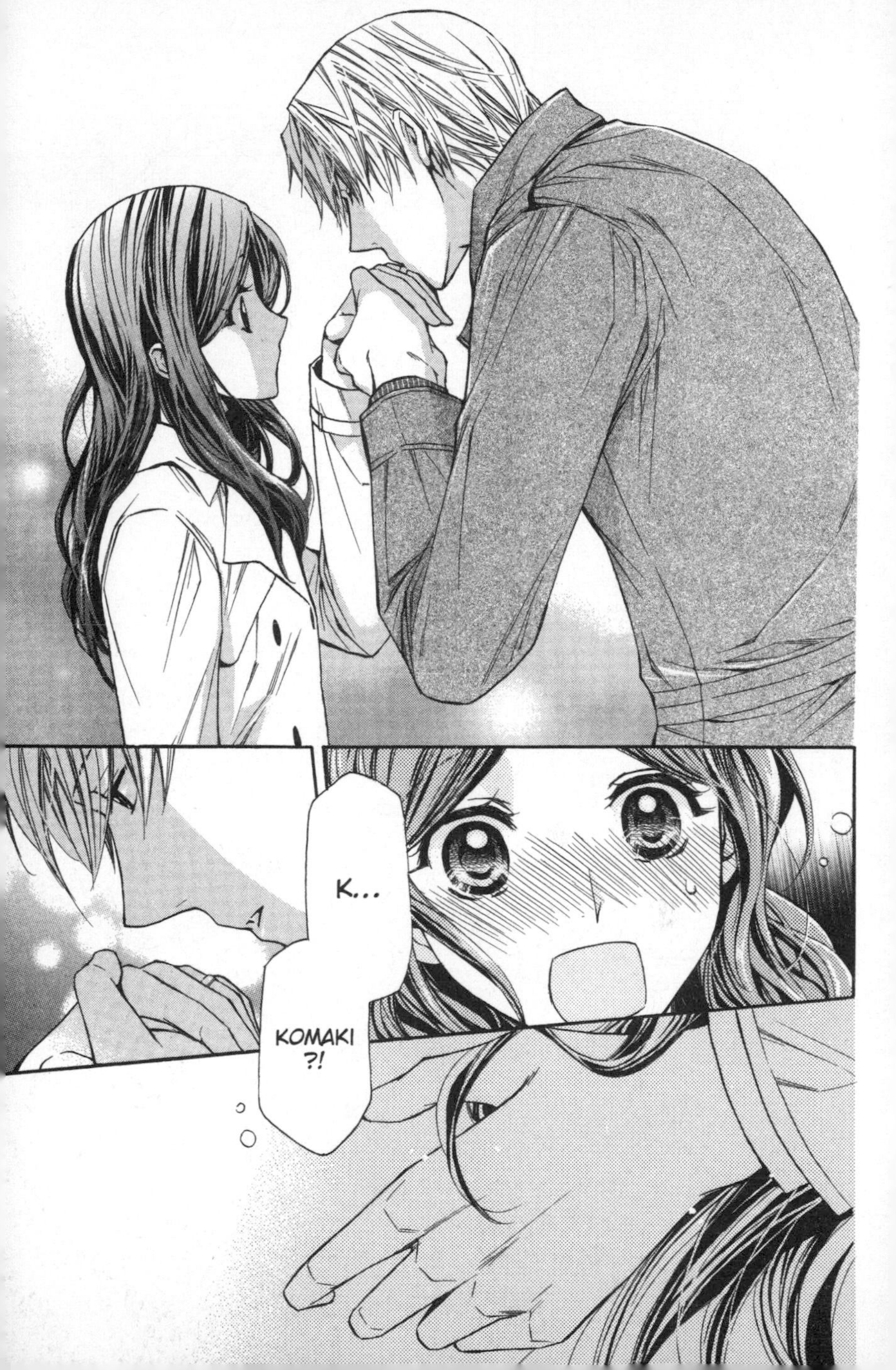
K...
KOMAKI ?!

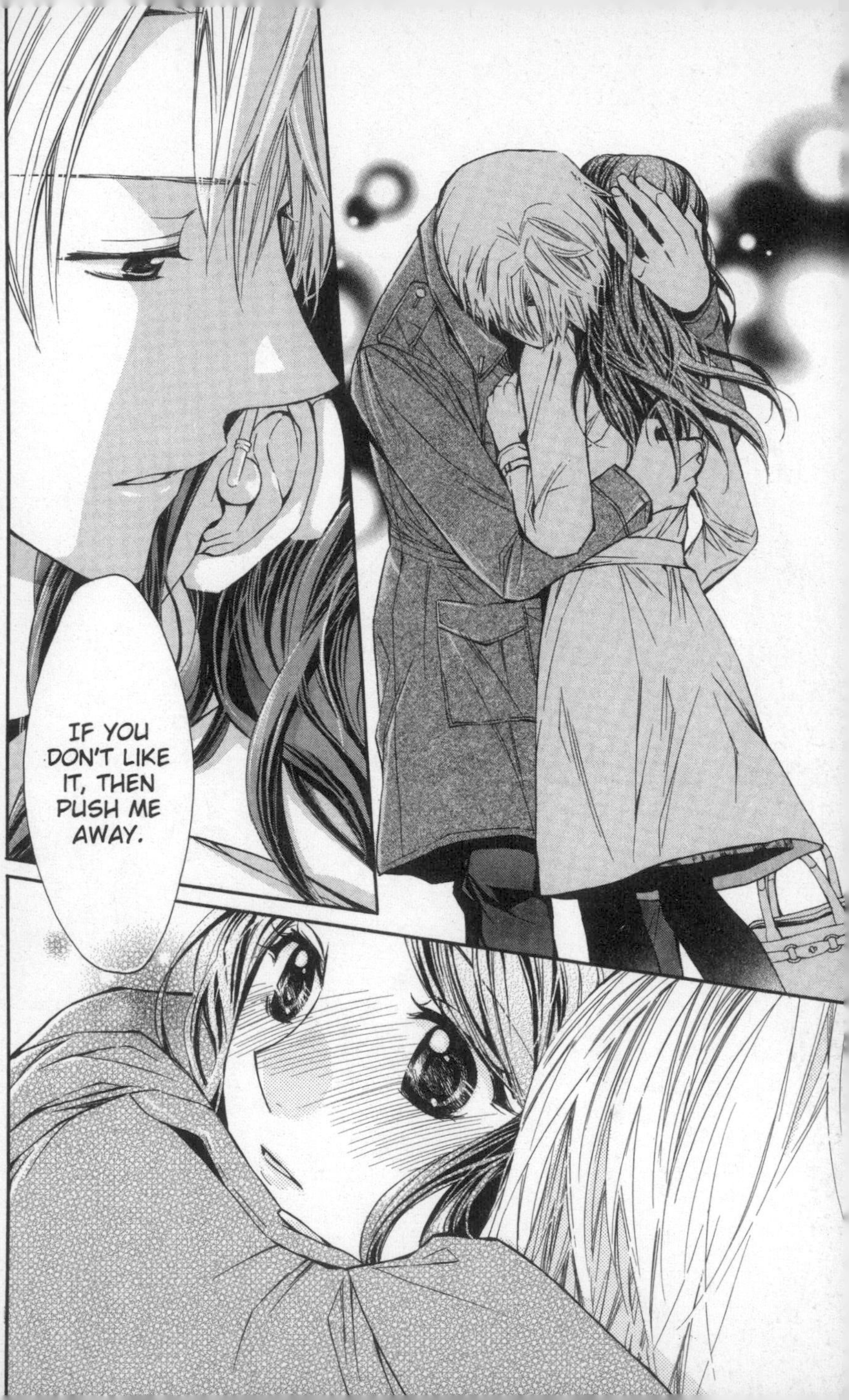
IF YOU DON'T LIKE IT, THEN PUSH ME AWAY.

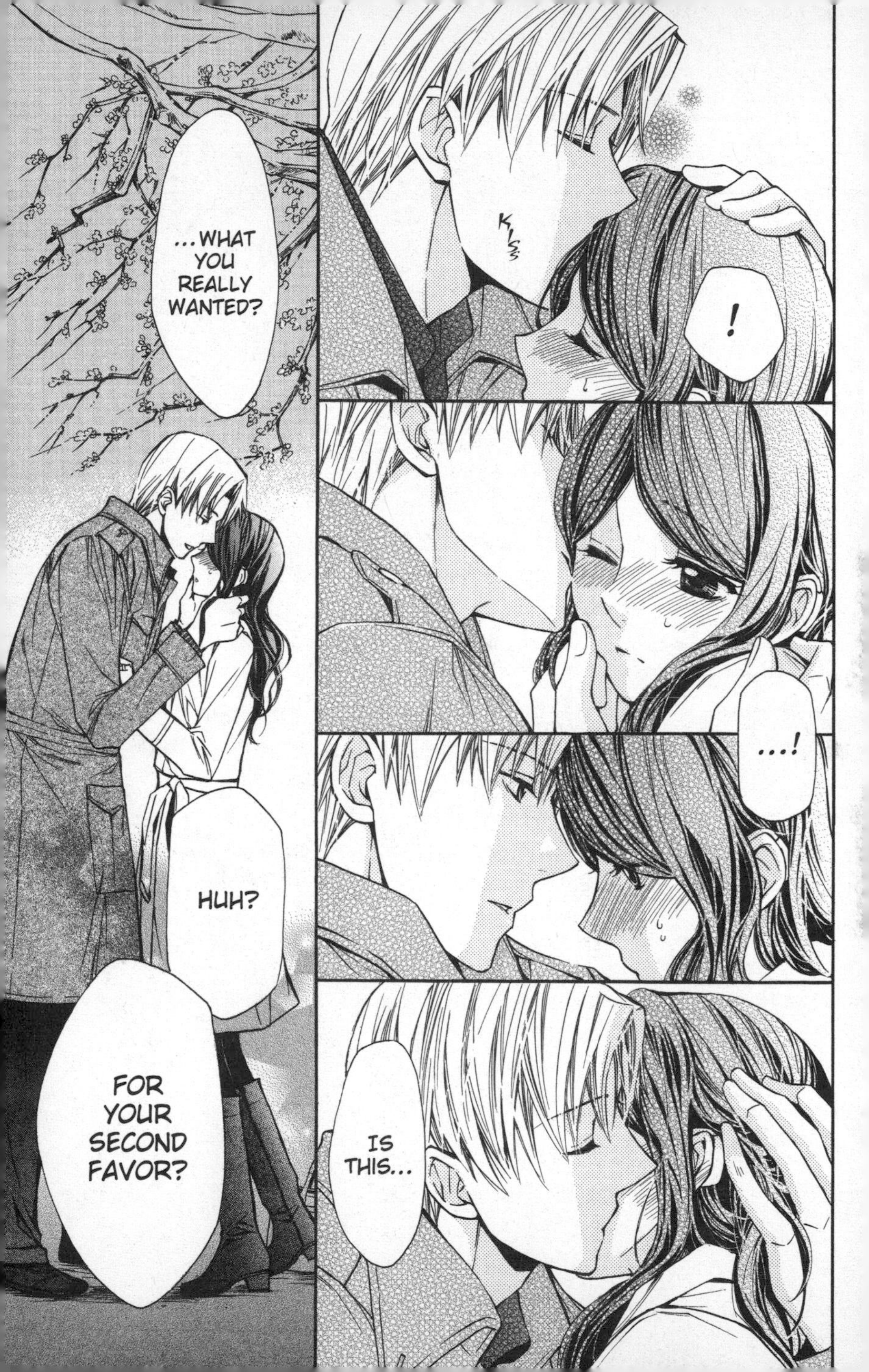
KISS
!
...!
IS THIS...
...WHAT YOU REALLY WANTED?
HUH?
FOR YOUR SECOND FAVOR?

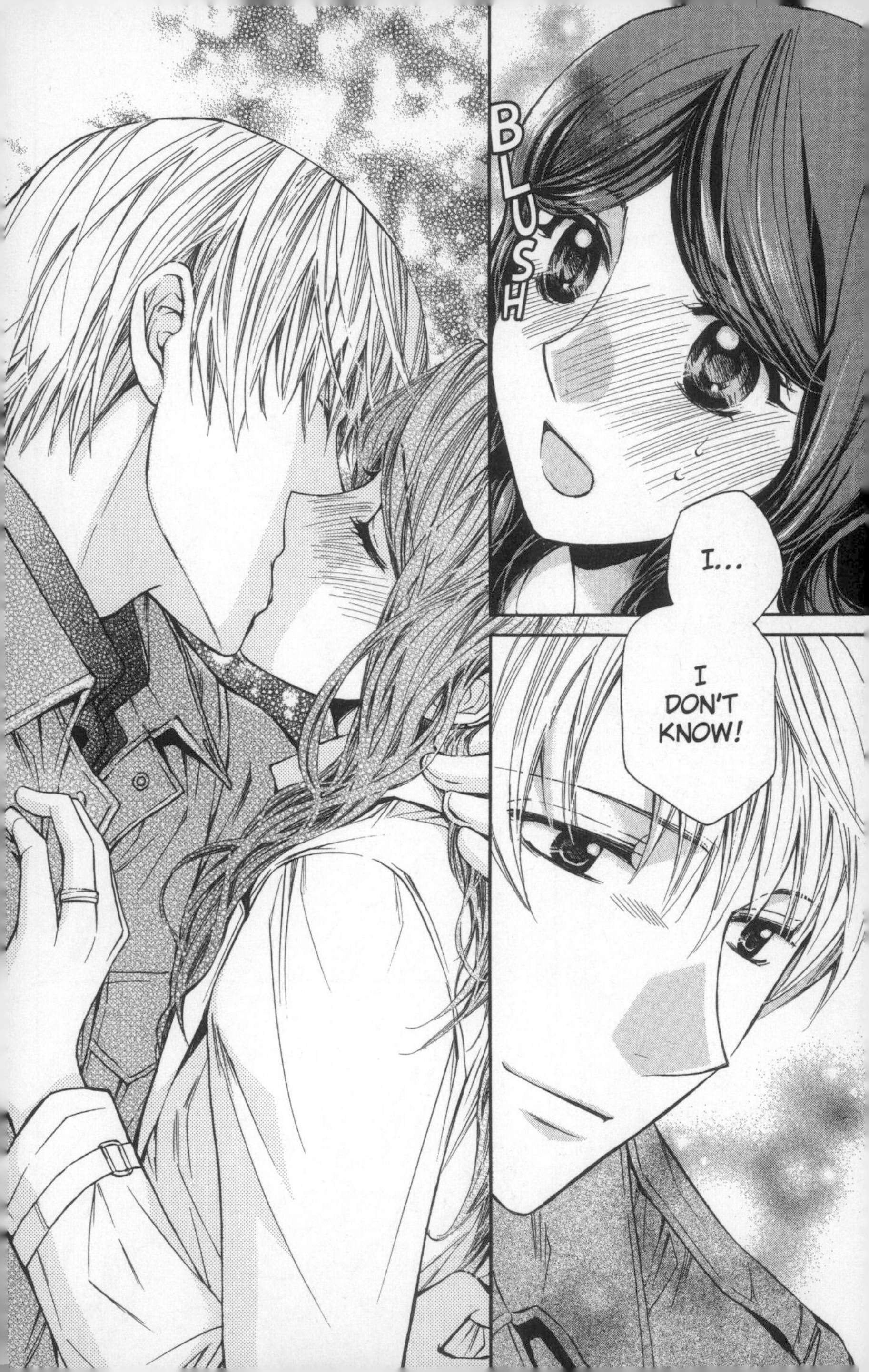
BLUSH
I...
I DON'T KNOW!

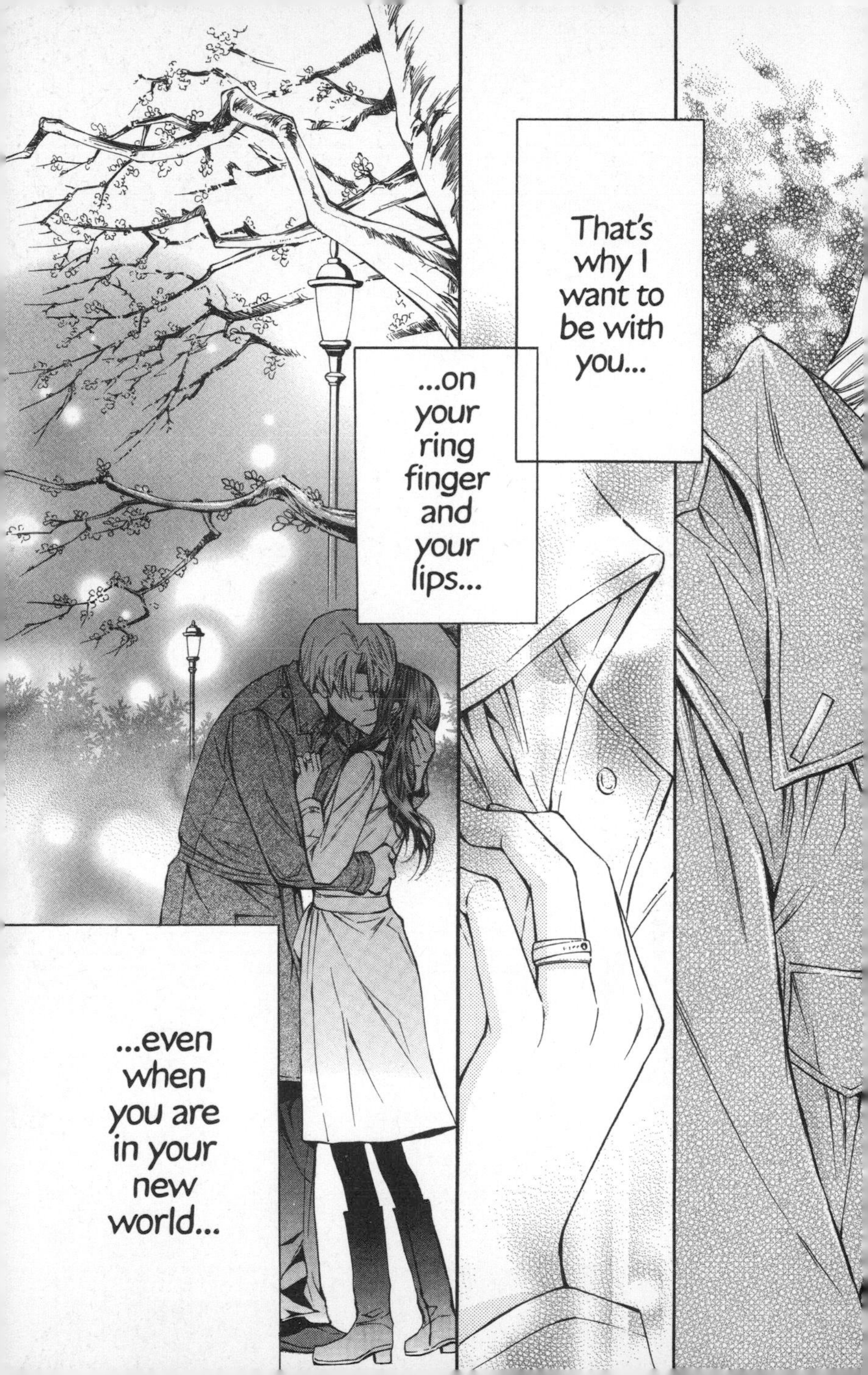
That's why I want to be with you...
...on your ring finger and your lips...
...even when you are in your new world...

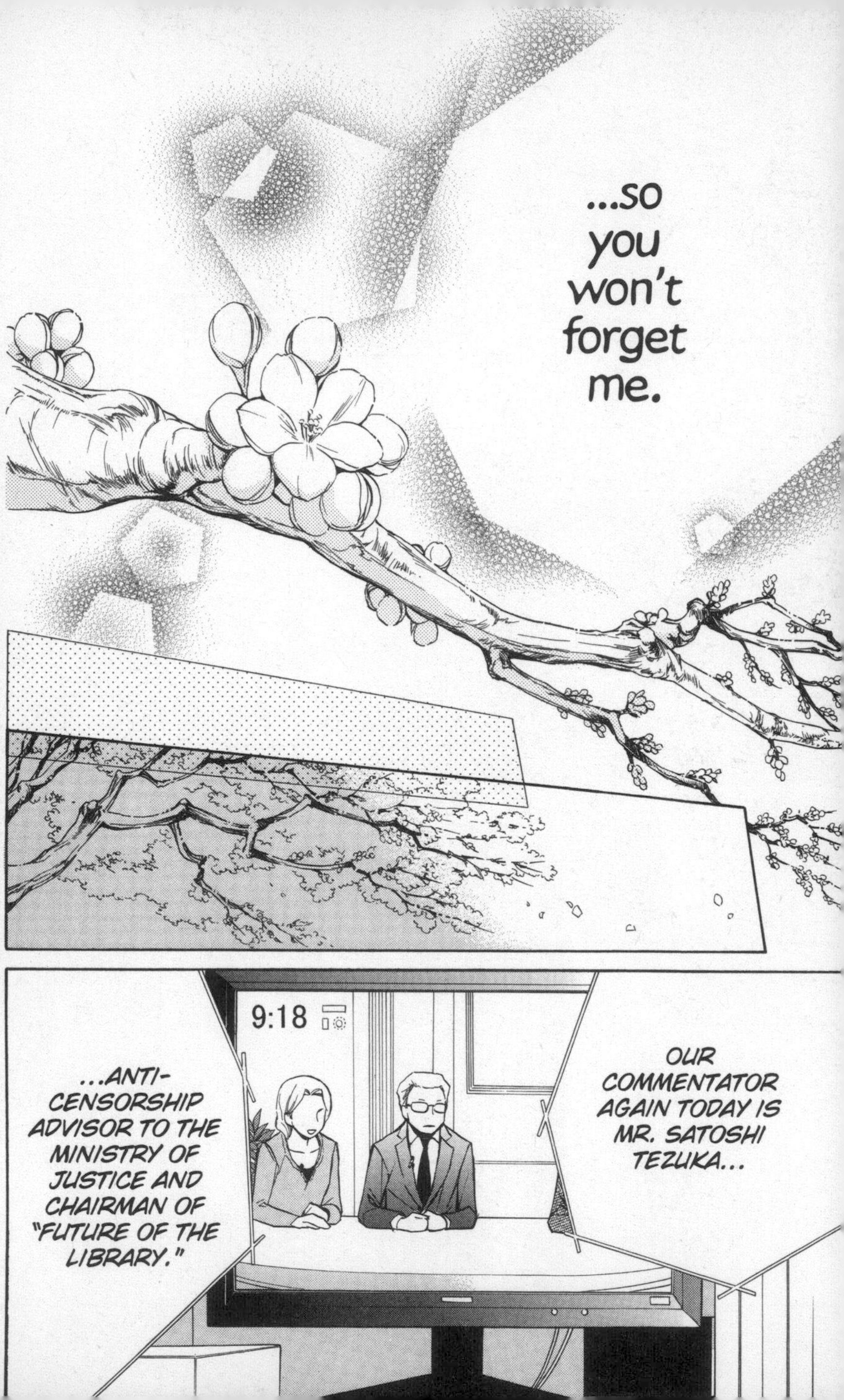
...so you won't forget me.
9:18
OUR COMMENTATOR AGAIN TODAY IS MR. SATOSHI TEZUKA...
...ANTI-CENSORSHIP ADVISOR TO THE MINISTRY OF JUSTICE AND CHAIRMAN OF "FUTURE OF THE LIBRARY."

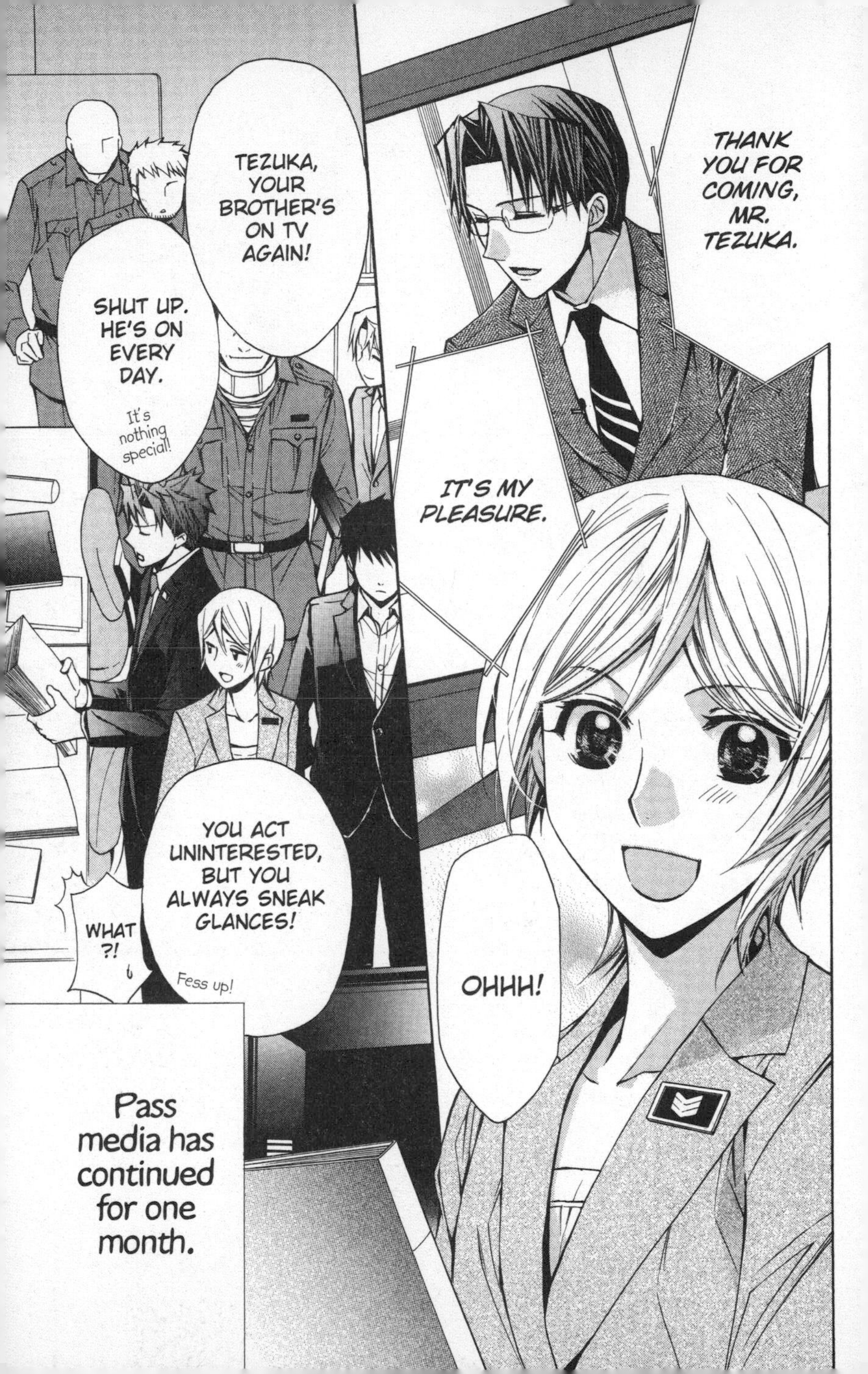
THANK YOU FOR COMING, MR. TEZUKA.
IT'S MY PLEASURE.
OHHH!
TEZUKA, YOUR BROTHER'S ON TV AGAIN!
SHUT UP. HE'S ON EVERY DAY.
It's nothing special!
YOU ACT UNINTERESTED, BUT YOU ALWAYS SNEAK GLANCES!
Fess up!
WHAT?!
Pass media has continued for one month.

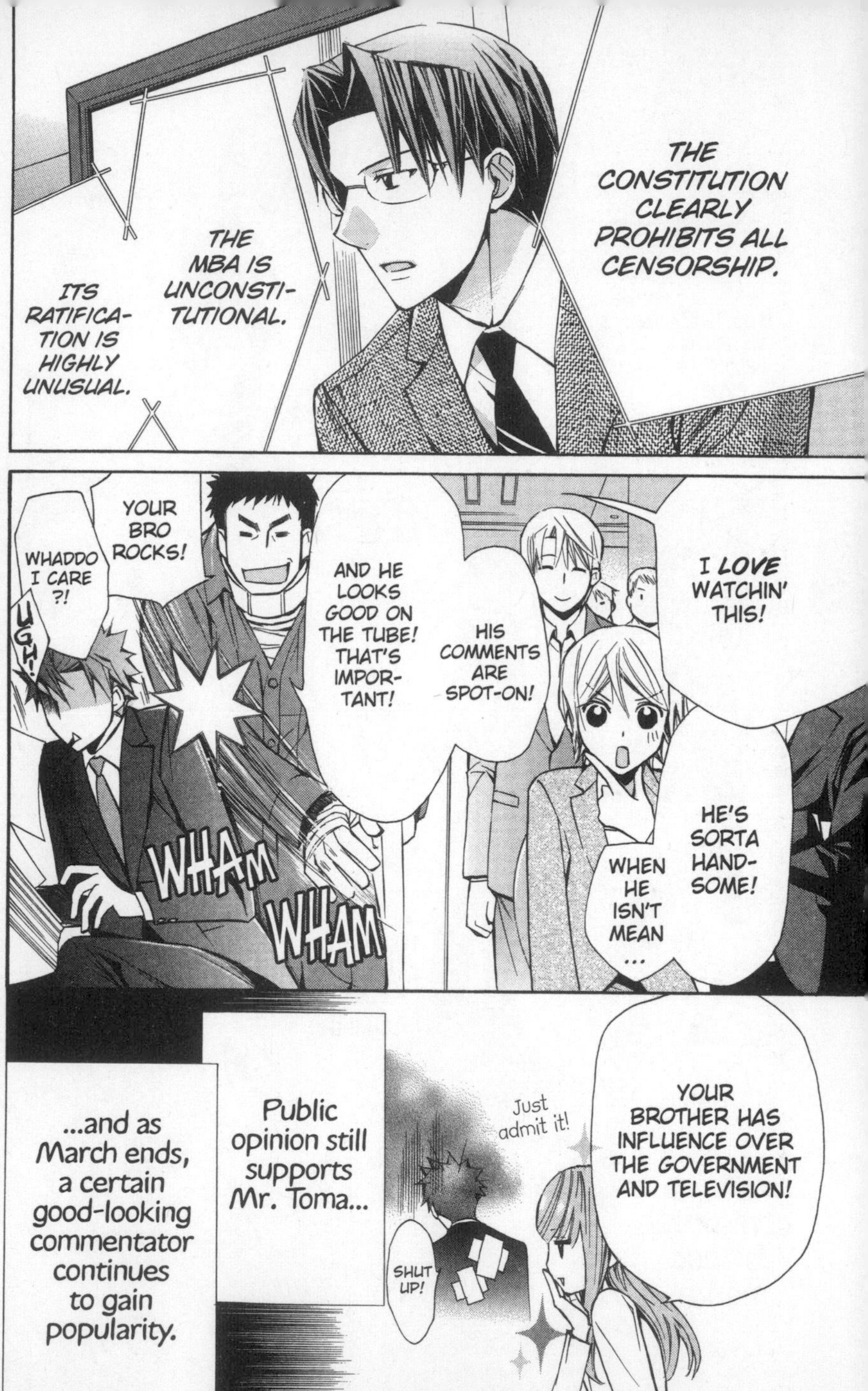
THE CONSTITUTION CLEARLY PROHIBITS ALL CENSORSHIP.
THE MBA IS UNCONSTITUTIONAL.
ITS RATIFICATION IS HIGHLY UNUSUAL.
I LOVE WATCHIN' THIS!
HE'S SORTA HANDSOME!
WHEN HE ISN'T MEAN ...
HIS COMMENTS ARE SPOT-ON!
AND HE LOOKS GOOD ON THE TUBE! THAT'S IMPORTANT!
YOUR BRO ROCKS!
WHADDO I CARE ?!
UGH!
WHAM
WHAM
YOUR BROTHER HAS INFLUENCE OVER THE GOVERNMENT AND TELEVISION!
Just admit it!
SHUT UP!
Public opinion still supports Mr. Toma...
...and as March ends, a certain good-looking commentator continues to gain popularity.

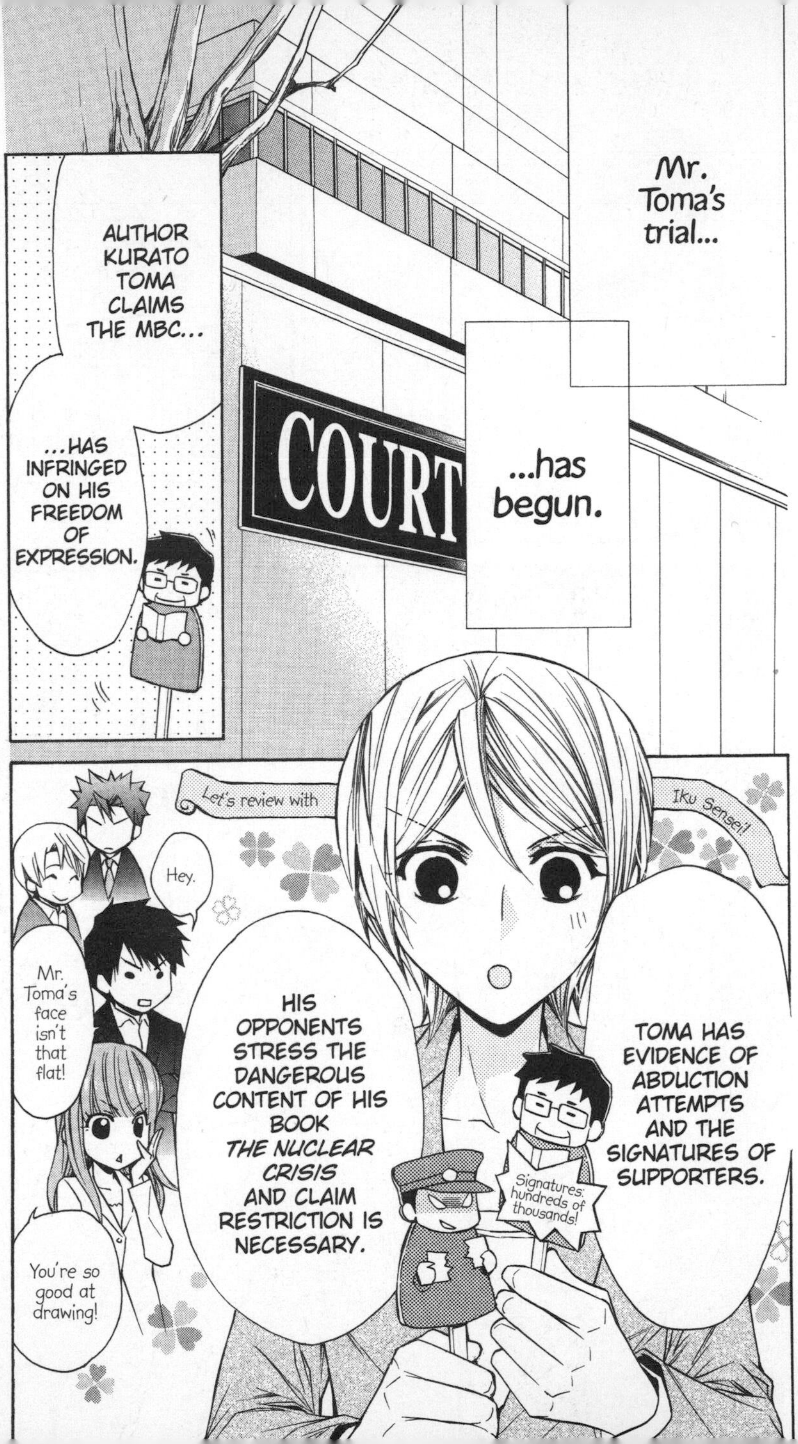
Mr. Toma's trial...
...has begun.
COURT
AUTHOR KURATO TOMA CLAIMS THE MBC...
...HAS INFRINGED ON HIS FREEDOM OF EXPRESSION.
Let's review with Iku Sensei!
TOMA HAS EVIDENCE OF ABDUCTION ATTEMPTS AND THE SIGNATURES OF SUPPORTERS.
Signatures: hundreds of thousands!
HIS OPPONENTS STRESS THE DANGEROUS CONTENT OF HIS BOOK *THE NUCLEAR CRISIS* AND CLAIM RESTRICTION IS NECESSARY.
Hey.
Mr. Toma's face isn't that flat!
You're so good at drawing!

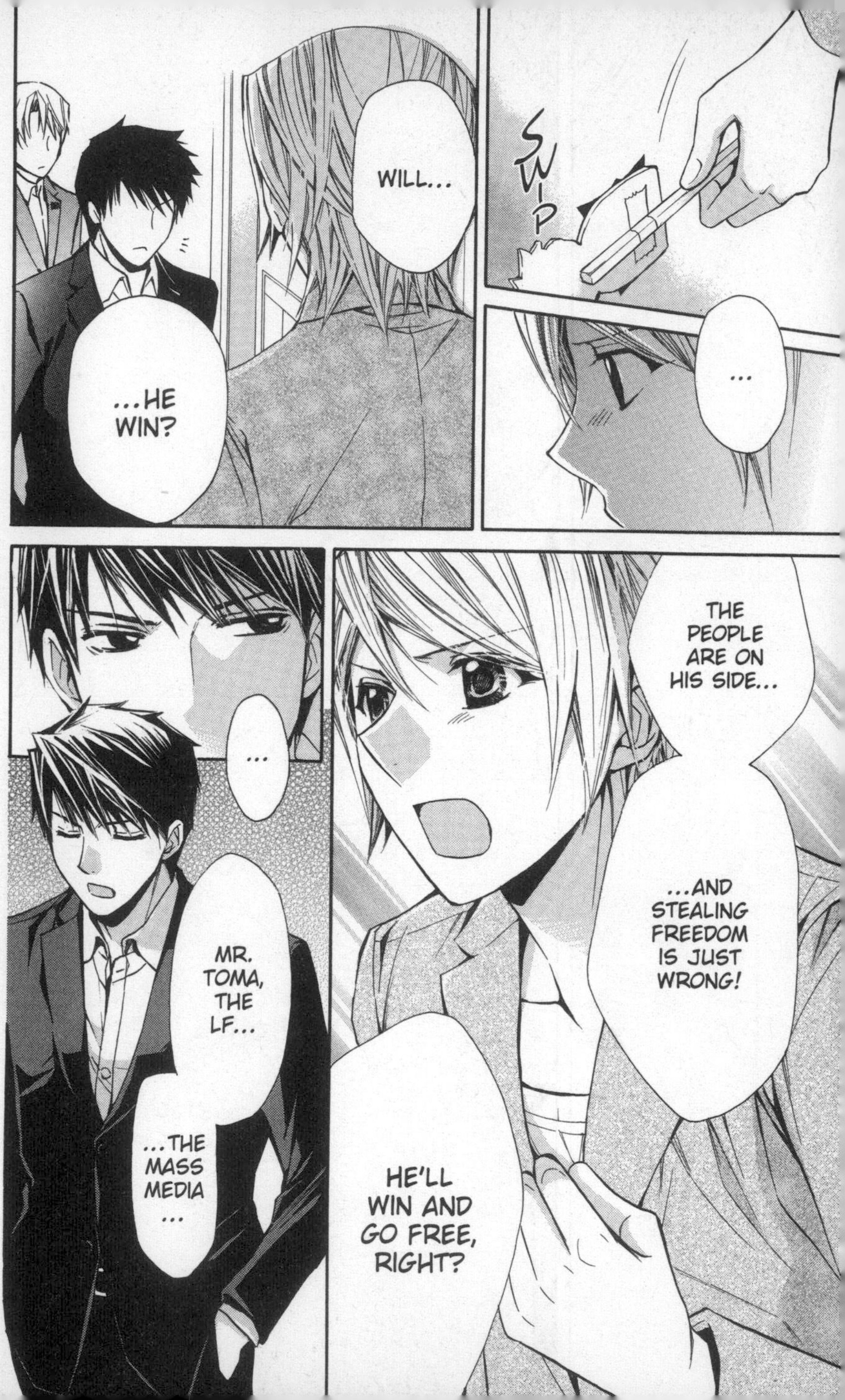
SWIP
...
WILL...
...HE WIN?
THE PEOPLE ARE ON HIS SIDE...
...AND STEALING FREEDOM IS JUST WRONG!
HE'LL WIN AND GO FREE, RIGHT?
...
MR. TOMA, THE LF...
...THE MASS MEDIA ...

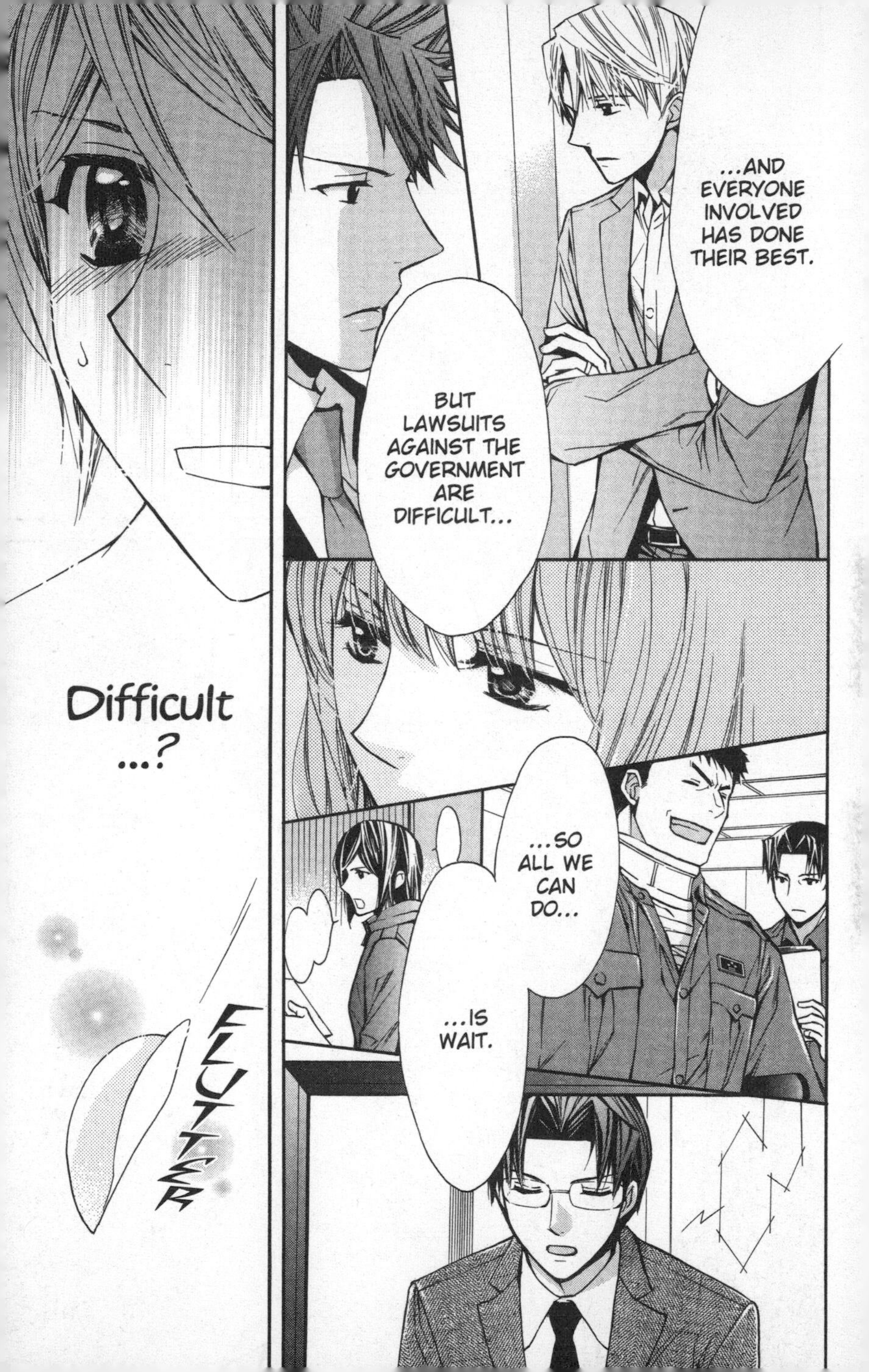
...AND EVERYONE INVOLVED HAS DONE THEIR BEST.
BUT LAWSUITS AGAINST THE GOVERNMENT ARE DIFFICULT...
...SO ALL WE CAN DO...
...IS WAIT.
Difficult ...?
FLUTTER

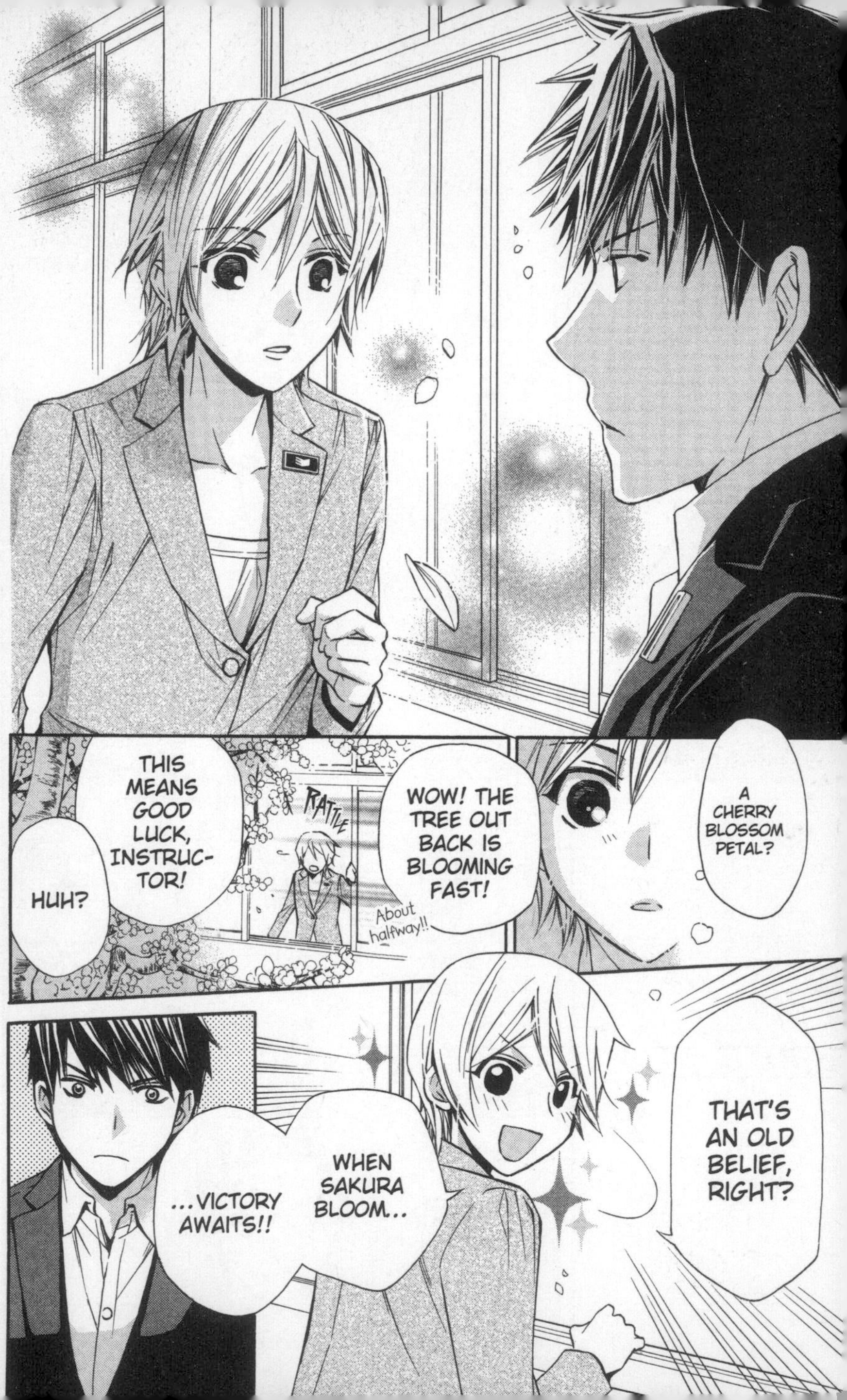
A CHERRY BLOSSOM PETAL?
WOW! THE TREE OUT BACK IS BLOOMING FAST!
RATTLE
About halfway!!
THIS MEANS GOOD LUCK, INSTRUCTOR!
HUH?
THAT'S AN OLD BELIEF, RIGHT?
WHEN SAKURA BLOOM...
...VICTORY AWAITS!!

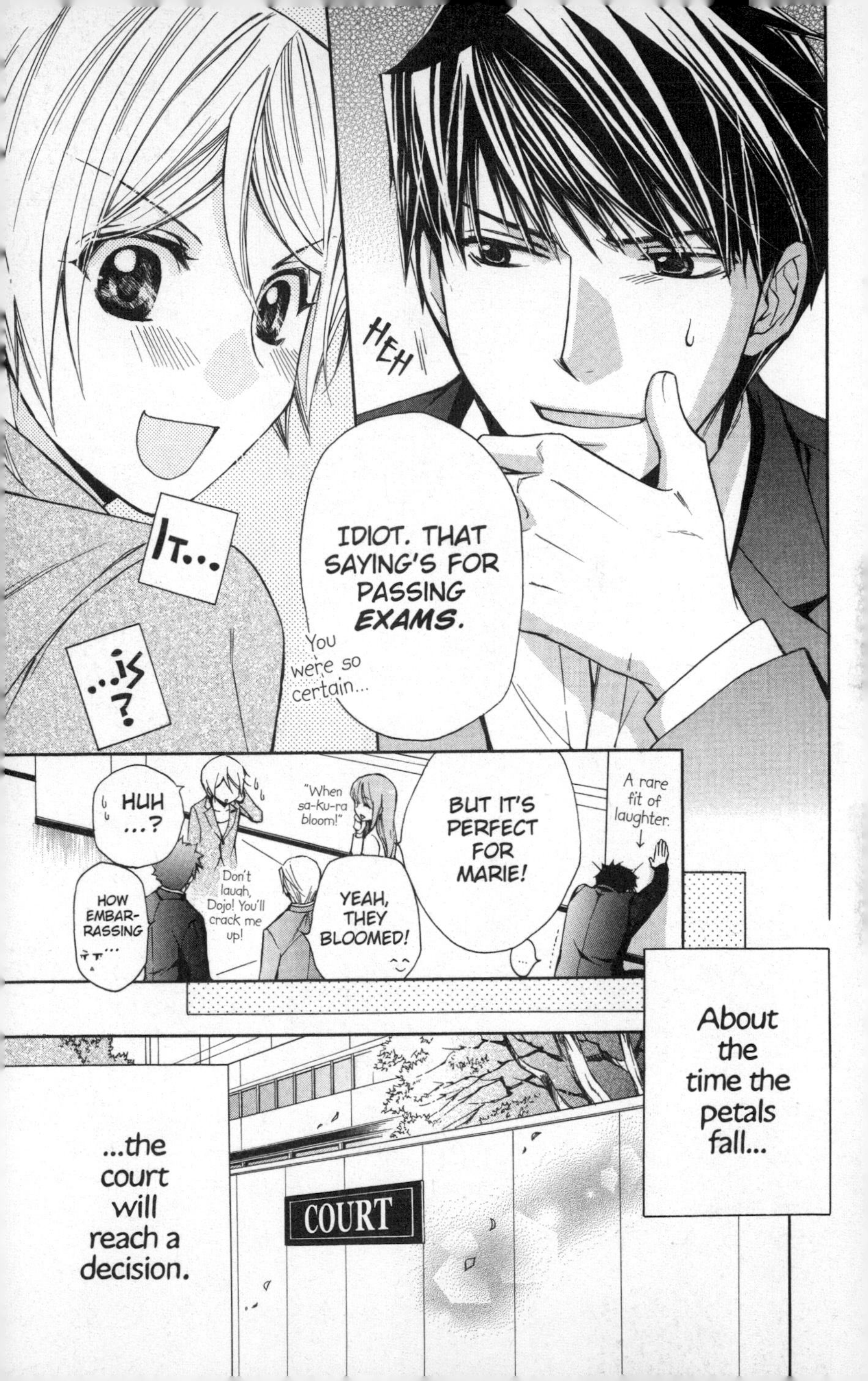
HEH
IDIOT. THAT SAYING'S FOR PASSING EXAMS.
You were so certain...
It...
...is ?
A rare fit of laughter.
...
BUT IT'S PERFECT FOR MARIE!
YEAH, THEY BLOOMED!
"When sa-ku-ra bloom!"
Don't laugh, Dojo! You'll crack me up!
HUH ...?
HOW EMBARRASSING...
About the time the petals fall...
COURT
...the court will reach a decision.

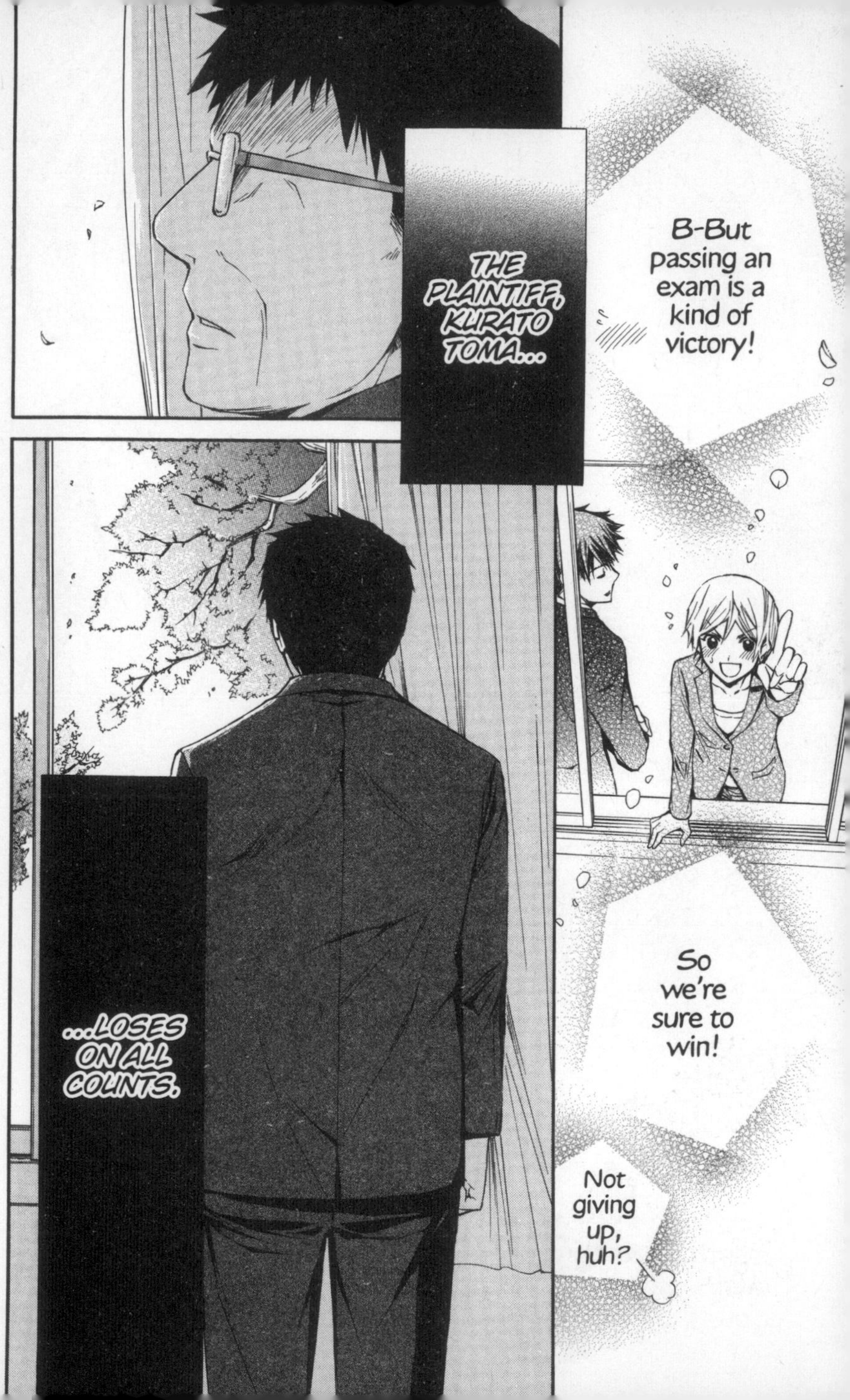
B-But passing an exam is a kind of victory!
So we're sure to win!
Not giving up, huh?
THE PLAINTIFF, KURATO TOMA...
...LOSES ON ALL COUNTS.

CHAPTER 63

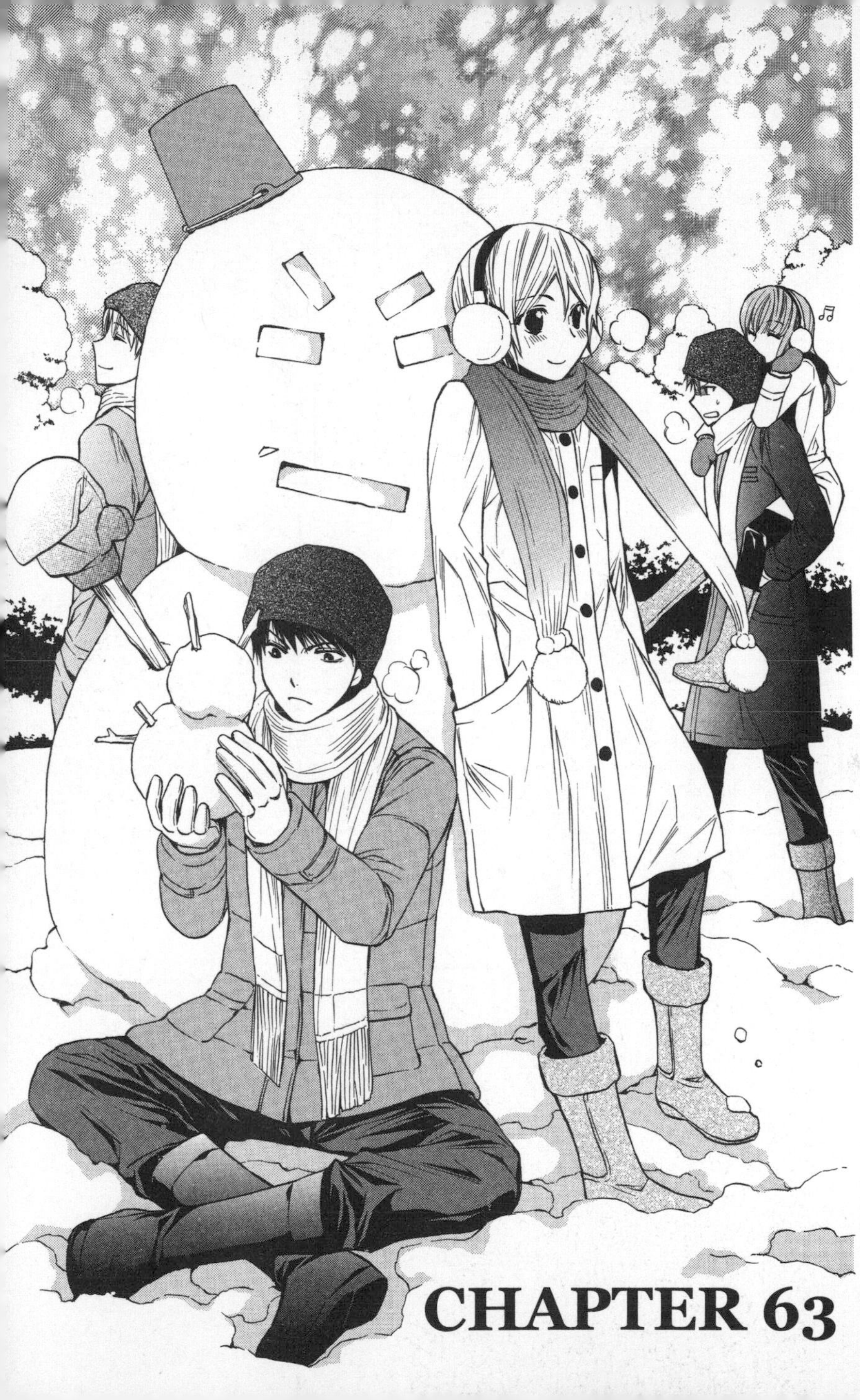

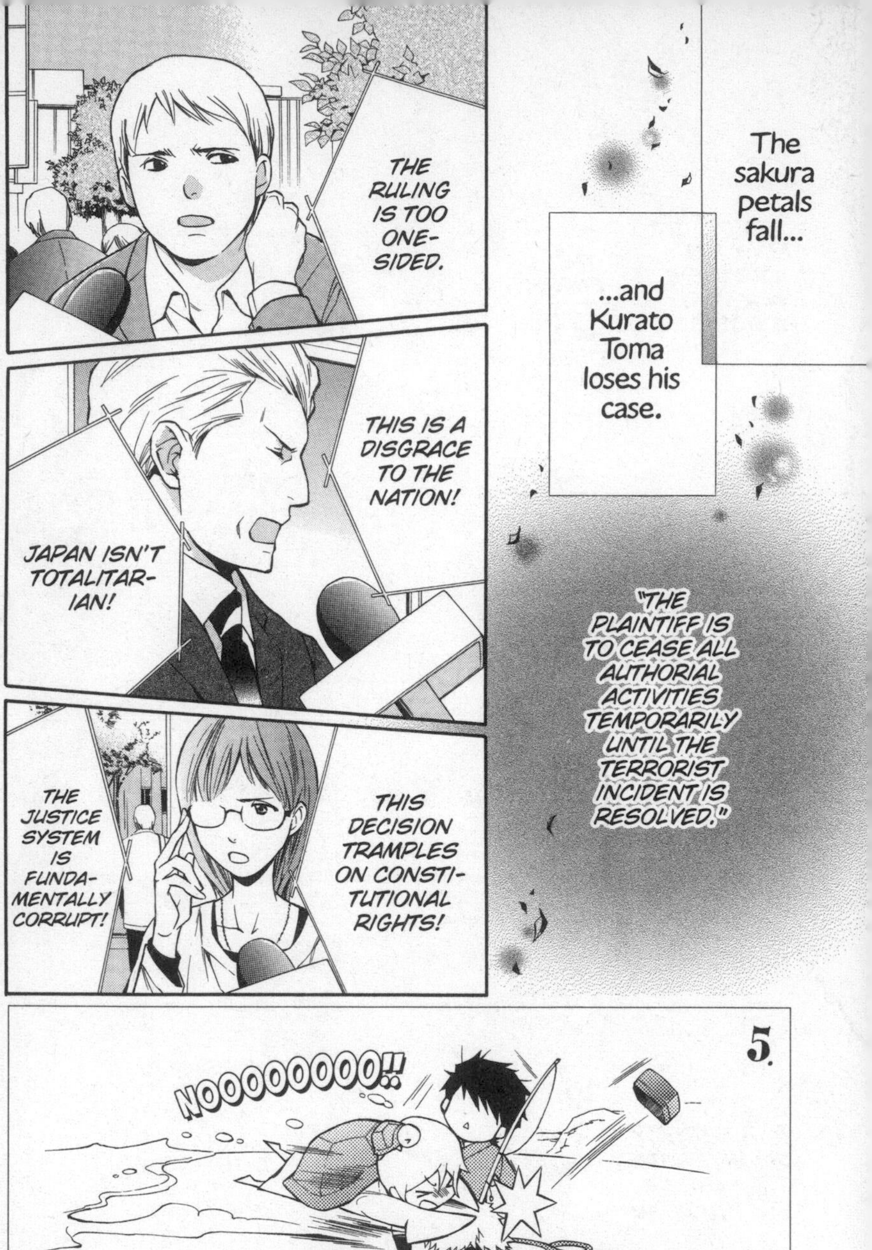
The sakura petals fall...
...and Kurato Toma loses his case.
"THE PLAINTIFF IS TO CEASE ALL AUTHORIAL ACTIVITIES TEMPORARILY UNTIL THE TERRORIST INCIDENT IS RESOLVED."
THE RULING IS TOO ONE-SIDED.
THIS IS A DISGRACE TO THE NATION!
JAPAN ISN'T TOTALITARIAN!
THIS DECISION TRAMPLES ON CONSTITUTIONAL RIGHTS!
THE JUSTICE SYSTEM IS FUNDAMENTALLY CORRUPT!
5.
NOOOOOOOO!!

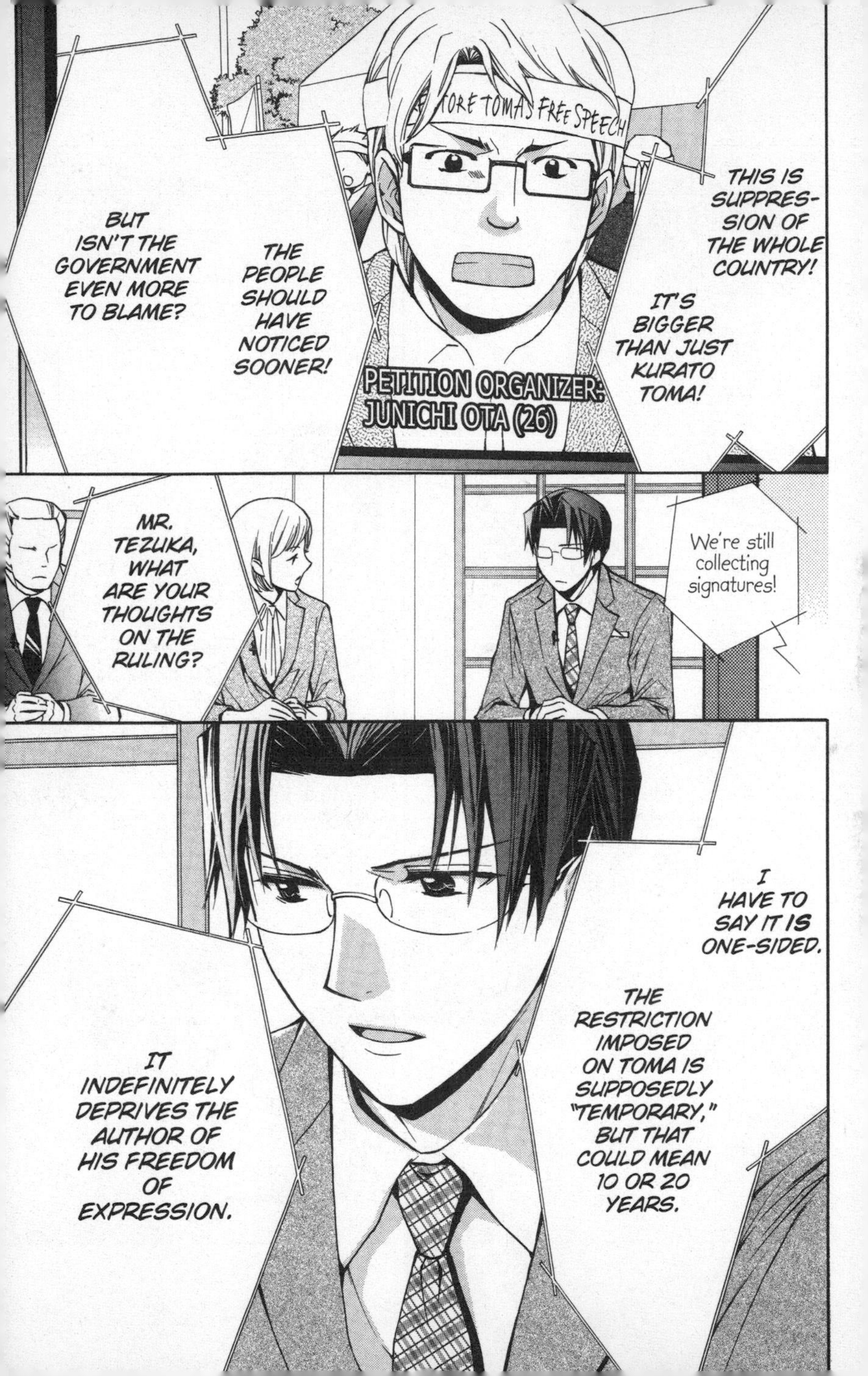
THIS IS SUPPRES-SION OF THE WHOLE COUNTRY!
IT'S BIGGER THAN JUST KURATO TOMA!
TORE TOMA'S FREE SPEECH
PETITION ORGANIZER: JUNICHI OTA (26)
THE PEOPLE SHOULD HAVE NOTICED SOONER!
BUT ISN'T THE GOVERNMENT EVEN MORE TO BLAME?
We're still collecting signatures!
MR. TEZUKA, WHAT ARE YOUR THOUGHTS ON THE RULING?
I HAVE TO SAY IT **IS** ONE-SIDED.
THE RESTRICTION IMPOSED ON TOMA IS SUPPOSEDLY "TEMPORARY," BUT THAT COULD MEAN 10 OR 20 YEARS.
IT INDEFINITELY DEPRIVES THE AUTHOR OF HIS FREEDOM OF EXPRESSION.

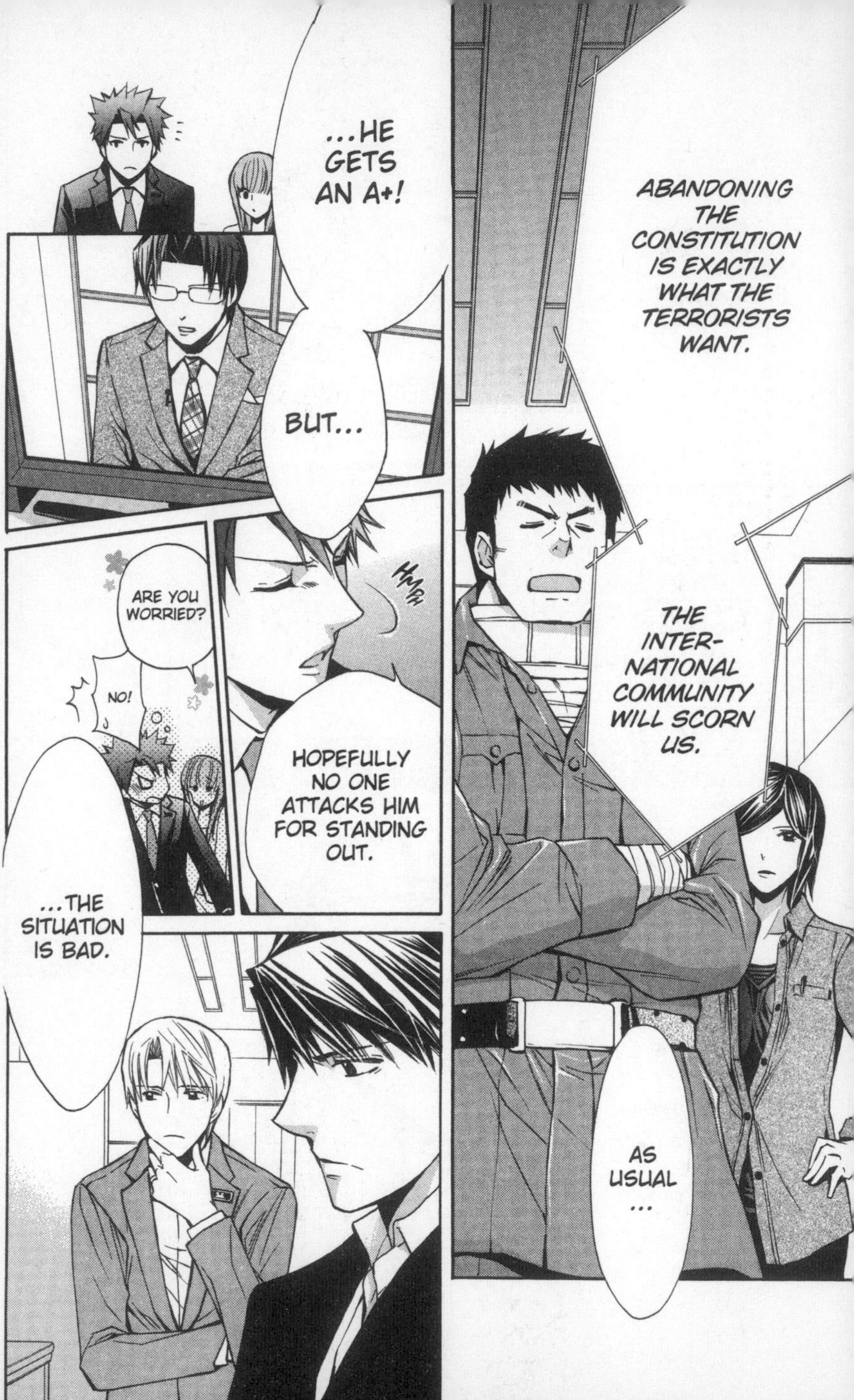
ABANDONING THE CONSTITUTION IS EXACTLY WHAT THE TERRORISTS WANT.
THE INTER-NATIONAL COMMUNITY WILL SCORN US.
AS USUAL...
...HE GETS AN A+!
BUT...
HMPH
HOPEFULLY NO ONE ATTACKS HIM FOR STANDING OUT.
ARE YOU WORRIED?
NO!
...THE SITUATION IS BAD.

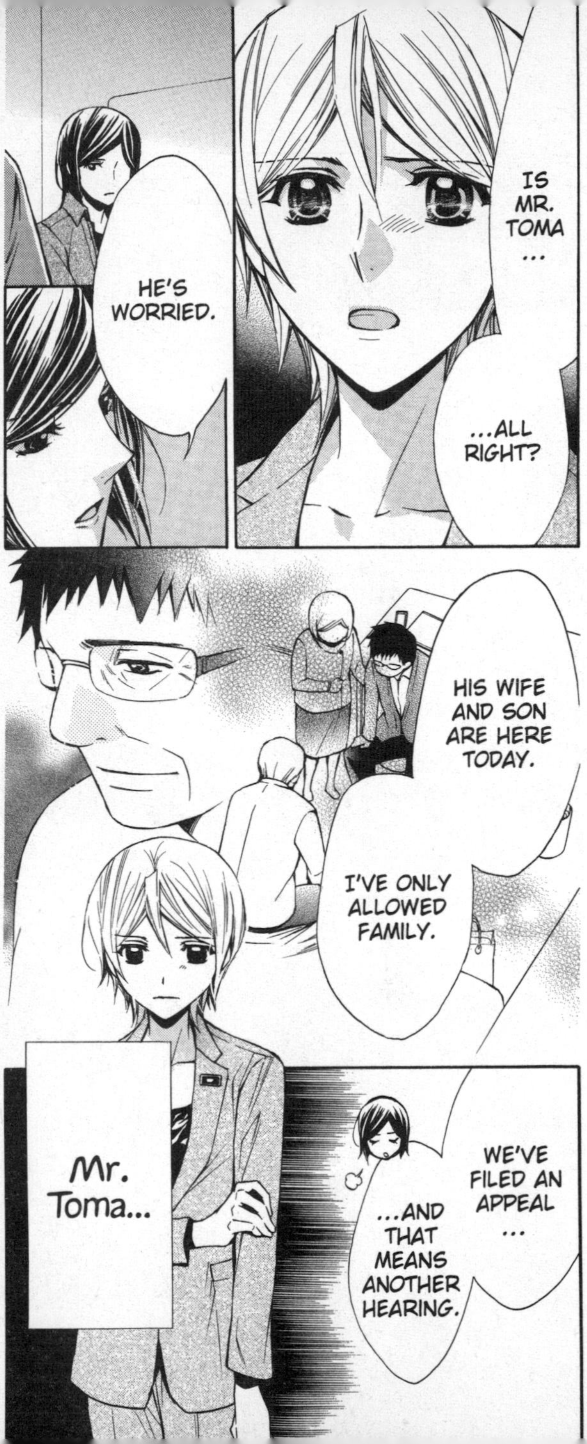
IS MR. TOMA ...
...ALL RIGHT?
HE'S WORRIED.
HIS WIFE AND SON ARE HERE TODAY.
I'VE ONLY ALLOWED FAMILY.
WE'VE FILED AN APPEAL ...
...AND THAT MEANS ANOTHER HEARING.
Mr. Toma...

5

As for *MonHun* 4, released in September of 2013... Right after it went on sale, I went to the hot springs at Shibu Onsen. I also went to MonHun Festa. When I'm not working, I do solo play and party play and at present I only have a few difficult awards left to win! It's so much fun that my new motto is "No hunt, no life!" Thank you, Capcom! If you get too into *MonHun*, it eats up time, so manga authors shouldn't play it!

Too late! (lol)

From now on... no hunt, no life!

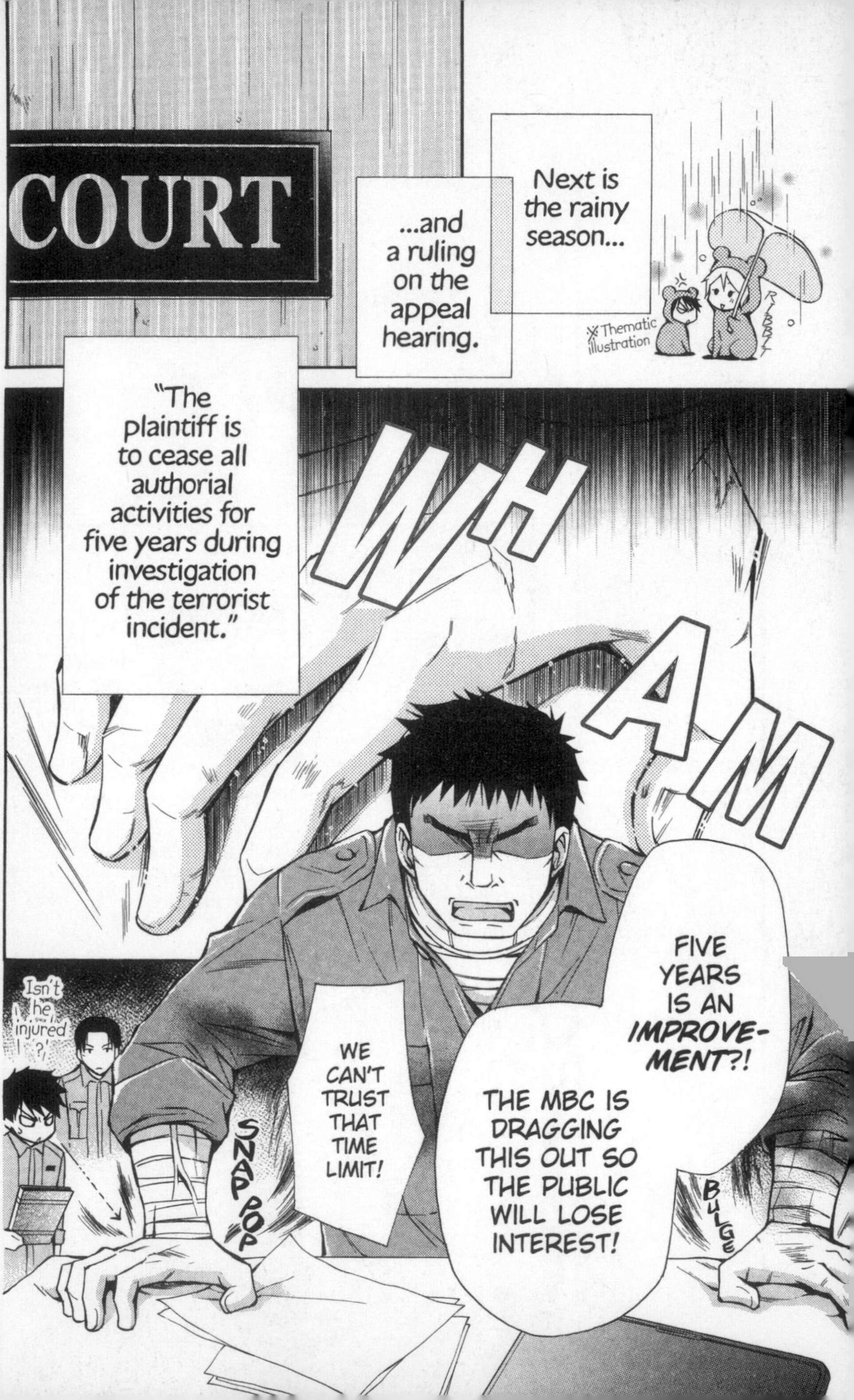

Next is the rainy season...
RIBBIT
※Thematic illustration
...and a ruling on the appeal hearing.
COURT
"The plaintiff is to cease all authorial activities for five years during investigation of the terrorist incident."
WHAM
FIVE YEARS IS AN IMPROVEMENT?!
THE MBC IS DRAGGING THIS OUT SO THE PUBLIC WILL LOSE INTEREST!
BULGE
WE CAN'T TRUST THAT TIME LIMIT!
SNAP POP
Isn't he injured?!

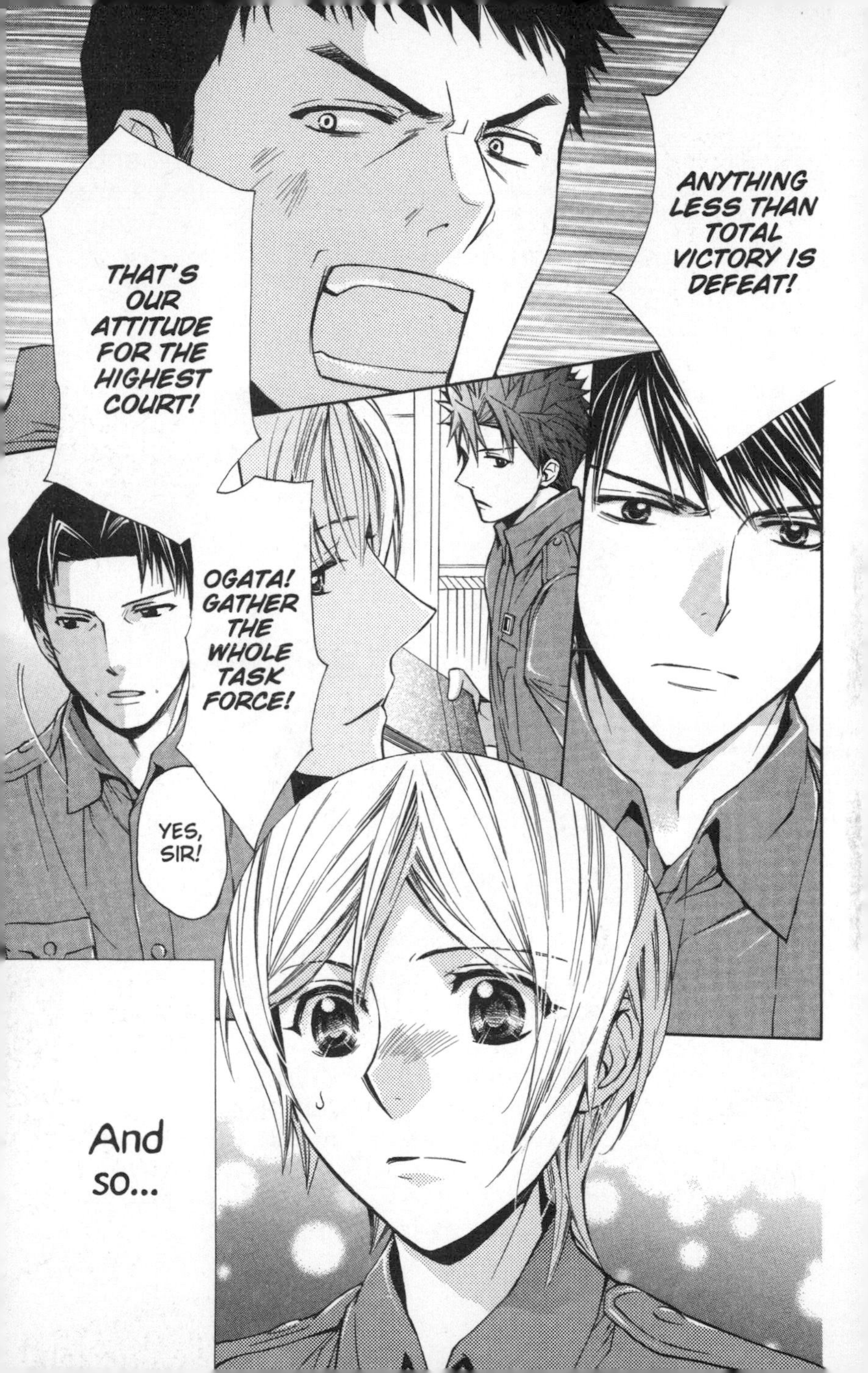
ANYTHING LESS THAN TOTAL VICTORY IS DEFEAT!
THAT'S OUR ATTITUDE FOR THE HIGHEST COURT!
OGATA! GATHER THE WHOLE TASK FORCE!
YES, SIR!
And so...

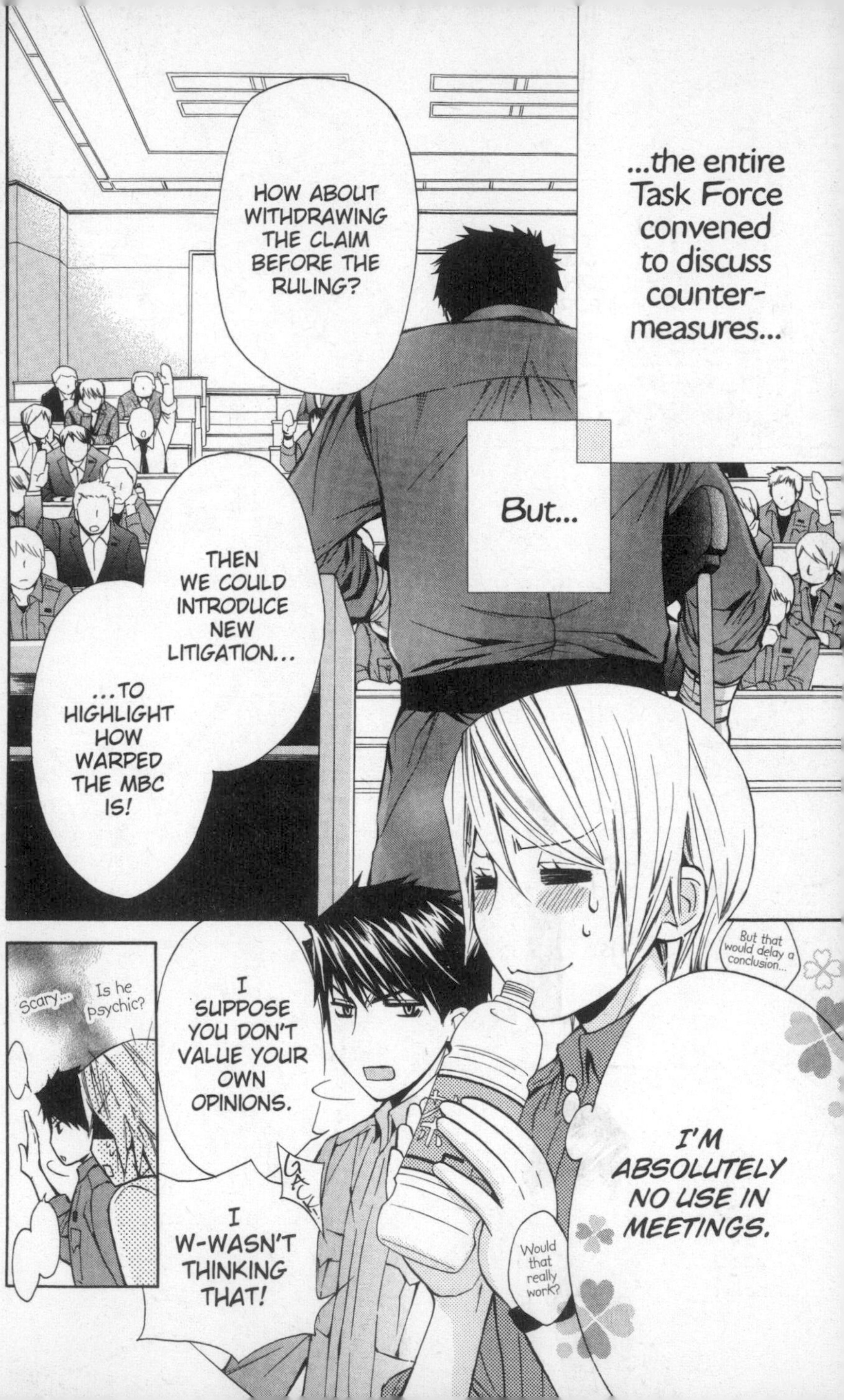
...the entire Task Force convened to discuss counter-measures...
HOW ABOUT WITHDRAWING THE CLAIM BEFORE THE RULING?
But...
THEN WE COULD INTRODUCE NEW LITIGATION...
...TO HIGHLIGHT HOW WARPED THE MBC IS!
But that would delay a conclusion...
I'M ABSOLUTELY NO USE IN MEETINGS.
Would that really work?
I SUPPOSE YOU DON'T VALUE YOUR OWN OPINIONS.
GACK
I W-WASN'T THINKING THAT!
Is he psychic?
Scary...

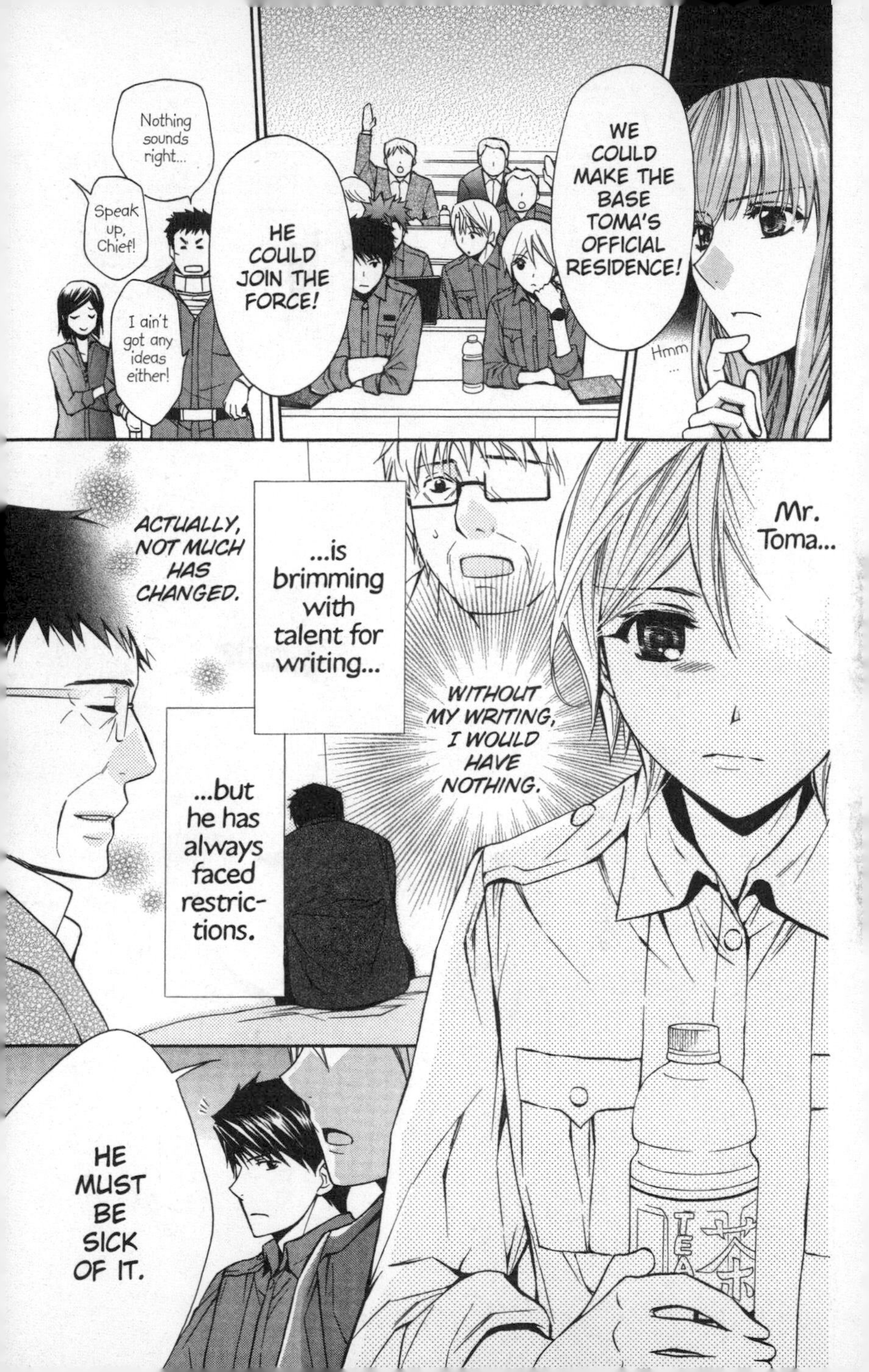
WE COULD MAKE THE BASE TOMA'S OFFICIAL RESIDENCE!
Hmm...
HE COULD JOIN THE FORCE!
Nothing sounds right...
Speak up, Chief!
I ain't got any ideas either!
Mr. Toma...
...is brimming with talent for writing...
...but he has always faced restrictions.
WITHOUT MY WRITING, I WOULD HAVE NOTHING.
ACTUALLY, NOT MUCH HAS CHANGED.
HE MUST BE SICK OF IT.

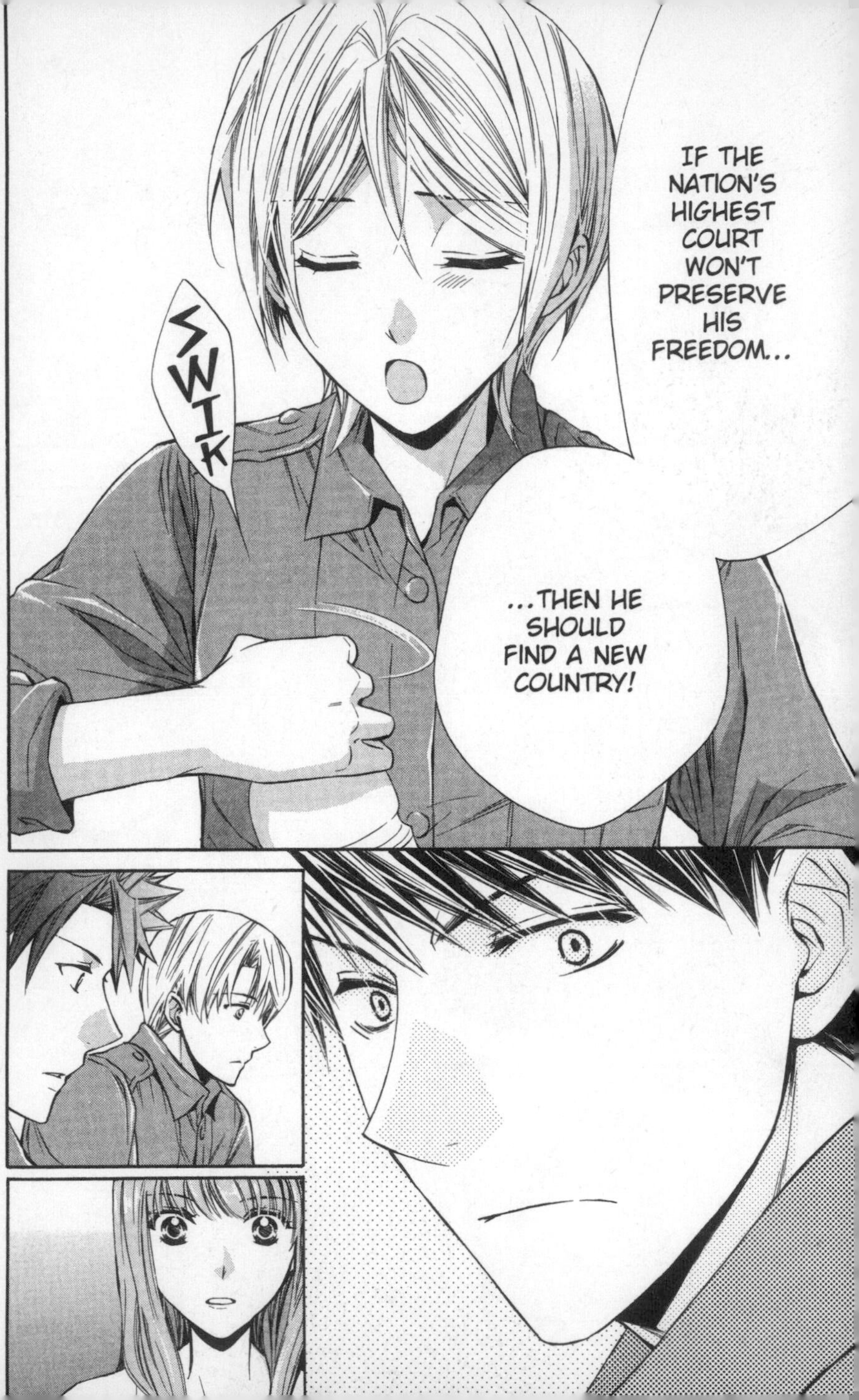
IF THE NATION'S HIGHEST COURT WON'T PRESERVE HIS FREEDOM...
SWIK
...THEN HE SHOULD FIND A NEW COUNTRY!

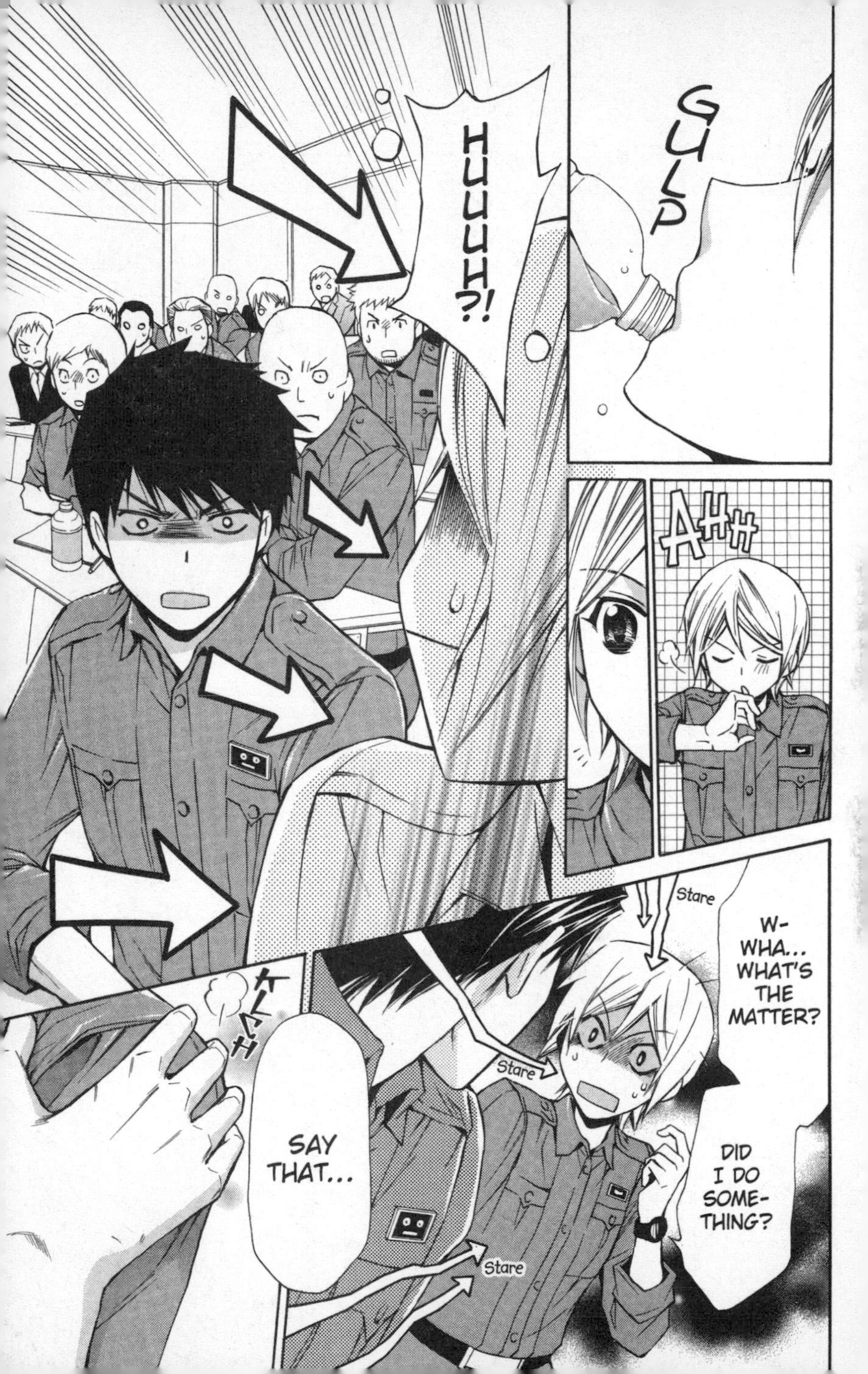
GULP
AHH
HUUUUH?!
Stare
W- WHA... WHAT'S THE MATTER?
DID I DO SOME- THING?
Stare
Stare
KLCH
SAY THAT...

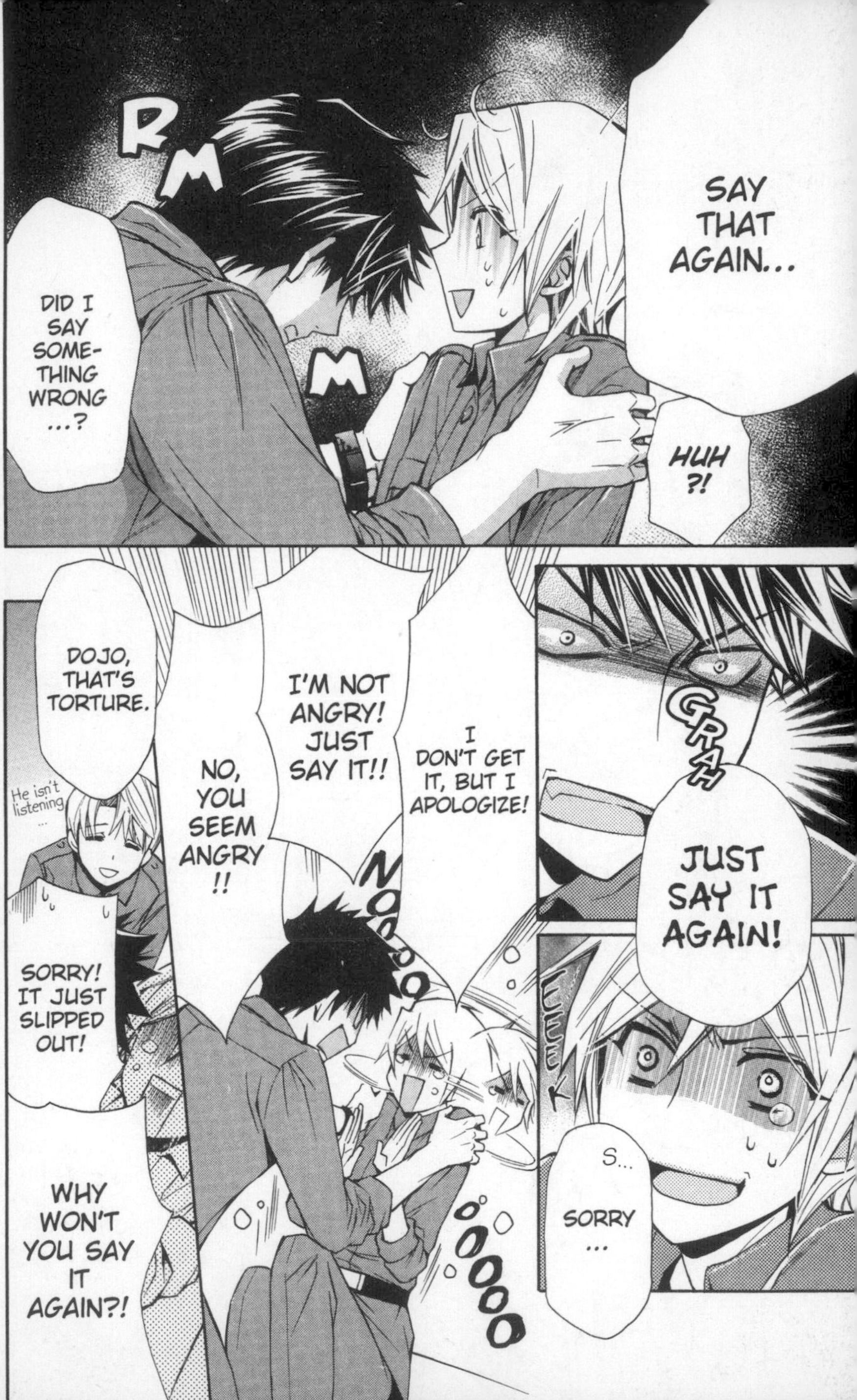
SAY THAT AGAIN...
RMM
HUH ?!
DID I SAY SOME-THING WRONG ...?
GRAH
JUST SAY IT AGAIN!
EEEK
S... SORRY ...
I DON'T GET IT, BUT I APOLOGIZE!
I'M NOT ANGRY! JUST SAY IT!!
NO, YOU SEEM ANGRY !!
DOJO, THAT'S TORTURE.
He isn't listening ...
NOOOO
SORRY! IT JUST SLIPPED OUT!
WHY WON'T YOU SAY IT AGAIN?!
OOOOOO

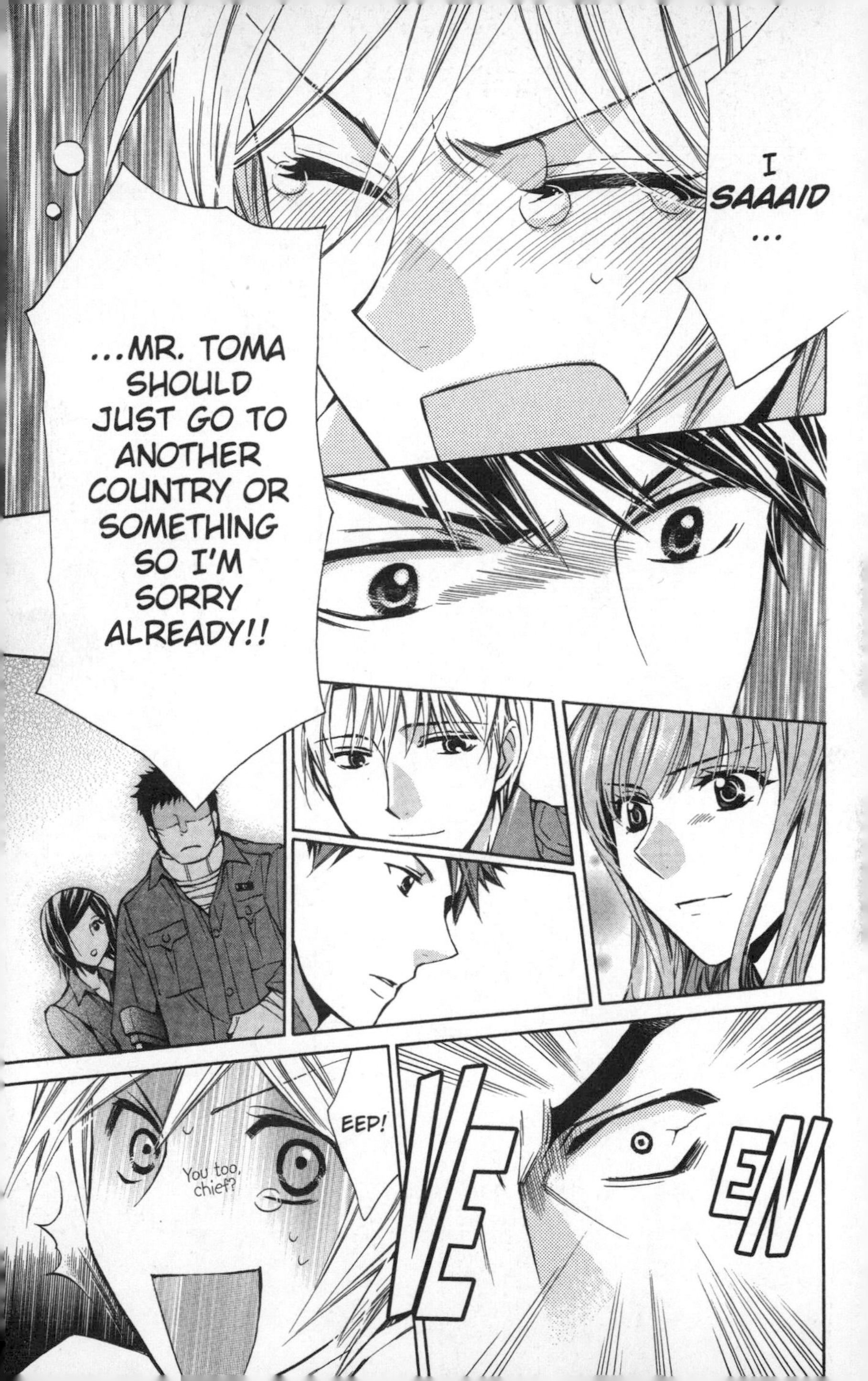
I SAAAID...
...MR. TOMA SHOULD JUST GO TO ANOTHER COUNTRY OR SOMETHING SO I'M SORRY ALREADY!!
VE
EN
EEP!
You too, chief?

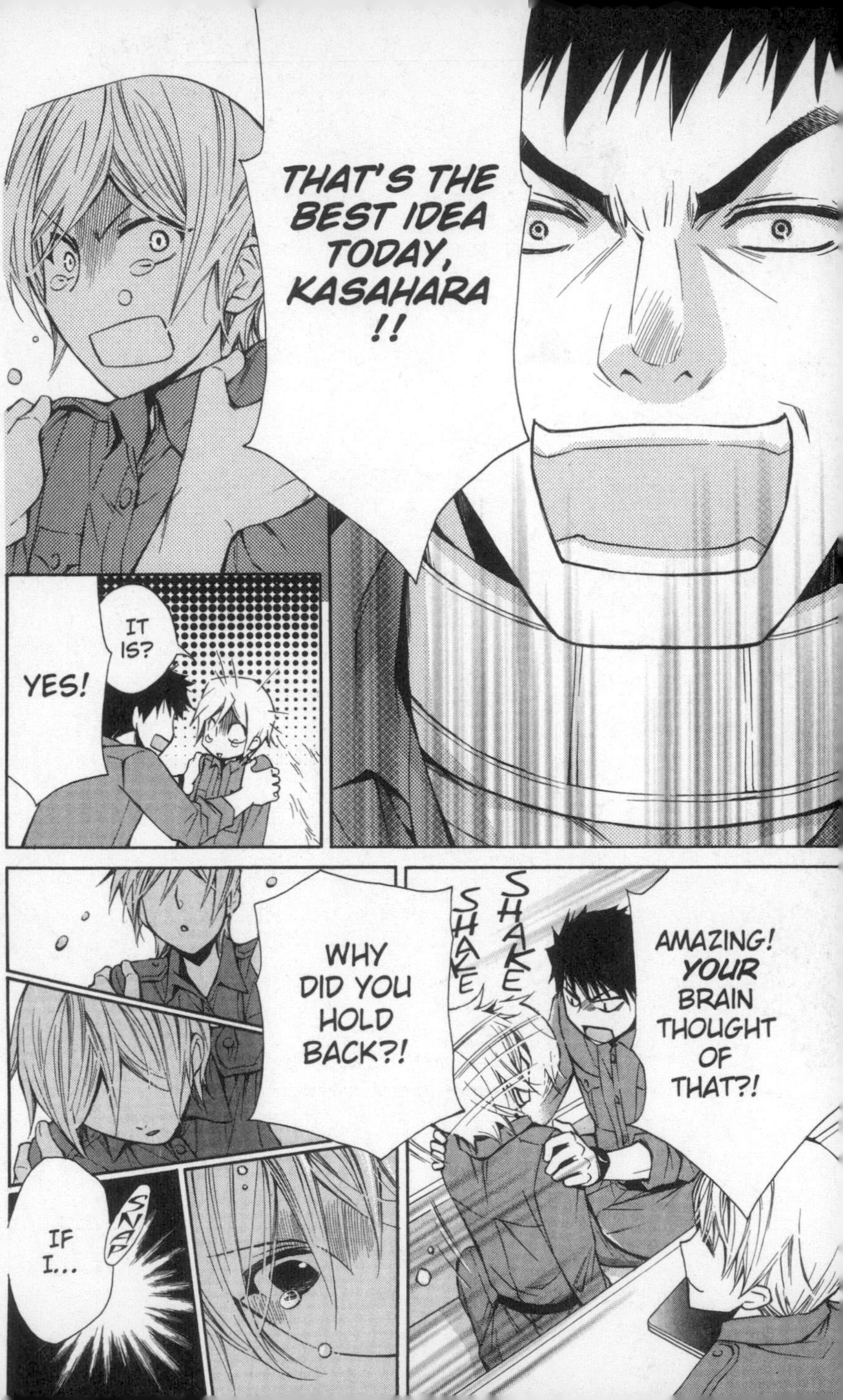
THAT'S THE BEST IDEA TODAY, KASAHARA!!
IT IS?
YES!
SHAKE SHAKE
AMAZING! YOUR BRAIN THOUGHT OF THAT?!
WHY DID YOU HOLD BACK?!
SNAP
IF I...

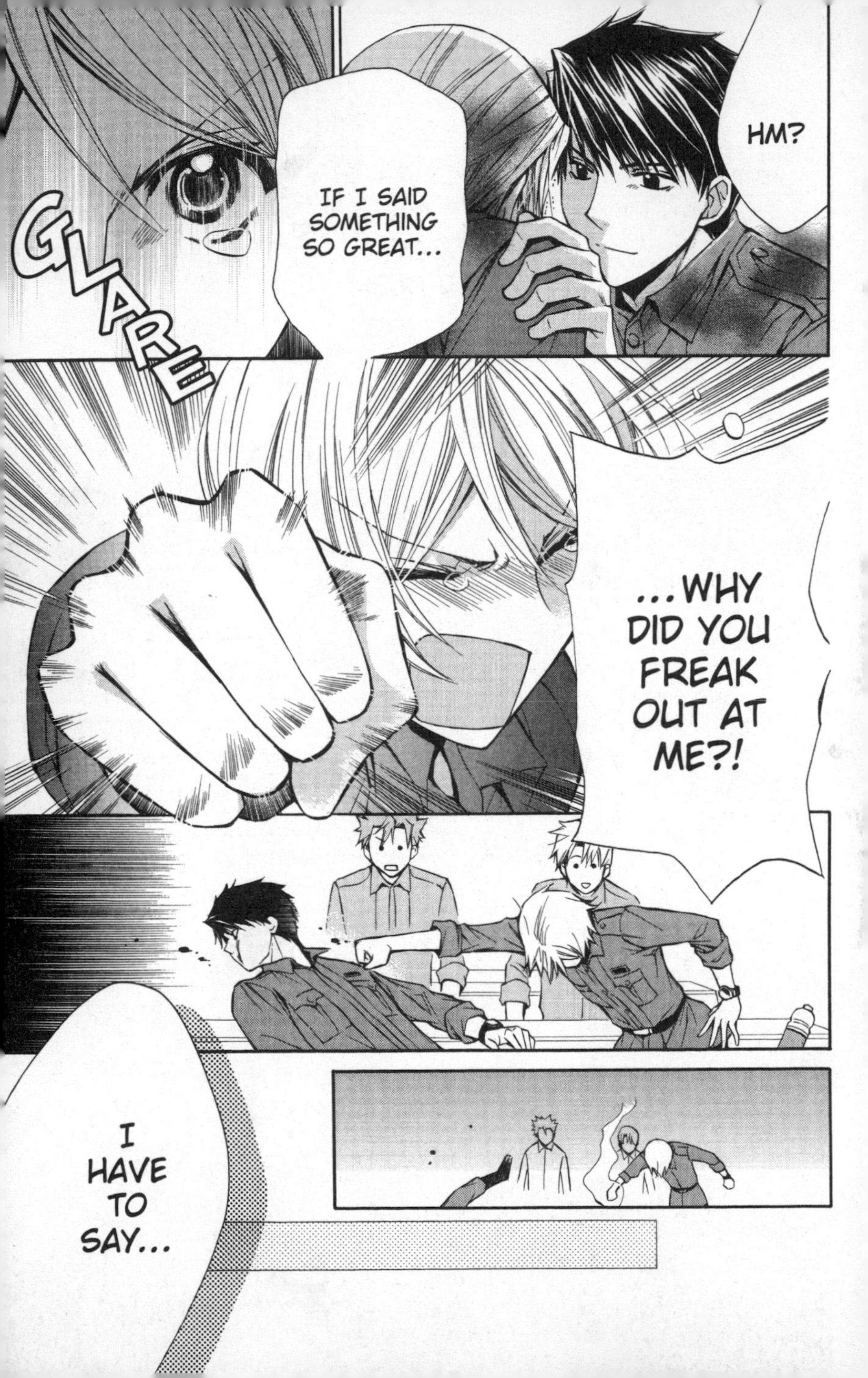
HM?
IF I SAID SOMETHING SO GREAT...
GLARE
...WHY DID YOU FREAK OUT AT ME?!
I HAVE TO SAY...

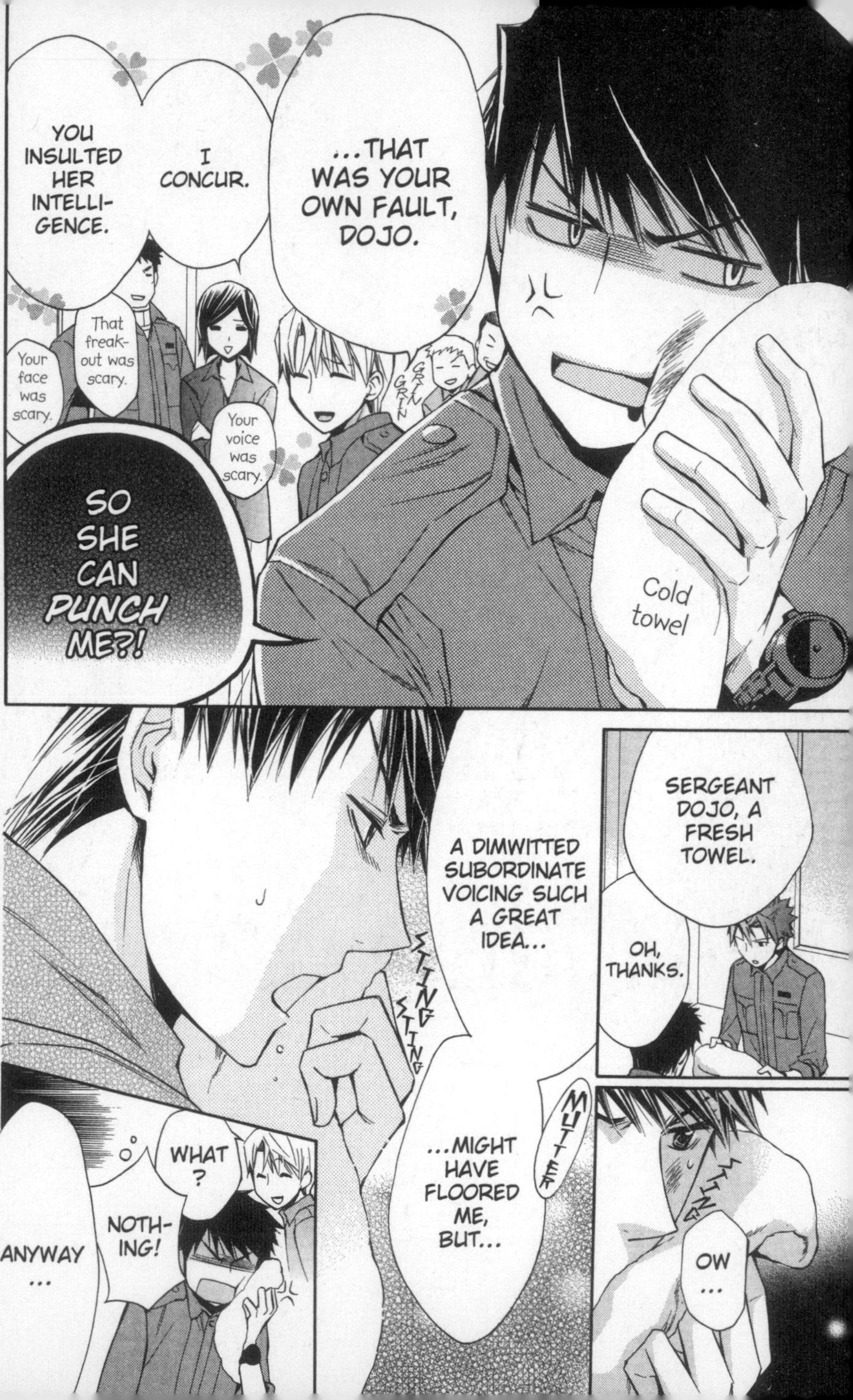
...THAT WAS YOUR OWN FAULT, DOJO.
I CONCUR.
YOU INSULTED HER INTELLIGENCE.
GRIN GRIN
That freak-out was scary.
Your face was scary.
Your voice was scary.
Cold towel
SO SHE CAN PUNCH ME?!
SERGEANT DOJO, A FRESH TOWEL.
OH, THANKS.
OW...
A DIMWITTED SUBORDINATE VOICING SUCH A GREAT IDEA...
STING STING
MUTTER
...MIGHT HAVE FLOORED ME, BUT...
WHAT?
NOTH-ING!
ANYWAY...

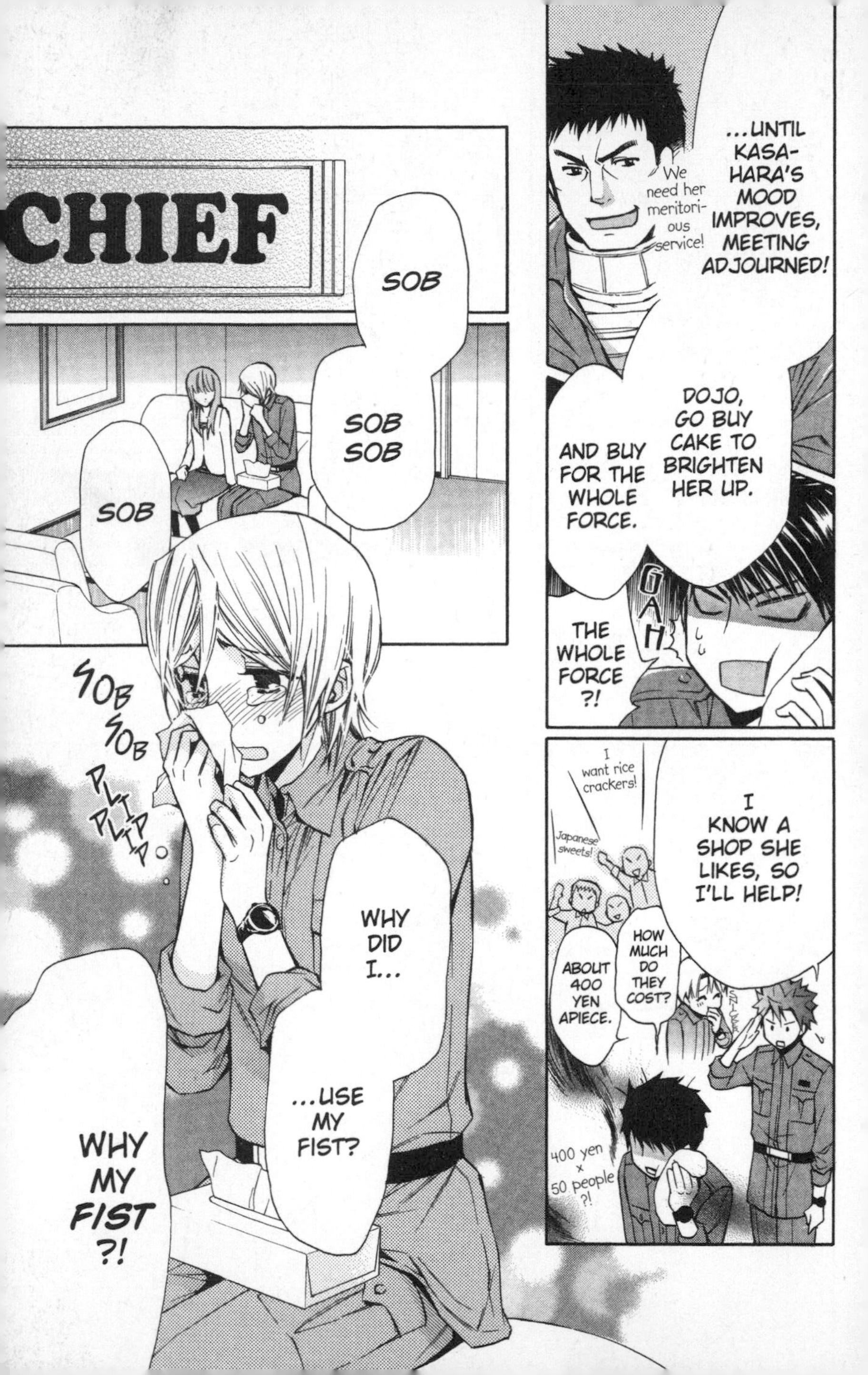
...UNTIL KASAHARA'S MOOD IMPROVES, MEETING ADJOURNED!
We need her meritorious service!
DOJO, GO BUY CAKE TO BRIGHTEN HER UP.
AND BUY FOR THE WHOLE FORCE.
GAAH
THE WHOLE FORCE?!
I KNOW A SHOP SHE LIKES, SO I'LL HELP!
I want rice crackers!
Japanese sweets!
HOW MUCH DO THEY COST?
ABOUT 400 YEN APIECE.
SNICKER
400 yen x 50 people?!
CHIEF
SOB
SOB SOB
SOB
SOB SOB
PLIP PLIP
WHY DID I...
...USE MY FIST?
WHY MY FIST?!

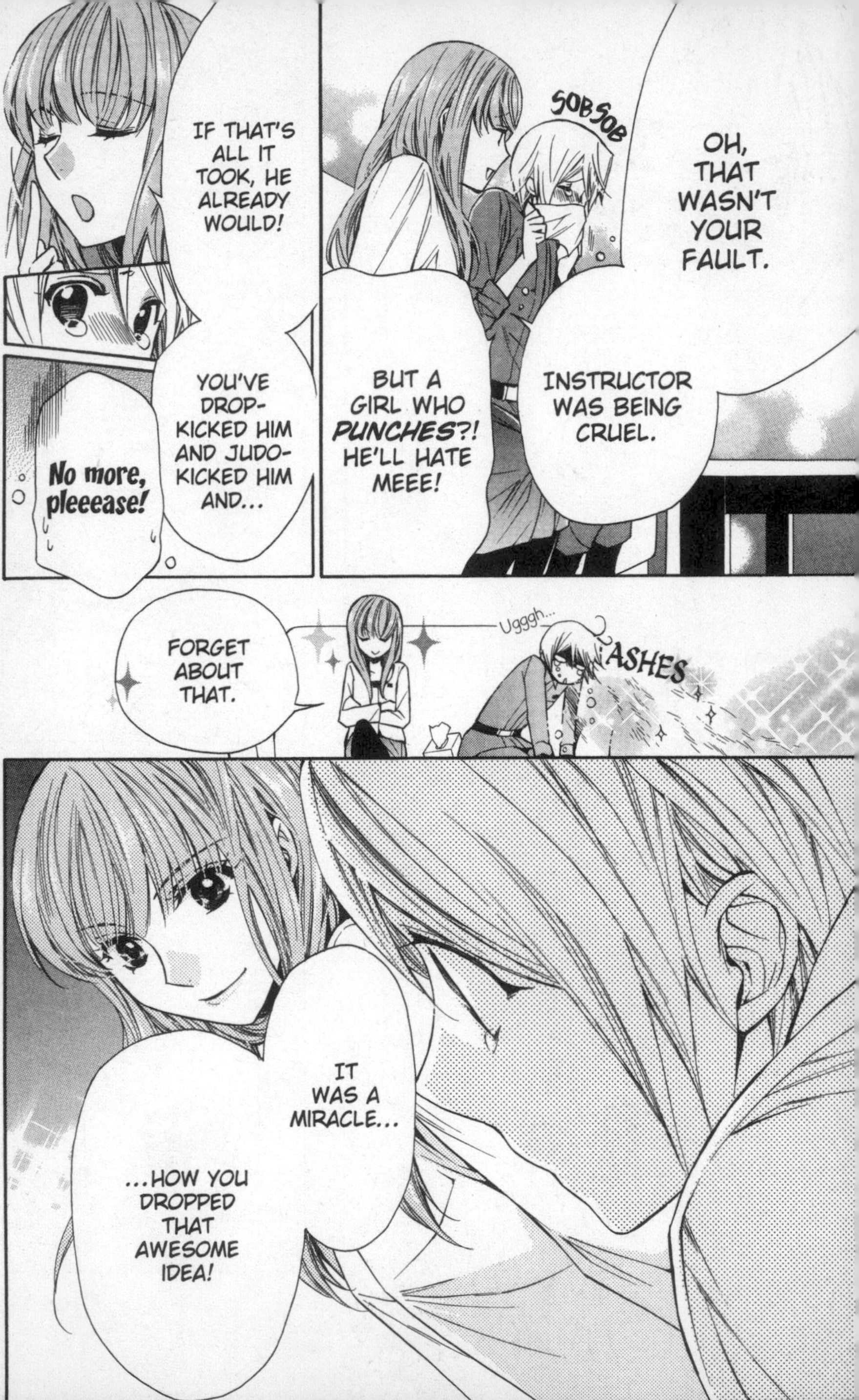
OH, THAT WASN'T YOUR FAULT.
SOB SOB
INSTRUCTOR WAS BEING CRUEL.
BUT A GIRL WHO *PUNCHES*?! HE'LL HATE MEEE!
IF THAT'S ALL IT TOOK, HE ALREADY WOULD!
YOU'VE DROP-KICKED HIM AND JUDO-KICKED HIM AND...
No more, pleeease!
ASHES
Ugggh...
FORGET ABOUT THAT.
IT WAS A MIRACLE...
...HOW YOU DROPPED THAT AWESOME IDEA!

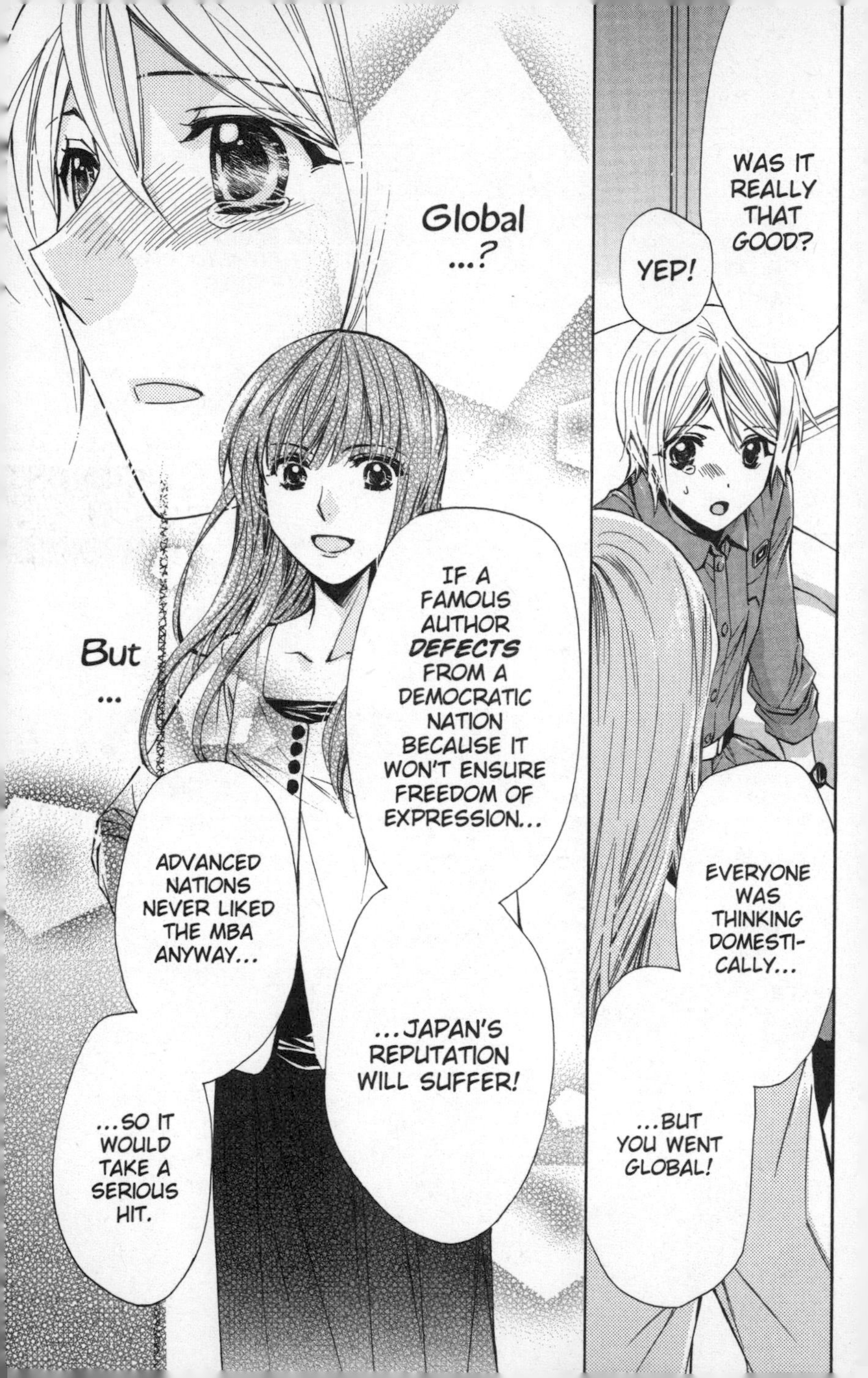
WAS IT REALLY THAT GOOD?
YEP!
EVERYONE WAS THINKING DOMESTI-CALLY...
...BUT YOU WENT GLOBAL!
Global ...?
IF A FAMOUS AUTHOR **DEFECTS** FROM A DEMOCRATIC NATION BECAUSE IT WON'T ENSURE FREEDOM OF EXPRESSION...
...JAPAN'S REPUTATION WILL SUFFER!
But ...
ADVANCED NATIONS NEVER LIKED THE MBA ANYWAY...
...SO IT WOULD TAKE A SERIOUS HIT.

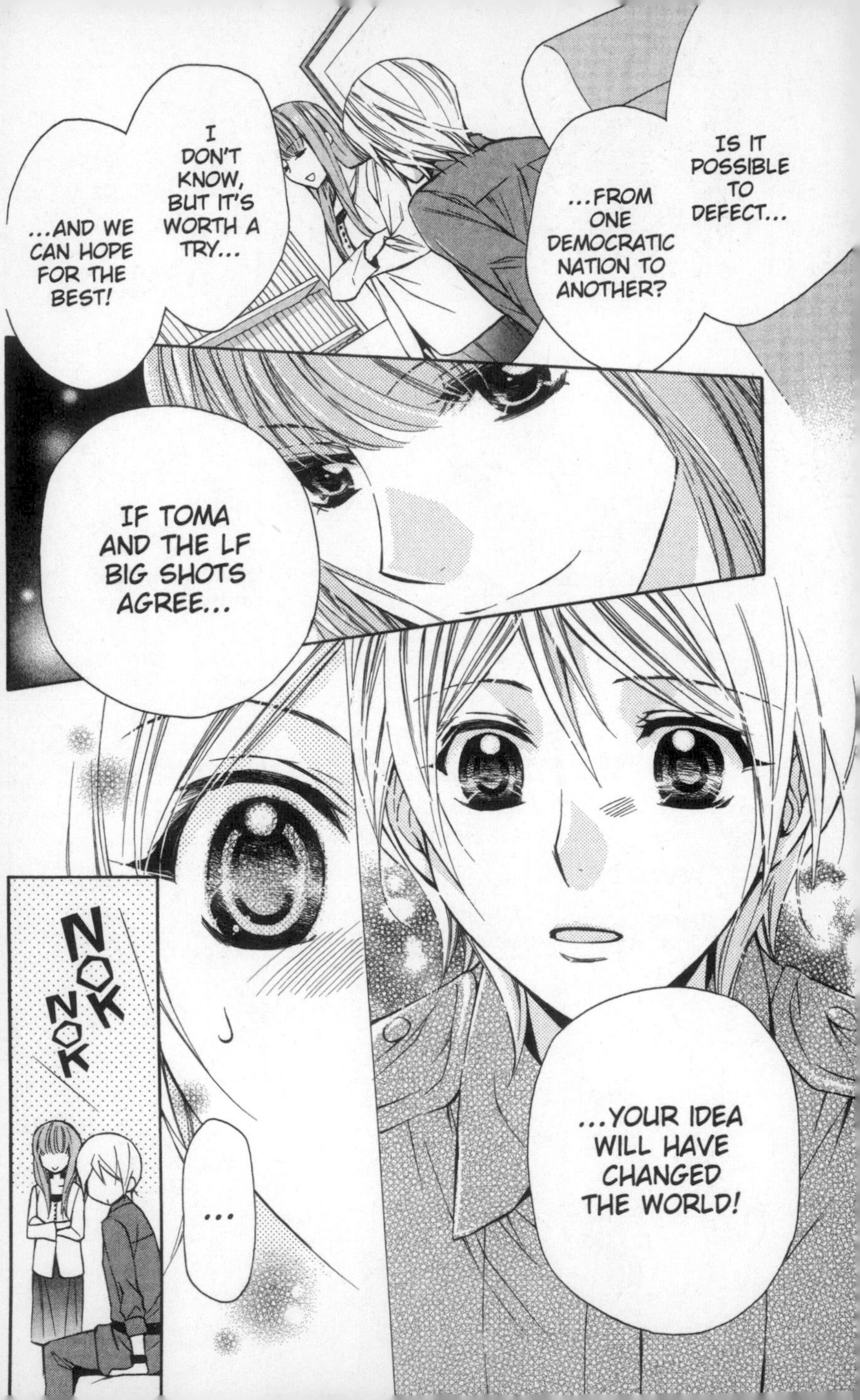
IS IT POSSIBLE TO DEFECT...
...FROM ONE DEMOCRATIC NATION TO ANOTHER?
I DON'T KNOW, BUT IT'S WORTH A TRY...
...AND WE CAN HOPE FOR THE BEST!
IF TOMA AND THE LF BIG SHOTS AGREE...
...YOUR IDEA WILL HAVE CHANGED THE WORLD!
...
NOK NOK

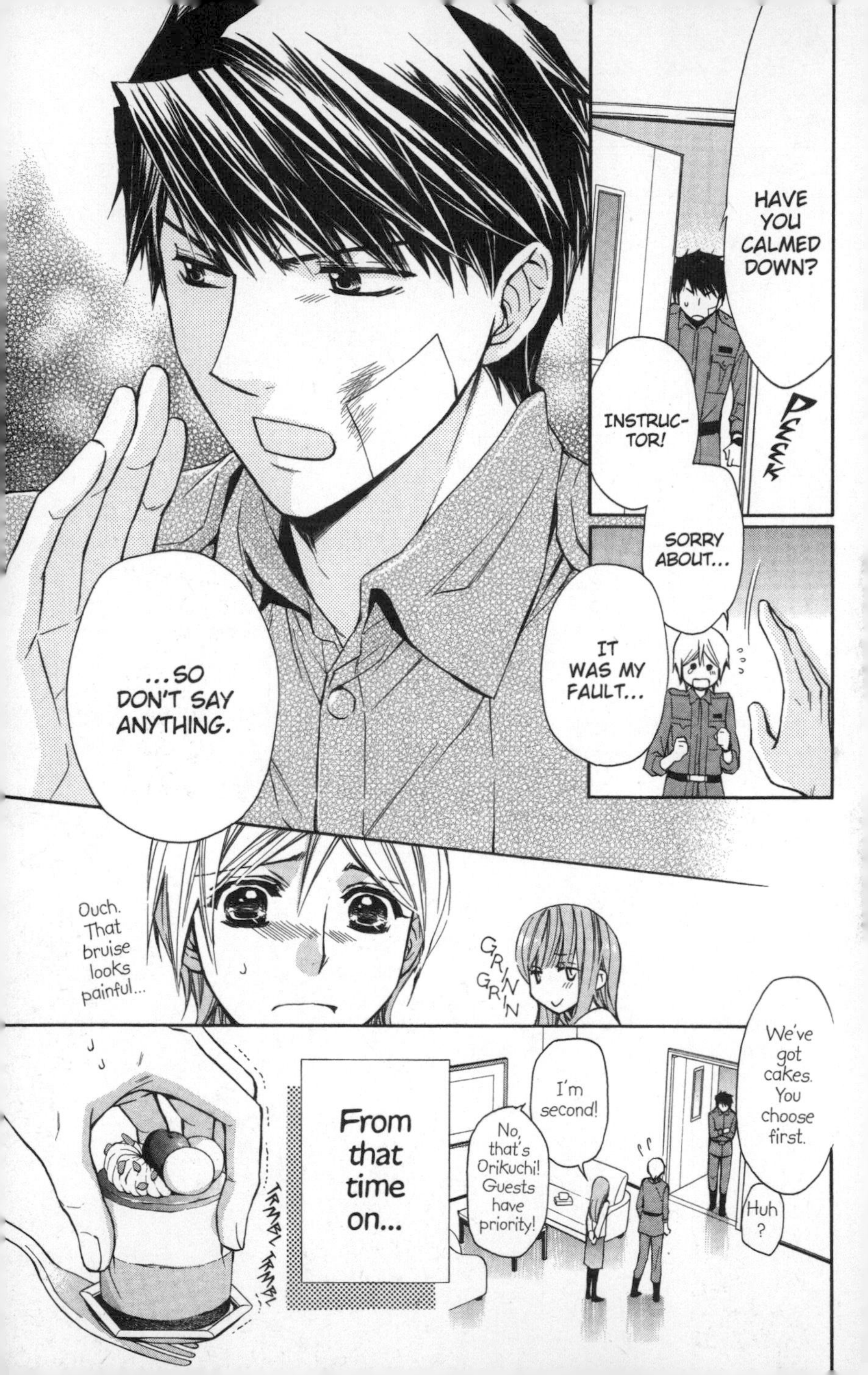
HAVE YOU CALMED DOWN?
INSTRUC-TOR!
SORRY ABOUT...
IT WAS MY FAULT...
...SO DON'T SAY ANYTHING.
GRIN GRIN
Ouch. That bruise looks painful...
We've got cakes. You choose first.
Huh?
I'm second!
No, that's Orikuchi! Guests have priority!
From that time on...
TREMBL TREMBL

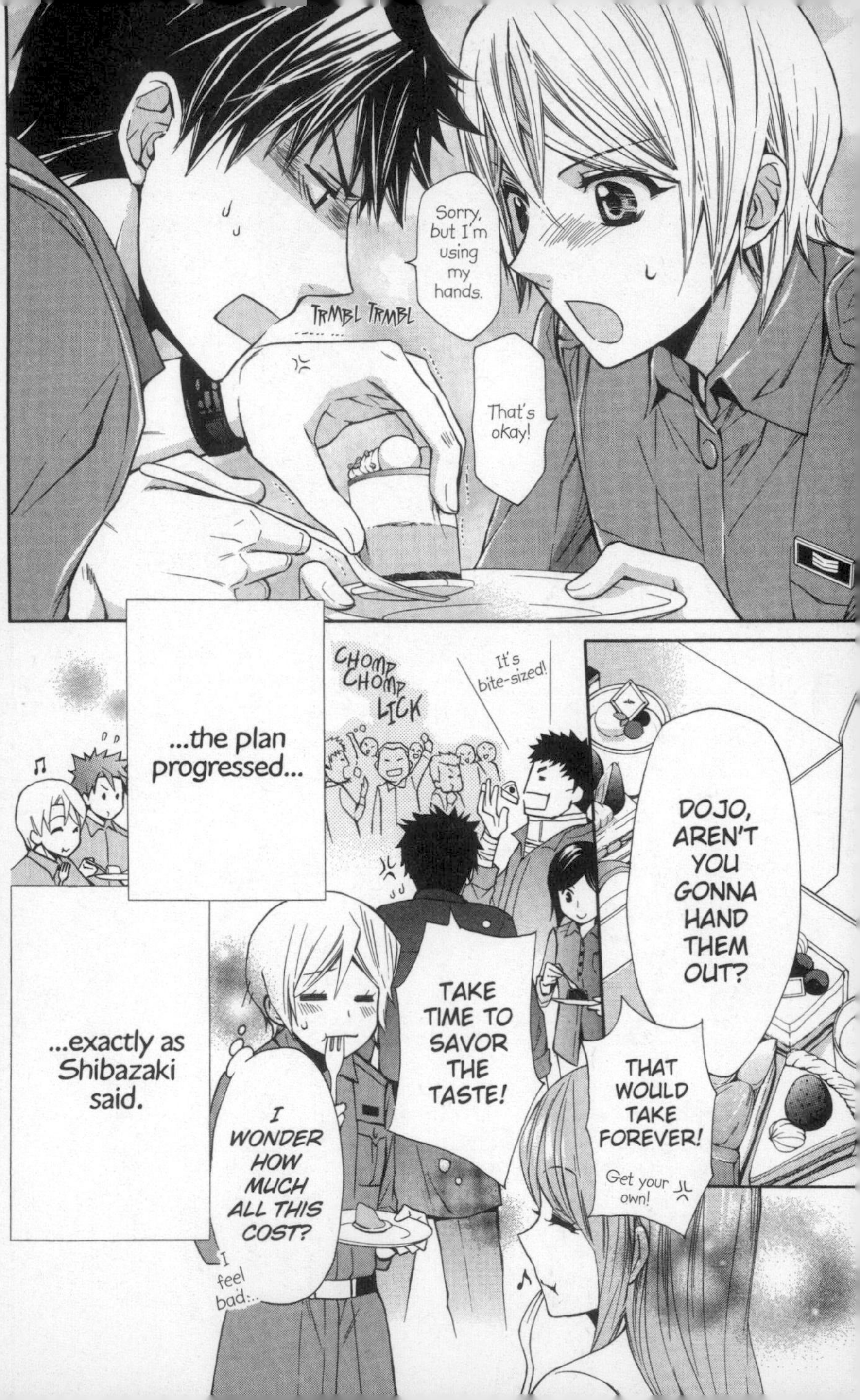

Sorry, but I'm using my hands.
TRMBL TRMBL
That's okay!
DOJO, AREN'T YOU GONNA HAND THEM OUT?
It's bite-sized!
CHOMP CHOMP LICK
...the plan progressed...
THAT WOULD TAKE FOREVER!
Get your own!
TAKE TIME TO SAVOR THE TASTE!
I WONDER HOW MUCH ALL THIS COST?
I feel bad...
...exactly as Shibazaki said.

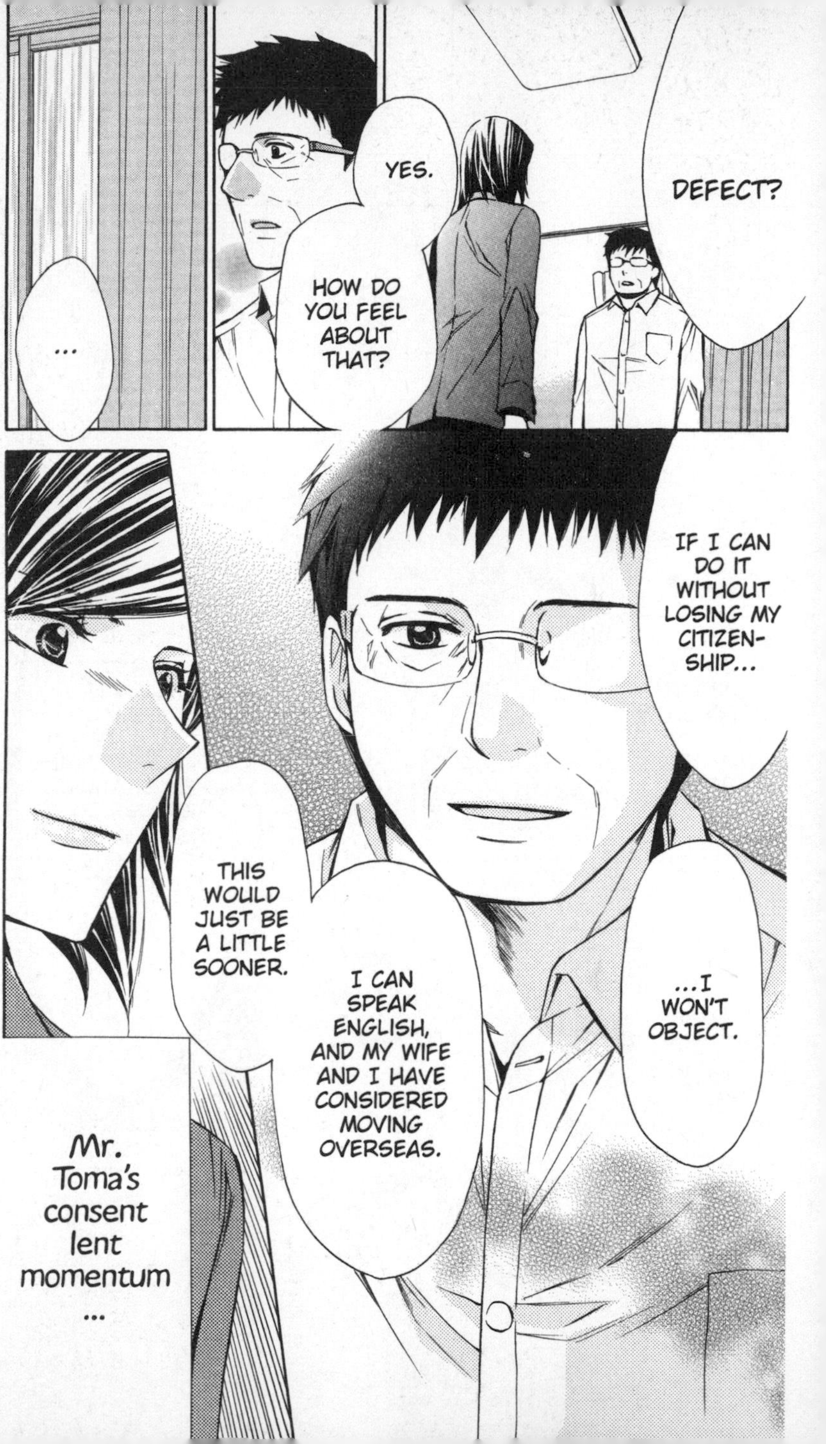
DEFECT?
YES.
HOW DO YOU FEEL ABOUT THAT?
...
IF I CAN DO IT WITHOUT LOSING MY CITIZEN-SHIP...
...I WON'T OBJECT.
I CAN SPEAK ENGLISH, AND MY WIFE AND I HAVE CONSIDERED MOVING OVERSEAS.
THIS WOULD JUST BE A LITTLE SOONER.
Mr. Toma's consent lent momentum ...

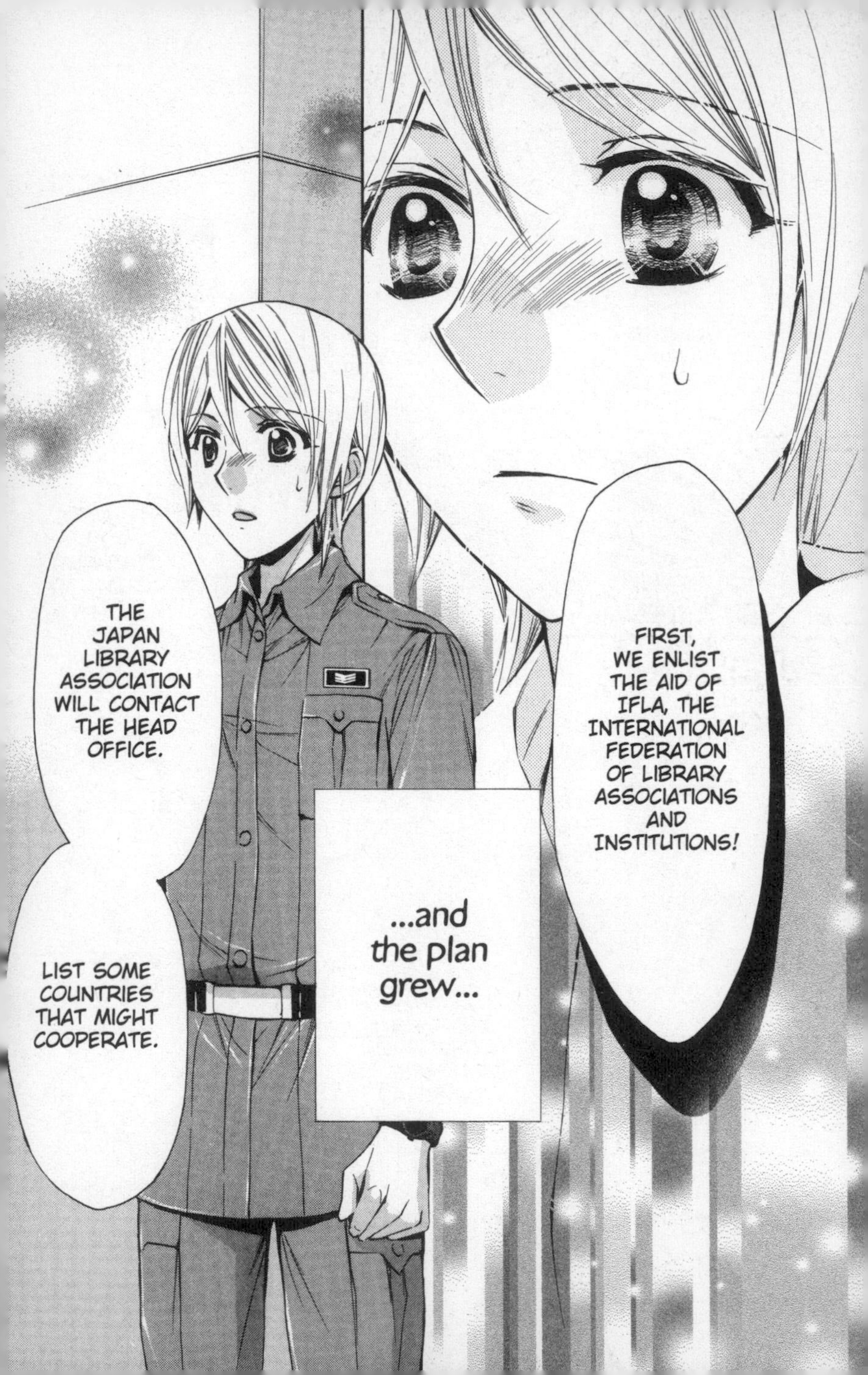
FIRST, WE ENLIST THE AID OF IFLA, THE INTERNATIONAL FEDERATION OF LIBRARY ASSOCIATIONS AND INSTITUTIONS!
THE JAPAN LIBRARY ASSOCIATION WILL CONTACT THE HEAD OFFICE.
...and the plan grew...
LIST SOME COUNTRIES THAT MIGHT COOPERATE.

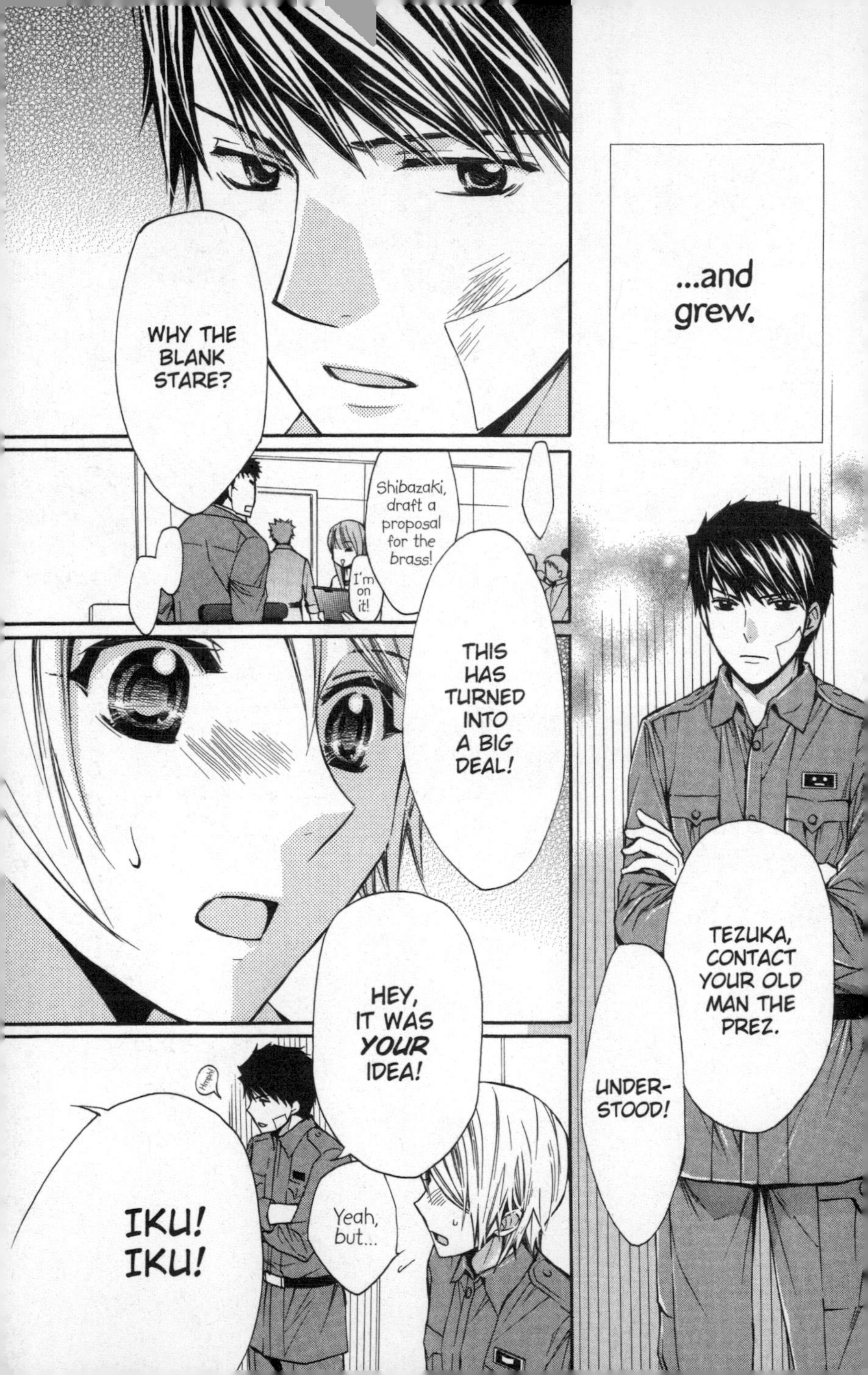

...and grew.
TEZUKA, CONTACT YOUR OLD MAN THE PREZ.
UNDER-STOOD!
WHY THE BLANK STARE?
Shibazaki, draft a proposal for the brass!
I'm on it!
THIS HAS TURNED INTO A BIG DEAL!
HEY, IT WAS *YOUR* IDEA!
Hmph!
Yeah, but...
IKU! IKU!

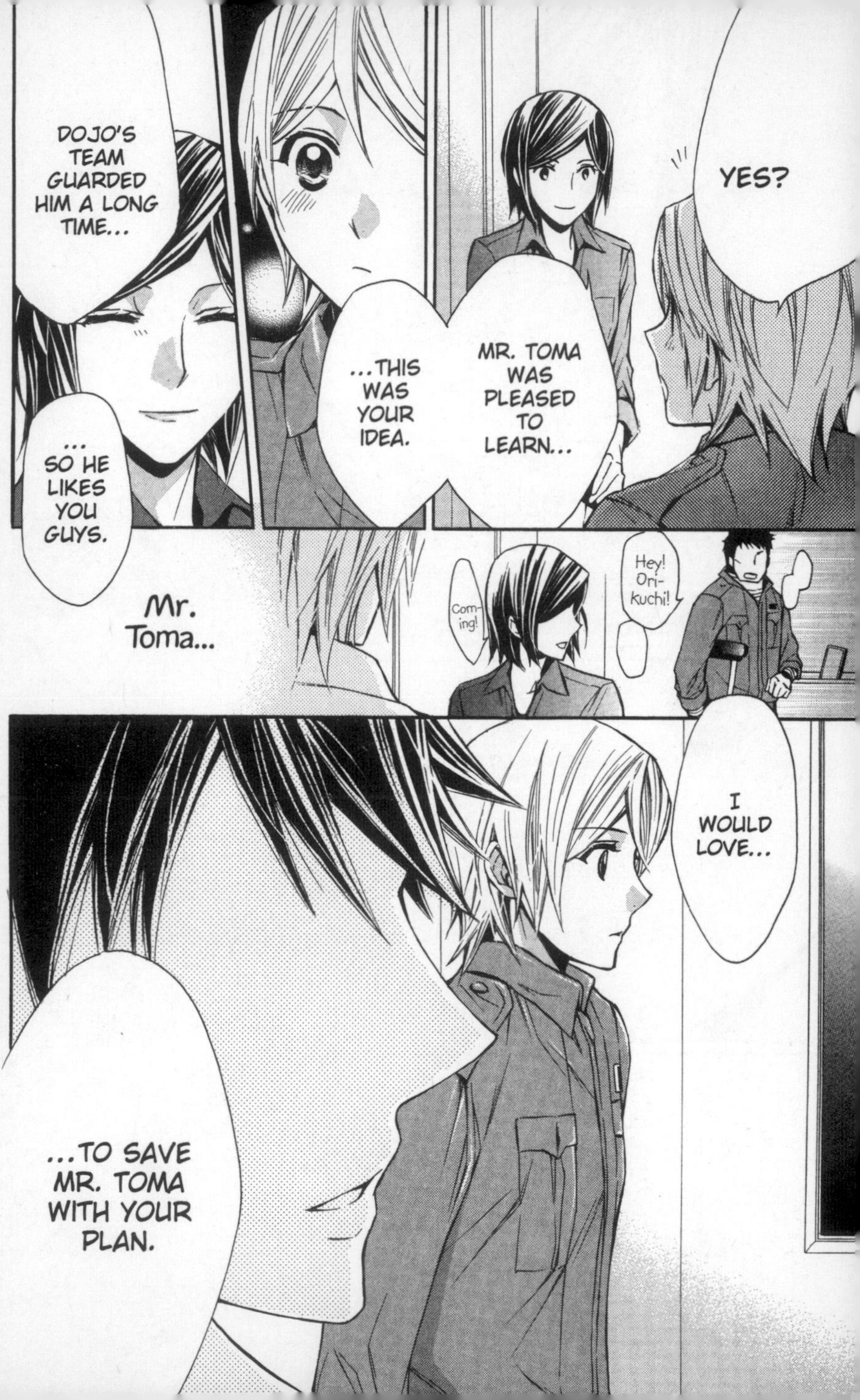
YES?
MR. TOMA WAS PLEASED TO LEARN...
...THIS WAS YOUR IDEA.
DOJO'S TEAM GUARDED HIM A LONG TIME...
... SO HE LIKES YOU GUYS.
Hey! Ori-kuchi!
Com-ing!
Mr. Toma...
I WOULD LOVE...
...TO SAVE MR. TOMA WITH YOUR PLAN.

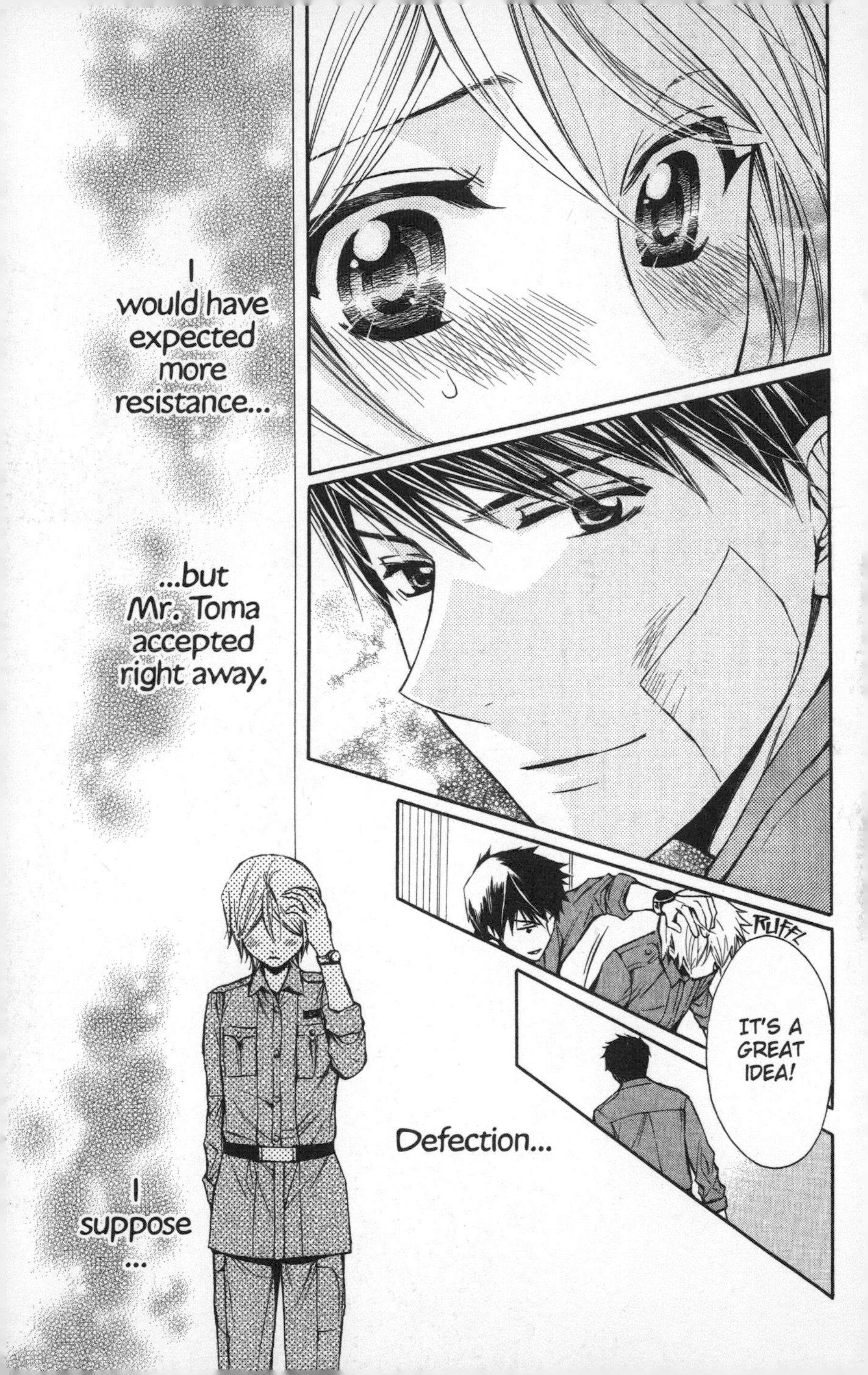

RUFFL
IT'S A GREAT IDEA!
Defection...
I would have expected more resistance...
...but Mr. Toma accepted right away.
I suppose ...

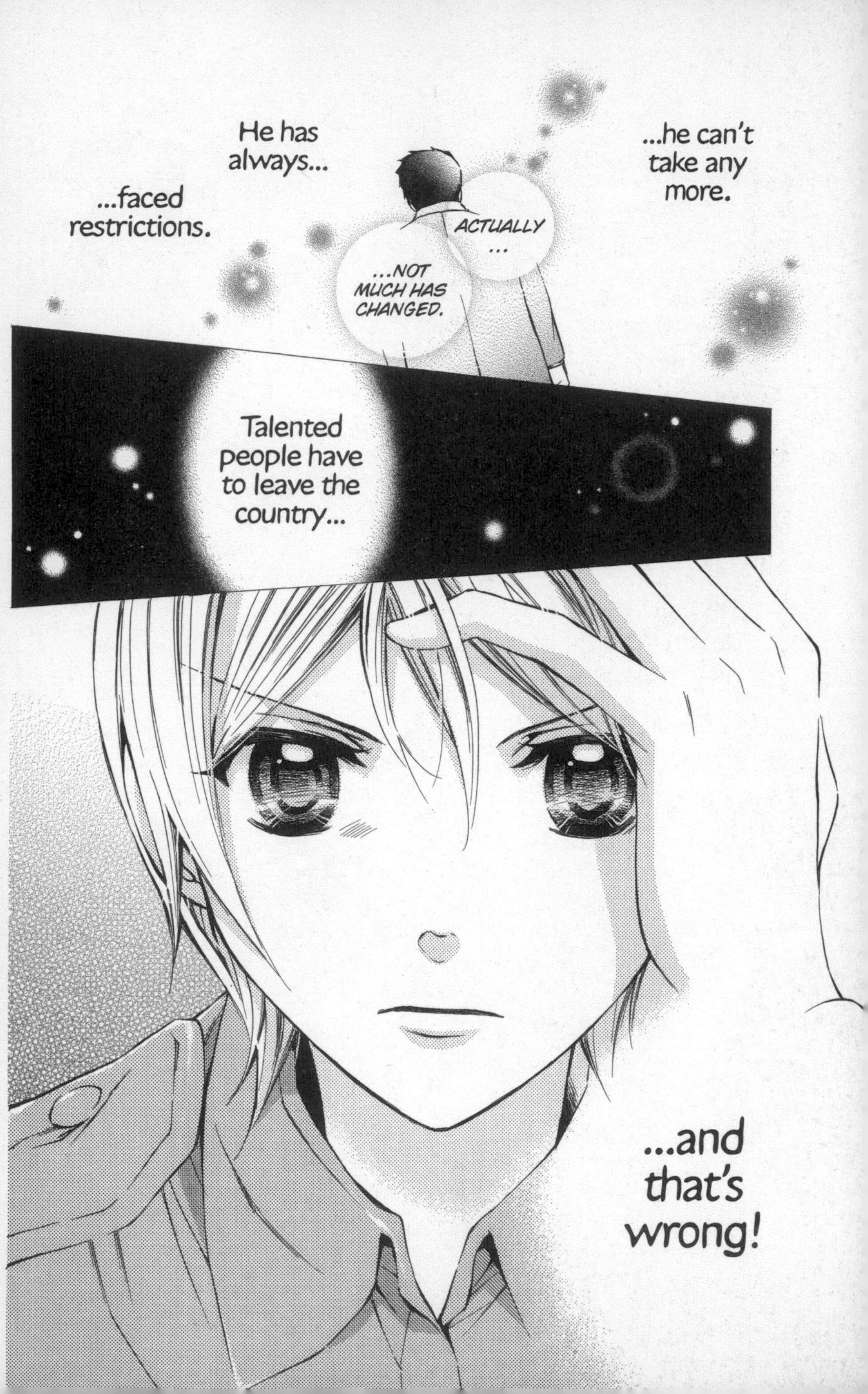
...he can't take any more.
He has always...
...faced restrictions.
ACTUALLY...
...NOT MUCH HAS CHANGED.
Talented people have to leave the country...
...and that's wrong!

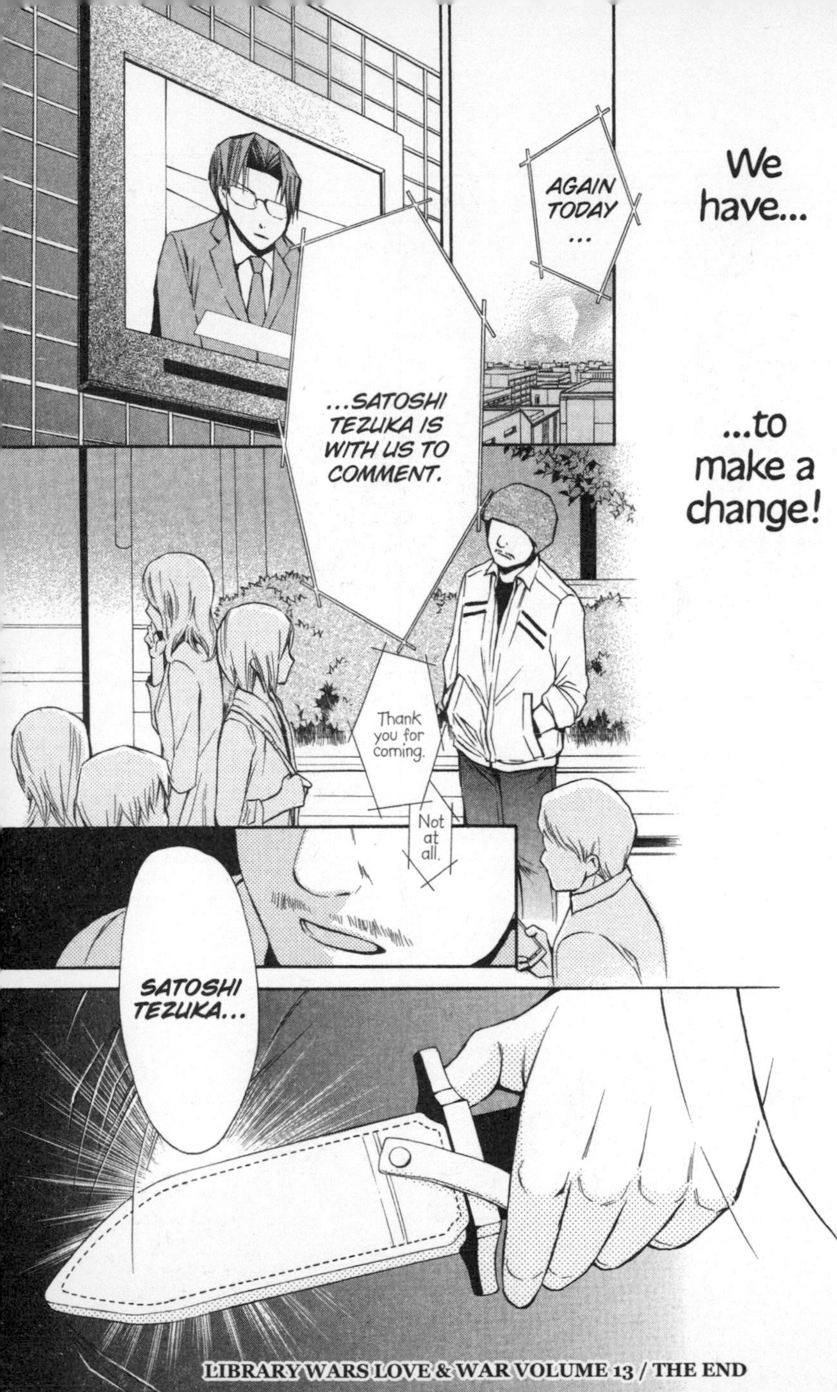
We have...
AGAIN TODAY ...
...SATOSHI TEZUKA IS WITH US TO COMMENT.
...to make a change!
Thank you for coming.
Not at all.
SATOSHI TEZUKA...

LIBRARY WARS LOVE & WAR VOLUME 13 / THE END

Secret Admirer Part 12

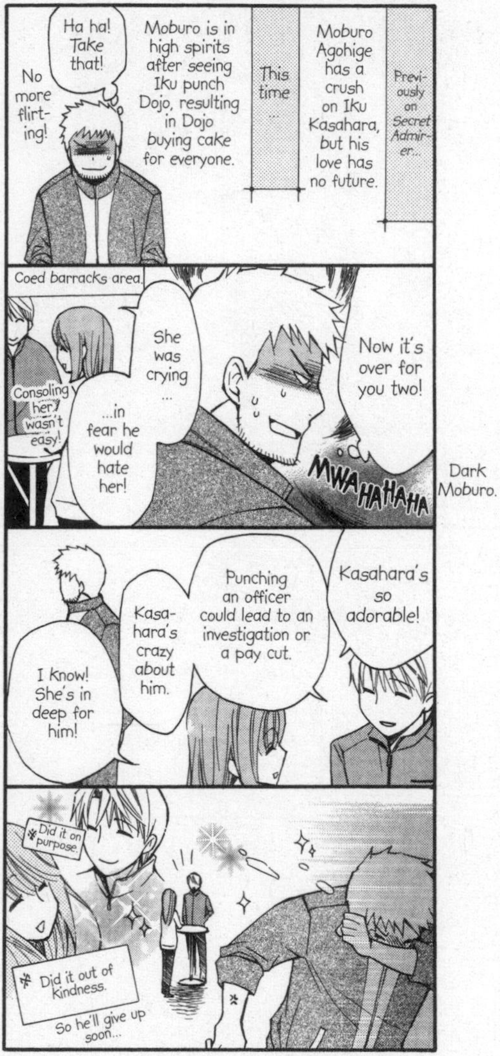
Previously on Secret Admirer...
Moburo Agohige has a crush on Iku Kasahara, but his love has no future.
This time...
Moburo is in high spirits after seeing Iku punch Dojo, resulting in Dojo buying cake for everyone.
Ha ha! Take that!
No more flirting!
Coed barracks area.
Now it's over for you two!
MWAHAHAHA
Dark Moburo.
She was crying...
...in fear he would hate her!
Consoling her wasn't easy!
Kasahara's so adorable!
Punching an officer could lead to an investigation or a pay cut.
Kasahara's crazy about him.
I know! She's in deep for him!
※Did it on purpose.
※Did it out of kindness.
So he'll give up soon...

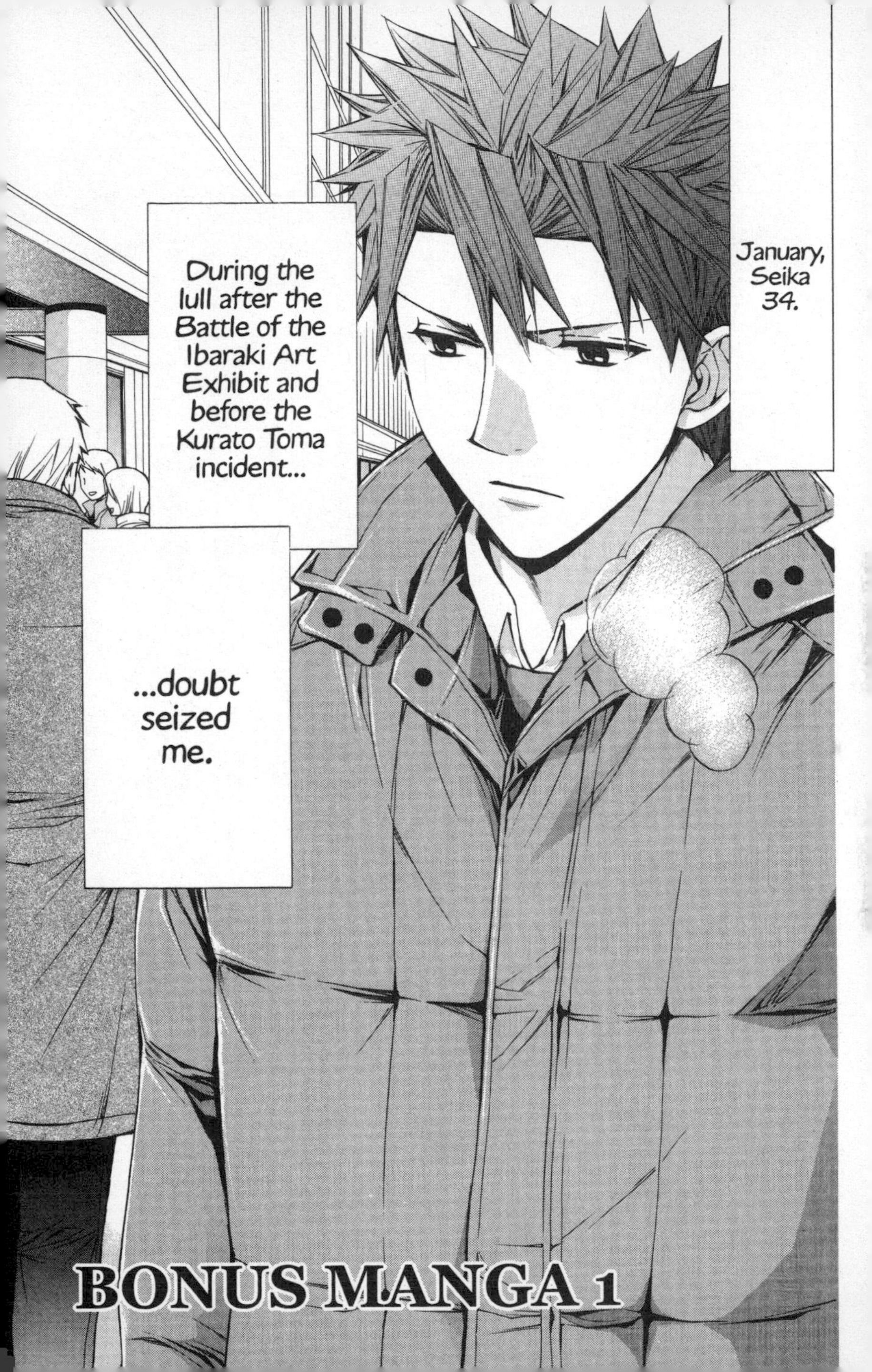
January, Seika 34.
During the lull after the Battle of the Ibaraki Art Exhibit and before the Kurato Toma incident...
...doubt seized me.
BONUS MANGA 1

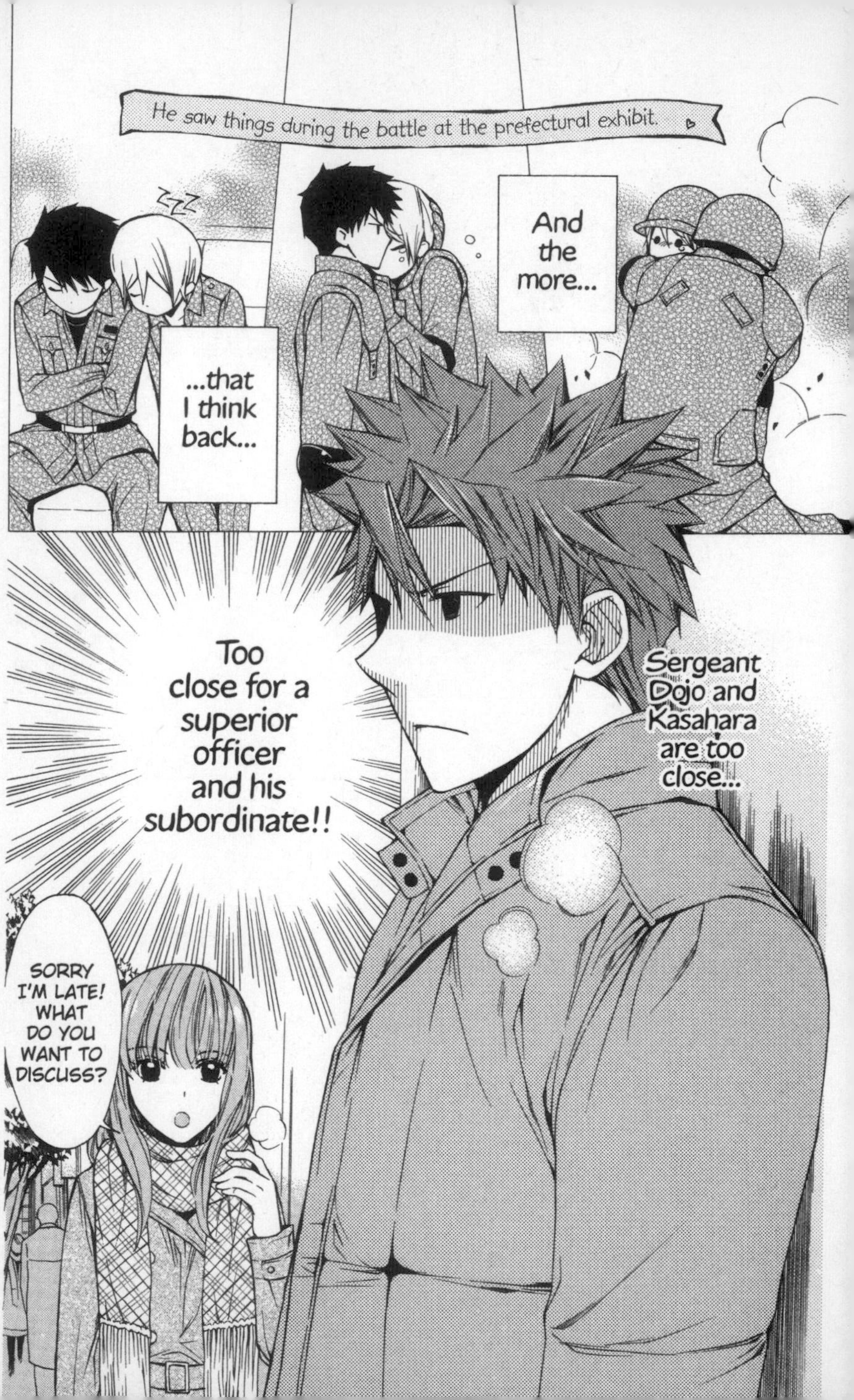
He saw things during the battle at the prefectural exhibit.
And the more...
...that I think back...
Sergeant Dojo and Kasahara are too close...
Too close for a superior officer and his subordinate!!
SORRY I'M LATE! WHAT DO YOU WANT TO DISCUSS?

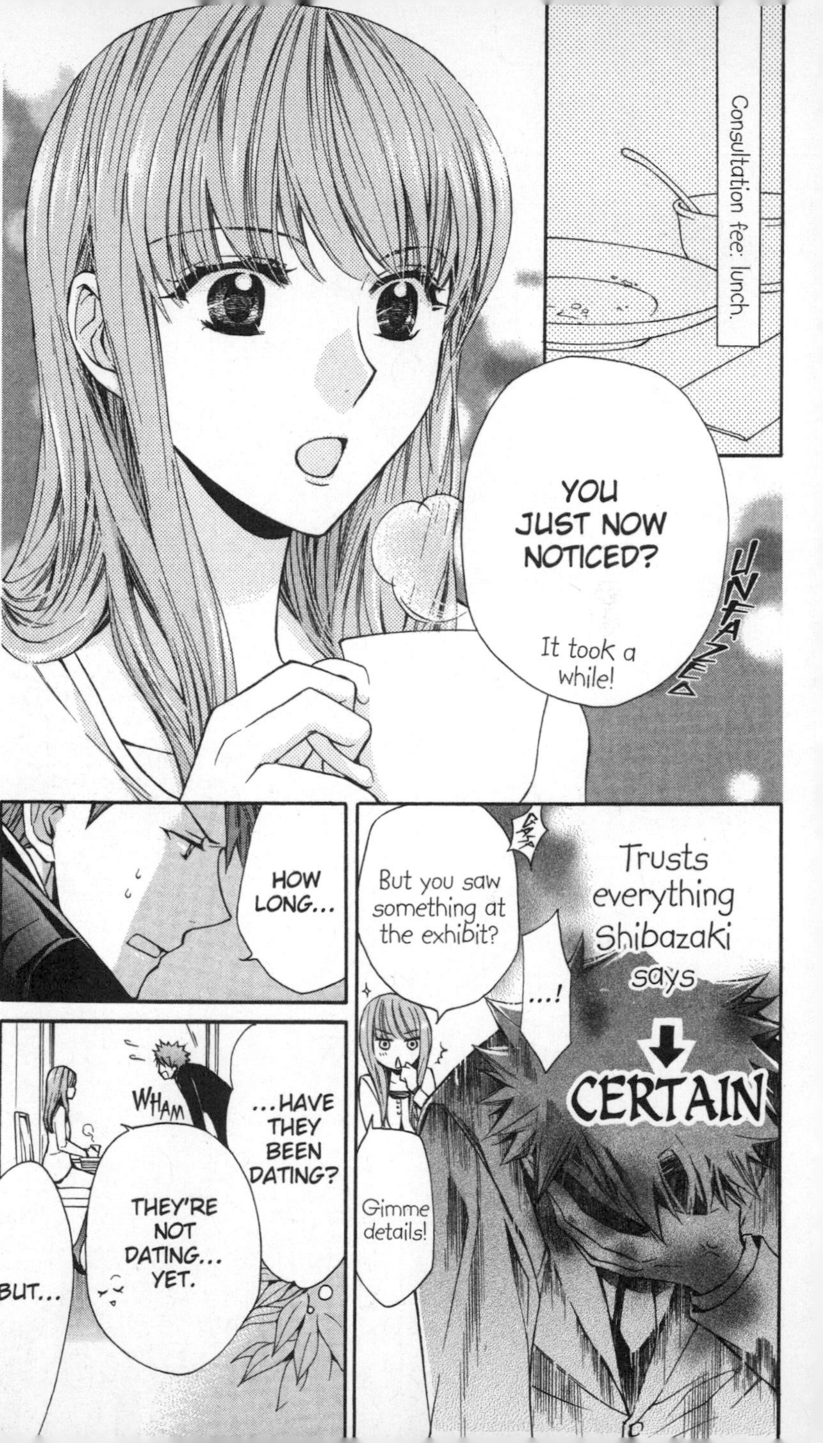
Consultation fee: lunch.
YOU JUST NOW NOTICED?
It took a while!
UNFAZED
Trusts everything Shibazaki says
CERTAIN
But you saw something at the exhibit?
...!
Gimme details!
HOW LONG...
...HAVE THEY BEEN DATING?
WHAM
THEY'RE NOT DATING... YET.
BUT...

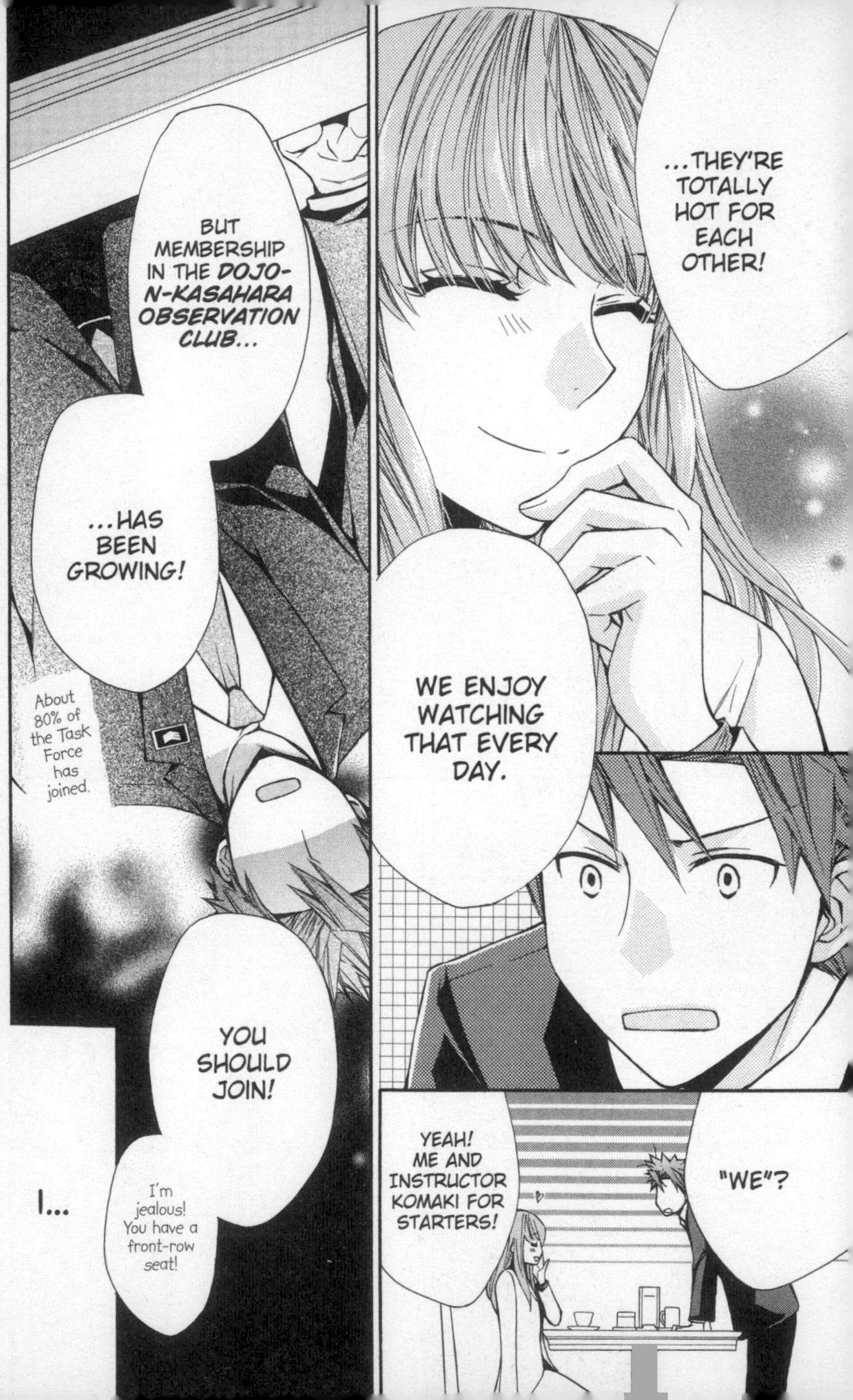
...THEY'RE TOTALLY HOT FOR EACH OTHER!
WE ENJOY WATCHING THAT EVERY DAY.
"WE"?
YEAH! ME AND INSTRUCTOR KOMAKI FOR STARTERS!
BUT MEMBERSHIP IN THE DOJO-N-KASAHARA OBSERVATION CLUB...
...HAS BEEN GROWING!
About 80% of the Task Force has joined.
YOU SHOULD JOIN!
I'm jealous! You have a front-row seat!
I...

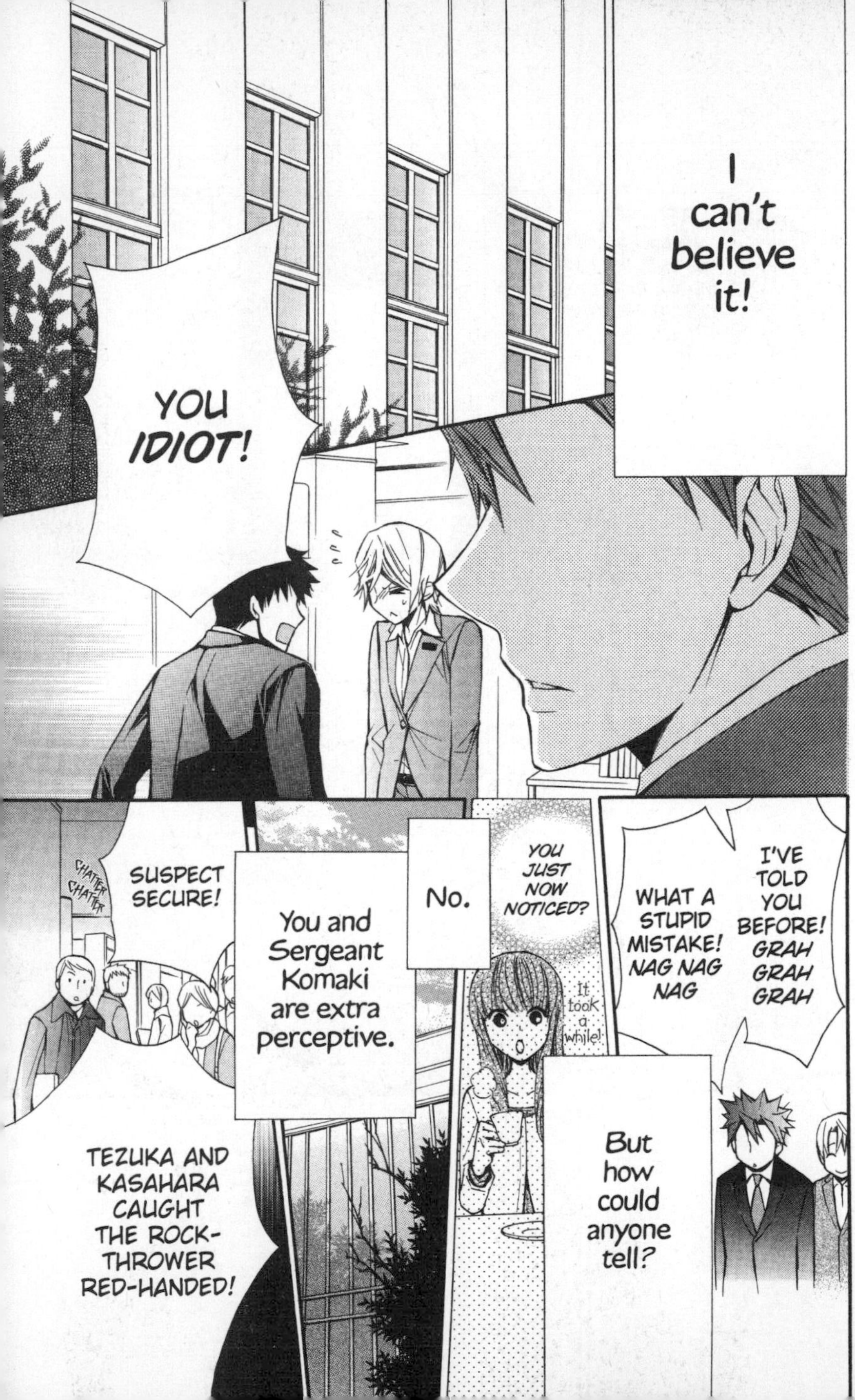
I can't believe it!
YOU IDIOT!
I'VE TOLD YOU BEFORE! GRAH GRAH GRAH
WHAT A STUPID MISTAKE! NAG NAG NAG
But how could anyone tell?
YOU JUST NOW NOTICED?
It took a while!
No.
You and Sergeant Komaki are extra perceptive.
SUSPECT SECURE!
CHATTER CHATTER
TEZUKA AND KASAHARA CAUGHT THE ROCK-THROWER RED-HANDED!

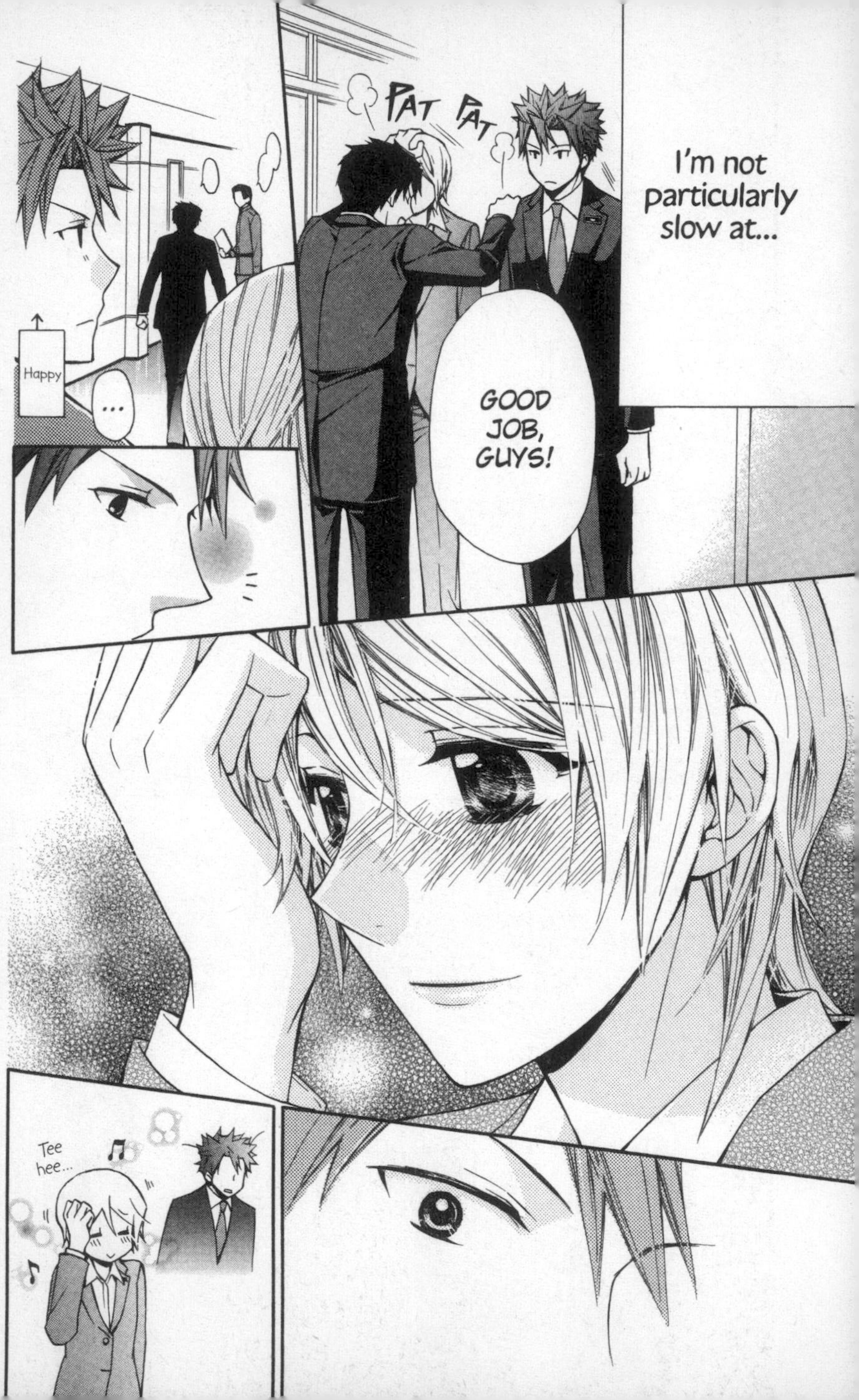
I'm not particularly slow at...
PAT PAT
GOOD JOB, GUYS!
Happy
...
Tee hee...

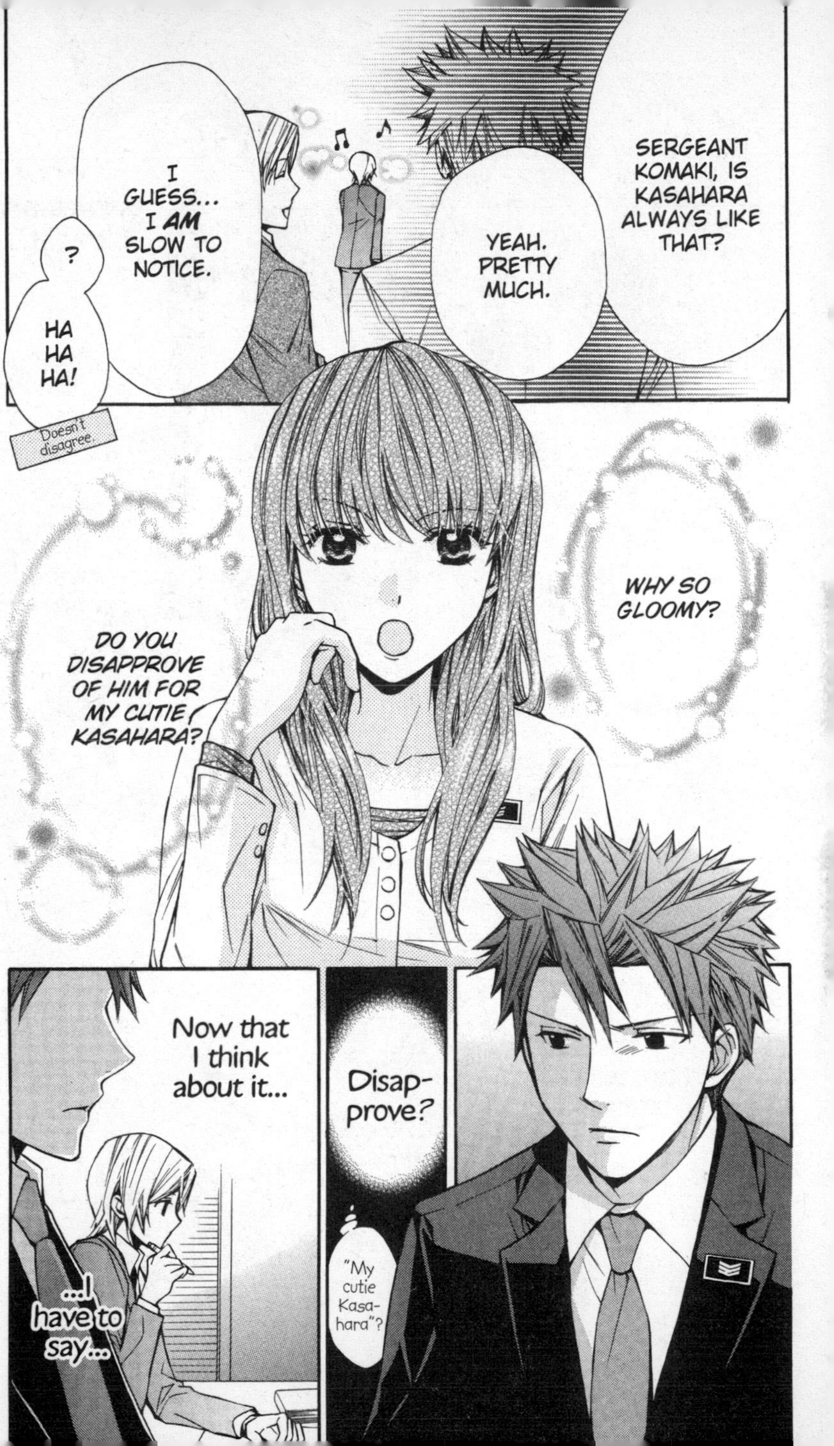
SERGEANT KOMAKI, IS KASAHARA ALWAYS LIKE THAT?
YEAH. PRETTY MUCH.
I GUESS... I *AM* SLOW TO NOTICE.
?
HA HA HA!
Doesn't disagree
WHY SO GLOOMY?
DO YOU DISAPPROVE OF HIM FOR MY CUTIE KASAHARA?
Disap-prove?
"My cutie Kasa-hara"?
Now that I think about it...
...I have to say...

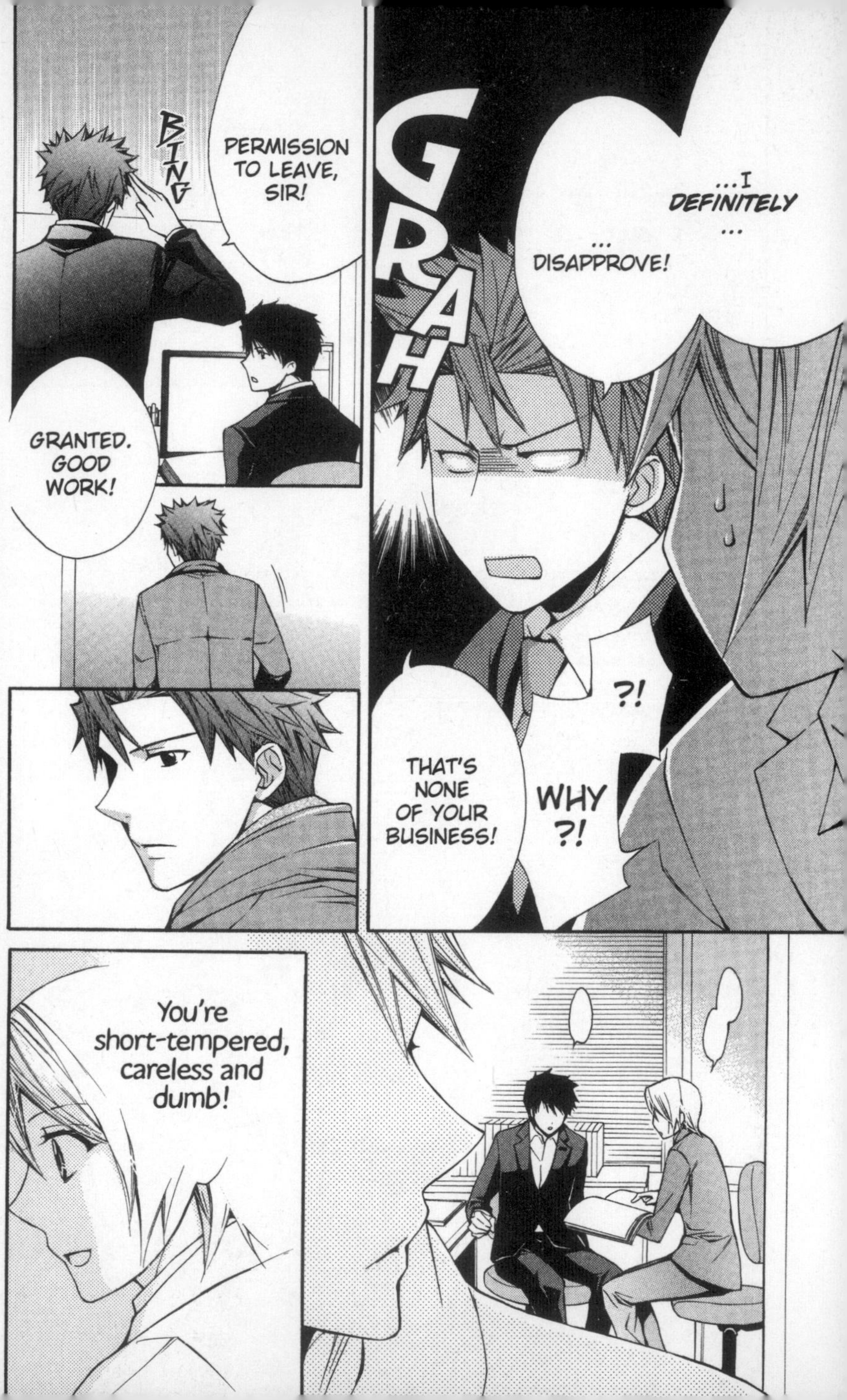
...I DEFINITELY ...
... DISAPPROVE!
GRAH
?!
WHY ?!
THAT'S NONE OF YOUR BUSINESS!
BING
PERMISSION TO LEAVE, SIR!
GRANTED. GOOD WORK!
You're short-tempered, careless and dumb!

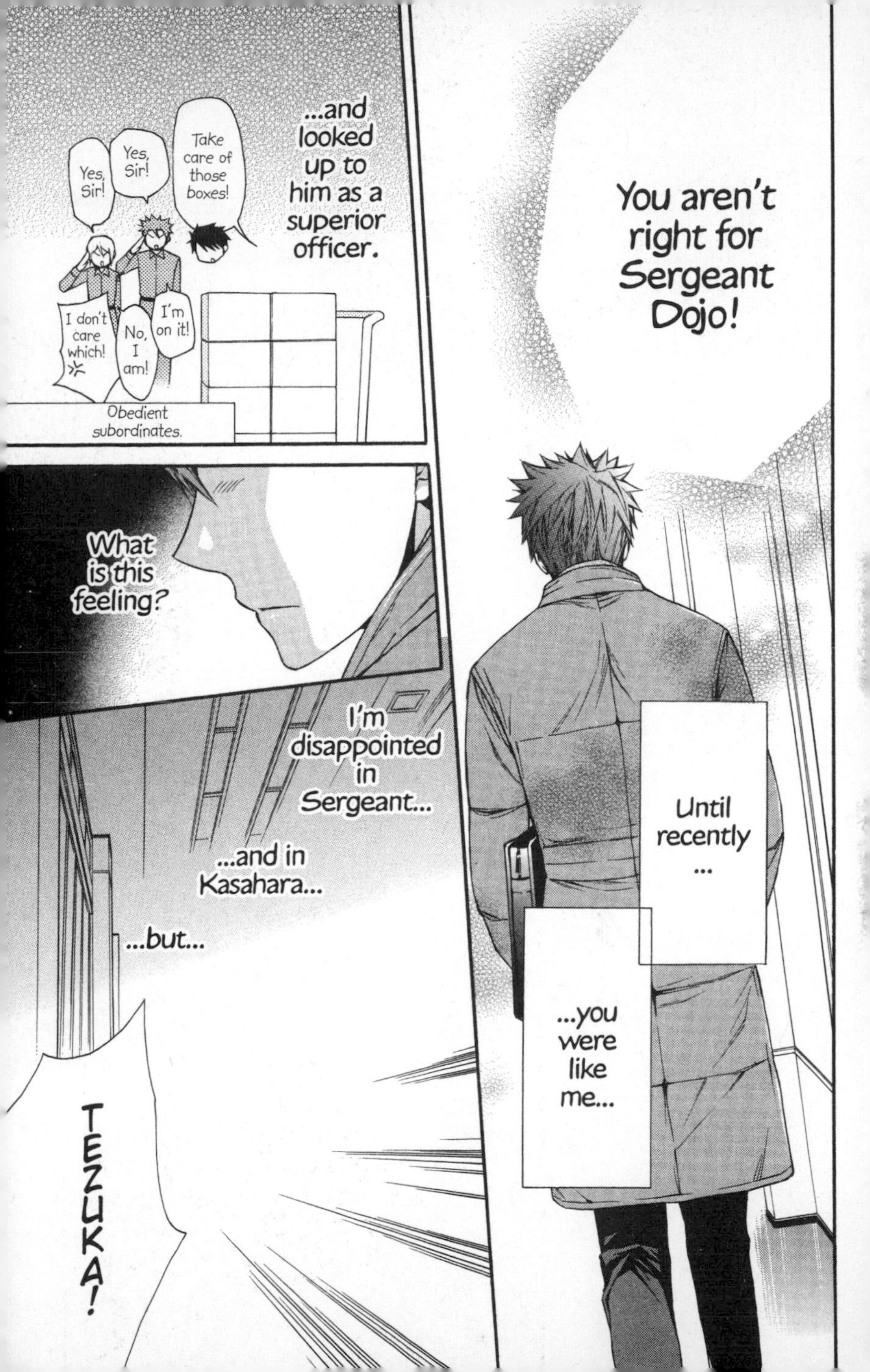
You aren't right for Sergeant Dojo!
Until recently...
...you were like me...
...and looked up to him as a superior officer.
Take care of those boxes!
Yes, Sir!
Yes, Sir!
I'm on it!
No, I am!
I don't care which!
Obedient subordinates.
What is this feeling?
I'm disappointed in Sergeant...
...and in Kasahara...
...but...
TEZUKA!

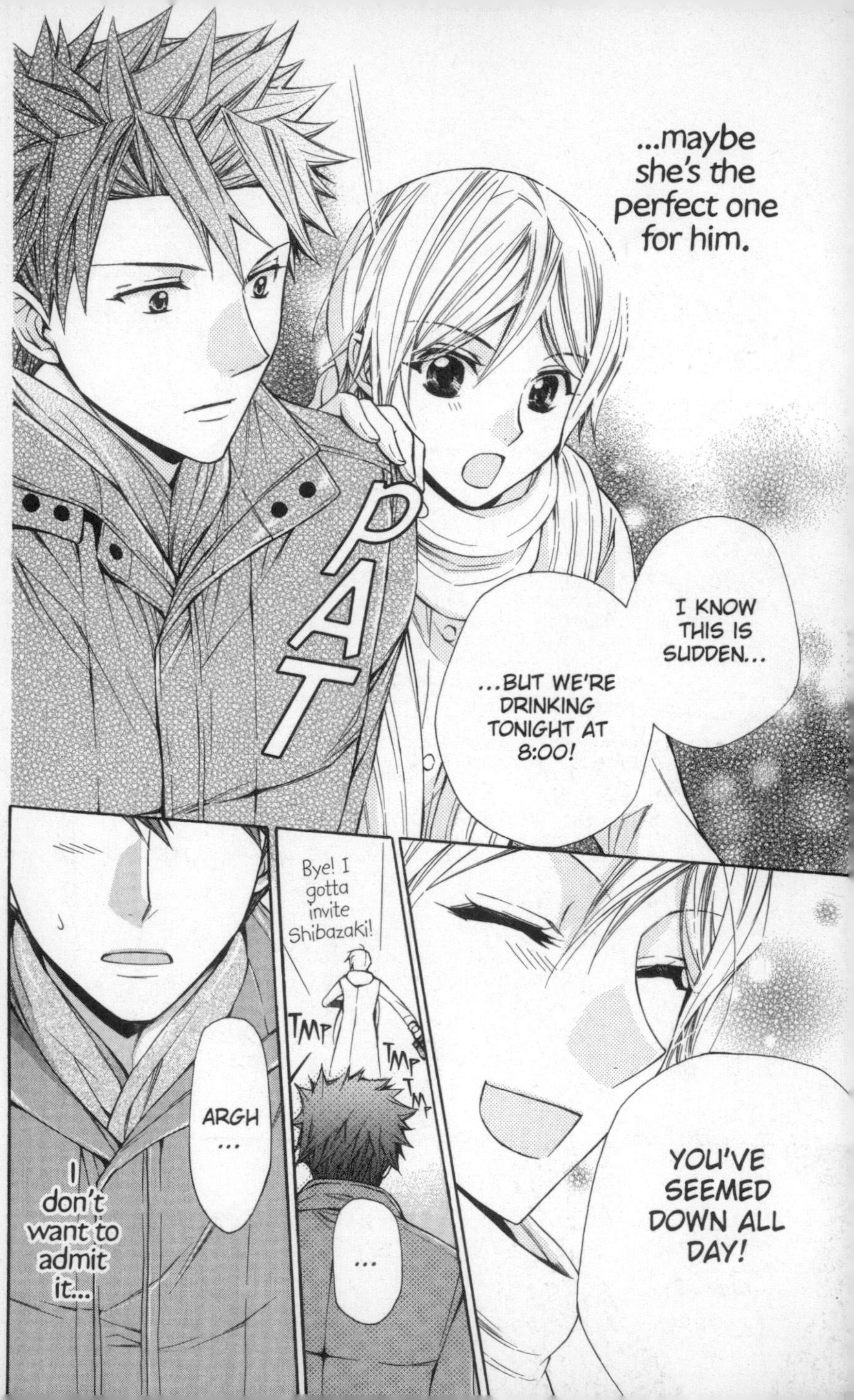
...maybe she's the perfect one for him.
I KNOW THIS IS SUDDEN...
...BUT WE'RE DRINKING TONIGHT AT 8:00!
PAT
YOU'VE SEEMED DOWN ALL DAY!
Bye! I gotta invite Shibazaki!
TMP
TMP
TMP
...
ARGH ...
I don't want to admit it...

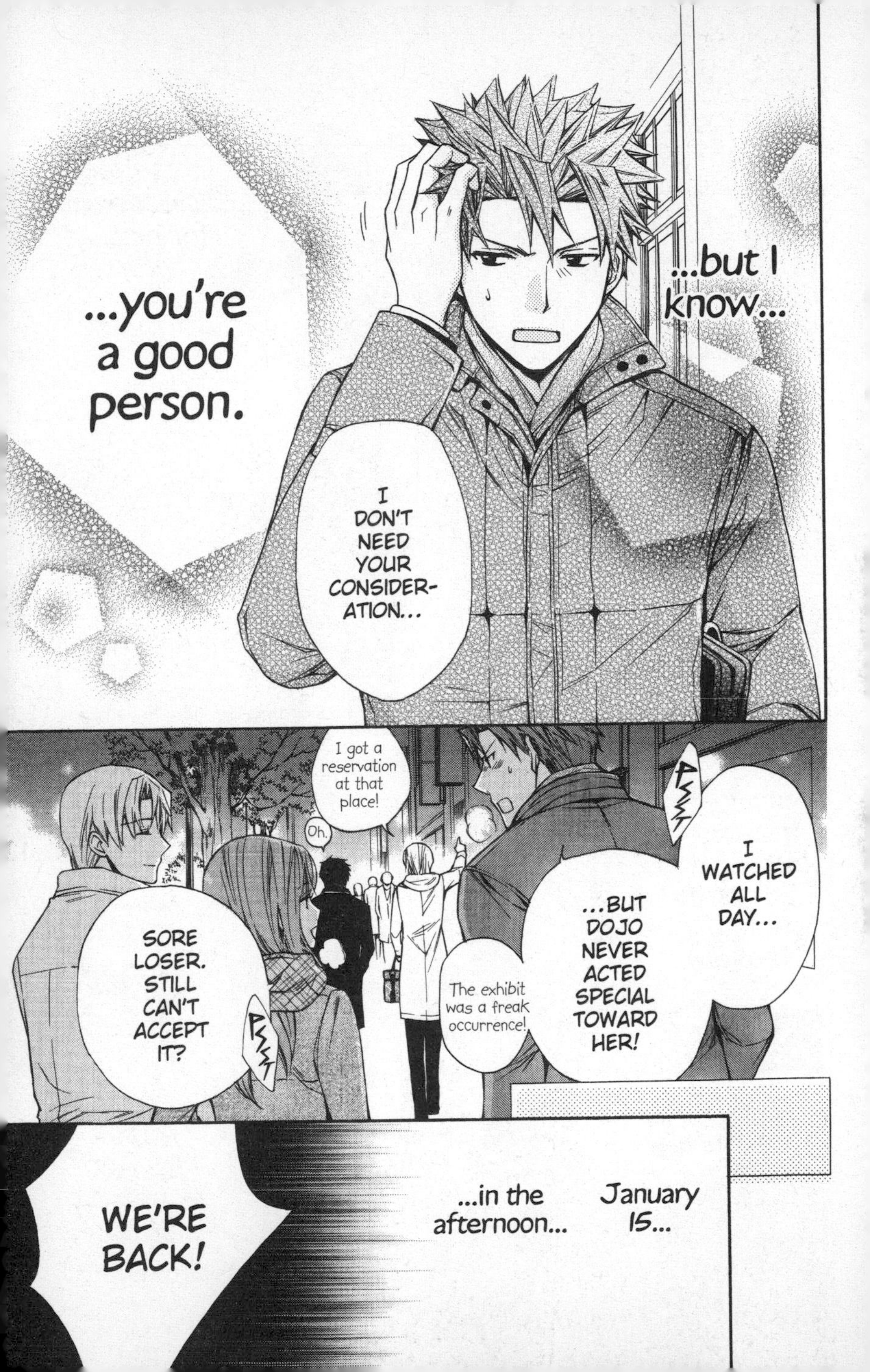
...but I know...
...you're a good person.
I DON'T NEED YOUR CONSIDERATION...
I WATCHED ALL DAY...
...BUT DOJO NEVER ACTED SPECIAL TOWARD HER!
The exhibit was a freak occurrence!
I got a reservation at that place!
Oh.
SORE LOSER. STILL CAN'T ACCEPT IT?
January 15...
...in the afternoon...
WE'RE BACK!

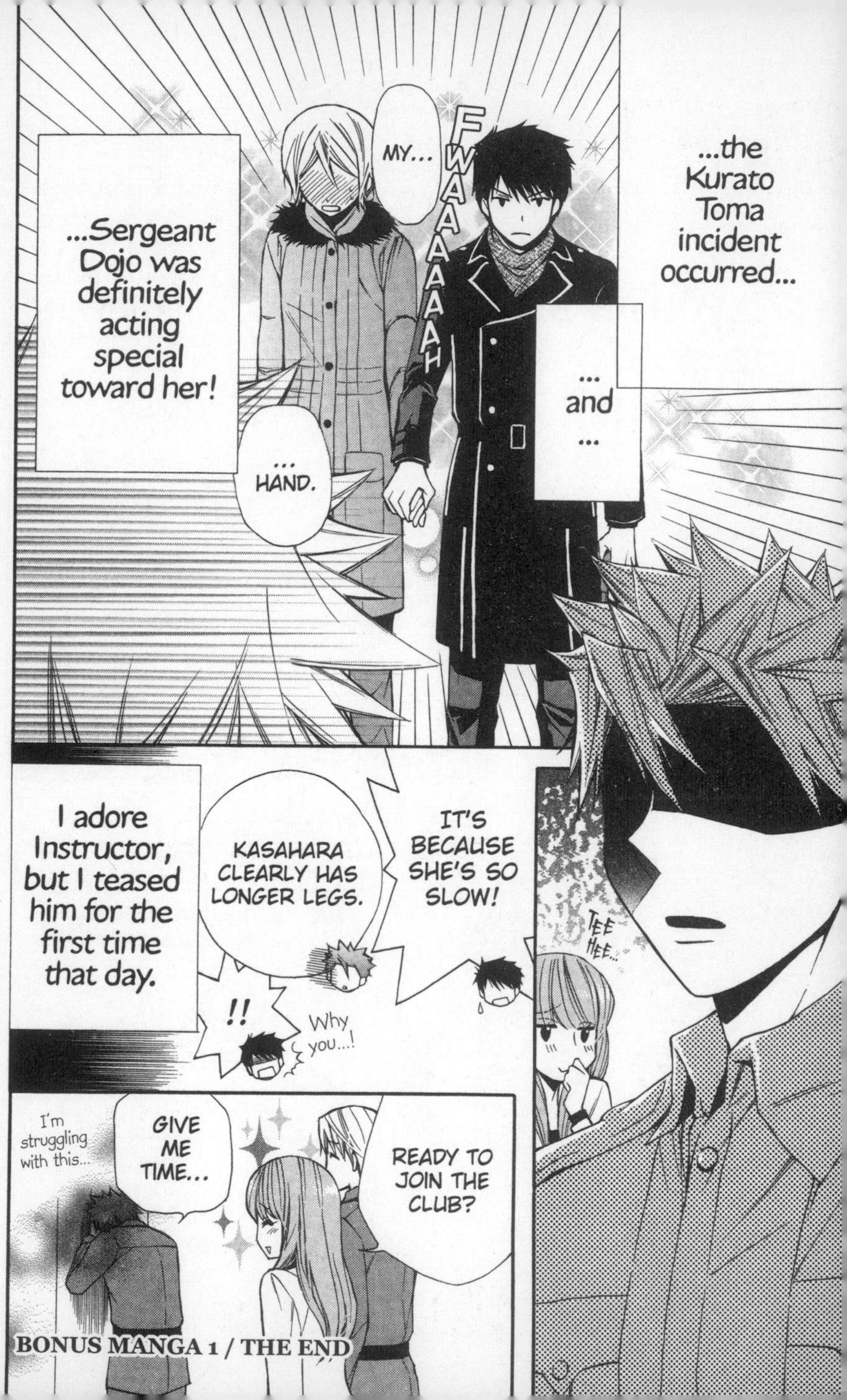
...the Kurato Toma incident occurred...
... and ...
TEE HEE...
MY...
FWAAAAAAAH
... HAND.
...Sergeant Dojo was definitely acting special toward her!
IT'S BECAUSE SHE'S SO SLOW!
KASAHARA CLEARLY HAS LONGER LEGS.
!!
Why you...!
I adore Instructor, but I teased him for the first time that day.
READY TO JOIN THE CLUB?
GIVE ME TIME...
I'm struggling with this...
BONUS MANGA 1 / THE END

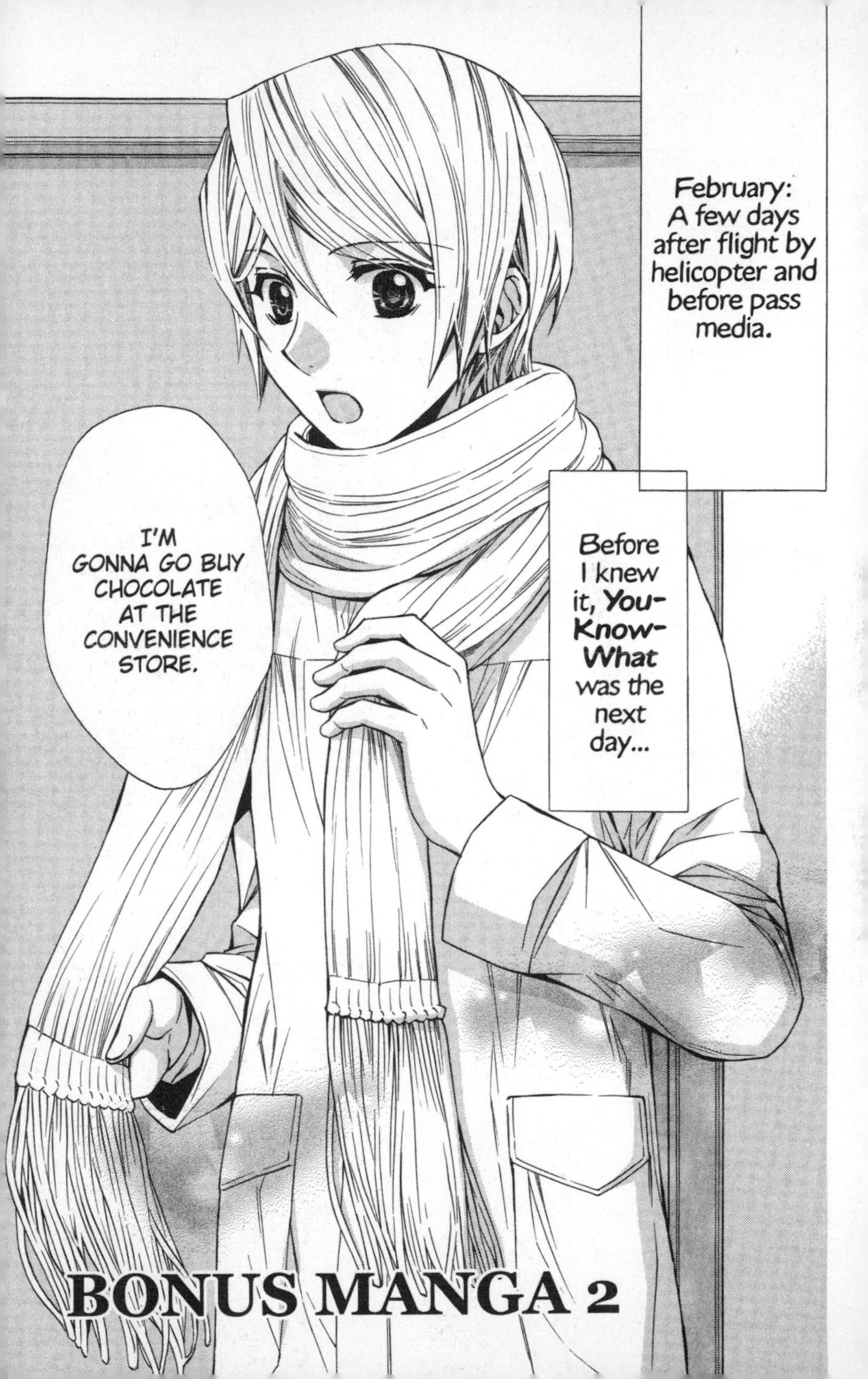
February: A few days after flight by helicopter and before pass media.
Before I knew it, **You-Know-What** was the next day...
I'M GONNA GO BUY CHOCOLATE AT THE CONVENIENCE STORE.
BONUS MANGA 2

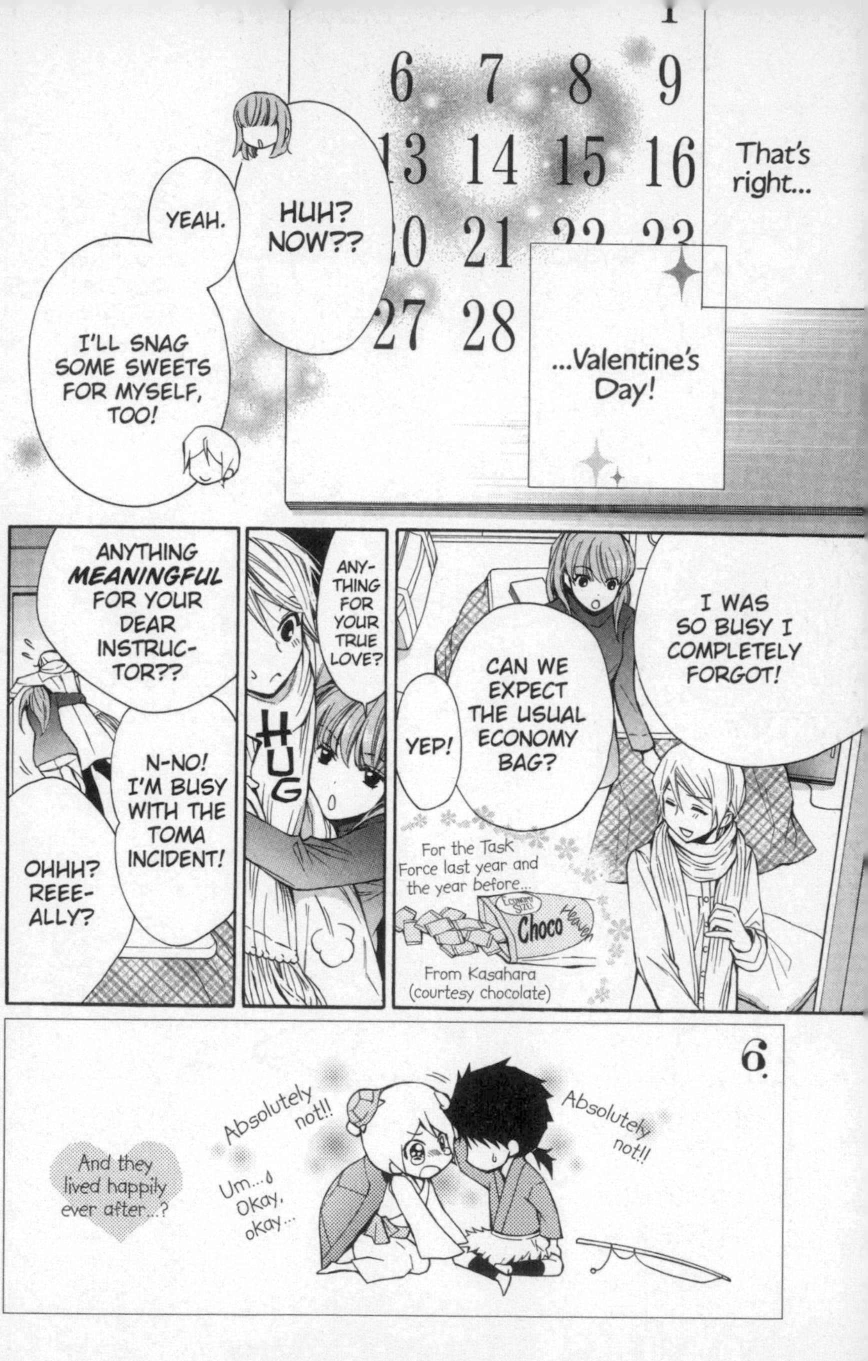
That's right...
...Valentine's Day!
HUH? NOW??
YEAH.
I'LL SNAG SOME SWEETS FOR MYSELF, TOO!
I WAS SO BUSY I COMPLETELY FORGOT!
CAN WE EXPECT THE USUAL ECONOMY BAG?
YEP!
For the Task Force last year and the year before...
ECONOMY SIZE!
Choco Heaven
From Kasahara (courtesy chocolate)
ANY-THING FOR YOUR TRUE LOVE?
HUG
ANYTHING MEANINGFUL FOR YOUR DEAR INSTRUCTOR??
N-NO! I'M BUSY WITH THE TOMA INCIDENT!
OHHH? REEE-ALLY?
6.
Absolutely not!!
Absolutely not!!
Um... Okay, okay...
And they lived happily ever after...?

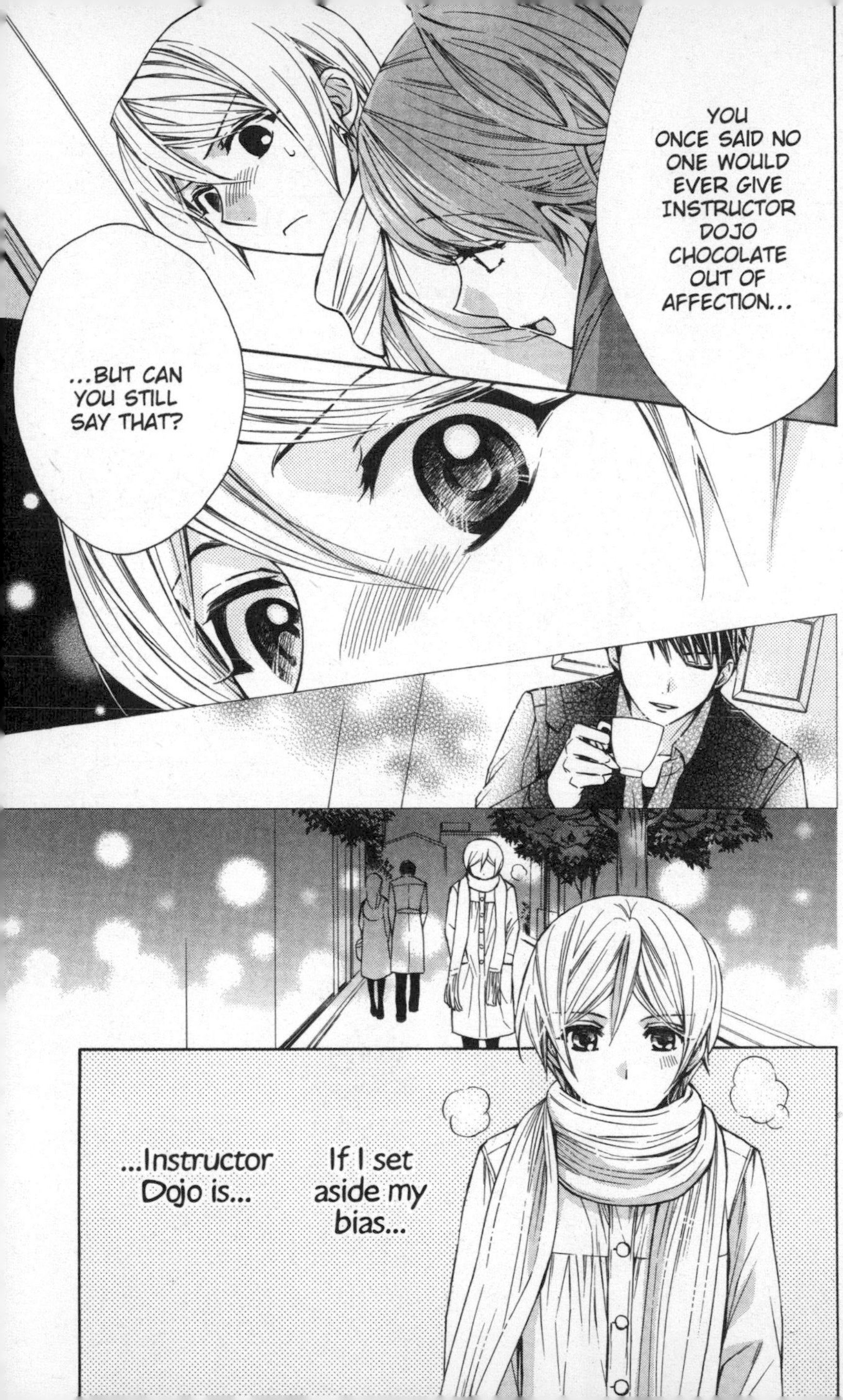
YOU ONCE SAID NO ONE WOULD EVER GIVE INSTRUCTOR DOJO CHOCOLATE OUT OF AFFECTION...
...BUT CAN YOU STILL SAY THAT?
If I set aside my bias...
...Instructor Dojo is...

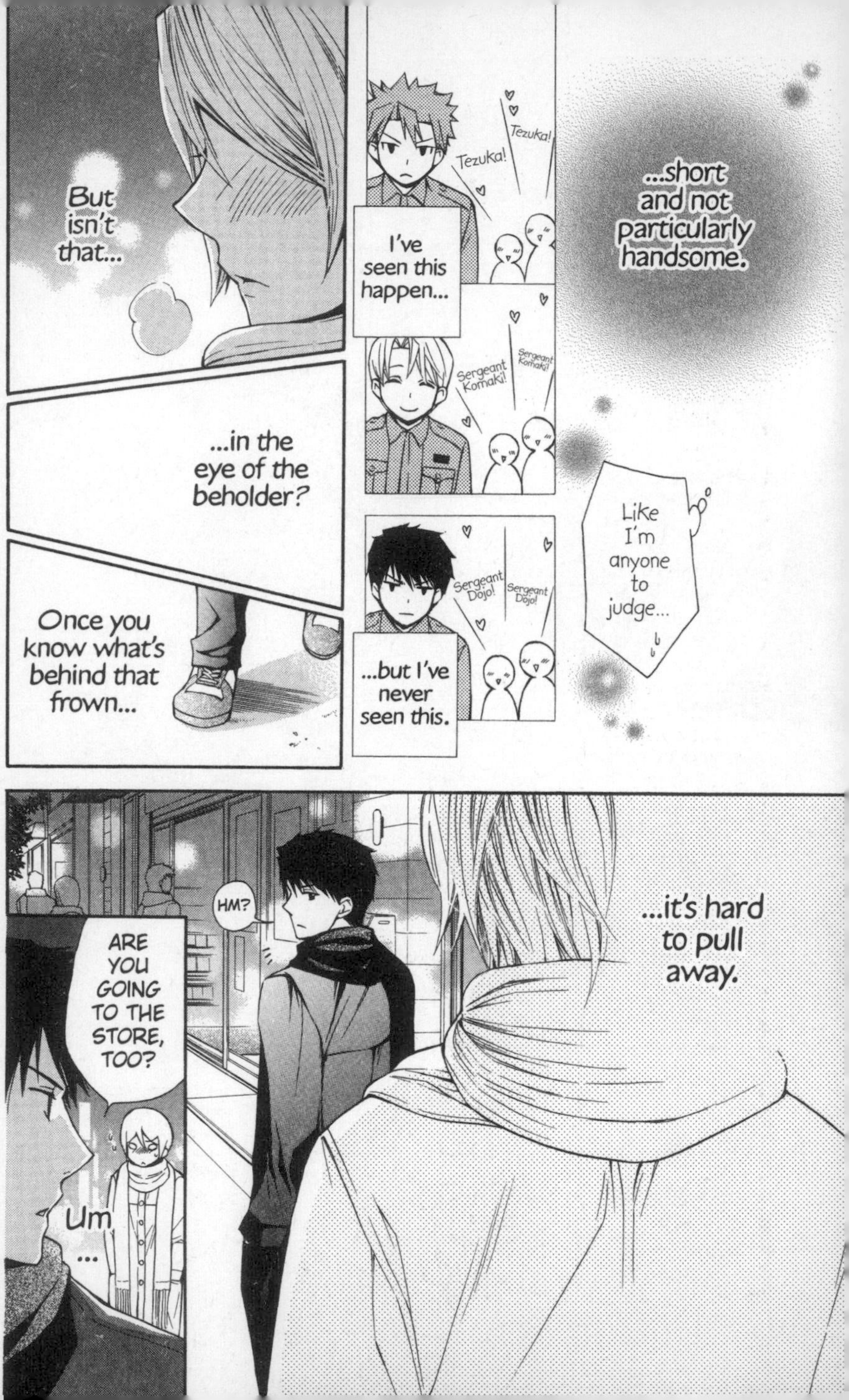
...short and not particularly handsome.
Like I'm anyone to judge...
Tezuka!
Tezuka!
I've seen this happen...
Sergeant Komaki!
Sergeant Komaki!
Sergeant Dojo!
Sergeant Dojo!
...but I've never seen this.
But isn't that...
...in the eye of the beholder?
Once you know what's behind that frown...
...it's hard to pull away.
HM?
ARE YOU GOING TO THE STORE, TOO?
Um...

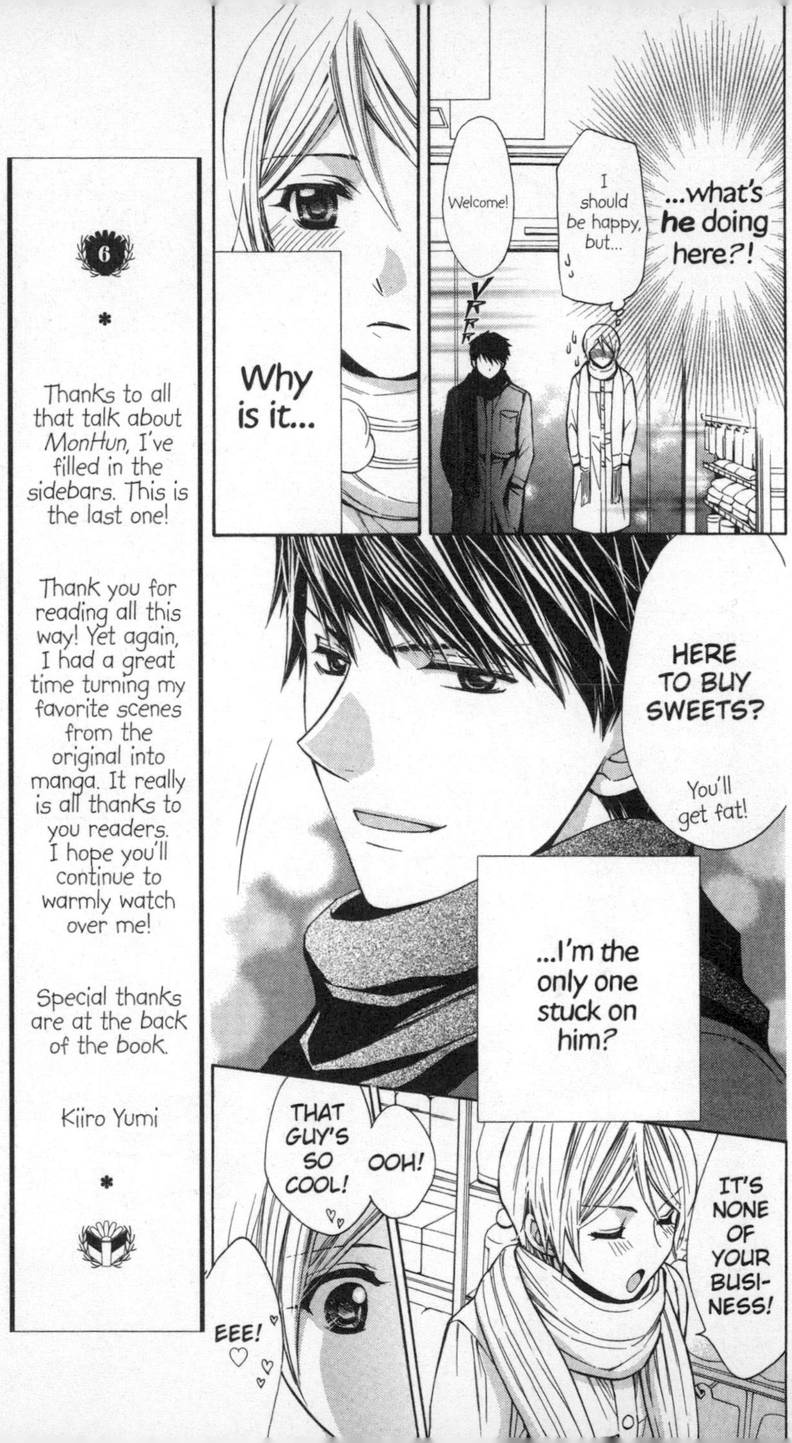
...what's he doing here?!
I should be happy, but...
Welcome!
VRRR
Why is it...
HERE TO BUY SWEETS?
You'll get fat!
...I'm the only one stuck on him?
IT'S NONE OF YOUR BUSINESS!
OOH!
THAT GUY'S SO COOL!
EEE!

6

*

Thanks to all that talk about *MonHun*, I've filled in the sidebars. This is the last one!

Thank you for reading all this way! Yet again, I had a great time turning my favorite scenes from the original into manga. It really is all thanks to you readers. I hope you'll continue to warmly watch over me!

Special thanks are at the back of the book.

Kiiro Yumi

*

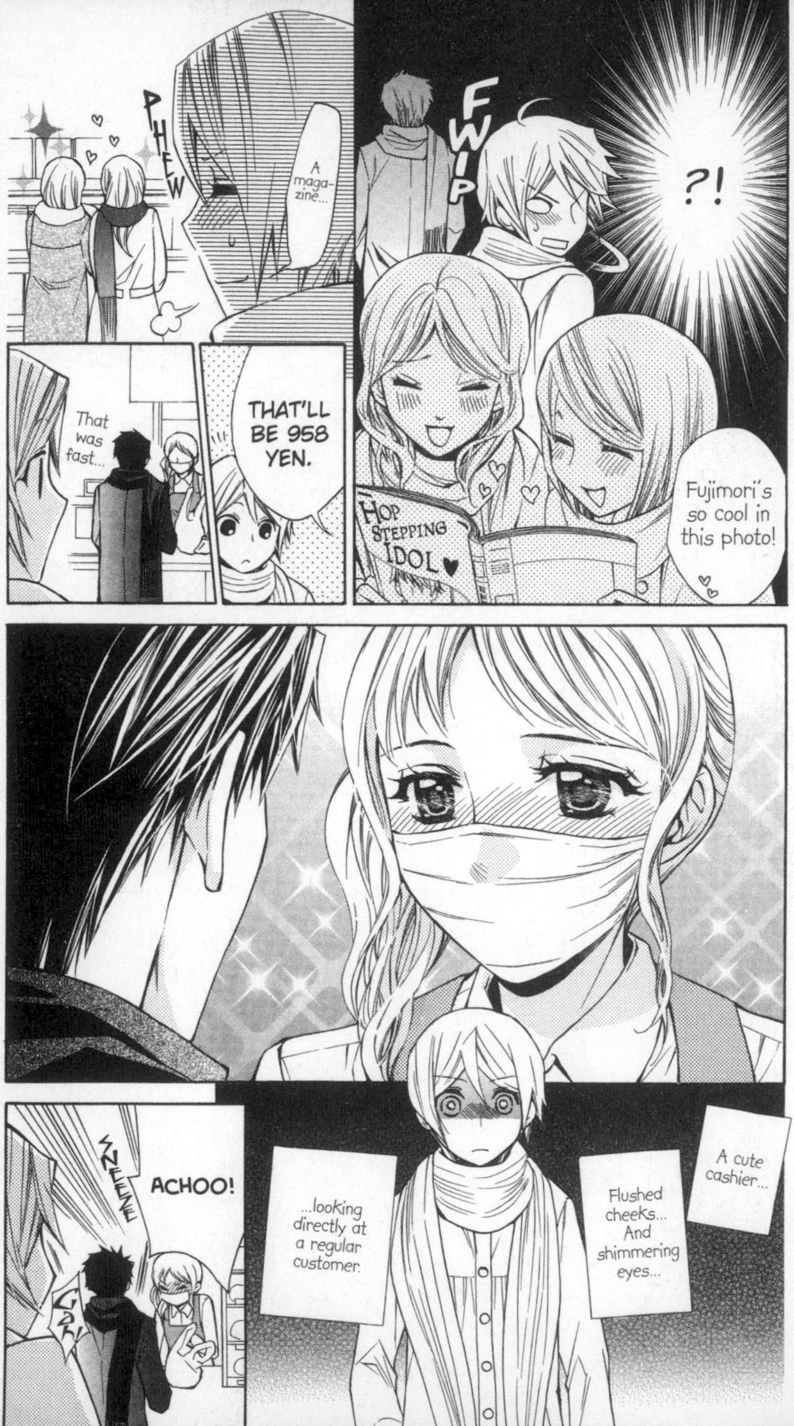
FWIP
?!
Fujimori's so cool in this photo!
HOP STEPPING IDOL
A magazine...
PHEW
THAT'LL BE 958 YEN.
That was fast...
A cute cashier...
Flushed cheeks... And shimmering eyes...
...looking directly at a regular customer.
SNEEZE
ACHOO!
Gah!

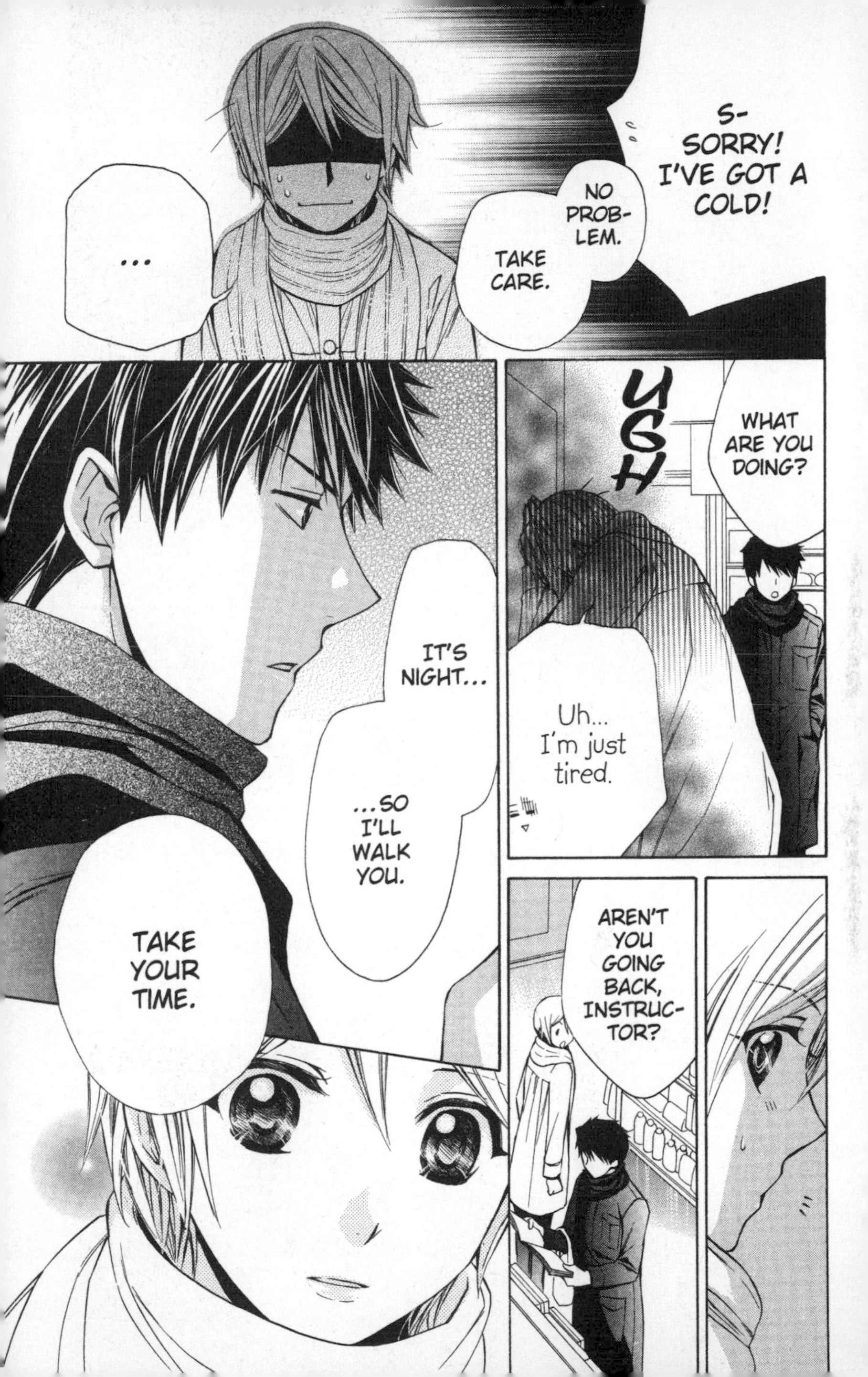
S-SORRY! I'VE GOT A COLD!
NO PROB-LEM.
TAKE CARE.
...
WHAT ARE YOU DOING?
UGH
Uh... I'm just tired.
AREN'T YOU GOING BACK, INSTRUC-TOR?
IT'S NIGHT...
...SO I'LL WALK YOU.
TAKE YOUR TIME.

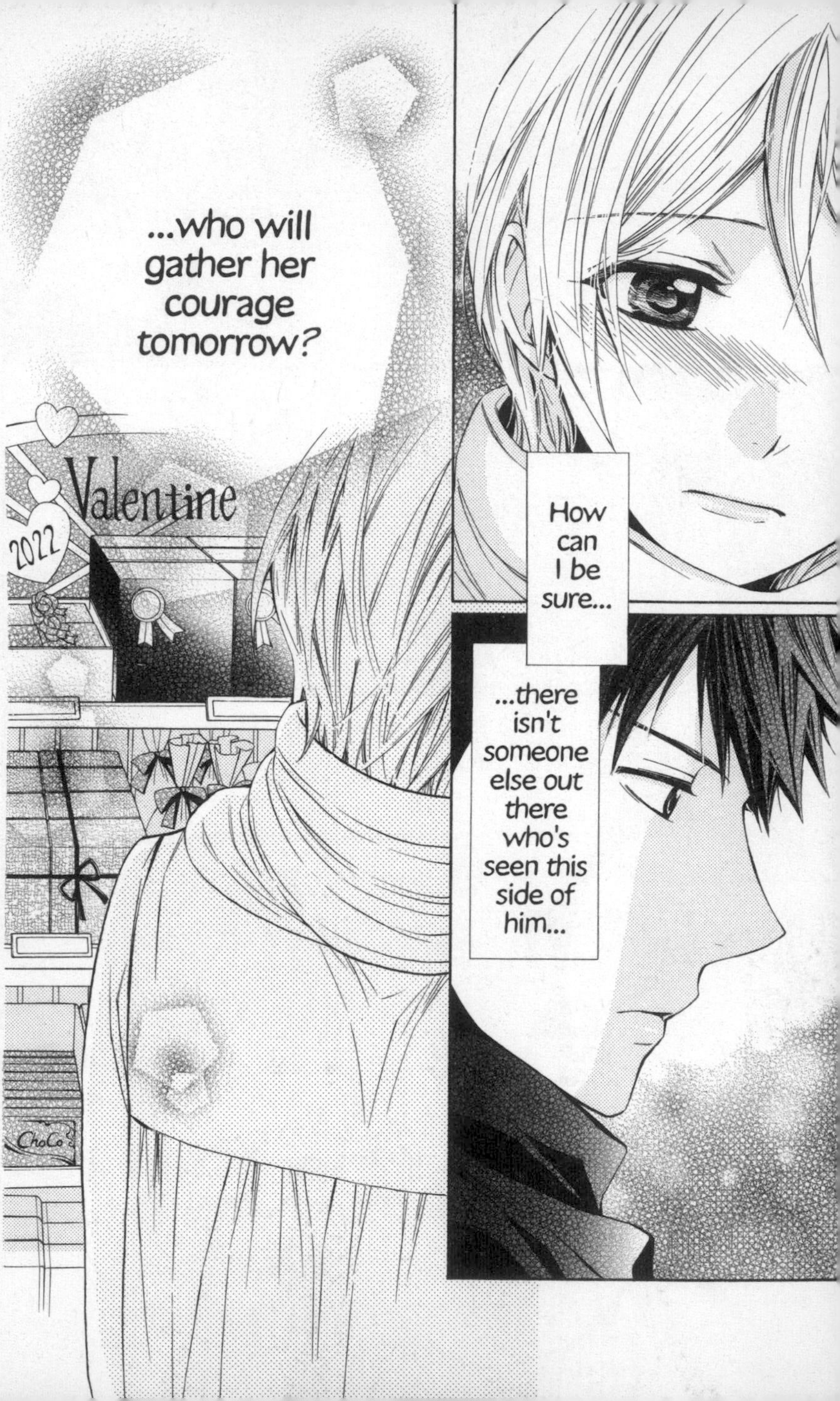
How can I be sure...
...there isn't someone else out there who's seen this side of him...
...who will gather her courage tomorrow?
Valentine
2022
ChoCo

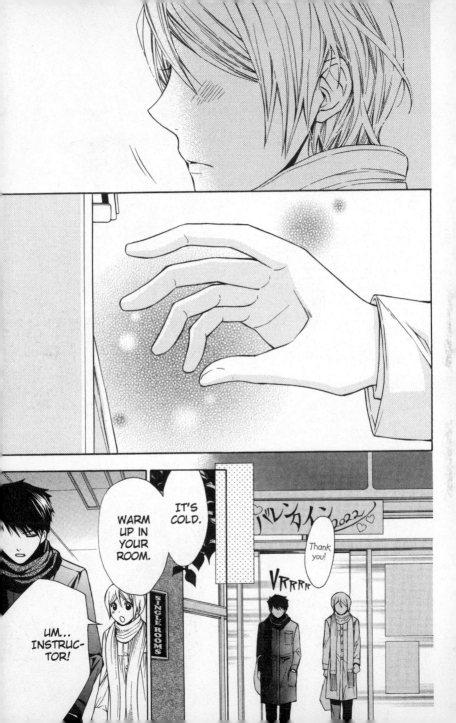

IT'S
COLD.

WARM
UP IN
YOUR
ROOM.

Thank
you!

VRRRR

UM...
INSTRUC-
TOR!

SINGLE ROOMS

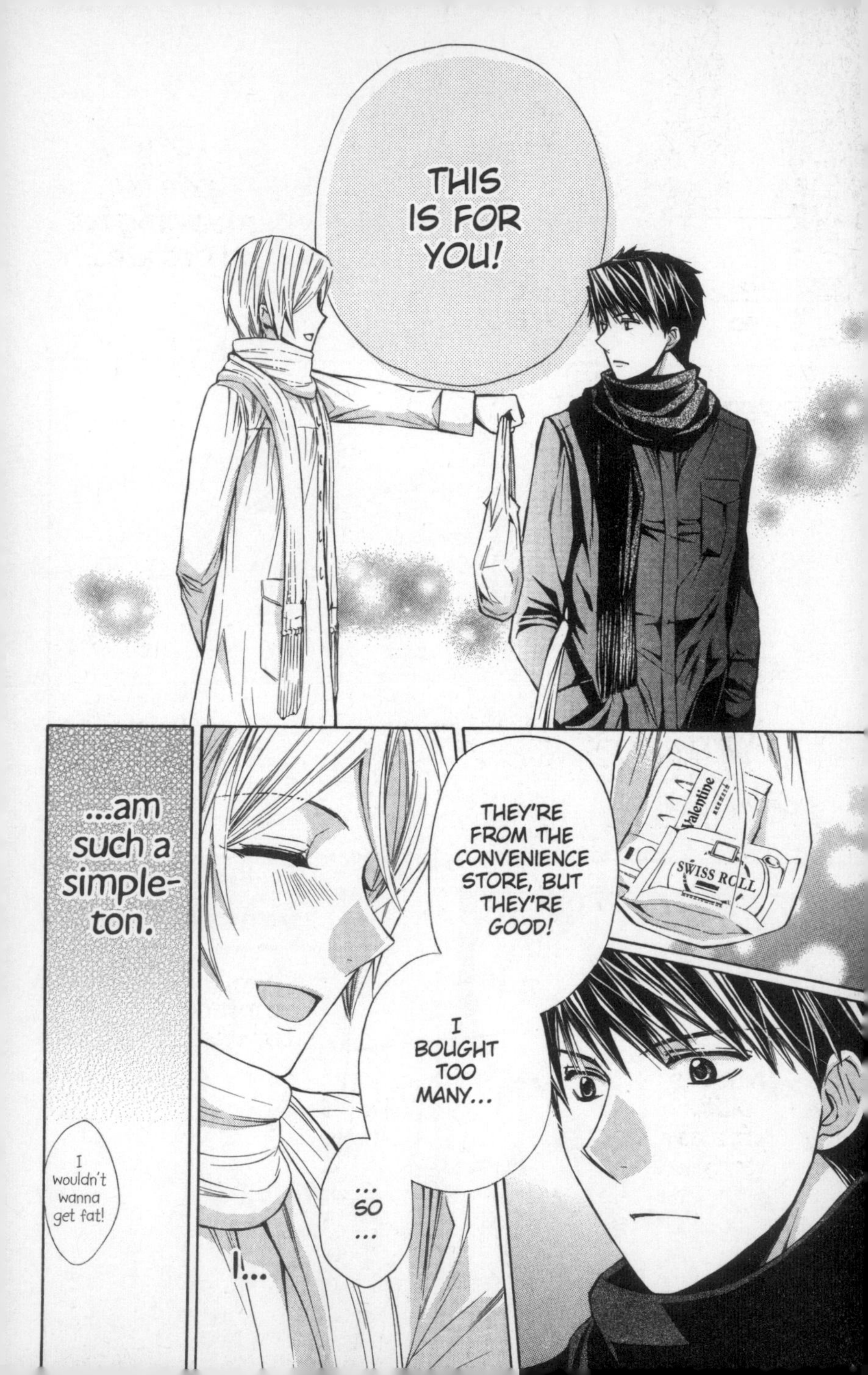
THIS IS FOR YOU!
Valentine
SWISS ROLL
THEY'RE FROM THE CONVENIENCE STORE, BUT THEY'RE GOOD!
I BOUGHT TOO MANY...
...SO...
I...
...am such a simpleton.
I wouldn't wanna get fat!

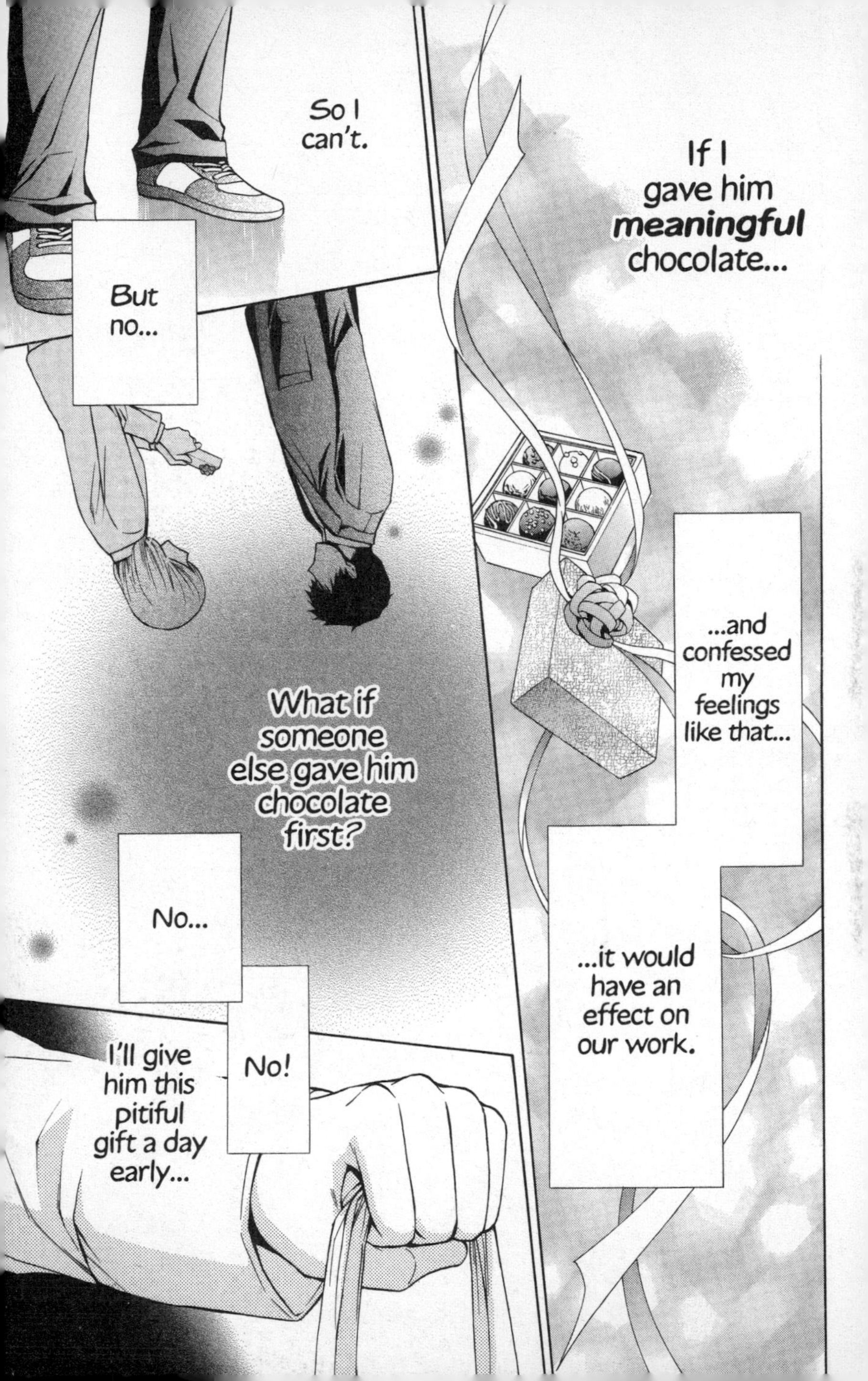
If I gave him meaningful chocolate...
...and confessed my feelings like that...
...it would have an effect on our work.
So I can't.
But no...
What if someone else gave him chocolate first?
No...
No!
I'll give him this pitiful gift a day early...

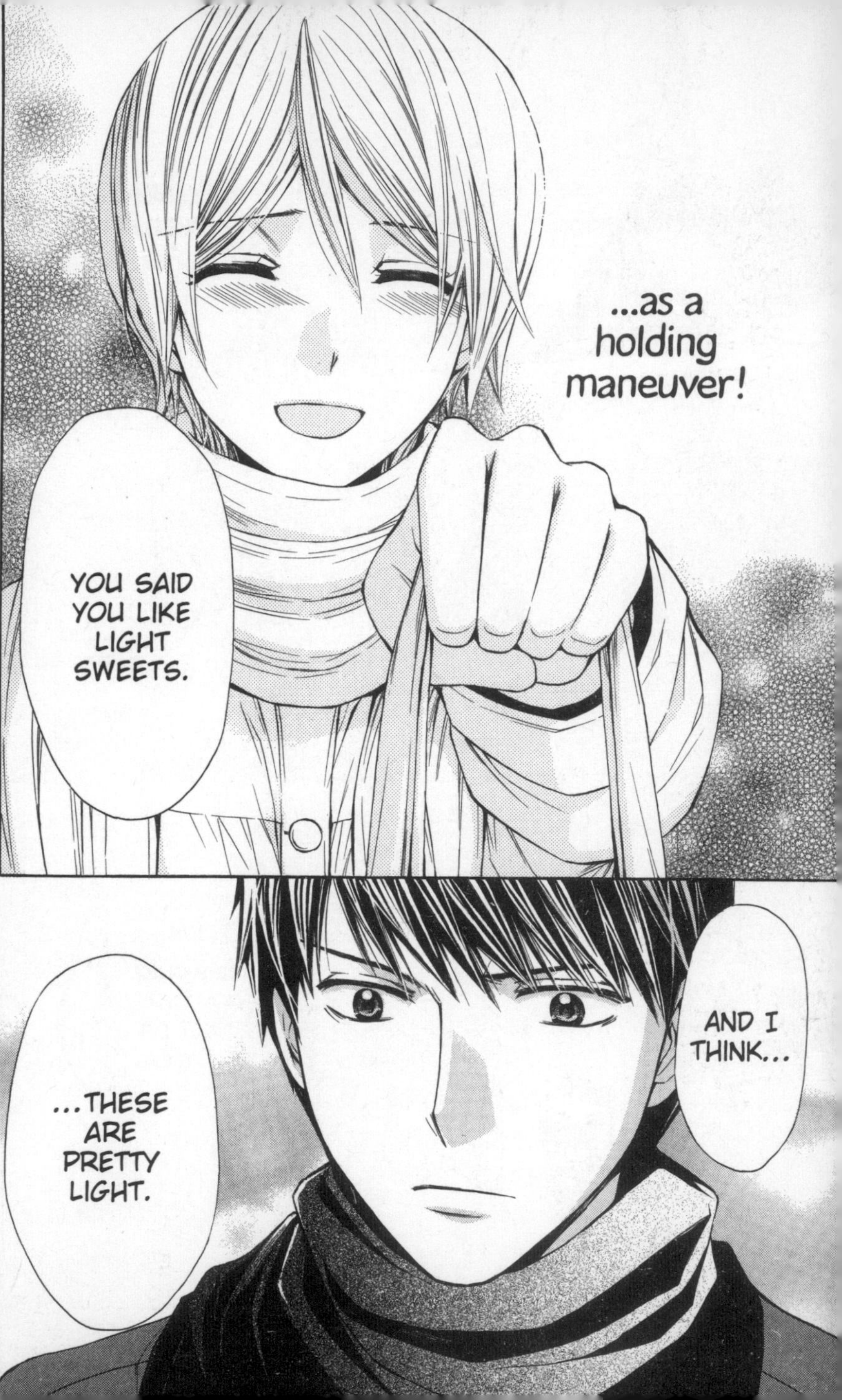
...as a holding maneuver!
YOU SAID YOU LIKE LIGHT SWEETS.
AND I THINK...
...THESE ARE PRETTY LIGHT.

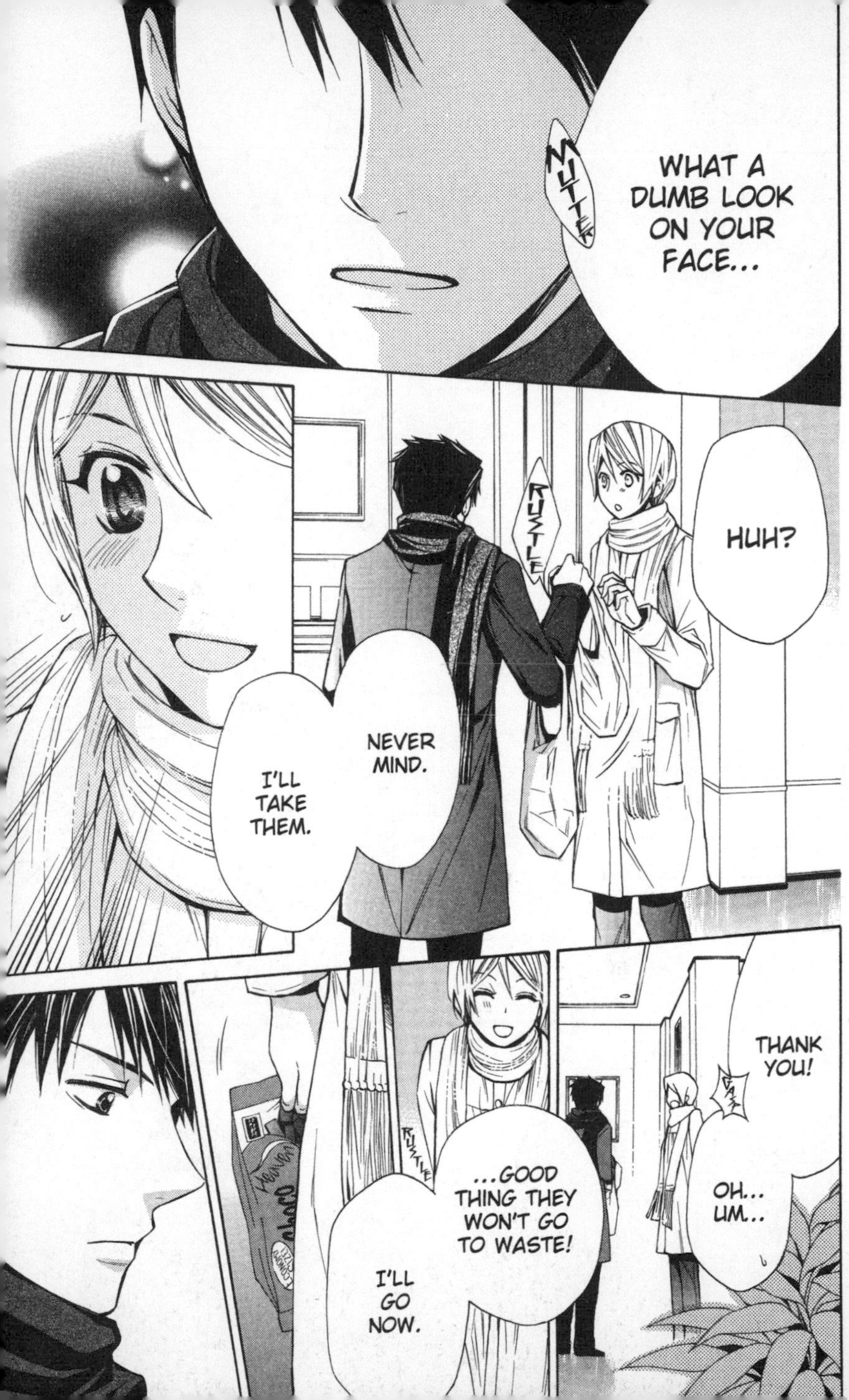
MUTTER
WHAT A DUMB LOOK ON YOUR FACE...
HUH?
RUSTLE
NEVER MIND.
I'LL TAKE THEM.
THANK YOU!
OH... UM...
...GOOD THING THEY WON'T GO TO WASTE!
RUSTLE
I'LL GO NOW.

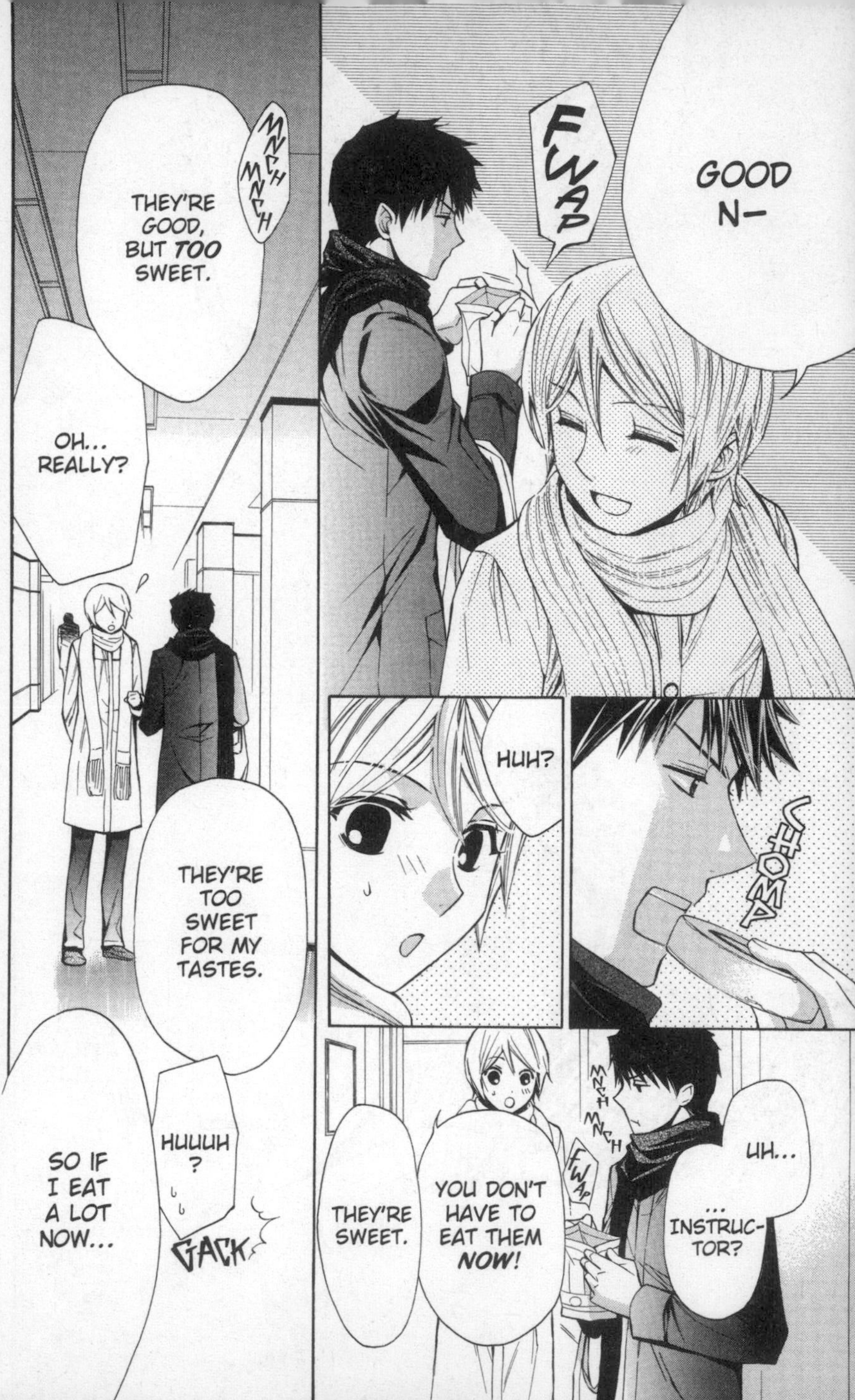
GOOD N-
FWAP
CHOMP
HUH?
UH...
... INSTRUCTOR?
MNCH MNCH
FWAP
YOU DON'T HAVE TO EAT THEM NOW!
THEY'RE SWEET.
THEY'RE GOOD, BUT TOO SWEET.
MNCH MNCH
OH... REALLY?
THEY'RE TOO SWEET FOR MY TASTES.
HUUUH?
SO IF I EAT A LOT NOW...
GACK

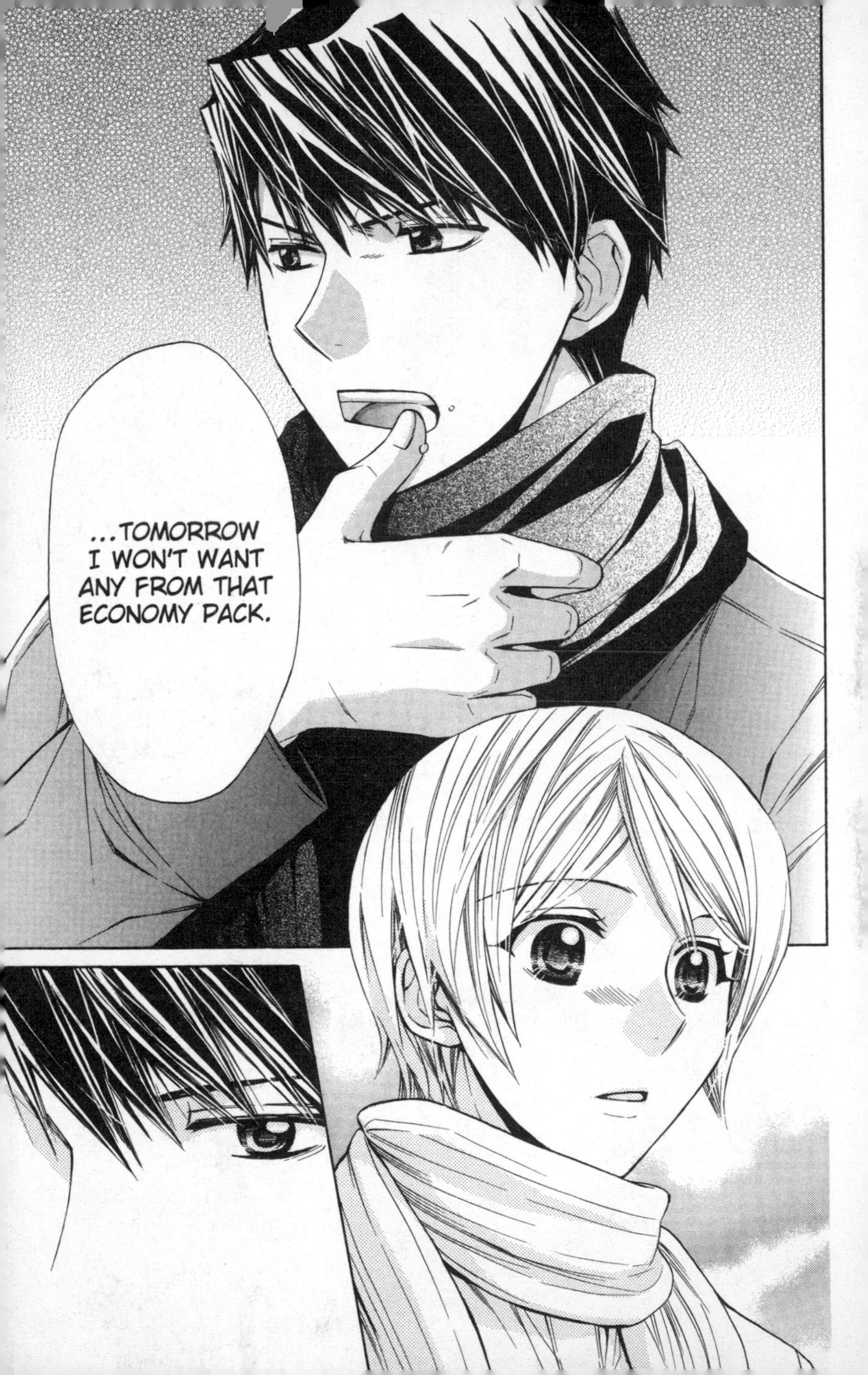
...TOMORROW I WON'T WANT ANY FROM THAT ECONOMY PACK.

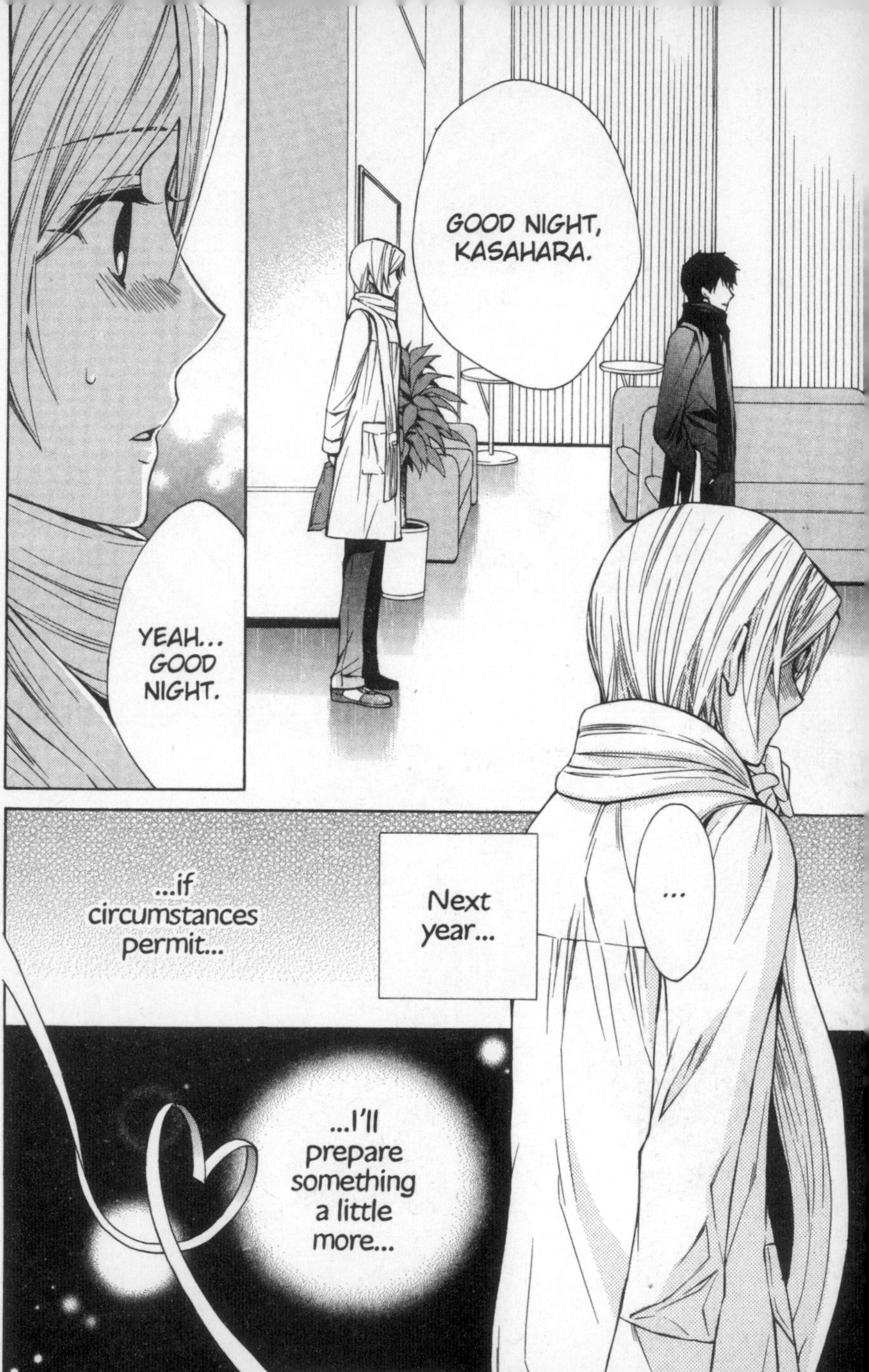
GOOD NIGHT, KASAHARA.
YEAH... GOOD NIGHT.
...
Next year...
...if circumstances permit...
...I'll prepare something a little more...

BONUS MANGA 2 / THE END

EXTRA BONUS MANGA

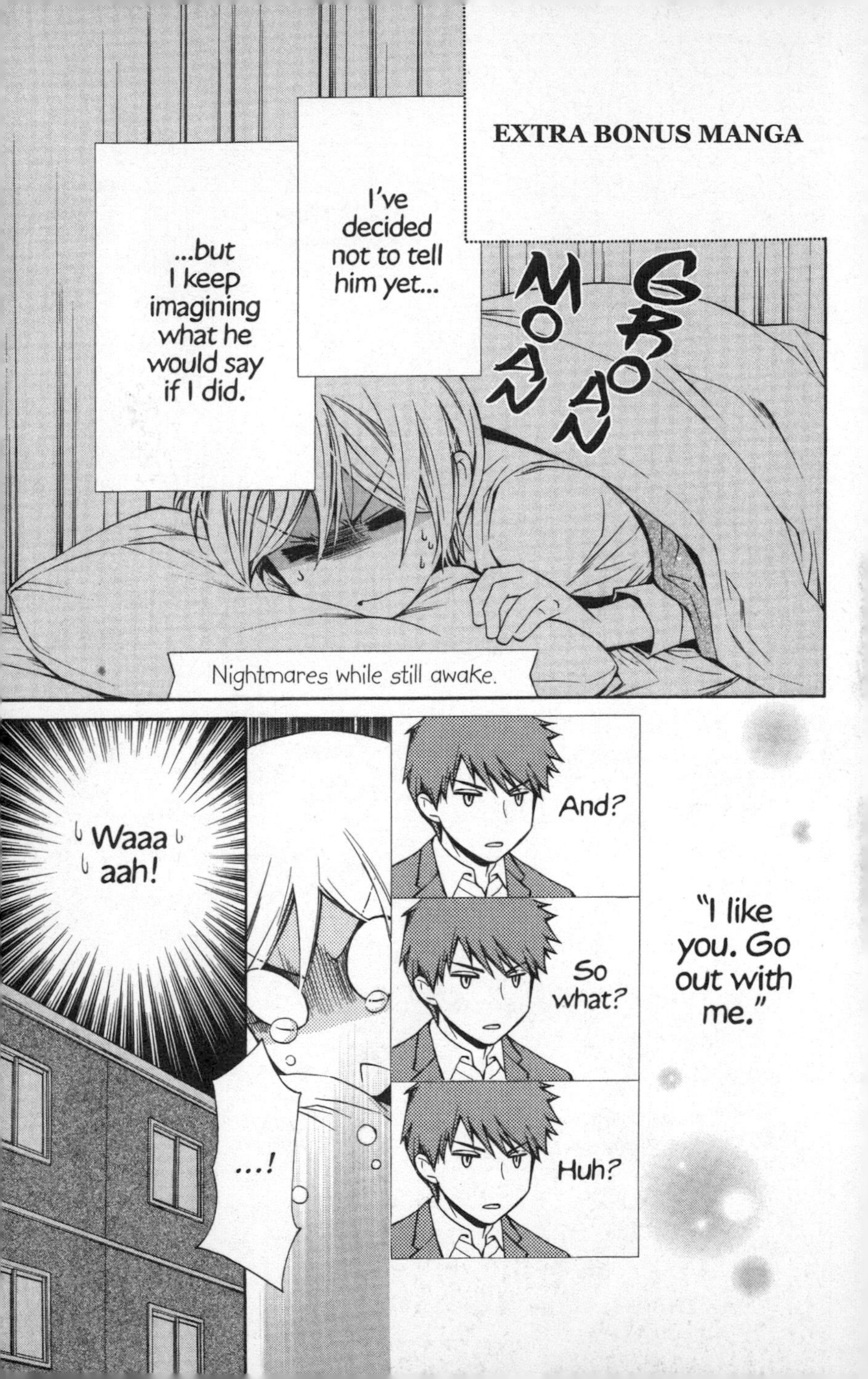
I've decided not to tell him yet...
...but I keep imagining what he would say if I did.
GROAN
MOAN
Nightmares while still awake.
"I like you. Go out with me."
And?
So what?
Huh?
...!
Waaa aah!

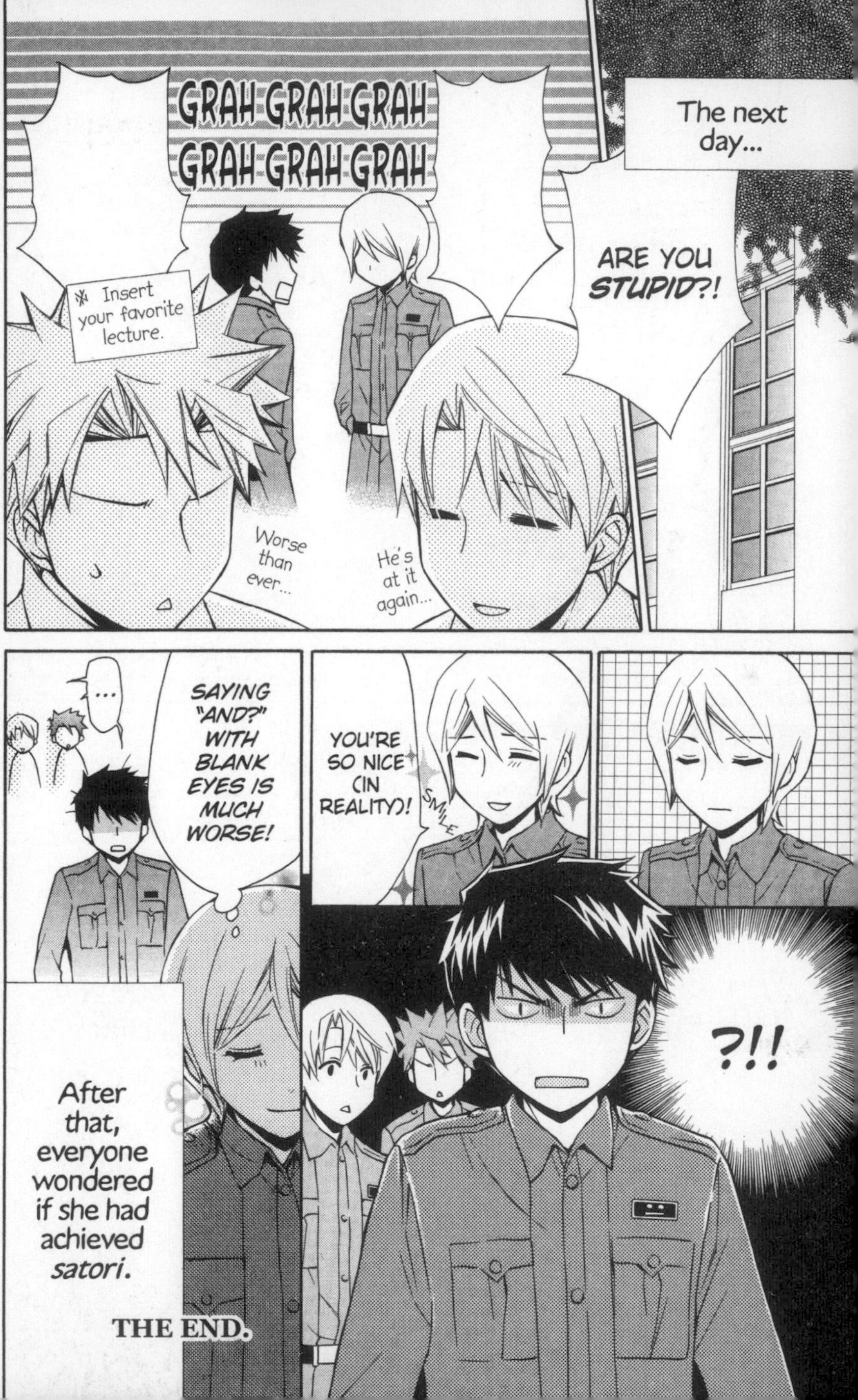
The next day...
ARE YOU STUPID?!
GRAH GRAH GRAH
GRAH GRAH GRAH
※ Insert your favorite lecture.
He's at it again...
Worse than ever...
YOU'RE SO NICE (IN REALITY)!
SMILE
SAYING "AND?" WITH BLANK EYES IS MUCH WORSE!
...
?!!
After that, everyone wondered if she had achieved satori.
THE END.

Special Thanks!!

Ms. Arikawa
Ms. Arikawa's editor
(ASCII Media)
★
Mamada, Murakami, Aoki
★
My family
★
My editor
★
Everyone who makes this series possible.
★★
Thanks so, so much!

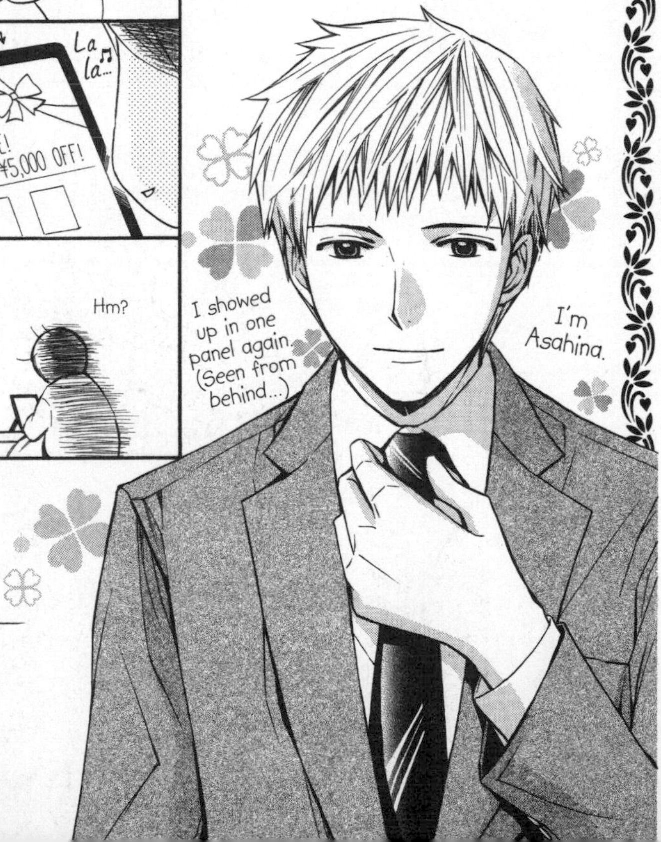
I'm Asahina.
I showed up in one panel again. (Seen from behind...)

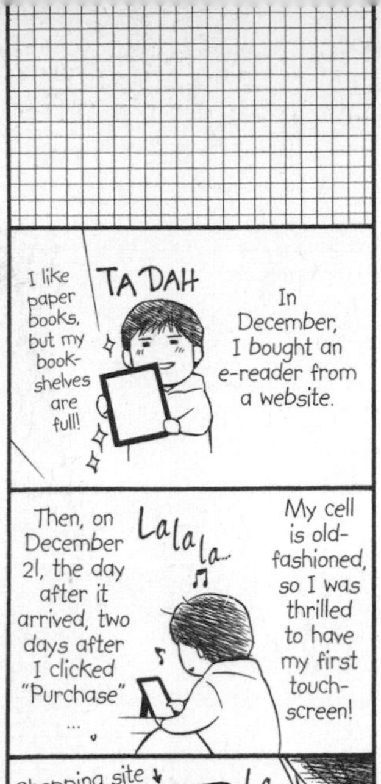
In December, I bought an e-reader from a website.
TA DAH
I like paper books, but my bookshelves are full!
My cell is old-fashioned, so I was thrilled to have my first touchscreen!
La la la...
Then, on December 21, the day after it arrived, two days after I clicked "Purchase"...
La la...
Shopping site
EC. 21, 22
TWO DAYS ONLY!
CHRISTMAS SALE!
ALL TABLETS ¥5,000 OFF!
Hm?
That isn't the price I paid...

Hope to see you again next volume!

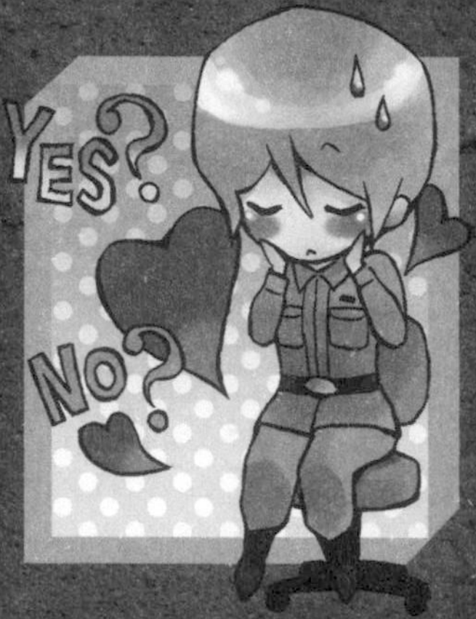
YES?
NO?

Kiiro Yumi won the 42nd *LaLa* Manga Grand Prix Fresh Debut award for her manga *Billy Bocchan no Yuutsu* (Little Billy's Depression). Her series *Toshokan Senso Love&War (Library Wars: Love & War)* ran in *LaLa* magazine in Japan and is published in English by VIZ Media.

Hiro Arikawa won the 10th Dengeki Novel Prize for her work *Shio no Machi: Wish on My Precious* in 2003 and debuted with the same novel in 2004. Of her many works, Arikawa is best known for the *Library Wars* series and her *Jieitai Sanbusaku* trilogy, which consists of *Sora no Naka* (In the Sky), *Umi no Soko* (The Bottom of the Sea) and *Shio no Machi* (City of Salt).

library wars

Volume 13
Shojo Beat Edition

Story & Art by **Kiiro Yumi**
Original Concept by **Hiro Arikawa**

ENGLISH TRANSLATION John Werry
LETTERING Annaliese Christman
DESIGN Amy Martin
EDITOR Megan Bates

Toshokan Sensou LOVE&WAR by Kiiro Yumi and Hiro Arikawa
© Kiiro Yumi 2014
© Hiro Arikawa 2014
All rights reserved.
First published in Japan in 2014 by HAKUSENSHA, Inc., Tokyo.
English language translation rights arranged with HAKUSENSHA,
Inc., Tokyo.

The stories, characters and incidents mentioned in this publication
are entirely fictional.

No portion of this book may be reproduced or transmitted in
any form or by any means without written permission from the
copyright holders.

Printed in the U.S.A.

Published by VIZ Media, LLC
P.O. Box 77010
San Francisco, CA 94107

10 9 8 7 6 5 4 3 2 1
First printing, April 2015

www.shojobeat.com   www.viz.com

RATED
T+
FOR OLDER TEEN

PARENTAL ADVISORY
LIBRARY WARS: LOVE & WAR is rated T+ for Older Teen
and is recommended for ages 16 and up. This volume
contains alcohol use, adult language and violence.
ratings.viz.com

SACRAMENTO PUBLIC LIBRARY
828 "I" Street
Sacramento, CA 95814
04/15

This is the last page.

In keeping with the original Japanese comic format, this book reads from right to left—so action, sound effects, and word balloons are completely reversed. This preserves the orientation of the original artwork—plus, it's fun! Check out the diagram shown here to get the hang of things, and then turn to the other side of the book to get started!

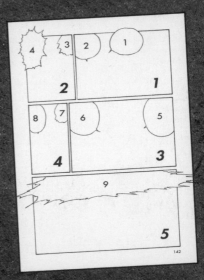